I0322890

STUDIES IN THE MASORETIC TRADITION OF THE HEBREW BIBLE

Studies in the Masoretic Tradition of the Hebrew Bible

edited by

Daniel J. Crowther, Aaron D. Hornkohl and Geoffrey Khan

UNIVERSITY OF CAMBRIDGE
Faculty of Asian and Middle Eastern Studies

OpenBook Publishers

https://www.openbookpublishers.com

Updated digital material and resources associated with this volume are available at https://doi.org/10.11647/OBP.0330#resources

Semitic Languages and Cultures 15.

ISSN (print): 2632-6906
ISSN (digital): 2632-6914

ISBN Paperback: 9781800649194
ISBN Hardback: 9781800649200
ISBN Digital (PDF): 9781800649217
DOI: 10.11647/OBP.0330

Cover images: A fragment of a Hebrew Bible manuscript (1 Sam. 25.44–26.8) from the Cairo Genizah containing vocalisation, accents, Masoretic notes and Masoretic marks (Cambridge University Library, T-S A8.10). Courtesy of the Syndics of Cambridge University Library.

Cover design: Jeevanjot Kaur Nagpal

CONTENTS

CONTRIBUTORS vii

PREFACE xi

ABSTRACTS xv

Elvira Martín-Contreras

Using the Masora for Interpreting the Vocalisation and Accentuation of the Biblical Text 1

Kim Phillips

The Masoretic Notes in RNL EVR II B 80+: An Initial Report 23

Vincent D. Beiler

The Marginal *nun/zayin*: Meaning, Purpose, Localisation 75

Aaron D. Hornkohl

Tiberian *ketiv-qere* and the Combined Samaritan Written-Reading Tradition: Points of Contact and Contrast 115

Estara J. Arrant

A Further Analysis of the 'Byzantine (Italian-Levantine) Triad' of Features in Common Torah Codices 163

Geoffrey Khan

Hebrew Vocalisation Signs in Karaite Transcriptions of the Hebrew Bible into Arabic Script 203

Yochanan Breuer

Dissonance between Masoretic Vocalisation and Cantillation in Biblical Verse Division 243

Daniel J. Crowther

Why are there Two Systems of Tiberian Ṭeʿamim? 289

Benjamin Williams

"Some Fanciful Midrash Explanation": *Derash* on the *Ṭeʿamim* in the Middle Ages and Early Modern Period 329

Joseph Habib

Does Saadya Refer to the Accents in his Introduction to the Pentateuch? 377

INDEX 417

CONTRIBUTORS

Elvira Martín-Contreras (PhD, Universidad Complutense, Madrid, 2000) is Senior Research Fellow at the Institute of Languages and Cultures of the Mediterranean and the Near East (ILC-CSIC). Her research is focused on the textual transmission and the reception of the Hebrew Bible text attested in the rabbinic literature and the Masora, i.e., the marginal annotations placed in medieval Hebrew Bible manuscripts. She is also interested in annotation practices in medieval Hebrew Bibles, as well as Hebrew palaeography. She is author of several monographs and many articles, including *Masora: La transmisión de la Tradición de la Biblia Hebrea* (Navarra, 2010). She is co-editor of *The Text of the Hebrew Bible: From the Rabbis to the Masoretes* (Vandenhoeck & Ruprecht, 2014).

Kim Phillips (PhD, University of Cambridge, 2016) is a Research Associate in the Taylor-Schechter Genizah Research Unit, Research Associate in Semitic Biblical Texts at Tyndale House, Cambridge, and an affiliated lecturer in Hebrew in the Faculty of Divinity of the University of Cambridge. His research focuses on Masoretic Studies, medieval Jewish biblical exegesis, and Christian Palestinian Aramaic.

Vincent D. Beiler (PhD forthcoming, University of Cambridge, 2022) works on early Masoretic Bibles, with a special focus on Bibles found in St Petersburg. His thesis is entitled 'The Small

Masorah: Genealogical Relationships in the Earliest Hebrew Bible Codices'. This is his first publication.

Aaron D. Hornkohl (PhD, The Hebrew University of Jerusalem, 2012) is the author of *Linguistic Periodization and the Language of Jeremiah* (Brill, 2013), a translated adaptation of his doctoral dissertation, and co-editor (with Geoffrey Khan) of *Studies in Semitic Vocalisation* (University of Cambridge and Open Book Publishers, 2020). He teaches Hebrew in the Faculty of Asian and Middle Eastern Studies at the University of Cambridge. His recent research focuses on the historical depth of the Tiberian reading tradition as manifested in dissonance between its written and recitation components, but he also deals with other ancient Hebrew traditions, such as Qumran Hebrew and Samaritan Hebrew, diachrony and linguistic periodisation, the Biblical Hebrew verbal system, and pragmatics.

Estara J Arrant (PhD, University of Cambridge, 2021) is a Research Associate at the Taylor-Schechter Genizah Research Unit at the Cambridge University Library, working as the digital humanities scholar for the ERC project *TEXTEVOLVE: A New Approach to the Evolution of Texts Based on the Manuscripts of the Targums*. Her research focuses on Semitic languages in contact, the development and transmission of scriptures in Semitic languages, Jewish and Islamic codicology and palaeography, and data science and digital humanities. Her PhD thesis, 'A Codicological and Linguistic Typology of Common Torah Codices from the Cairo

Genizah', analysed the features of 1,500 everyday medieval Torah fragments using machine learning

Geoffrey Khan (PhD, School of Oriental and African Studies, London, 1984) is Regius Professor of Hebrew at the University of Cambridge. His research publications focus on three main fields: Biblical Hebrew language (especially medieval traditions), Neo-Aramaic dialectology, and medieval Arabic documents. He is the general editor of *The Encyclopedia of Hebrew Language and Linguistics* and is the senior editor of *Journal of Semitic Studies*. His most recent book in the field of Hebrew is the two-volume *The Tiberian Pronunciation Tradition of Biblical Hebrew* (University of Cambridge and Open Book Publishers, 2020).

Yochanan Breuer (PhD, The Hebrew University of Jerusalem, 1993) is the Ch. N. Bialik Professor of the Hebrew Language at the Hebrew University of Jerusalem and a member of the Academy of the Hebrew Language. His research interests include Biblical Hebrew and the *Masora*, Mishnaic Hebrew, Babylonian Aramaic, and Modern Hebrew (especially the language of S. Y. Agnon). He is the co-editor of the series *Language Studies* (Jerusalem: Mandel Institute). His most recent book is *From Aramaic into Hebrew: The Method of Translation in the Book Hilkhot Re'u* (The Academy of the Hebrew Language, 2020).

Daniel J. Crowther (PhD, University of Bristol, 2015) is an Assistant Director for Langham Scholars' Ministry and a Research Associate of the Centre for Muslim and Christian Studies, Oxford.

He co-edited *Reading the Bible in Islamic Context* and has published a number of articles in journals and collected volumes. His present research concerns the Muslim historical setting of the Tiberian Masoretic endeavour, the Ashkenazi handling of the Tiberian heritage and the varied and various interconnections between the Psalms and the Qurʾān.

Benjamin Williams (PhD, University of Oxford, 2012) is Senior Lecturer in Biblical and Rabbinic Studies at Leo Baeck College and James Mew Lecturer in Rabbinic Hebrew at the University of Oxford. His research focuses on the development of rabbinic Bible interpretation, including the dating of late antique exegetical traditions; the transmission of midrash in manuscript and print, particularly in the Ottoman Sephardi communities in which the *editiones principes* were published; and the interpretation of midrash in Jewish and Christian commentarial traditions. He is the author of *Commentary on Midrash Rabba in the Sixteenth Century: The* Or ha-Sekhel *of Abraham ben Asher* (OUP, 2016).

Joseph Habib (PhD, University of Cambridge, 2021) is an independent researcher. His doctoral thesis was entitled 'Accents, Pausal Forms and *Qere/Ketiv* in the Bible Translations and Commentaries of Saadya Gaon and the Karaites of Jerusalem'. He currently works in the areas of medieval Jewish exegesis, Hebrew accents, Judaeo-Arabic literature, and Hebrew philology. He has published a number of articles on these topics in collected volumes and journals.

PREFACE

This volume brings together papers on topics relating to the transmission of the Hebrew Bible from Late Antiquity to the Early Modern period. We refer to this broadly in the title of the volume as the 'Masoretic Tradition'. The term 'Masoretic' is sometimes used in a narrower sense to refer to the activities of circles of scholars known as Masoretes in the early Islamic period. The most prestigious circle of Masoretes were those of Tiberias, who produced some of the most authoritative medieval codices of the Hebrew Bible, such as the Aleppo Codex (generally referred to by the abbreviation A). The Tiberian Masoretes were associated with the so-called Palestinian *Yeshiva*, which was the main seat of authority in Palestine from Late Antiquity to the Middle Ages. We have records of the activity of several generations of Tiberian Masoretes from the eighth to the tenth centuries CE. By the second half of the tenth century, the school of Masoretes in Tiberias was discontinued for reasons that are not entirely clear.

The objective of the Tiberian Masoretes was the careful preservation of the transmission of a stabilised form of the Hebrew Bible. They achieved this through the textualisation of the oral reading that was received from antiquity in the form of vowel and cantillation signs and the development of textual notes, known as Masoretic notes. The Masoretic notes related to differences in orthography, with statistical information about their distribution, dissonances between orthography and oral reading, and occasionally also differences in the interpretation of words of similar form.

 https://doi.org/10.11647/OBP.0330.11

The activities of stabilisation of the transmission of the Hebrew Bible, however, predate the formation of the Masoretic school in Tiberias. Already in the Second Temple Period, authoritative forms of both the written transmission and oral reading tradition had begun to be fixed. Moreover, Masoretic activities and the production of authoritative Masoretic Bible codices continued after the discontinuation of the Tiberian Masoretic School in the tenth century. Indeed, the Codex Leningradensis (generally referred to by the abbreviation L), which is the basis of modern scholarly editions of the Hebrew Bible such as BHS and BHQ, was produced in the eleventh century in Egypt. These Masoretic activities continued in various centres in the Middle East and Europe down to the Early Modern Period.

Furthermore, despite the process of stabilisation, there has always been some degree of diversity in the transmission of the Hebrew Bible. This diversity can be seen in differences between the authoritative oral reading tradition and the authoritative written tradition, in differences in the systems of cantillation across various parts of the Bible, and also in differences between various written streams of transmission reflected by the extant manuscripts. In the Middle Ages and beyond the written transmission was more fixed, but minor differences, mainly in orthography, are found across manuscripts. There were differences in oral reading traditions and in systems of their textualisation. There were also differences in the form and content of Masoretic notes. Moreover, the engagement with the Masoretic tradition is found in many rabbinic exegetical and grammatical works.

The papers in this volume are studies on a range of aspects of this Masoretic tradition of the Hebrew Bible in its broad sense, ranging from the Second Temple Period to the Early Modern Period. They focus on traditions of vocalisation signs and accent signs, traditions of oral reading, traditions of Masoretic notes, as well as rabbinic and exegetical texts.

We thank Estara Arrant and Vince Beiler, who helped choose the images for the cover of the volume. We would like to express our gratitude also to Open Book Publishers for all their efficient help in publishing the volume. Their open-access initiative will allow this publication to be widely read throughout the world.

The Editors, Cambridge, September 2022

ABSTRACTS

Elvira Martín-Contreras, Using the Masora for Interpreting the Vocalisation and Accentuation of the Biblical Text

The marginal annotations that appear with the biblical text in most medieval biblical manuscripts—called by the technical term Masora—are hardly taken into account when interpreting the biblical text. Their idiosyncratic characteristics (they are formulated briefly, concisely, and, on many occasions, elliptically) make it nearly impossible to appreciate the content of the annotation and its possible interpretive relevance on a first reading. All these difficulties can be resolved, however, by establishing implicit information and formulating a clear methodology as to how to analyse the Masoretic annotations. This allows us to study them and apply them to the interpretation of the biblical text. This article shows the benefits of using the Masora for the interpretation of the biblical text through some selected examples, all of them related to vocalisation and stress. The content of these Masora annotations is explained and applied to textual interpretation.

Kim Phillips, The Masoretic Notes in RNL EVR II B 80+: An Initial Report

RNL EVR II B 80 is a Torah codex, quintessentially Tiberian in text and layout. Nonetheless, the masoretic notes reveal extensive and sustained influence from the Babylonian masoretic tradition.

This influence can be detected in the technical terms employed in the masoretic notes, the structure of the notes themselves, and the biblical text-form implied by the content of the notes. This article serves as a preliminary report demonstrating the nature and extent of the Babylonian masoretic material in the manuscript and illustrates some of the ways in which this material can be used to consolidate and expand our existing knowledge of the Babylonian Masora.

Vincent D. Beiler, The Marginal *nun/zayin*: Meaning, Purpose, Localisation

In some early masoretic Bible codices, a large letter resembling *nun* or *zayin* occurs in the margin, often in conjunction with the marking of *qere/ketiv*. Occurring in some codices, but not in others, the letter represents a bit of a cipher. Drawing on a database of ca. 15,000 *masora parva* notes, taken from 81 different classmarks, I propose that the letter, possibly a *zayin*, had (or acquired) a practical purpose, viz. as a means of avoiding certain types of copyist mistakes when recording *qere/ketiv* notes. Because the sign occurs in certain script types more than others, I also show that the notation can function as something of a regional identifier.

Aaron D. Hornkohl, Tiberian *ketiv-qere* and the Combined Samaritan Written-Reading Tradition: Points of Contact and Contrast

Both the Tiberian and Samaritan biblical traditions are composite in nature. In the Tiberian tradition this manifests most clearly in the phenomenon of *ketiv-qere*. Against the backdrop of the normally harmonious relationship between the written (i.e., consonantal, orthographic) and pronunciation (i.e., vocalisation, recitation) components of the Tiberian biblical tradition, *ketiv-qere* instances are a clear indication of divergence between what is written and what is read—divergence which, it should be emphasised, exceeds acknowledged cases of *ketiv-qere*. A similar relationship obtains between the Samaritan written tradition and its oral recitation, with the latter regularly deviating from what was evidently intended by the former. Both the Tiberian and Samaritan reading traditions are commonly characterised as later than their respective written traditions. The present study examines a series of *ketiv-qere* cases in the Pentateuch, seeking to explain the various forms reflected by the Tiberian and Samaritan written and reading traditions and to assess the relative antiquity of each.

Estara J Arrant, A Further Analysis of the 'Byzantine (Italian-Levantine) Triad' of Features in Common Torah Codices

This study analyses the distinctive features of a group of eleven Torah fragments from the Taylor-Schechter collection of Cairo Genizah manuscripts, which appear to come from related regions and use the signs *dagesh* and *shewa* in three related ways to reinforce a standard of pronunciation of the biblical text. The three uses of these signs have, individually, been associated with Palestino-Tiberian vocalisation, or labelled as 'Extended Tiberian'. I contribute a fresh analysis by contextualising the signs with each other, showing how they work together to preserve a standard form of pronunciation of the biblical text through reinforcing the syllabification when the text is read aloud. I also examine the codicological features of each of these fragments, which appear very similar to each other. I conclude that they constitute a group, and I infer what their physical and linguistic features reveal about their practical function in the reading and study of the Hebrew Bible in the medieval period.

Geoffrey Khan, Hebrew Vocalisation Signs in Karaite Transcriptions of the Hebrew Bible into Arabic Script

In the 10th and 11th centuries CE many Karaite scribes in the Middle East used Arabic script to write not only the Arabic language, but also the Hebrew language. Such Hebrew texts in Arabic transcription were predominantly Hebrew Bible texts. The transcriptions reflect the oral reading tradition of the biblical text. Most manuscripts reflect the Tiberian reading tradition. Some reflect an imperfect performance of the Tiberian reading tradition. This imperfect performance may be attributed to the impact of the phonological system of the vernacular language of the scribes. In this paper I discuss aspects of imperfect performance discernible in the distribution of Hebrew vocalisation signs that are used in the manuscripts. The paper focuses in particular on (a) deviations in the distribution of vowel signs that reflect imperfect performance of Tiberian vowel qualities and (b) deviations in the distribution of *shewa* and *ḥaṭef* signs that reflect imperfect performance of Tiberian syllable structure.

Yochanan Breuer, Dissonance between Masoretic Vocalisation and Cantillation in Biblical Verse Division

The Masoretic text is the final stage of a process during which the Masoretes had to decide between numerous various readings in order to produce a fixed and consistent text. Although the final production is a remarkable achievement, the Masoretic text still contains cases of inconsistencies. The prominent example is the discrepancy between the *ketiv* (the way the word should be written) and the *qere* (the way the word should be pronounced), where we find two contradictory readings in the same word. In this article, a similar phenomenon is described regarding the vocalisation and the cantillation. Although the vocalisation and the cantillation usually reflect division of a verse according to the same interpretation, there are also cases where they reflect two opposing divisions based on different interpretations. Awareness of this may enrich our understanding of the complexity that was involved in the fixing of the Masoretic text.

Daniel J. Crowther, Why Are There Two Systems of Tiberian Ṭeʿamim?

Why might it be that a dedicated system of accentuation is used for 'the Three'—the 'poetic' books of Job, Proverbs, and Psalms—but not for the many other 'poetic texts' found scattered throughout the 'Twenty-One' (the rest of the books of the Hebrew Bible)? The earliest commentators associate the two types of Tiberian accentuation with differences in verse-length. More modern commentators attribute it to the essence of poetry. Following these two ideas, two different methods of presenting poetry can be observed in the Twenty-One. One is appropriate to poetic texts with short verses (of fewer than eight words per verse) and the other is appropriate to poetic texts with long verses (of more than ten words per verse). Within this double system, the practical challenges of presenting short-verse poetic texts under the accentuation system of the Twenty-One can be observed in the one text that attempts this feat (2 Sam. 22). This observation suggests a rationale for a different system of accentuation that is more appropriate to extended texts of exclusively short-verse poetry, as found in the books of Psalms, Proverbs, and Job, but not in the books of Chronicles, Lamentations and Song of Songs.

Benjamin Williams, "Some Fanciful Midrash Explanation": *Derash* on the *Ṭeʿamim* in the Middle Ages and Early Modern Period

This chapter examines the history of the idea that the shapes, names, and sounds of the *ṭeʿamim* convey information about biblical narratives, including twists and turns in the plot, the thoughts and motivations of the characters, and the way direct speech was delivered. This exegetical technique is examined first by enquiring into its relationship with the midrashic method of deriving such information from the graphic features of the consonantal text of the Hebrew Bible. Turning to the approach of Tobias ben Eliezer, Joseph ibn Caspi, and Baḥya ben Asher, attention is focused on interpretations of unusual and irregular cantillation marks, including the *shalshelet*, according to the principles of *derash*. Finally, examples from the commentaries of Moses Alsheikh of Safed are examined to show how sixteenth-century Sephardi interpreters treated the Masoretic system of accentuation more broadly as a source of information concerning biblical narratives.

Joseph Habib, Does Saadya Refer to the Accents in His Introduction to the Pentateuch?

In the introduction to his long commentary on the Pentateuch, the Rabbanite scholar Saadya Gaon discusses the importance of word groupings. The possibility has been raised that here Saadya is referring to the biblical accents. The purpose of this article is to determine whether or not Saadya has the accents in mind. This is done through a close analysis of select key terms and the biblical passages mentioned in the passage.

USING THE MASORA FOR INTERPRETING THE VOCALISATION AND ACCENTUATION OF THE BIBLICAL TEXT[1]

Elvira Martín-Contreras

Strictly speaking, the term Masoretic Text (MT)[2] refers to any Hebrew biblical codex that is accompanied by a corpus of marginal annotations known as *masora*.[3] Each codex has its own set of marginal annotations and there are no two *masoras* that are the same

[1] This article was completed under the auspices of a research project entitled 'Legado de *Sefarad* II. La producción material e intelectual del judaísmo sefardí bajomedieval', which is based at the ILC-CSIC in Madrid and funded by the Plan Nacional de I + D + i (FFI2015-63700–P).

[2] For the use of the term, see Martín-Contreras (2016, esp. 420).

[3] In this paper the terms *masora* and *Masorah* are used according to the distinction made by Aron Dotan. He divided written *Masorah* into two categories: (1) the masoretic notes in the margins of the text and the longer lists which accompany the text or are appended to it—the *masora* in the narrow sense; (2) the graphemes which, by their nature, are of two types: (a) vocalisation signs; (b) accentuation signs. See Dotan (2007, 614). The term is written *Masorah* (with uppercase *M* and final *h*) when it is the generic name, and *masora* (with lower case m) when it refers to the marginal masoretic annotations of a particular manuscript.

 https://doi.org/10.11647/OBP.0330.01

(Orlinsky 1966, esp. xxxvi). The marginal annotations are found in the intercolumn, top and bottom margins of each folio, and also collected at the end of the biblical books, where they are arranged in lists.[4] All of them contain varied information about the words of the biblical text with which they appear, such as: spelling, enumeration, vocalisation, accentuation, grammatical rules, meaning, etc. (see Martín-Contreras 2021, 178–81). However, all this information is rarely taken into account when the biblical text is interpreted.[5]

The roots of 'neglecting' the interpretative value of these marginal annotations lie in (a) lack of knowledge about this source (additional specialised training is needed to decipher the annotations), (b) the way the annotations work, and (c) how the information is provided.

These textual annotations are found in manuscripts vocalised in the three systems of Hebrew vocalisation. Consequently, it is possible to distinguish three kinds of Masoras: Tiberian, Palestinian, and Babylonian. On Palestinian Masora see Kahle (1959); Weil (1963, 68–80); Yeivin (1963); Revell (1970; 1974; 1977); Chiesa (1978). For a general view of Babylonian Masora see Ofer (2001). An additional *masora* is attached to the text of Targum Onkelos; see Klein (2000).

[4] This information is sometimes denominated *Masora Finalis*; however, as the Masoretic material arranged by Jacob ben Ḥayyim at the end of the Second Rabbinic Bible is called *Masorah Finalis*, it is better to avoid this term.

[5] For the benefits of using the *masora* for interpretation, see Freedman and Cohen (1974); Fernández Tejero (1984); Barthélemy (1992, lxix–xcvii); Mynatt and Crawford (2001); Martín-Contreras (2009; 2013); Dotan (2010).

Usually, each marginal annotation is linked to one or more words of the biblical text written on the same folio. A graphic symbol—a small circle called a *circellus* (˚)—is often placed over a word or between two or more words of the biblical text. The *circellus* alerts us to the presence of extra information on the word to be found in a marginal annotation.[6]

Annotations are connected to their lemmas through (a) their placement next to the line of the text (this is the case with annotations placed in the intercolumnar margins, which are called collectively *masora parva*, MP) and (b) the repetition of the lemma in the annotation itself. This latter technique is typically used for those annotations written in the top and bottom margins (all of which are called collectively *masora magna*, MM), as well as for annotations found at the end of a biblical book or a collection of biblical books.

The denominations *masora magna* and *masora parva* merely express an external-technical division of the annotations. This division does not imply differences in the function and nature of the annotations placed in each. Both types annotate the same kinds of information, but they differ in how they represent this information in writing. It has been said that the MM can be regarded as an expansion of the information that is collected in the MP. This is only partially true. There are many MP annotations with no parallel MM, and vice versa. Therefore, it is better to

[6] Alternatively, a lemma may have a *circellus*, but no corresponding annotation; or, conversely, a lemma may have an annotation, but no corresponding *circellus*.

regard both types, MP and MM, as parallel entities (see Dotan 2010, 59, n. 9).

The masoretic annotations are characterised by (a) their expression of information in a mixture of Rabbinic Hebrew and Aramaic (Hyvernat 1902–1905) and (b) their brief and concise presentation of information (generally using abbreviations) that is, on many occasions, even elliptical (part of the information remains implicit). There is no standardised form for these abbreviations, or a single way of expressing similar information: they vary between manuscripts and, sometimes, even within the same manuscript (see Fernández Tejero and Ortega Monasterio 1981; 1983; Martín-Contreras 2012; Ortega Monasterio 1986; 1993; 1997; Fernández Tejero 2009). Those placed in the intercolumn margins show the briefest form, with the words often represented only by their initial letters. The ultimate expression of this ellipsis are annotations that give only a number (a letter of the Hebrew alphabet with a supralinear dot).

In most cases, these characteristics make it impossible on first reading to appreciate the content of the annotation and its possible relevance to interpretation. However, all these difficulties can be resolved by supplying the information that was left implicit and by formulating a clear methodology of how to analyse masoretic annotations. This enables us to apply the information they contain to the interpretation of the biblical text (Martín-Contreras 2013).

Once the apparent difficulties posed by the Masora have been explained, the best way to learn about its benefits for the interpretation of the biblical text is to use it. The following selected examples show how to decipher the content of a masoretic annotation so as to apply it thereafter to textual interpretation. All of these examples concern vocalisation and accentuation.

1.0. Judg. 6.37

The following information on the word חֹרֶב 'dryness' (Judg. 6.37) is given in the *masora* of Leningrad codex (L).

Figure 1: Leningrad codex, f. 140r (courtesy of The National Library of Russia)

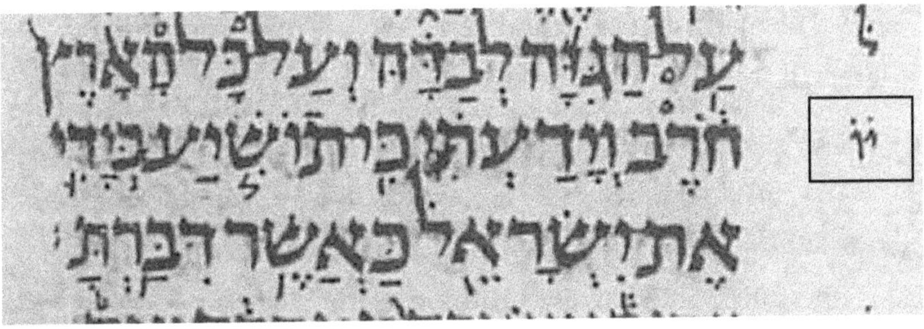

The MP annotation says: יו̇ 'sixteen'. There is no annotation in the MM. At first glance, the annotation could be classified as one of numerical type, stating the number of times the word appears in the Bible. However, a concordance search reveals that this word appears eleven times (Even-Shoshan 1996, 398). Is the annotation wrong? Or does it give information of a different type?

According the methodology to be followed in the analysis of any masoretic annotation, the next step is to confirm the reliability of the information given in the annotation. For this purpose, it is necessary to consult the *masoras* in the main Tiberian biblical manuscripts (B.L. Or. 4445, the Cairo codex of the Prophets, the Aleppo Codex, and the 'Leningrad Codex') and the major masoretic lists and treatises (Frensdorff 1864; Dotan 1967; Díaz Esteban 1975; Ginsburg 1975; Ognibeni 1995). I have searched in the Cairo (C) and Aleppo (A) codices, but none of them have masoretic annotations on this word in this verse. I then searched in Ginsburg's masoretic compilation. There is one list where the lemma and the information match the annotation here (Ginsburg 1975, 497–98).

We have all the information collected in the process of analysing the annotation: the MP information, the MM information, the identification of the masoretic signs (*simanim*), other evidence. This can help to explain the overall meaning of the annotation and its purpose.

According to the list in Ginsburg's compilation, the sixteen references are: Gen. 31.40; Judg. 6.37, 39, 40; Jer. 36.30; 49.13; 50.38; Ezek. 29.10; Isa. 4.6; 25.4; 25.5, 5; 61.4; Zeph. 2.14; Hag. 1.11; and Job 30.30. After careful examination of the references, we can infer two facts. First, the number sixteen includes occurrences of this word both with and without prefixes. This additional information is stated explicitly in the MP annotation on this word at Job 30.30 in L: י֗ו בלי֗ש 'sixteen in the meaning'. Second, the word is vocalised with *segol* under the *resh* in all the instances. In other words, there are sixteen occurrences of the word חרֶב and similar forms vocalised with *segol*.

But, why is it necessary to provide this information? Because the word חרב, with and without prefixes, also appears vocalised with *ṣere* in the Bible: חֹרֵב 'Horeb'.[7] The purpose of the

[7] Sixteen times in the Hebrew Bible plus one case where the word is written *plene*, חוֹרֵב (Exod. 33.6); cf. Even-Shoshan (1996, 352).

annotation is to distinguish these consonantal homographs with different meanings. The distinction is made via the vocalisation and accentuation: those with *segol* and penultimate stress are cases of the common noun חֹ֫רֶב 'drought, parching heat, desolation/dryness' (Brown 1952), and those with *ṣere* and stress on the ultima are instances of the proper name חֹרֵ֫ב 'Horeb'.

2.0. Zech. 6.10

The following information on the word וּבָאתָ from Zech. 6.10 is found in the *masora* of C.

Figure 2: Cairo codex, Zech. 6.10 (photographs held by the Masora team at the CSIC)

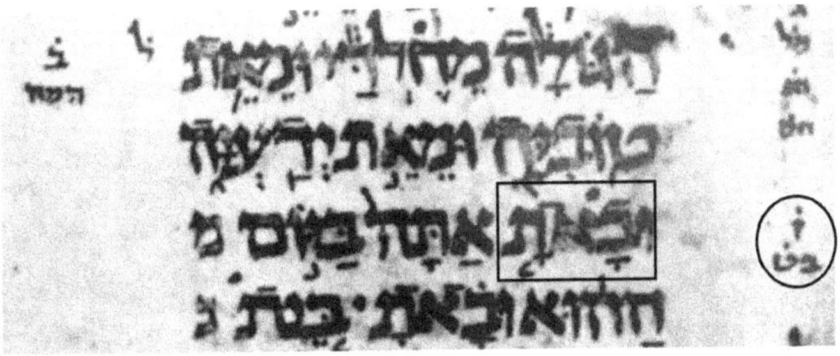

The MP annotation says: ז̇ בט̇. There is also a MM annotation:

ובאת ז̇ בטע̇ וסימנהון והקימתי ושמעו הכהנים הכהן וקראת במגלה ושלשת תרדמאך לקוח מאת הגולה.

The textual information comes after the lemma and it explicitly says *we-simanehon*. This is the introductory formula for saying that the next words are the *simanim*, the catchwords that make it possible to identify the verses involved. I have identified them as: Gen. 6.18; Exod. 3.18; Deut. 17.9; 26.3; Jer. 36.6; 1 Sam. 20.19; and Zech. 6.10.

Similar information is found in the MP annotation on this word at Zech. 6.10 in L and in Ginsburg's Masoretic compilation (Ginsburg 1975, 167). All this information is going to help us to understand the annotation, the next step.

So, what does this annotation mean? Firstly, we translate the MP annotation ז̇ בטע̇ 'seven times with the accent'. According to this translation, the first hypothesis is that the annotation relates to the accent in the word, *pashṭa*; in other words, to the seven times that the word appears with this accent. But if we check the word in each of the verses given in the MM annotation, we can see that this accent does not occur in all of them. It is therefore necessary to pursue other clues.

The list in Ginsburg's compilation adds a very important piece of information: the word is accented these seven occurrences on the letter *taw*.

According to the concordances (Even-Shoshan 1996, 154), the word וּבָאתָ, the 2ms *qal* perfect with the prefix *waw*, appears nineteen times in the entire Bible. A careful examination of the references confirms that: the word וּבָאתָ in the seven verses listed in the masoretic annotation has the accent on the ultima, and in the other twelve instances on the penultima. In other words, the meaning of the annotation is that the word occurs seven times with stress on the ultima.

But, why is it necessary to give this information? What is the purpose of the annotation? Is it merely statistical? Those who think that the *masora* has a numerical character may answer 'yes'. But, my answer is 'no'. The position of the word stress is often used to distinguish similar words with different tense meanings:

in the case of ובאת, those with an ultima stress usually have future meaning—the so-called *waw* consecutive perfect—while those with penultima have past meaning (Revell 1985; Khan 2000, 92). So, the purpose of the annotation is to ensure that the word is not interpreted as a past tense form in the seven relevant verses.

3.0. Josh. 2.3

The word הוֹצִיאִי 'bring out' (Josh. 2.3) has the following MP annotation in A.

Figure 3: Aleppo codex, Josh. 2.3 (courtesy of the Ben-Zvi Institute, Jerusalem. Photographer: Ardon Bar Hama)

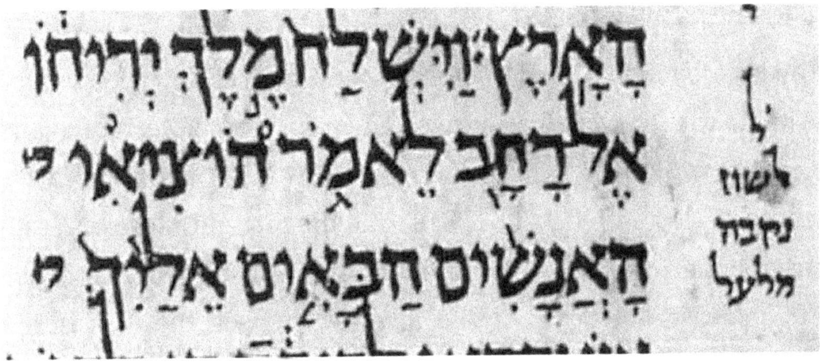

There is no MM annotation. Similar information is found in the MP annotation on this word in L.

What does this annotation mean? It can be translated as: 'unique[8] in feminine; penultimate stress'. However, the word has the accent *telisha gedola* and the sign of this accent is not usually

[8] I prefer to translate the term לית *let* as 'unique' because it may refer to words or expressions that appear once in the Bible (*hapax* in *sensu strictu*) as well as to words or expressions that are unique in some other sense (spelling, vocalisation, accentuation, meaning, location, etc.).

used to indicate stress position (Yeivin 1980, 102). Codex L helps to elucidate this matter.

The word in that codex has two signs of this accent, one over the letter *he* and other over the letter *ṣade*: הֹ֠וצִ֠יאִי.

Figure 4: Leningrad codex, f. 122r (courtesy of The National Library of Russia)

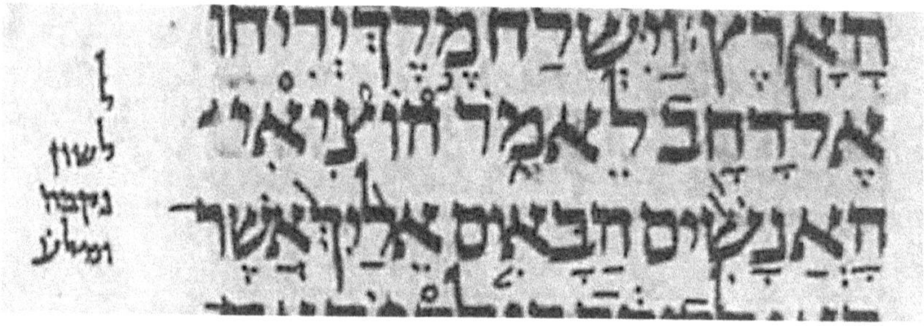

The sign over the letter *ṣade* is not reproduced in the standard printed edition or the electronic ones (such as Bible Works and Accordance), with the exceptions of the *Biblia Hebraica Leningradensia* (Dotan [ed.] 2001, 318) and the module 'Masora Tesaurus' (Dotan [ed.] 2014), both edited by Aron Dotan. This is one of the reasons it is advisable always to check the manuscript when working on the *masora*. The editions do not always offer all the details exactly as they appear in the manuscripts.

The *telisha* sign is generally not repeated on the stressed syllable in manuscripts with standard Tiberian pointing, although there are some exceptions, and this case is one of them (Yeivin 1980, 211). And, what does the repetition mean? According to Israel Yeivin (1980, 102), the sign is repeated on this word to indicate the stress position.

And, what is the purpose of the annotation? The word הוֹצִיאִֽי appears three times in the Bible: Jer. 7.22 (*qere*); 11.4; and here.[9] The word is stressed on the ultima in the two verses in Jeremiah. This information is confirmed by a list from the masoretic compendium *ʾOḵla we-ʾOḵla*, according to the Paris MS version, on words that occur once with penultimate stress while everywhere else they have ultimate stress (Frensdorff 1864, 171, 372). The ultimate purpose of the annotation is to distinguish homographs. The position of the word stress is used to do this: those with ultimate stress are infinitives with the 1CS suffix, while the one with penultimate stress is a FS imperative.

4.0. Deut. 32.5

An analysis of the accents and *masora* of Deut. 32.5 in L illustrates its role and importance in interpreting the biblical text. This is a difficult text, with a great variety of renderings attested in the ancient versions. The accentuation of the first part of the verse is: שִׁחֵ֨ת ל֛וֹ לֹ֖א בָּנָ֣יו מוּמָ֑ם. According to the accents, לוֹ לֹא should be read together and a literal translation of the first three words would thus be—as odd as it may sound—'they behaved corruptly towards him not'. This accentuation is unusual and the trend has, therefore, been to disregard it and follow the more 'logical' reading proposed by the consonantal text. Accordingly, the translation found in the New American Standard Bible is: 'They have acted corruptly toward Him, They are not His children, because

[9] There is one further case where the word is written defectively, i.e., without the *yod* in the second syllable, Jer. 34.13; cf. Even-Shoshan (1996, 484).

of their defect'. However, the reading proposed by the accents is supported by the Targumim and the *masora*. What does the *masora* teach us about this?

There is a MP annotation to לֹא לֹו in L:

Figure 5: Leningrad codex, f. 118v (courtesy of The National Library of Russia)

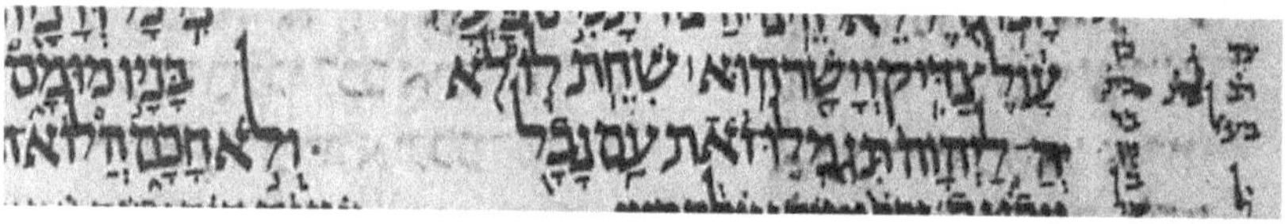

It says: ו בת̇ 'six [times] in the Torah'. There is no MM note. Manuscripts Or 4445 (B) and A have no masoretic annotation here, but according to a list in Ginsburg's (1975, 120) compilation the references could be: Gen. 28.1; 47.18; Exod. 28.32; Deut. 23.17; 25.5; 32.5. Apart from the case in Deut. 32.5, these two words do not appear to be linked conjunctively by the accents in any of the remaining occurrences. It seems that this annotation merely states the number of times that these two words appear together, in this order, irrespective of the accentuation.[10]

However, I have found others annotations in L which may be relevant to the accentuation. The sequence לא לו in Gen. 38.9 has two marginal annotations:

[10] This sequence is found also in Deut. 21.16.

Figure 6: Leningrad codex, f. 23v (courtesy of The National Library of Russia)

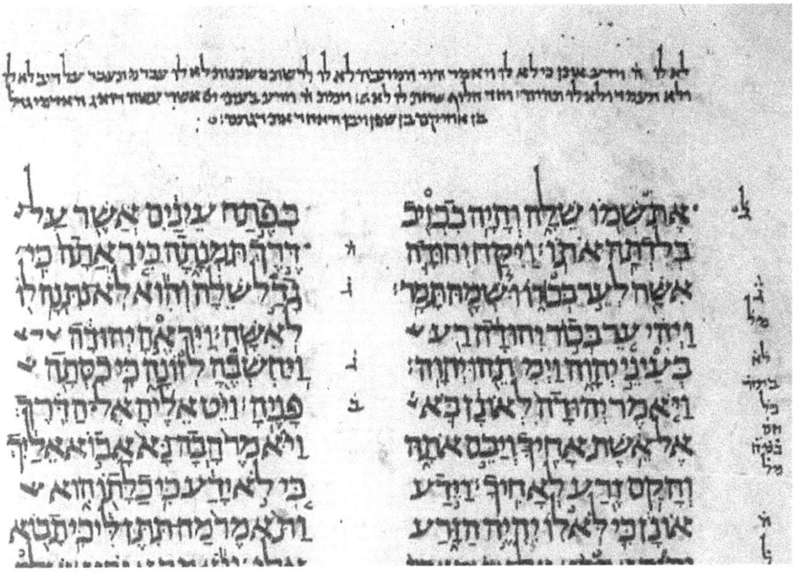

The MP annotation says: ה̇ 'five'. Additional information and the references are given in the MM annotation:

> לא לו ה̇ וידע אונן כי לא לו ויאמר הוי המרבה לא לו לרשת משכנות לא לו עבר מתעבר על ריב לא לו ולא תעמד ולא לו תהיה וחד חלף שחת לו לא

> לא לו five [times]: וידע אונן כי לא לו (Gen. 38.9); ויאמר הוי המרבה לא לו (Hab. 1.6); לרשת משכנות לא לו (Hab. 2.6); עבר מתעבר על ריב לא לו (Prov. 26.17); ולא תעמד ולא לו תהיה (Dan. 11.17); and one [with the order] reversed, שחת לו לא (Deut. 35.2).

Careful examination of the references allows us to infer that in all of them these two words appear side by side, in either order, and linked—twice by the accents *merkha* and *ṭarḥa* and four times by *maqqef*. So, these two words should be read together.[11]

This MM annotation not only confirms the unusual accentuation of the sequence in Deut. 32.5, but also demonstrates the Masoretes' concern that it be interpreted correctly. By listing this case together with the occurrences that have *maqqef*,[12] they ensured that it would be treated in the same way.

5.0. Judg. 5.8

The word לָחֶם 'fighting, war' (Judg. 5.8) has a MP annotation in A.

Figure 7: Aleppo codex, Judg. 5.8 (courtesy of the Ben-Zvi Institute, Jerusalem. Photographer: Ardon Bar Hama)

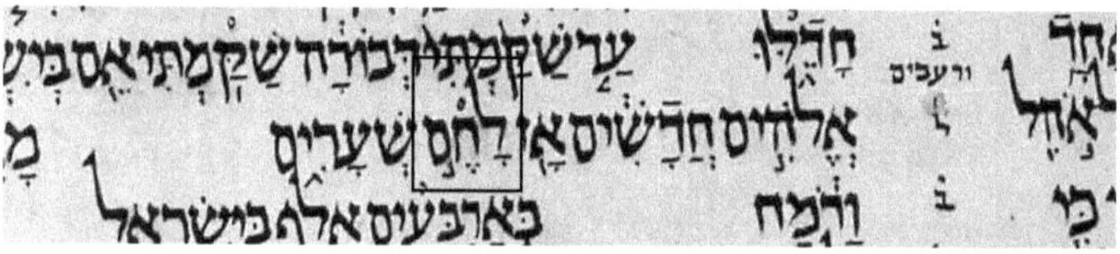

The same information is given in the MP annotations of codices C and L to the same verse.

According to this annotation, the word is 'unique'. However, we find in the concordances that this word appears 38 times in the entire Bible.[13] What, then, does the annotation mean? In

---

[11] For a different understanding of the Masoretic notes and of the verse see McCarthy (2002).

[12] On the use of *maqqef* with words consisting of a single open syllable see Yeivin (1980, 230–31).

[13] Omitting occurrences of this word with prefixes; cf. Even-Shoshan (1996, 596–97).

what sense is the word is unique? List 373 of the masoretic compendium *ʾOkhla we-ʾOklah*, according to the Paris ms version, helps us with this dilemma (cf. Frensdorff 1864, 172). This is one of the words that occur once with an ultimate stress while everywhere else they have a penultima stress.

By drawing our attention to the unusual stress position, the annotation supplies the clue to properly understand this word in context.[14] It tells us that this is not another instance of the word לֶ֨חֶם 'bread' in the pausal form לָ֨חֶם—which is vocalised identically to our word in Deut. 32.5, but with penultimate stress—but a different word. The distinction between the two words is made by the stress position. So the essential purpose of this annotation is to avoid misunderstanding of the word as 'bread'. Here the word means 'war', from the root לח"ם 'fighting'.

6.0. Conclusion

To conclude, I hope these examples help to show why the *masora* is an indispensable tool in our attempts to achieve a more profound understanding of the Hebrew biblical text. It constitutes a historical record that accompanies the biblical text: a window onto the past. Why not use it?

[14] On the difficulty of interpreting this word in context, cf. Fernández Marcos (2011, 56*–57*).

References

Barthélemy, Dominique. 1992. *Critique textuelle de l'AT*, vol. 3. Orbis Biblicus et Orientalis 50/3. Fribourg: Éditions Universitaires and Göttingen: Vandenhoeck & Ruprecht.

Brown, Francis, Samuel Rolles Driver, and Charles A. Briggs. 1906. *A Hebrew and English lexicon of the Old Testament: With an appendix containing the Biblical Aramaic. Based on the Lexicon of William Gesenius as translated by Edward Robinson.* Oxford: Clarendon Press.

Chiesa, Bruno. 1978. *L'Antico Testamento Ebraico secondo la tradizione palestinense.* Turin: Bottega d'Erasmo.

Díaz Esteban, Fernando. 1975. *Sefer Oklah we Oklah. Colección de listas de palabras destinadas a conservar la integridad del texto hebreo de la Biblia entre los judíos de la Edad Media.* Textos y estudios "Cardenal Cisneros" 4. Madrid: CSIC.

Dotan, Aron. 1967. *Sefer Diqduqe ha-Teʿamim of Aharon ben Moshe ben Asher, with a Critical Edition of the Original Text from New Manuscripts.* Jerusalem: The Academy of the Hebrew Language.

——— (ed.). 2001. *Biblia Hebraica Leningradensia: Prepared According to the Vocalization, Accents, and Masora of Aaron ben Moses ben Asher in the Leningrad Codex.* Peabody, MA: Hendrickson.

———. 2007 (1971). 'Masorah'. In *Encyclopaedia Judaica*, 2nd edition, 23: 603–56.

———. 2010. 'Masora's Contribution to Biblical Studies: Revival of an Ancient Tool'. In *Congress Volume Ljubljana 2007*, edited by André Lemaire, 57–69. Vetus Testamentum Supplements 133. Leiden: Brill.

——— (ed.). 2014. *Masora Thesaurus*. Accordance electronic edition. Altamonte Springs, FL: OakTree Software, Inc.

Even-Shoshan, Avraham. 1996. *A New Concordance of the Bible. Thesaurus of the Language of the Bible Hebrew and Aramaic Roots, Words, Proper Names, Phrases and Synonyms*. Jerusalem: Kiryat Sefer.

Fernández Marcos, Natalio (ed.). 2011. *The Bíblia Hebraica Quinta, vol. 7, Judges*. Stuttgart: Deutsche Bibelgesellschaft.

Fernández Tejero, Emilia. 1984. 'Masora y Exégesis'. In *Simposio Bíblico Español*, edited by Natalio Fernández Marcos, Julio C. Trebolle Barrera, and Javier Fernández Vallina, 183–91. Madrid: Universidad Complutense.

———. 2009. 'Se equivocó el masoreta. ¿Se equivocaba?'. *Sefarad* 69: 303–13;

Fernández Tejero, Emilia, and María Teresa Ortega Monasterio. 1981. 'Las masoras de A, C y L en el libro de Nahum'. *Sefarad* 41: 1–43.

———. 1983. 'Las masoras de A, C y L en el libro de Joel'. In *Estudios Masoréticos (V Congreso de la IOMS). Dedicados a Harry M. Orlinsky*, edited by Emilia Fernández Tejero, 205–42. Textos y estudios "Cardenal Cisneros" 33. Madrid: Instituto "Arias Montano".

Freedman, David Noel, and Miles B. Cohen. 1974. 'The Masoretes as Exegetes: Selected Examples'. In *1972 and 1973 Proceedings IOMS,* edited by Harry Orlinsky, 35–46. Missoula, MT: Scholars Press.

Frensdorff, Solomon. 1864. *Ochlah W'ochlah.* Hannover: Hahn.

Ginsburg, Christian David. 1966 (1897). *Introduction to the Massoretico-Critical Edition of the Hebrew Bible.* New York: Ktav Publishing House; originally published London: Trinitarian Bible Society.

———. 1975. *The Massorah Compiled from Manuscripts Alphabetically and Lexically Arranged.* With an Analytical Table of Contents and Lists of Identified Sources and Parallels by A. Dotan. 4 vols. New York: Ktav Pub. House.

Hyvernat, Henri. 1902–1905. 'Petite Introduction à l'Étude de la Massore'. *Revue Biblique* 11: 551–63; 12: 529–42; 13: 521–46; 14: 203–34, 515–42.

Kahle, Paul E. 1959. *The Cairo Geniza.* 2nd edition. Oxford: Blackwell.

Khan, Geoffrey. 2000. *The Early Karaite Tradition of Hebrew Grammatical Thought.* Studies in Semitic Languages and Linguistics 32. Leiden: Brill.

Klein, Michael L. 2000. *The Masorah to Targum Onqelos: As Preserved in Mss Vatican Ebreo 448, Rome Angelica Or. 7, Fragments on the Cairo Genizah in Earlier Editions by A. Berliner and S. Landauer—Critical Edition with Comments and Introduction.* Binghamton, NY: Targum Studies.

Martín-Contreras, Elvira. 2009. 'Masoretic and Rabbinic Lights on the word הבי, Ruth 3:15: יהב or בוא?' *Vetus Testamentum* 59: 244–56.

———. 2012. 'The Phenomenon *Qere we la' ketib* in the Main Biblical Codices: New Data'. *Vetus Testamentum* 6: 77–87.

———. 2013. 'Masora and Masoretic Interpretation'. In *The Oxford Encyclopedia of Biblical Interpretation*, edited by Steven L. McKenzie, I: 542–50. Oxford: Oxford University Press.

———. 2016. 'Medieval Masoretic Text: Overview Article'. In *The Textual History of the Bible*, edited by Armin Lange, 1A: 420–29. Leiden: Brill.

———. 2021. 'Annotations in the Earliest Medieval Hebrew Bible Manuscripts'. In *Scribal Habits in Near Eastern Manuscript Traditions*, edited by George A. Kiraz and Sabine Schmidtke, 167–88. Piscataway, NJ: Gorgias Press.

McCarthy, Carmel. 2002. 'Masoretic Undertones in the Song of Moses'. *Proceedings of the Irish Biblical Association* 25: 42–45.

Mynatt, Daniel S., and Timothy G. Crawford. 2001. 'Integrating the Masorah into the Classroom: A Tribute to Page Kelley'. *Perspectives in Religious Studies* 28: 373–79.

Ofer, Yosef. 2001. *The Babylonian Masora of the Pentateuch its Principle and Methods*. Jerusalem: Magnes Press.

Ognibeni, Bruno. 1995. *La seconda parte del Sefer Oklah weOklah. Edizione del ms. Halle, Universitätsbibliothek Y v 4º, ff. 68–124*. Textos y estudios "Cardenal Cisneros" 57. Madrid: CSIC.

Orlinsky, Harry M. 1966. 'Prolegomenon. The Masoretic Text: A Critical Evaluation'. In Ginsburg 1966 (1897), i–xlv.

Ortega Monasterio, María Teresa. 1986. 'Las masoras de A, C y L en el libro de Habacuc'. *Henoch* 8: 149–84.

———. 1993. 'Some Aspects of the Masora of the Codices Or. 4445 and Aleppo'. In *Estudios Masoreticos (X Congreso de la International Organization for Masoretic Studies), en memoria de Harry M. Orlinsky*, edited by Emilia Fernández Tejero and María Teresa Ortega Monasterio, 89–98. Madrid: Instituto de Filología del CSIC.

———. 1997. 'Some Masoretic Notes of Mss. L and Or 4445 Compared with the Spanish Tradition'. *Sefarad* 57: 127–33.

Revell, E. J. 1970. *Hebrew Texts with Palestinian Vocalization*. Toronto: University of Toronto Press.

———. 1974. 'The Relation of the Palestinian to the Tiberian Massora'. In *1972 and 1973 Proceedings IOMS*, edited by Harry Orlinsky, 87–98. Masoretic Studies 1. Missoula: MT: Scholars Press.

———. 1977. *Biblical Texts with Palestinian Pointing and their Accents*. Masoretic Studies 4. Missoula, MT: Scholars Press.

———. 1985. 'The Conditioning of Stress Position in *Waw* Consecutive Perfect Forms in Biblical Hebrew'. *Hebrew Annual Review* 9: 277–300.

Weil, Gérard E. 1963. 'Un fragment de Okhlah Palestinienne'. *Annual of the Leeds University Oriental Society* 3: 68–80.

Yeivin, Israel. 1963. 'A Palestinian Fragment of Haftaroth and Other MSS with Mixed Pointing'. *Textus* 3: 121–27.

———. 1980. *Introduction to the Tiberian Masorah.* Translated and edited by E. J. Revell. Masoretic Studies 5. Missoula, MT: Scholars Press.

THE MASORETIC NOTES IN RNL EVR II B 80+: AN INITIAL REPORT

Kim Phillips

From Second Temple times until the end of the first millennium CE, the Hebrew Bible was preserved and transmitted in two major Jewish cultural centres: Tiberias and 'Babylon' (i.e., Iraq) (Khan 2020, 6–33). The consonantal texts preserved in each of these two centres differed in a great many small details one from the other. Likewise, the reading traditions preserved and transmitted in each centre differed one from the other, mainly at the levels of phonetics, phonology, and morphology (i.e., different dialects of Hebrew), but also—to a far lesser degree—at the level of the semantic content of the texts (Chiesa 1979, 9–36; Yeivin 1985, 21–36).

Each centre also developed its own distinct apparatus as an aid to the preservation of minute details of the biblical text (consonants + reading tradition)—its own *masora*, in the narrow sense of the term. These textual commentaries differed one from the other not only with respect to the texts they were designed to preserve, but also in terms of the methods used, terminology employed, and even the way each commentary was preserved and transmitted. The Tiberian Masora (t.Mas) exists as a vast nebula of distinct notes and comments, which was drawn on according to

 https://doi.org/10.11647/OBP.0330.02

need, taste, and availability, on a codex-by-codex basis (Yeivin 2003, 60–92). There is no authoritative standard text-form of the t.Mas. By contrast, there *is* an authoritative standard text-form of the Babylonian Masora (b.Mas), at least of the Pentateuch. The b.Mas of the Pentateuch (b.MasP) was transmitted as a distinct text, not usually 'appended' to the biblical text itself. Where separate copies of the same portions of this text have been preserved, they are functionally identical. Some Babylonian biblical MSS do contain individual masoretic comments in the margins, but these comments have their origin in a text with a fixed form (Ofer 2019, 151–57).[1]

In the same way that the Hebrew biblical commentaries of R. David Qimḥi and Abraham Ibn Ezra condemned the Judaeo-Arabic commentaries of their forebears to obscurity for centuries,

---

[1] Abbreviations used throughout this article: A = Aleppo Codex; b.Mas = The Babylonian Masora, referring to the entirety of the fixed text of this textual commentary; b.MasP = The Babylonian Masora of the Pentateuch (referring to the entire, perhaps unrecoverable, text of this textual commentary, rather than Ofer's edition, which is fragmentary); DP = Damascus Pentateuch; L = Firkowich B 19a, i.e., the 'Leningrad' Codex; L^{m} = Pentateuch MS, written by Samuel b. Jacob (scribe of L), containing a large proportion of Babylonian masoretic notes (the *masora magna* of the MS has been edited by Breuer 1992; also known as Gottheil 14; see Gottheil 1905); Mm = Masora Magna; Mp = Masora Parva; Of.b.MasP = Ofer's (2001) edition of the Babylonian Masora to the Pentateuch; Or. 4445 = 'The London Pentateuch', located in the British Library; S^{1} = Sassoon 1053; t.Mas = the Tiberian Masora: the vast, nebulous, collection of individual notes designed to preserve the Tiberian recension of the biblical text.

so the rapid triumph of the Tiberian biblical text and reading tradition among the various Jewish communities quickly led to the demise and obscuring of the once-influential Babylonian text and reading tradition—and the b.Mas with it (Yeivin 1985, 22–24). However, since the uncovering of the Cairo Geniza, the study of the Babylonian biblical tradition in general, and the study of the b.Mas in particular, have flourished.

The study of the masoretic notes from the Babylonian tradition is very much a work in progress. Over the course of the last century many individual fragments of b.Mas have been edited. This labour culminated in Ofer's 600-page annotated edition of the Babylonian Masora of the Pentateuch (Ofer 2001). This edition incorporates all the currently known fragments of MSS containing the b.MasP text itself (though not the individual notes found in various biblical MSS). Nevertheless, he estimates that his edition comprises only about one sixth of the original b.MasP text. There is, to date, no edition of the b.Mas of the Prophets and Writings, though Ofer is at work on the latter (see Ofer 2011, 148 n. 42).[2] For obvious reasons, the present article will make constant reference to Ofer's edition of the b.MasP.

Part of the difficulty in studying the b.Mas is that the majority of the relevant manuscripts are from the Cairo Geniza, with all the fragmentariness involved with documents from this source. However, a crucially important exception to this is the manuscript known as L^m. L^m is a Tiberian Torah MS in terms of

---

[2] Weil (1963) and Yeivin (1982) have each edited small portions of the b.Mas of the Prophets, but compared to the b.MasP, the manuscript remains are few and far between.

text and layout, yet a very high proportion of its Mm seems to have come from a Babylonian source. Breuer (1992) has edited and annotated the Mm of L^m in two volumes, but the MS itself remains inaccessible to scholars.[3] Ofer (2001, 13–25) devotes an entire chapter to the discussion of L^m, and uses it throughout b.MasP.Ofer as a supplementary source to help clarify difficult portions of the MSS containing the formal b.MasP text.

L^m is not the only Tiberian MS that makes use of the b.Mas (or at least Babylonian graphemes and masoretic terminology). Indeed, Yeivin (1968, 72–75), Breuer (1992), Ofer (2001, 260–74), and Dotan (2005) have demonstrated that most of the well-known Tiberian MSS contain a certain amount of masoretic material originating from a Babylonian source. At one end of the spectrum, this Babylonian influence is very slight (e.g., in A); in other MSS (e.g., BL Or. 4445) the influence is more pronounced; and in still other MSS the influence is rather substantial (e.g., S^1). This phenomenon raises further questions, therefore, regarding the nature of the interaction between, and mutual influence, of the Tiberian and Babylonian masoretic traditions. At any rate, to date, L^m is thought to stand alone in terms of the massive extent to which the *masran* behind a Tiberian codex made use of Babylonian material in his *masora*.[4]

---

[3] For the purposes of the present article this inaccessibility is a particular frustration, inasmuch as the Mp notes of the MS are highly relevant to our topic here.

[4] The question of what 'counts' as a Babylonian masoretic note can be answered in various ways. Breuer (1992) adopts a minimalist approach, and classifies Mm notes in L^m as Babylonian only if he can demonstrate that the content of the note does not match the Tiberian biblical text,

However, it now appears that another Tiberian MS must be placed close to L^m with regard to the extent of the Babylonian influence on the masoretic notes: MS RNL EVR II B 80+.[5] Though quintessentially Tiberian in text-form and layout, the masoretic notes of this Torah MS show very extensive and sustained influence of the b.Mas.[6]

---

but does match what is known about the Babylonian biblical text and dialect (Ofer 1992, 272–73). There are at least two obvious difficulties with this approach. First, a great deal of the Babylonian biblical text and dialect is identical with the Tiberian text and dialect. Therefore, one would expect that a large proportion of the Babylonian masoretic notes would be identical in content (even if different in form and terminology) to the Tiberian notes. Breuer's approach makes no allowance for this, and therefore can only be expected to catch a relatively small subset of the Mm notes in L^m taken from a Babylonian source. Secondly, much about the Babylonian consonantal text (and, to some extent, dialect) remains uncertain, and so, once again, Breuer's approach can only positively identify a subset of the genuinely Babylonian notes. Yeivin (1968) is similarly cautious about identifying Babylonian notes in Tiberian codices purely based on the appearance of Babylonian vowel signs and masoretic terms, such as של' or even דק'. However, by comparing the Mm notes in L^m with the content of his edition of b.Mas.P, Ofer found that the great majority of the notes in L^m derived from the b.Mas.P, even when the content of the notes matched the Tiberian text just as well as the Babylonian text. In turn, this fully justifies taking a broader approach to identifying Babylonian notes. This broader approach (relying on not only the content of the notes, but also their form) is adopted by Ofer (2001) and Dotan (2005), and is the approach followed in this article.

[5] The + sign indicates additional shelfmarks (see §1.0, below).

[6] To the best of my knowledge, the masoretic notes of this MS have drawn scholarly attention twice before. Strack (1897) mentions two

The purpose of this article is to present a preliminary report on the masoretic notes (Mm and Mp) of this MS. The report will demonstrate the nature and extent of the Babylonian masoretic material therein, and begin to illustrate some of the ways in which this material can be used to consolidate and expand our existing knowledge of the b.Mas. Thus, the article is selective and illustrative, and makes no attempt at comprehensiveness. It is hoped that it will alert other students of the b.Mas to the riches of this MS, until a full edition and analysis of its *masora* (already underway) is completed.

After a brief description of the codex, the discussion of the masoretic notes is divided into three sections: structural features, external features, and internal features.

- Structural features: The b.Mas has a set of distinctive patterns, or formats, in the way its notes are structured. Some of these are scarcely attested in the t.Mas, but commonplace in the b.Mas. In the first section of this study, I show

notes (one Mm, one Mp) from the MS (which he refers to by its old numbering: Cod. Tschuf. 51), both of which discuss variant readings between the Easterners (Sura and Nehardea) and the Westerners. I am grateful to Prof. Yosef Ofer for bringing this article to my attention. The second discussion of the masoretic notes of this MS appears in Penkower's (2020) recent study of the textual variants between Sura and Nehardea. The frequent Mm and Mp notes discussing textual variants between the Eastern schools of Sura and Nehardea is further evidence of the Babylonian influence on the *masora* of this MS. Nonetheless, since so many examples have already been adduced by Penkower in his study, this aspect of the masoretic notes will not be considered further in this initial report.

that almost all the quintessentially Babylonian note-formats are found with great frequency throughout the MS.[7]

- External features: there are other (non-structural) Babylonian aspects that are visible 'on the surface' of the notes (i.e., self-evident to the eye, without having to analyse the content of the notes). These include terminology from the b.Mas, aspects of Babylonian Aramaic in the notes, etc. These features are reviewed in the second section of this chapter.
- Internal features: the final section of this chapter shows that when the content of many of the notes is analysed, it often only matches the Babylonian biblical text, or the Babylonian dialect of Hebrew.

1.0. Description of RNL EVR II B 80+[8]

The codex here referred to as RNL EVR II B 80+ is currently preserved under at least three shelfmarks. EVR II B 80 preserves the lion's share of the remains of the codex: 124 leaves.[9] EVR II B 170

[7] Ofer's (2001) monumental study of the b.MasP has been immensely instructive throughout this whole study. In particular, this section on the various common formats of Babylonian masoretic notes relies almost exclusively on his descriptions and analyses of the various note types.

[8] A full description of this MS (rather than simply its *masora*) is currently in preparation as a separate article. The brief description here, therefore, is intended only to orient the reader regarding the most general aspects of the MS, before focussing on the masoretic notes.

[9] In its current presentation on the Ktiv website, as well as in the descriptions in Beit-Arié et al. (1997, 13–14) and Dukan (2006, 310–11),

and EVR II B 14 each contain an additional three leaves. Thus, 130 leaves of the original codex are currently available to us. Throughout this article, individual shelfmarks are used where relevant, but generally the entire codex is referred to, using the label EVR II B 80+.[10] For ease, I will refer to the relevant image number when giving examples from the codex. All the examples below happen to be taken from EVR II B 80, which contains 256 images on the Ktiv website.[11] Thus, references take the form: 'image x/256'.

---

the MS has 125 folios, and fol. 125 contains two colophons, including a date (which has signs of tampering). However, it appears that this folio is not, in fact, part of the same MS as the rest of RNL EVR II B 80+. The most obvious evidence for this comes from the fact that although the double-dot *sof-pasuq* sign is used regularly and systematically throughout EVR II B 80+, it is virtually never used on fol. 125. Additional evidence pointing towards the fact that fol. 125 is not from our MS is to be found in the line-fillers employed, the positioning of the *masora circellus*, the shape of the *ḥaṭef-pataḥ* sign, and the use of *rafe*. More details will be provided in the full description of the MS.

[10] For the purposes of this study, I have searched through RNL EVR II B 1–600, looking for other fragments from this same MS. It is entirely plausible that when the scope of the search is expanded (as it must be before an edition of the notes can be produced), other portions of the MS will be found. For this initial report, however, the 130 leaves found thus far offer ample material for description.

[11] Accessible at https://web.nli.org.il/sites/nlis/he/manuscript.

RNL EVR II B 80+ is a monumental (42 × 36cm), three-column Model Torah Codex, probably from the 10th or 11th century.[12] The column height is 29cm, with 21 lines per column.[13] The margins are wide, with Mm in the upper and lower margins of virtually all the pages (typically one or two lines of Mm in the upper margin, and one to four lines in the lower margin). Mp notes occupy the outer vertical margin, and the two inter-columnar margins, but rarely the gutter margin of the page. The Mm contains some collative masoretic notes; these appear only in the upper margin of the page and occasionally include select Tiberian signs of cantillation and vocalisation (for example, the upper margin of fol. 4r and again on 31r). The rest of the Mm and Mp is sporadically vocalised and/or cantillated, with Tiberian accent signs and Tiberian or Babylonian vowel signs. These Babylonian vowel signs are from the simple (rather than the compound) line system (see Yeivin 1985, 54–55). Occasionally, the *pataḥ* sign from the dot system is employed (e.g., 55/256, 109/256). Many of the Babylonian vowel signs are placed over the inter-consonantal space, a clear marker of antiquity, according to Yeivin (1985, 55).

The biblical text is written in an accomplished Eastern hand, with Tiberian vocalisation and cantillation signs. Consonantally, the text is very close to that of A.

The extant portions of the MS comprise 130 folios. Of these, the majority are well preserved, such that almost all the biblical text on each leaf is extant and legible. Nonetheless, most of the

[12] See n. 9 above regarding the dated colophon that has been hitherto ascribed to this MS.

[13] These dimensions are taken from Dukan (2006, 310–11).

leaves contain some damage to the top margin and inner corner, such that the upper Mm is frequently obliterated, partially or completely, and often much of the Mp has also been lost. Fols 31–33 (images 65/256–70/256) and (especially) 46–49 (images 95/256–102/256) have suffered more extensive damage, such that significant portions of the biblical text itself are no longer legible on these leaves.

The following portions of the biblical text have been preserved in the MS (references in *italics* are from EVR II B 14; references underlined are from EVR II B 170; other references are from EVR II B 80):

> Gen. 27.20–42.4; *42.4–33*; 42.33–44.13; 46.10–50.26; Exod. 1.1–2.3; 10.15–12.25; 13.2–14.28; 16.19–20.17; 21.28–30.38; 32.33–36.7; 39.15–42; Lev. 13.57–14.51; 14.51–15.24; 15.24–16.16; 17.6–18.21; 23.18–44; *25.8–37*; *26.42–27.23*; Num. 1.23–51; 4.7–9.12; 10.20–13.23; 14.14–18.28; 20.1–28; 22.19–36.13; Deut. 1.1–31:14; 33.18–34.12.

In other words, almost all of Numbers and Deuteronomy have been preserved, together with about two thirds of Exodus, half of Genesis, and about a quarter of Leviticus.

Having been introduced to the MS itself, we can now focus our attention on the masoretic notes therein. As mentioned above, I will describe the Babylonian aspects of the notes from three different angles: structural features (the typically Babylonian ways many of the notes are constructed), external features (other aspects of the notes that reveal their Babylonian origins, without having to analyse the content of the notes), and internal features (the ways the notes reveal, when their content is analysed, that they refer to the Babylonian form of the biblical text and the Babylonian dialect of Hebrew).

2.0. Structural Features

Ofer (2001, 75–123) gives an extremely helpful overview and description of the different types of masoretic notes that are typical of the b.Mas. In this first section I simply demonstrate that almost all of the quintessential forms of Babylonian notes are found, often in great profusion, in EVR II B 80+.

2.1. All-Inclusive Description[14]

One of the foundational differences between the Tiberian and Babylonian *masorot* lies in the way each system counts and lists whatever textual element is under discussion. The simplest way to explain this difference is via an example.

(1) ויירא̇ו האנשים...

‘**And** the men **feared**…’ (Gen. 43.18 [Image 42/256])

‘They feared’ occurs 6 times	ויירא̇ו ו'
	של' בע וסימנהון

[14] Ofer (2001) refers to this as התיאור הכולל, and gives a comprehensive discussion of the phenomenon. In Ofer (2019) this phrase is translated in two ways: ‘general description’ and ‘all-inclusive description’. The latter translation is more helpful, pointing towards the fact that the count in these notes refers to the entirety of the Hebrew Bible, rather than dividing the text into discrete sections and dealing with each section in isolation, as is common in the t.Mas.

plene in the Scriptures, thus:[15]

All the Torah	כוליה אוריתא
Josh. 10.2	כי עיר גדולה
1 Sam. 17.24	בראותם את האיש
2 Kgs 17.7	ויהי כי חטאו בני ישראל
The Minor Prophets	תרי עשרה
All the Writings, excluding:	וכוליה כתיבי חוץ מן
Neh. 6.16.[16]	וַיִּרְאוּ כל הגוים

This note from EVR II B 80+ is concerned with the *plene* spelling of *wayyiqṭol* ויירא. Note in particular how the count of six includes not only three individual verses, but also three large stretches of text: 'all the Torah', 'the Minor Prophets', and 'all the Writings, except…' By my count, the *plene* spelling of the *wayyiqṭol* ויירא occurs six times in the Torah, four times in the Minor Prophets, and twice in the Writings (Psalms). In this Babylonian masoretic note, however, the entire Torah, all the Minor Prophets, and all the Writings each increase the count by only one.

---

[15] Translating masoretic notes into meaningful English is notoriously difficult, due to the highly codified and condensed language in which the notes are expressed. In the translations offered in this article I have aimed at a lucid, idiomatic rendering of the sense of the notes, rather than any sort of isomorphic formal equivalence.

[16] This note also appears in L^m at Gen. 20.8 (Breuer 1992, 124). There, however, the language of the note has been 'Tiberianised', as has the structure of the note, in such a way that the count no longer fits the lemmata. In addition, the reference to 'all the Torah' has been omitted. EVR II B 80+ thus preserves a more original Babylonian form of the note, as well as its accuracy.

There are here two distinctive features of the Babylonian All-Inclusive Description: (i) the count is all-inclusive—all the Bible is covered by the one count; (ii) entire books, or collections of books, with multiple individual instances of the relevant textual phenomenon, can be grouped together as 'one' instance for the sake of the count.[17]

---

[17] By contrast, the typical Tiberian way of describing the same phenomenon would be to break down the biblical text into sections and deal with those sections separately. For example, the note above could be 'Tiberianised' as follows:

'They feared' occurs three times *plene*, thus:	וייראו ג' מל' וסימנהון
Josh. 10.2	כי עיר גדולה
1 Sam. 17.24	בראותם את האיש
2 Kgs 17.7	ויהי כי חטאו בני ישראל
And all [occurrences in] the Torah, the Twelve, and the Writings are likewise *plene*, apart from one instance:	וכל תור' ותרי עש' וכתיביא דכותהון בר מן א
Neh. 6.16	וַיִּרְאוּ כל הגוים

Note how this Tiberian-style note divides the biblical text into two distinct sections. The first section (whose boundaries are typically unstated and must be inferred from the note as a whole) consists of the Prophets, apart from The Twelve. For this section, the count of *plene* occurrences of 'they feared' is three (the clear minority—there are eight defective forms in the same section). In the latter section: the Torah, the Twelve, and the Writings, the situation is reversed: all the occurrences of 'they feared' are *plene*, apart from Neh. 6.16. Thus, in the Tiberian-style note, the biblical text is divided into suitable distinct sections, and each section is dealt with separately. The note as a whole intertwines the discussion of the two sections using the term דכותהון. For an overview of the issues of counting and structure in masoretic notes (not specific to the b.Mas), see Breuer (1976, 193–283).

The Mm notes in EVR II B 80+ contain many dozens of examples of the All-Inclusive Description. Here is one more instance:

(2) ...וַיֹּאמְרוּ אֶל־פַּרְעֹה רֹעֵה צֹאן עֲבָדֶיךָ גַּם־אֲנַחְנוּ גַּם־אֲבוֹתֵינוּ׃
'..."Your servants are shepherds, as **our fathers** were."' (Gen. 47.3 [Image 47/256])

'Our fathers' occurs 11 times *plene* in the Scriptures, thus:	אבותינו י'א' של' בע' וסימנהון
Gen. 47.3 (end of verse)	גם אבותינו סוף פסוקא
All of Joshua	וכוליה יהושע
All of Judges	וכוליה שפטי
Jer. 3.24...	והבשת אכלה
...and following (Jer. 3.25)	ושלאחריו
Jer. 14.20	ידענו ייי
Jer. 16.19	נחלו אבותינו
All of Psalms, excluding:	וכוליה תילתא בר מן
Ps. 22.5	בך בטחו אבתינו
1 Chron. 12.18[18]	ירא אלהי אבותינו ויוכח
2 Chron. 29.9	והנה נפלו אבותינו
2 Chron. 34.21.	על אשר לא שמרו אבותינו

Once again, in this note, the count of 11 refers to the entire Bible, rather than simply to one section thereof. Joshua, Judges and

[18] Notice how the citations from Chronicles appear *after* the citations from Psalms. This reflects the Babylonian arrangement of the biblical books, rather than the Tiberian arrangement. See below, §3.4, for further details.

Psalms are each included in their entirety, even though they encompass multiple individual occurrences.[19]

2.2. Partial Count Preceding the All-Inclusive Description

Example (2) immediately above illustrates one of the systemic dangers inherent in the All-Inclusive Description. Consider the final five lines of the note:

וכוליה תילתא בר מן
בך בטחו אבתינו
ירא אלהי אבותינו ויוכח
והנה נפלו אבותינו
על אשר לא שמרו אבותינו

When one deciphers the biblical references behind the lemmata, it becomes clear that only one exceptional verse from the book of Psalms is mentioned. The subsequent three lemmata, from Chronicles, are part of the overall count of eleven *plene-plene* occurrences of אבותינו. However, if one does not carefully locate the references behind the lemmata, these lines could easily be misunderstood as presenting four exceptional verses from the book of Psalms. The problem, in other words, lies in the fact that

[19] Breuer (1976, 209) discusses the oddities of the equivalent Tiberian form of this note. In a very important chapter, Ofer (2001, 75–100) shows how our growing knowledge of the b.Mas has the capacity to explain many such oddities outlined by Breuer. Neither Breuer (1976) nor Ofer (2001) had access to this note in its Babylonian form. Now it has come to light, it is clear that Ofer's explanation perfectly fits in this instance, too.

there is no obvious boundary indicating the end of the list of exceptional verses, and the resumption of the list of verses making up the primary content of the note.

Ofer (2001, 79–81) suggests that this inherent source of potential confusion was the motivation behind an alternative form of the All-Inclusive Description also found frequently in the b.Mas: the Partial Count Preceding the All-Inclusive Description. Once again, this alternative form is found frequently in the Mm of EVR II B 80+. The example below, from EVR II B 80, is also found in b.Mas.P.Of:

(3) אֵ֣לֶּה קריאי (K) קְרוּאֵ֣י (Q) הָעֵדָ֔ה נְשִׂיאֵ֖י מַטּ֣וֹת **אֲבוֹתָ֑ם**...

'These were the ones chosen from the congregation, the chiefs of the tribes of **their fathers**...' (Num. 1.16 [Image 111/256])

'Their fathers' appears twice *plene* in the Torah, thus:	אבותם ב' מל' באוריתא וסימנהון
Num. 1.16	אלה קרואי העדה
Num. 17.18	ואת שם אהרן תכתב
[But] all [the rest of] the Torah	וכוליה אוריתא
1 Kgs 9.9	ואמרו
1 Kgs 14.22	ויקנאו
1 Kgs 17.41	גם בניהם
Ezra 10.16	ויבדלו עזרא
Neh. 7.61[20]	ולא יכלו להגיד בתרא'

[20] The term בתראה 'the latter' indicates, in this instance, that that verse in Nehemiah is being referred to, rather than the nearly identical verse from the parallel list in Ezra 2.

These are all the defectively spelled occurrences. הלין חס' בע'

This note could have been phrased as a normal All-Inclusive Description: 'Their fathers' is spelled defectively six times in the Scriptures: All the Torah apart from [two lemmata] + five more lemmata from Kings and Ezra-Nehemiah. The problem with this, as described above, is the potential confusion in moving immediately from the two exceptional *plene* spellings in the Torah, back to the five defective spellings in Kings and Ezra-Nehemiah. Instead, the Partial Count Preceding the All-Inclusive Description relocates the two exceptional verses from the Torah to the very beginning of the note, then continues with the normal All-Inclusive Description (minus the count) thereafter.

This note, in the same form, appears in b.Mas.P.Of (Ofer 2001, 495–96). The two notes are functionally identical, except that: (i) של' has been Tiberianised to מל' in our MS; (ii) וסימנהון has been added before the initial two lemmata in our MS; and (iii) the order of citations from Kings is canonical in our MS, whereas the first two are inverted in b.Mas.P.Of.

2.3. Rule-Stating Notes[21]

The b.Mas pays considerable attention to noting spellings in the Hebrew Bible that are *uniform* throughout the entire biblical text.[22] These observations are then phrased in short notes

[21] הערות כלל in Ofer's (2001, 105–7) terminology.

[22] By contrast, the t.Mas pays far less attention to words with consistent spellings, focusing instead on words whose spelling is variable.

throughout the b.Mas text. The Mm of EVR II B 80+ contains many dozens of such notes. Here are just a couple of examples, neither of which appears in L^{m} or in Ofer's edition:

(4) וַיְעַנְךָ֮ וַיַּרְעִבֶ֒ךָ֒ וַיַּאֲכִלְךָ֤ אֶת־הַמָּן֙ אֲשֶׁר לֹא־יָדַ֔עְתָּ וְלֹא יָדְעוּן אֲבֹתֶיךָ לְמַעַן הוֹדִיעֲךָ֗ כִּ֠י לֹא עַל־הַלֶּחֶם לְבַדּוֹ֙ יִחְיֶה הָאָדָ֔ם...

'And he humbled you and let you hunger and fed you with manna, which you did not know, nor did your fathers know, in order **to make you know** that man does not live by bread alone...' (Deut. 8.3 [Image 202/256])

The forms הודיעך and להודיעך are always written *plene*.

הודיעך להודיעך
כול' שלי'

(5) לֹא בְצִדְקָתְךָ֗ וּבְיֹ֙שֶׁר֙ לְבָבְךָ֔ אַתָּה בָא לָרֶשֶׁת אֶת־אַרְצָם...

'Not because of your righteousness **or the uprightness of** your heart are you going in to possess their land...' (Deut. 9.5 [Image 204/256])

Every occurrence of the forms ובישר, ישר, and וישר is spelled defectively.

ובישר ישר וישר
כול' חס'

In addition to these Rule-Stating Notes in the Mm, the *masran* behind EVR II B 80+ has also reworked many such observations from the b.Mas into *masora parva* notes.[23] For example, the following Mp notes all appear on image 79/256 (Exod. 25). Each of them appears to have been taken directly from the b.Mas, which is largely extant at this point:

---

[23] In Dotan's (2005, 36) overview of the traces of the b.Mas extant in Or. 4445, he mentions the existence of many Mp notes of the format: כול' + [מל'/חס'/כת' כן]. He sees these notes as one of the most prominent aspects of the Babylonian 'residue' in the *masora* of the MS.

Table 1: Mp notes in EVR II B 80

Reference	Biblical Text	Mp note in EVR II B 80	Equivalent note in Babylonian Masora (Ofer 2001, 450–51)
Exod. 25.12	פַּעֲמֹתָ֑יו	כול' חס'	פעמתיו פעמני הפעמנים פעמן כול' חס'
Exod. 25.17	כַפֹּ֖רֶת	כול חס'	כפרת הכפרת כול' חס'
Exod. 25.19	כְּר֨וּב	כול' מל'[24]	כרוב וכרוב לכרוב כול' של'
Exod. 25.19	וּכְרוּב־	כול' מל'	כרוב וכרוב לכרוב כול' של'
Exod. 25.20	הַכַּפֹּ֔רֶת	כול' חס'	כפרת הכפרת כול' חס'

To iterate the point: the t.Mas (*magna* and *parva*) does not tend to focus on uniform spellings, but variable spellings. None of the notes above appear in L (at all), or in Or. 4445 or DP (*ad loc.*). In fact, Yeivin (1968, 74) finds only one 'כול' חס note (which he, too, recognises as Babylonian in character) in the whole of A, and no כול' מל'/של'/כת' כן notes at all. The *masran* of EVR II B 80 +, though creating a genuinely Tiberian MS with typical Tiberian format for the *masora* (i.e., the distinction between Mm and Mp), nonetheless populates the Tiberian MS with many notes from the Babylonian masoretic tradition.[25]

---

[24] Here, the *masran* has semi-Tiberianised the note by converting 'של to 'מל. Nonetheless, the note remains quintessentially Babylonian, in that it attends to a uniform, rather than a variable, spelling.

[25] These Rule-Stating Notes are certainly not the only Babylonian notes to be found in the Mp of EVR II B 80 +. At present (until the MS is made available for scholarly examination) we do not have access to the Mp notes of L^m, and thus cannot tell to what extent reworked Babylonian masoretic content is to be found therein. Until access to L^m becomes available, EVR II B 80 + appears to be the most significant MS currently

2.4. Rule-Stating Notes, with Exceptions

If a particular word has a uniform spelling apart from one or two exceptions, the b.Mas has a typical formula for describing both the regular spelling and the exceptions:

> [מילה] כול' של"/חס' [-/בר מן/חוץ מ-] [פסוק חריג] חס'/של' בע'
>
> [the word] all *plene*/defective [except from] [select verses] defective/*plene*...[26]

First, the majority spelling is noted, in the typical format of the Rule-Stating Note. Thereafter, the exception is noted. According to Ofer (2001, 106), the two parts of the note are not usually linked by any sort of prepositional phrase, e.g., בר מן or חוץ מ-, and one is left to infer that the latter citation is an exception to the previously stated rule, by means of the concluding clause: חס'/של' בע'. In Ofer's list, only 5 out of the 14 notes contain a linking prepositional phrase.

EVR II B 80+ contains a great many Rule-Stating Notes, with Exceptions. The evidence of the initial survey suggests that, unlike in the pure b.Mas, the two parts of the note are usually joined with the prepositional phrase בר מן.[27] Nonetheless, some maintain the pure form dominant in Ofer's edition, such as the

available for examining the process of embedding Babylonian masoretic content into Tiberian-style Mp notes. I hope to carry out a full study of this phenomenon soon.

[26] This is a slightly emended citation of Ofer's (2001, 106) formulation.

[27] Possibly, this is evidence of an attempt to render the unfamiliar Babylonian form more readily understandable to a Tiberian user of the MS.

following (this particular example is found in neither b.Mas.P.Ofer nor L^m):

(6) תָּכִין לְךָ הַדֶּרֶךְ...

'**You shall prepare** yourself a way...' (Deut. 19.3 [Image 225/256])

The forms תכין and יכין are always *plene* [except for:]	תכין יכין כול' מל'
Ps. 89.3,	שמים תכן אמונתך בהם
which is the only defective spelling of תכן in the Scriptures.[28]	חס' בע'

2.5. Classifying Notes[29]

If a particular word in the biblical text has two optional *matres lectionis*, this results in *four* possible spellings for that word. The b.Mas has a distinctive type of note for such forms. First, the various minority spellings are grouped, and their references listed. Then, the note ends with the formula 'and the rest are spelled + [most frequent spelling]'.[30] Thus, the note serves as a guide to all the various spellings of that particular word in all its occurrences. Ofer (2001, 108) notes that in the formal b.Mas text these notes are usually introduced with the formula: [מילה] + של' וחס',

[28] Once again, this note shows a token effort at Tiberianisation. Nonetheless, the content and structure of the note, and the use of the term בע' are all quintessentially Babylonian.

[29] הערות המסורה הממיינות in Ofer's (2001, 108–10) terminology.

[30] Note that, because of the b.Mas's distinctive way of counting (see §2.1, above), the 'minority' and 'majority' spellings may well not be classified on a purely numerical basis.

whereas in L^m^ this formula has usually been removed (perhaps in an effort to Tiberianise the notes).

EVR II B 80+ contains dozens of these Classifying Notes. In almost all cases it seems that the introductory formula has been removed (as with L^m^), though other typically Babylonian terminology within the note itself often remains. The example below (the only example I have thus far found with the introductory formula still extant) also appears in Of.b.MasP and L^m^, thereby offering an excellent opportunity to compare the three sources:

(7) אֶת־בֶּ֫צֶר בַּמִּדְבָּ֛ר בְּאֶ֥רֶץ הַמִּישֹׁ֖ר לָרֻֽאוּבֵנִ֑י וְאֶת־**רָאמֹ֤ת** בַּגִּלְעָד֙ לַגָּדִ֔י...

'Bezer in the wilderness on the tableland for the Reubenites, **Ramoth** in Gilead for the Gadites…' (Deut. 4.43 [Image 195/256])

The *plene* and defective spellings of רמות:	רמות של' וחס'
Deut. 4.43…	את בצר במדבר
…and its parallel in Josh. [20.8]	ודומ' דיהושע
Ezek. 27.16	וראמׄת וכדכׄד
These occurrences are spelled ראמת:	ראמׄת כת':
1 Sam. 30.27	ולאשר ברׄמׄוׄת
Ps. 18.28	ועינים רׄמׄוׄת
Prov. 6.17	עינים רׄמׄוׄת
Ezra 10.29	ושאל ורׄמׄוׄת
2 Chron. 18.19	ויׄׄעל ויׄפׄל דדברי הימים
2 Chron. 22.5	גם בעצׄתׄם
All of these are spelled רמות:	כולהון רׄמׄוׄת כת':
Job 28.18	ראמות וגׄבׄיש
Prov. 24.7	רׄאמות לאויל

(2 Chron. 18.19?)[31] יפ֫ת֫ה

[31] Breuer also finds this lemma at this point in the note in L^{m}. However, there it is written as יפתח and unpointed. Breuer (1992, 687) interprets this as a second lemma from the same verse as the preceding lemma: Prov. 24.7. He offers no explanation as to why two lemmata are given for the same verse, nor why the rather indistinctive form יפתח would be used as a lemma at all. In Ofer's (2001, 552) version of the same note the lemma יפתח and the following lemma וישׂשכר are both listed after the end of the note, quite out of place. Ofer, too, interprets יפתח as referring to Prov. 24.7, and suggests that the repetition of references to this verse points to the coupling together of originally separate masoretic notes.

The present manuscript seems to have had a similar *Vorlage* to Ofer's and (particularly) Breuer's MSS. However, the relevant word has been read and interpreted differently. Consonantally, ה is read at the end of the word, rather than ח. Additionally, the lemma in the present MS has been vocalised as the equivalent of Tiberian יְפַתֶּה. This seems to refer to either 1 Kings 22:20, or 2 Chronicles 18:19: וַיֹּ֣אמֶר יְהֹוָ֗ה מִ֤י יְפַתֶּה֙ אֶת־אַחְאָ֔ב וְיַ֕עַל וְיִפֹּ֖ל בְּרָמֹ֣ת גִּלְעָ֑ד (Kings; the Chronicles version adds מלך ישראל after אחאב, and spells Ramoth with *plene vav*).

The evidence of the present MS, taken together with the textual witnesses offered by Breuer and Ofer, offers another way to interpret the presence of this puzzling lemma. First, note the unexpected spelling in part of Ofer's version of the note:

...רמות כת'
רמות וגביש
רמות לאויל...
ראמות כת'

The forms רמות וגביש and רמות לאויל are spelled without א, even though they are part of the section of the list that concludes: ראמות כת'. It is plausible that a copyist, momentarily confused by the lemmata רמות וגביש and רמות לאויל, and perhaps also noting the reference to Chronicles immediately following, mistakenly added the lemma יפתה, as a reference to 2 Chron. 18.19, in which 'Ramoth' is genuinely spelled רמות.

1 Chron. 6.58	וישׂשכר
1 Chron. 6.65	וגד דדברי הימים
These occurrences are spelled ראמות.	ראמות כת'
All the other occurrences are spelled רמת.	ושאר' רׄמֹת כת'

The above examples illustrate my claim that a large proportion of the Mm notes in EVR II B 80+ are quintessentially Babylonian in their structure. Before moving on to discuss other Babylonian facets of the masoretic notes in this MS, it is worth pointing out that at least one typically Babylonian note-type is seemingly absent from the *masora* of the MS: the Cross-Referencing Note.[32] The reason for this lack appears to be the fact that the *masran* behind our MS abandoned the b.Mas' 'principle of the first occurrence' in the process of fitting the Babylonian notes to his Tiberian MS.[33]

3.0. External Features

So far, the discussion has focussed on the structural aspects of the masoretic notes in EVR II B 80+, i.e., how occurrences are counted and how the masoretic information is structured in the notes themselves. I hope to have demonstrated that almost all the patterns and formats considered by Ofer to be characteristic of the Babylonian Masora (as opposed to the Tiberian) are found in the MS—often with great frequency. We now proceed to what I call the External Babylonian Features. By this I mean non-structural aspects of the notes suggesting their Babylonian origin that

[32] Regarding this type of note, see Ofer (2001, 60–74).

[33] On the principle of first occurrence, see Ofer (2001, 26–29).

are visible 'on the surface' of the note, that is, without any need to analyse the structure of the note or what information it provides about the biblical text. Most obviously, this category includes the use of Babylonian masoretic terminology, some of which occurs in great profusion throughout the MS. Also included in this section are evidence of Babylonian, rather than Palestinian, Aramaic features in the wording of the notes; evidence of the Babylonian pronunciation tradition when lemmata are vocalised; the Babylonian arrangement of the biblical books in lists of lemmata; references to the *parašot* and *pisqot* in the masoretic notes.

3.1. Babylonian Terminology

The terms most distinctive of the b.Mas—'דק, 'בע, and 'של—are found in great profusion in this MS, each occurring hundreds of times, usually in the Mm, though to a far lesser extent also in the Mp.[34] Samuel b. Jacob, in L^m, attempted to remove as many of

[34] The term 'דק is an abbreviation of דקרן; it clarifies that it is the *reading* of a particular form that is of interest, rather than its written form. 'בע is an abbreviation of בעלמא; it clarifies that the note pertains to the entire Bible, rather than a subset thereof. The interpretation of these two signs has a long and somewhat tortuous history (see, among others, Kahle 1902, 15–18; 1913, 177–79; Yeivin 1966; 1973). Ofer (2001, 46–53) provides a helpful overview of the use of these terms, and the history of scholarship pertaining thereto. These terms lack precise Tiberian masoretic terminological equivalents. By contrast, the term 'של, i.e., שלמא *'plene'* is simply the Babylonian equivalent of the Tiberian term 'מל, i.e., מלא *'plene'*.

Some scholars, particularly Yeivin (1968, 74–75) have argued that the value of the term 'של as an indicator of the Babylonian origin of a

these Babylonian masoretic terms as possible or to replace them with their Tiberian equivalents. The scribe behind EVR II B 80+, by contrast, was far less concerned about removing these terms. Consequently, there are many notes whose Babylonian origin is revealed by EVR II B 80+ for the first time, sometimes with surprising ramifications. Here is a particularly fruitful example:

(8) **אֵיכָ֥ה** אֶשָּׂ֖א לְבַדִּ֑י טָרְחֲכֶ֥ם וּמַשַּׂאֲכֶ֖ם וְרִֽיבְכֶֽם׃

‘**How** can I bear by myself the weight and burden of you and your strife?’ (Deut. 1.12 [Image 183/256])

The forms איכה איך היך	איכה איך היך
are always spelled *plene*.	כול' של'
The word חך is always spelled defectively.	חך חס'

Everything about this note is distinctively Babylonian, from the terminology כול' של', to the fact that it concerns consistent, rather than variable, spellings, to the use of Babylonian vowel

masoretic note is rather limited. Rather, he suggests that the term was known to the Tiberian masoretes, and that at least some of them used it simply as a synonym for the more usual מל'. Dotan (2005, 35–36), too, appears to downplay the probative value of the appearance of the term in Or. 4445. Ofer (2001, 265–66) articulates an alternative interpretation of the evidence. He suggests that the appearance of Babylonian terms in an otherwise ‘pure’ Tiberian MS (such as A) could be seen as residual evidence of large-scale borrowing of quondam Babylonian masoretic notes into the t.Mas, where they were generally Tiberianised, thus obliterating the evidence of their Eastern origins. In any case, in EVR II B 80+ the point is moot. The frequent appearance of של' must be considered alongside the mass of other evidence of the Babylonian nature of many of the notes. The argument is cumulative.

signs, to the fact that it shows a characteristically Babylonian interest in the ח/ה distinction (Ofer 2001, 285–97). It does not appear in b.Mas.P.Ofer or L^{m}, but it does appear in a modified and Tiberianised form in none other than the Aleppo Codex:

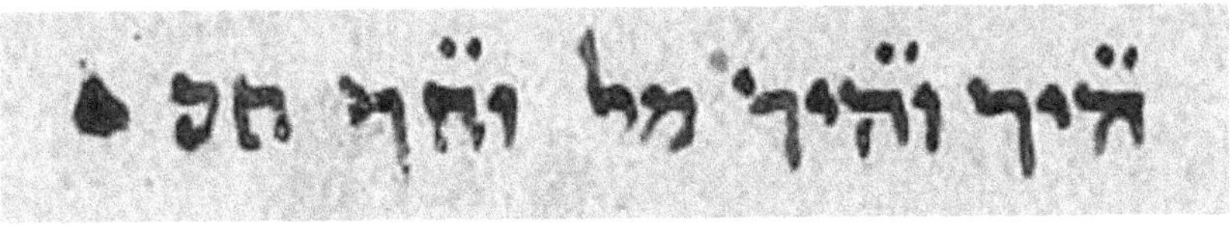

Figure 1: Snippet from Aleppo Codex, fol. 213v

The forms הי̈ך and והי̈ך are spelled *plene*	הי̈ך והי̈ך מל
whereas ח̈ך is spelled defectively.	וח̈ך חס

Yeivin (1968, 73) denies that the presence of Babylonian vocalisation in the Mm of A implies "any dependence on the b.Mas on the part of A." Ofer (2001, 267), however, considers this particular note in A, and is more hesitant. Based on the interest in the ח/ה distinction and the Babylonian vowel signs, he suggests "it is possible… that the masoretic note was copied from a Babylonian source." Ofer could not be more definite in his claim, since at that point there was no direct evidence of such a note in the b.Mas. However, now that such a similar note has been found in EVR II B 80+, we can conclude with a greater level of confidence that this note in A is indeed of Babylonian origin. This, in turn, reopens the larger question of the extent of the influence of the b.Mas on the *masora* of A.[35]

---

[35] In fact, the context of the note on the page itself, in A, may provide some further corroboration of the note's Babylonian origins; the details of this point, however, would drift too far beyond the scope of the current paper.

The terms 'דק, 'בע, and 'של are the most frequently occurring Babylonian terms in EVR II B 80+, but are by no means the only such terms. Particularly probative are cases where there is clear linguistic opposition between the Tiberian and Babylonian *masorot*. The following four examples of Babylonian masoretic terms all occur regularly in EVR II B 80+ (alongside their Tiberian counterparts):[36]

---

[36] For lists of Babylonian masoretic terms, see Kahle (1902, 15–18), Yeivin (2003, 93–95), and especially Ofer (2001, 39–59). Several of the terms that seem to have started out as Babylonian have made their way so thoroughly into the t.Mas that it is debatable whether they should be considered as distinctively Babylonian at all. Ofer's list, for example, contains far more 'Babylonian' terms than does Yeivin's.

Table 2: B.mas terms in EVR II B 80+

Babylonian Term	Tiberian Equivalent	Example of Babylonian term in EVR II B 80+	Location of example (text and image)
שלאחריו (Kahle 1902, 86 n. 7)	בתרא/בתריה	אותך י'ו' של בנקבות... והפשיטו אותך ושלאחריו השאטות אותך ושלאחריו ושלאחריו...	Gen. 39.9 (33/256)
ודומיה	וחברו	כה אמר ייי אלהי ישראל... התפללת אמרו ודומ'... למלך יהודה ודומ'...	Exod. 32.27 (95/256)
בתוכו	ביה	יסיף ב' באוריתא... ארבעים יכנו שנים בתוכו...	Deut. 25.3 (236/256)
אוריתא	תורה	See example immediately above.	
דהוא	—	כול' קריה אלה הדברים בר מן חד ואלה הדברים דפלגיה דירמיה דהוא דק'	Deut. 1.1 (182/256)

Additionally, scattered throughout the MS there are many other distinctively Babylonian masoretic terms, albeit occurring sporadically. Some examples: (ד)גבי 'next to, adjacent to' (243/256); לבד—Babylonian name for the letter *lamed* (24/256); במתואתא 'location'—when a particular word can refer either to a place, or to something else, this term is used to specify that the form is being referred to in its sense as a location (45/256); דמשתבשין—the Babylonian equivalent of the Tiberian term *sevirin* (76/256); דטען ביה—another equivalent to *sevirin* (38/256).

To give some idea of the frequency with which one encounters Babylonian masoretic terminology in this MS, a random sample of 50 pages was taken, across the full extent of the MS. Three pages contained no distinctively Babylonian terminology; 16

pages contained between one and four Babylonian terms; 31 pages contained five or more terms from the b.Mas.

Before finishing this section on Babylonian masoretic terminology in EVR II B 80+, it is worth noting which terms do *not* appear in the MS.[37] Most prominent among these are the Babylonian terms for the vowels and accents, which appear to be totally absent from the MS. Instead, the *masran* consistently uses the Tiberian names for vowels and accents, in both the Mm and Mp. Here is a stark example:

(9) ...עַד הִשָּׁמֶדְךָ וְעַד־אֲבָדְךָ מַהֵר מִפְּנֵי **רֹעַ מַעֲלָלֶיךָ** אֲשֶׁר עֲזַבְתָּנִי׃

‘...until you are destroyed and quickly perish because of **the evil of your deeds**, in that you have forsaken me.’ (Deut. 28.20b [Image 243/256])

Every time they occur next to	כול גבי מעלליך
the nouns ‘your (MS/PL)/their deeds’	מעלליהם מעלליכם
the form of רע has *ḥolem*,	רֹע מֹרֹע ומֹרֹע
apart from a single counterexample:	בר מן חד
1 Sam. 25.3,	והאיש קשה וַרֹע מעללים
where רע, uniquely, has *pataḥ*.	דק' בפתחא

This note has many Babylonian distinctives. Structurally, it is a Rule-Stating Note, with Exception (see §2.4, above). The terms גבי and דק' are Babylonian, and the vowel signs are Babylonian. Despite all this, the vowel at the end of the note is referred to using the Tiberian (though also appearing in Babylonian) פתחא, rather than the more distinctively Babylonian מיפתח פומה.

---

[37] Until an exhaustive analysis of the manuscript has been carried out, the following observations are somewhat provisional.

3.2. Babylonian Linguistic Elements

As with b.Mas.P (Ofer 2001, 46), the Aramaic of the masoretic notes in EVR II B 80+ frequently contains phonetic and morphological elements typical to Babylonian Aramaic, rather than Jewish Palestinian Aramaic. To give three illustrative examples: (1) The Babylonian determined plural suffix abounds in the forms: נביי 'the Prophets', e.g., 21/256, כתיבי 'the Writings', e.g., example (1) above. Likewise, this suffix appears in some of the names of the biblical books: שפטי 'Judges, e.g., example (2) above, מלכי 'Kings', e.g., 132/256. (2) *ʾAlef*, rather than *yod*, is regularly used in the gentilic suffix, e.g., קדמא[ה] (113/256), בתרא[ה] (132/256), תליתאה (133/256). (3) There is an example of a Babylonian Aramaic *aqṭel* infinitive (*aqṭole*) on image 237/256:

These are all the occurrences of the form יוסף with the sense 'increase, do again'.	...הלין יוסף דק' באוסופי...

3.3. Vocalisation Reflecting Babylonian Pronunciation

Closely related to these linguistic elements are the occasional vocalisations found in the Mm notes that reflect the Babylonian pronunciation tradition of Hebrew. Many of the Mm notes in EVR II B 80+ are vocalised (at least partially) with Babylonian vocalisation signs. This is not in and of itself a definitive mark of the direct influence of the b.Mas, as most of the key early Tiberian codices occasionally employ the Babylonian vocalisation signs in their Mm notes (Yeivin 1968, 72–74).[38] Moreover, Yeivin (1968, 74) is careful to note that, although the *graphemes* used are occasionally Babylonian, the *dialect* those graphemes represent is regularly Tiberian: “In all the MSS I have examined, the dialect reflected in the Babylonian graphemes is the Tiberian dialect.”

In EVR II B 80+, by contrast, an initial overview has revealed at least two loci where the Babylonian vocalisation signs reflect the *Babylonian*, rather than the Tiberian, pronunciation tradition:

(10) וַיִּ֗קֶן אֶת־חֶלְקַ֤ת הַשָּׂדֶה... בְּמֵאָ֖ה קְשִׂיטָֽה׃

‘And he bought the piece of land… for a hundred ***qasita***.’ (Gen. 33.19 [Image 21/256])

The form קשיטה occurs three times,	קשיטה ג'
thus:	וסימנהון
Gen. 33.19	את חלקת
Josh. 24.32	בחלקת השדה
Job 42.11.	ואיש נזם זהב

It appears that in the first lemma cited, a Babylonian *ḥiriq* is marked over the *ḥet* of חלקת. This accords well with the Babylonian pronunciation tradition (see Yeivin 1985, 814), in which

[38] Having said that, the extent of the use of Babylonian vocalisation signs in the Mm (and, rarely, the Mp) of the MS is pronounced—somewhere between a third and a half of the notes containing vocalisation signs employ Babylonian, rather than Tiberian, signs. (This count excludes the many collative *masora* notes, which are typically *Tiberian*, and are always vocalised with Tiberian signs.) Such a high proportion of Babylonian vowel sign usage does appear to point to the Babylonian origins of much of the MS’s *masora*.

the lowering of the original *ḥiriq* to a *segol* (as found in the Tiberian tradition) is less operative, presumably due to the weakening of the guttural *ḥet* in the Babylonian pronunciation.[39]

(11) וְאֶכְתֹּב֙ עַל־הַלֻּחֹ֔ת אֶת־הַדְּבָרִ֔ים...

'**so that I may write** on the tablets the words' (Deut. 10.2 [Image 206/256])

The forms וְאִכתֹב and וַיִכתֹב	ואכתב ויכתב
are always written defectively, except	כול' חס' בר מן
for Hos. 8.12, where אכתוב is *plene*.	אכתוב לו רבי תורתי של'

The biblical text itself at this point in the MS is written, as expected, according to the Tiberian pronunciation tradition, וְאֶכְתֹּב with the expected *segol* as the preformative vowel of the 1CS imperfect. However, the Babylonian vocalisation in the masoretic note marks this preformative vowel as a *ḥiriq*, as is regularly found in the early and middle forms of the Babylonian dialect (Yeivin 1985, 449).

3.4. Babylonian Arrangement of the Biblical Books

The arrangement of the books of the Latter Prophets and Writings differs somewhat between the Tiberian tradition and the Babylonian.[40] The most prominent differences pertain to the locations of Isaiah and Chronicles (though there are various additional differences regarding the order of the shorter books of the Writings).

---

[39] On this weakening in Jewish Babylonian Aramaic, see Morgenstern (2011, 73–76).

[40] The order of the biblical books in the Babylonian tradition follows the order found in the famous *baraita* in b. Baba Bathra 14b–15a.

In the Tiberian tradition, the order of the Latter Prophets is Isaiah, Jeremiah, Ezekiel, The Twelve; and Chronicles is located at the beginning of the Writings.[41] In the Babylonian tradition, the order of the Latter Prophets is Jeremiah, Ezekiel, Isaiah, The Twelve; and Chronicles is located at the end of the Writings.

These differences in sequencing crop up regularly in the masoretic notes. In general, masoretic notes arrange their lemmata in canonical sequence.[42] Thus, if a particular note happens to cite both Psalms and Chronicles—in that order—this is evidence that the note has been drawn from the b.Mas.[43] Example 2 above illustrates this Psalms-Chronicles sequence of lemmata. Or if, to give another example, a particular note cites from Jeremiah or Ezekiel, followed by Isaiah, this is likewise evidence of Babylonian origin. Such a note is found, for example, on image 133/256. After citing eight verses from Jeremiah, the note continues: 'And all of Ezekiel, and all of Isaiah, and all of The Twelve'.

---

[41] This is the order of the books in the great Tiberian codices, such as L and A. BHS locates Chronicles at the end of the Writings, and thus is not a faithful reflection of L in this respect.

[42] This rather general statement has many exceptions—not least given the 'interwoven' nature of many longer masoretic notes from the Tiberian tradition, and the arrangement of the Babylonian Classifying Notes (see §2.5, above).

[43] Breuer (1992, 12), followed by Ofer (2001, 16, 124–25), see this as one of the most significant identifiers of notes from the b.Mas.

3.5. Reference made to *Pisqot/Parashiyyot* and *Parashot*

The b.Mas includes far more references to *pisqot/parashiyyot* and *parashot* than the t.Mas.[44] They play a double role in the b.Mas: sometimes rules are framed such that they pertain to just a single *pisqa* or *parasha*; on other occasions they are used as reference points to help identify the precise location of a given lemma (Ofer 2001, 126–34, 151–52). Both uses are found in the masoretic notes of EVR II B 80+, more often in connection with *pisqot*, though in isolated instances also with reference to *parashot*. In the first example below, a note is formulated with reference to just one *pisqa*. In the second example, a *pisqa* is used as a reference point to identify the particular occurrence of a given collocation. In the third example the term פרשתא is used, referring to *Parashat Balaq*.

(12) **לְמַטֵּ֣ה** יְהוּדָ֑ה... **וּלְמַטֵּה֙ בְּנֵ֣י** שִׁמְע֔וֹן... **לְמַטֵּ֣ה** בִנְיָמִ֔ן... **וּלְמַטֵּ֥ה בְנֵי־**
דָ֖ן... **לְמַטֵּ֥ה בְנֵֽי־**מְנַשֶּׁ֖ה... **וּלְמַטֵּ֥ה בְנֵֽי־**אֶפְרַ֖יִם... **וּלְמַטֵּ֥ה בְנֵֽי־**זְבוּלֻ֖ן...
וּלְמַטֵּ֥ה בְנֵֽי־יִשָּׂשכָ֖ר... **וּלְמַטֵּ֥ה בְנֵֽי־**אָשֵׁ֖ר... **וּלְמַטֵּ֥ה בְנֵֽי־**נַפְתָּלִ֖י...
'**of the tribe of** Judah... **and of the tribe of thc sons of** Simeon... **of the tribe of** Benjamin... **and of the tribe of the sons of** Dan... **of the tribe of the sons of** Menasseh...

[44] Ofer (2001, 151) suggests that the reason the *parashiyyot* play a far larger role in the b.Mas than in the t.Mas is that the b.Mas specifically attends to the preservation of the *parashiyyot*. At each relevant point in the text, the b.Mas notes the presence of a new *parasha*, and the nature of that *parasha* (*petuḥa* or *setuma*). By contrast, the t.Mas is seemingly 'blind' to the *parashiyyot*, not attending to the accurate preservation of that aspect of the biblical text.

and of the tribe of the sons of Ephraim... **and of the tribe of the sons of** Zebulon... **and of the tribe of the sons of** Issachar... **and of the tribe of the sons of** Asher... **and of the tribe of the sons of** Naphtali... (Num. 34.19–29 [Image 178/256])

In the *pisqa* of ‘These are	כוליה פיסקא דאלה
the names of the men who	שמות האנשים אשר
will divide for you’ (Num. 34.16–29)	ינחלו לכם
conjunctive *waw* always precedes the	ולמטה
phrase ‘of the tribe of’, except in three	בר מן ג' למטה
cases, as follows:	וסימנהון
‘of the tribe of Judah’ (v. 19);	למטה יהודה
‘of the tribe of Benjamin’ (v. 21);	למטה בנימן
‘of the tribe of the sons of Manasseh’ (v. 23).	למטה בני מנשה
These make the mnemonic 'י'ב'ם'.	י'ב'ם' סימן
Judah and Benjamin alone	יהודה ובנימן דלית
among them omit ‘the sons of’.	בהון בני בכולן
These make the mnemonic 'י'ב'.	י'ב' סימן:
Judah, Simeon, and Benjamin	יהודה שמעון בנימן
alone among them omit ‘a chief’.	דלית נשיא בכולן
These make the mnemonic 'י'ש'ב'.	י'ש'ב' סימן

The phraseology of the list of cis-Jordan tribal chiefs responsible for the distribution of the land inheritance is highly stylised and repetitive. Nonetheless, there are many fine-grained deviations. This long note, pertaining only to this single *parasha*, codifies these deviations to preserve the list from future modifications.[45]

(13) וְהָיִ֣יתָ לְשַׁמָּ֔ה לְמָשָׁ֖ל וְלִשְׁנִינָ֑ה בְּכֹל֙ הָֽעַמִּ֔ים אֲשֶֽׁר־יְנַהֶגְךָ֥ יְהוָ֖ה שָֽׁמָּה׃

'And you shall become **a horror, a byword, and a taunt** among all the peoples where the LORD will lead you away.' (Deut. 28.37 [Image 244/256])

cf. וּנְתַתִּים֙ לזועה (K) לְזַעֲוָה (Q) לְרָעָ֔ה לְכֹ֖ל מַמְלְכ֣וֹת הָאָ֑רֶץ לְחֶרְפָּ֤ה וּלְמָשָׁל֙ לִשְׁנִינָ֣ה וְלִקְלָלָ֔ה בְּכָל־הַמְּקֹמ֖וֹת אֲשֶֽׁר־אַדִּיחֵ֥ם שָֽׁם׃

'I will make them a horror to all the kingdoms of the earth, to be **a reproach and a byword, a taunt and a curse** in all the places where I shall drive them. (Jer. 24.9)

In the Torah, the phrase is:	אוריתא
'A horror, a byword, and a taunt'	לשמה למשל
(Deut. 28.37).	ולשנינה
The mnemonic for this is ש'מ'ן'.	ש'מ'ן' סימן:
[But in the *pisqa*]	
'Like the [bad] figs' (Jer. 24.8–10)	וכתאנים
the phrase is: 'And you will make them	ונתתים
a reproach and a byword,	לחרפה ולמשל
a taunt and a curse' (v. 9).	לשנינה ולקללה
The mnemonic for this is פ'מ'ש'ק'.	פ'מ'ש'ק' סימן:

---

[45] This note, in a similar form, also appears in L^m (Breuer 1992, 662). However, in L^m, the introductory phrase פיסקא כוליה has been modified to כל עניני. Ofer (2001, 129–30) observes a similar tendency: notes in the b.Mas mentioning weekly *parashot* are sometimes emended when taken over into the t.Mas, with the reference to a *parasha* being replaced by a more general reference to the ʿ*inyan*.

In this Comparative Masoretic Note,[46] the issue is the similarity between some of the language of the covenant curses in Deut. 28 and Jeremiah's 'fig-oracle' (Jer. 24). The note compares the wording of a particular phrase between the two texts, so as to preserve the precise details of each, and prevent the one contaminating the other. The point for our purposes here is that the reference is to the *siman* of the *pisqa* and not to the verse.

(14) וְעַתָּה לְכָה־נָּא... עַתָּה לְכָה... וּלְכָה־נָּא... לְכָה אָרָה־לִּי יַעֲקֹב וּלְכָה... לְכָה־נָּא... לְכָה...

'So now, **come** please... Now, **come**... **And come** please... **Come** curse for me Jacob **and come**... **Come** please... **Come**...' (Num. 22.6–25.14 [Image 153/256])

[The lengthened imperative	[לכה ז' מל'
לכה occurs 7 times in *Parashat Balaq*:	בפרש' וסימנהון]
Num.] 22.6	[ועתה ל]כה נא
Num. 22.11	הנה העם היצא
Num. 22.17	כי כבד אכבדך
Num. 23.7 twice in the verse	מן ארם ינחני שנים בפסוק
Num. 23.27	אקחך
Num. 24.14	איעצך

---

46 Comparative Masoretic Notes are very common in the b.Mas, and there are many such notes in EVR II B 80+. However, since they also occur with some frequency in the t.Mas, this type of note has not been adduced as particular evidence of the Babylonian quality of the *masora* of EVR II B 80+.

The beginning of this partially obliterated Mm note has been reconstructed on the basis of its associated Mp note, which appears several times throughout the *parasha*: ז' מל' בפרש'.

There are many other instances of the lengthened imperative לכה throughout the biblical text; the scope of this note, however, is limited to one weekly *parasha*.

This completes the overview of the external Babylonian features of the masoretic notes in EVR II B 80+. Some of these features, e.g., the use of Babylonian masoretic terminology, are extremely common in the MS, while others, e.g., references to the *parashot*, are rare. Taken together, however, these external Babylonian features colour almost every page of the MS.

4.0. Internal Features: Notes Reflecting the Babylonian Textual Tradition

The discussion thus far has focused on the Babylonian elements of the masoretic notes themselves. We have not yet 'peered through' the notes, using them like a window, to examine the consonantal text they aim to preserve, or the dialect of Hebrew they presuppose. When the notes are interpreted in this manner, they sometimes point to the Babylonian consonantal text and dialect, rather than the Tiberian.

An initial overview of the MS reveals that a number of the masoretic notes reflect the Babylonian recension of the biblical text, rather than the Tiberian. Many of these notes appear in the Mp, rather than the Mm. As Ofer (2001, 264) has already suggested, this is likely due to the fact that it is easier to 'Tiberianise' the Mm notes than the Mp notes, since the former include the relevant biblical references, and can thus be relatively easily cross-checked to confirm that they match the Tiberian text. Nonetheless, there are also some Mm notes in the MS that apparently reflect the Babylonian recension of the MT. Space constraints limit me to offering a single example each from the Mp and the Mm. The first is already known to scholarship, whereas the second appears to be hitherto unknown.

(15) לָ֤מָּה נַחְבֵּ֙אתָ֙ לִבְרֹ֔חַ וַתִּגְנֹ֖ב אֹתִ֑י וְלֹא־הִגַּ֣דְתָּ לִּ֔י וָֽאֲשַׁלֵּחֲךָ֛ בְּשִׂמְחָ֥ה **וּבְשִׁרִ֖ים** בְּתֹ֥ף וּבְכִנּֽוֹר׃

‘Why did you flee secretly and trick me, and did not tell me, so that I might have sent you away with mirth **and songs**, with tambourine and lyre?’ (Gen. 31.27 [Image 16/256])

The Mp note related to ובשרים ‘and with songs’ reads: ה' חס' בליש' ‘This word, and those like it, occurs 5 times written defectively with this vocalisation, i.e., a *hireq* without a *mater lectionis*’.

Breuer (1992, 15, 183) has already discussed this note, which appears in the Mm of L^{m}. The count of five seems to match only the Babylonian text, rather than the Tiberian. The equivalent Tiberian note counts only four such defective forms. The additional occurrence in the Babylonian version of the note occurs at Jdg. 5.1. The Tiberian text reads וַתָּ֣שַׁר דְּבוֹרָ֔ה ‘and Deborah sang’, but it seems that the Babylonian text must have read וַתָּשִׁר with *ḥiriq*.[47]

[47] As Breuer himself notes (*ad loc*), Yeivin (1985, 654) catalogues an equivalent phenomenon with the root סו"ר in the Babylonian tradition.

(16) לְֹא־יִמָּצֵא בְךָ מַעֲבִיר בְּנוֹ־וּבִתּוֹ בָּאֵשׁ **קֹסֵם** קְסָמִים...

‘There shall not be found among you anyone who burns his son or his daughter as an offering, **anyone who practices divination**…’ (Deut. 18.10 [Image 223/256])

Forms of the verb קסם are always spelled	קסם כול'
defectively, [apart from]	חס
Ezek. 17.9	ואת פריה יקוֹסֹם
Zech. 10.2,	והקוסמים חזו
the only *plene* forms in all the Scriptures.	של' בע'

This intriguing Mm note appears to preserve a different consonantal text of Ezek. 17.9 to that known from the Tiberian tradition. First, observe that the formulation of the note is quintessentially Babylonian: a Rule-Stating Note, with Exceptions (see §2.4, above). Likewise, fully Babylonian are the terminology, 'כול, 'של, 'בע, and the vocalisation signs. There is little doubt, therefore, that this formulation is a genuine part of the b.Mas. The note is concerned with the root קס"ם. It claims that words formed from this root are always spelled defectively, save two exceptions, which are then listed. The first exception is from Ezek. 17.9. In the Tiberian text the relevant clause reads: וְאֶת־פִּרְיָהּ ׀ יְקוֹסֵס וְיָבֵשׁ ‘and its fruit cut off’. The Babylonian text, by contrast, apparently read יקוסם. This cannot simply be a *lapsus calami* on the part of the *masran*, since the inclusion of Ezek. 17.9 in a note dealing with the root קס"ם makes sense only on the basis of the reading יקוסם rather than יקוסס.[48] Thus, this consonantal difference should be added to the

[48] The *masran* of EVR II B 80+ seems to have struggled with this word when writing the note: a *samekh* and final *mem* are visible, superimposed, at the end of יקוסם. The image quality is not sufficiently high to

growing list of textual differences between the Babylonian and Tiberian recensions of the biblical text.[49]

These examples (and many others like them) notwithstanding, it must be noted that the great majority of the Mm and Mp notes in the MS are consistent with the Tiberian text and dialect—including those notes with distinctively Babylonian structural and external features. This may simply be because the Babylonian and Tiberian recensions of the biblical text share a large amount of material. Alternatively, it might be that the *masran*, while content to keep the Babylonian form and language of the notes, was careful to try to use only such notes as are consistent with the Tiberian text. It is also possible that the *masran* kept the Babylonian form and language of the notes, but actively altered the content of the notes, when necessary, to match the Tiberian text and dialect. For example, consider the following note:

---

determine which letter was written first, and which is the supposed correction.

[49] I am very grateful to Prof. Yosef Ofer, who (after a lecture in which I presented this Mm note) checked the three known Babylonian biblical MSS containing this verse and confirmed that one of them (Oxford Bod. Heb. d.49 18v) does indeed read יקוסם. This consonantal variant will be considered from a text-critical angle elsewhere.

(17) וְאֶת־יְהוֹשׁ֣וּעַ צִוֵּ֔יתִי בָּעֵ֥ת הַהִ֖וא לֵאמֹֽר...

‘And I commanded **Joshua** at that time…’ (Deut. 3.21 [Image 190/256])

The Westerners spell ‘Joshua’ *plene*	יהושוע ב' מל למע'
twice, as follows:	וסימנהון
Deut. 3.21	ואת יהושוע צויתי
Josh. 24.31	ויעבדו העם דשפטי
(the second occurrence in the verse).	תינינא דפסוקא

The same note appears in b.Mas.P.Ofer and L^{m}, except that in these sources the count is given as three, rather than two, and the final line of the note reads 'שנ' בת (Ofer 2001, 541) or its equivalent, 'ב' בפסוק (Breuer 1992, 679). In Ginsburg (1880, 213) the beginning of the note reads 'יהושוע ב' מל' וסימ, omitting the reference to the Westerners. Obviously, one cannot form generalisations based on such slight evidence, but it is plausible to interpret the note here in EVR II B 80+ as a self-conscious reworking of the Babylonian note in light of the Tiberian text. Hopefully, the full analysis of the *masora* of this MS will enable more clarity on this point.

5.0. Conclusion

In this article I have attempted to show that the masoretic notes (Mm and Mp) of RNL EVR II B 80+ have been deeply influenced by the Babylonian masoretic tradition—perhaps more so than in any other Tiberian MS (apart from L^{m}) of which we are currently aware. In fact, the extent of this influence is so pronounced, that there is scarcely a page which does not reveal at least some trace of Babylonian Masora. The Babylonian nature of the notes is apparent in the structure of the notes, the language and terminology employed, and sometimes the content of the notes—i.e., what the notes claim about the biblical text. On the basis of an initial sample of 35 Mm notes from Num. 31–34, about half of the notes were also found in b.Mas.P.Ofer. Moreover, about two-thirds of all the notes were either found in b.Mas.P.Ofer or showed clear external signs of having been drawn from the b.Mas. This survey ignored Mp notes, some of which also showed clear Babylonian traces.

Despite the extent of the Babylonian influence, the *masran* responsible for the codex was apparently very accomplished at making the *masora* compatible with the Tiberian nature of the MS. This is perhaps most obvious in the apparently total absence of Babylonian names for the vowels and accents. There is also some evidence that the *masran* may have moved beyond simply choosing Babylonian notes compatible with the Tiberian text, to emending Babylonian notes such that they fit the Tiberian text rather than the Babylonian text, even though their style and terminology remain Babylonian. Nevertheless, this process of filtering and possible emending was not accomplished perfectly, and a small but important proportion of these Mm and Mp notes remain incompatible with the Tiberian text. These notes provide a window into the Babylonian text and reading tradition.

The nature of the codex—Tiberian in text and *mise-en-page*, but with Babylonian masoretic notes—invites particular comparisons between this MS and L^{m}. Pending fuller examination of the

MS, all such comparisons remain provisional. Nonetheless, some initial observations can be made:

(a) The present MS retains the quintessential Babylonian terms 'דק, 'של, and 'בע to a far greater degree than L^m. This may allow us to identify a Babylonian background to many more masoretic notes than has hitherto been possible.

(b) The present MS contains many Mp notes influenced by the b.Mas, and the question of the reworking of the b.Mas into Tiberian-style Mp notes requires significant further study. This reconfirms the desideratum of gaining access to digital images of L^m, such that the Mp notes therein can be similarly studied.

(c) L^m is well-known for the many errors in its masoretic notes (Breuer 1992, 12–15). The evidence thus far suggests that the notes in EVR II B 80+ have been far more carefully and competently copied. Several of the examples above have already shown that the present MS has the potential to resolve some of the outstanding difficulties in the notes of L^m, and even in Ofer's edition of the b.Mas itself.

I will finish with one final example where the present MS resolves a minor difficulty in b.Mas.P.Ofer by filling in a series of lacunae.

(18) מֵהֹ֣ר הָהָ֔ר תְּתָא֖וּ לְבֹ֣א חֲמָ֑ת וְהָי֛וּ **תּוֹצְאֹ֥ת** הַגְּבֻ֖ל צְדָֽדָה׃

'From Mount Hor you shall draw a line to Lebo-hamath, and **the limit of** the border shall be at Zedad.' (Num. 34.8 [Image 177/256])

תוצאות דכת' תוצאת	There are two occurrences of תוצאות
ב' וסימנהון	spelled *plene*-defective:
מהר ההר תתאו	Num. 34.8
ואלה תוצאת העיר:	Ezek. 48.30.
כי ממנו תוצאות של'	Prov. 4.23 is the only occurrence
בע' בתרין ווי	spelled *plene* with two *vavin*.
ושאר' כוליה תצאות	All the other occurrences are written
כת':	תצאות.

This same note is found, with three substantial lacunae, in EVR II B 1549, the largest of the fragments of b.Mas that Ofer uses for his edition, and which was previously edited by Ginsburg (1885). These lacunae render possible widely differing reconstructions of the note, as comparison between Ginsburg's and Ofer's editions shows:

ת[וצאת של וחס] מהר ההר ואלה תוצאת העיר תוצא[ת כת בית חגלה]
של בע בית [חרין תצא]תו כת

(Ginsburg 1885, 242)

The citation of בית חגלה refers to Josh. 18.19, and the citation of בית חרין refers to Josh. 16.3. The reconstruction of the third lacuna is particularly unconvincing: the two letters preceding the lacuna are clearly בת rather than בית, and after the lacuna the letters ת כת (without a *vav*) are certain. Similarly, at the end of the first lacuna a ת is clearly visible, which Ginsburg ignores.

ת[וצאות של וחס ?]ת מהר ההר ואלה תוצאת העיר תוצא[ת כת חיים]
של בע בת[רא דיהודה?? תצאת כת ושארא תצאו]ת כת

(Ofer 2001, 518)

Ofer expresses hesitations regarding his proposed reconstruction of this note. The words בתרא דיהודה are a reference to Josh. 15.11, where Ofer found this defective-defective reading in a Babylonian MS. However, reconstructing the three lacunae according to Ofer's proposal reveals that his hesitations were well-founded. Here is a reconstruction of the first lacuna in EVR II B 1549 according to Ofer's proposal:[50]

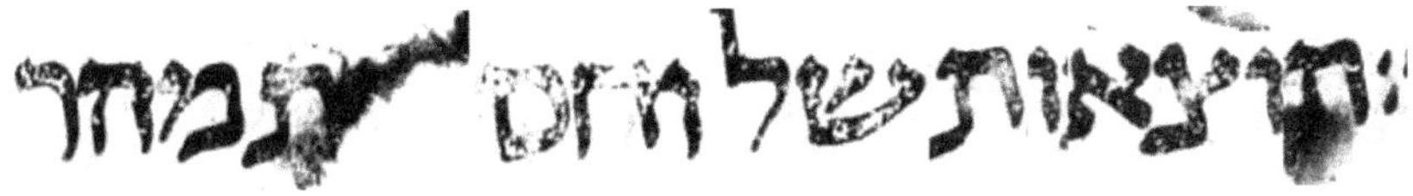

As the image shows, there is plenty of space to fit Ofer's proposed reading between the *tav* at the beginning of the line and the *tav* at the end. However, the reading leaves a small amount of space at the end of the lacuna, and it is not at all obvious what might fill that space and connect to the *tav* immediately after the lacuna.

Ofer's proposed reconstruction of the second lacuna fits the available space, narrowly, but his proposal regarding the third lacuna does not:

In the reconstruction above, I have abbreviated Ofer's בתרא to בתר, but even so, the text is substantially too long for the available space.

[50] All the reconstructions below were created using combinations of letters and words from the same side of the same leaf of EVR II B 1549 in which the lacunae are found.

Based on the note in EVR II B 80+, emended in light of the typical phraseology and scribal tendencies in EVR II B 1549, I suggest the following reconstruction:

ת[וצאות דכת תוצא]ת מהר ההר ואלה תוצאת העיר תוצא[ות חיים]של
בע בת[רין ווי ושארא תצאו]ת כת

The proposed reconstruction of the first lacuna fits the available space well:

The proposal for the second lacuna is plausible, but does

leave a small amount of free space:

The reconstruction of the third lacuna fits very well:

If this reconstruction proves persuasive, then this note from EVR II B 80+ has solved one small mystery regarding the text of the b.Mas, and also gone some way to clarifying the Babylonian *biblical* text itself. It is to be hoped that a full edition and examination of the masoretic notes in this important MS, already underway, will yield a great many further insights of a similar nature.

References

Beit-Arié, Malachi, Colette Sirat, and Mordechai Glatzer. 1997. *Codices hebraicis litteris exarati quo tempore scripti fuerint exhibentes*. Vol. 1. 4 vols. Monumenta Palaeographica Medii Aevi, Series hebraica 1. Belgium: Brepols.

Breuer, Mordechai. 1976. *The Aleppo Codex and the Accepted Text of the Bible*. Jerusalem: Mosad Harav Kook. [Hebrew]

——— (ed.). 1992. *The Masorah Magna to the Pentateuch by Shemuel ben Yaʿaqov*. 2 vols. The Manfred and Anne Lehmann Foundation Series 16. New York: Manfred and Anne Lehmann Foundation. [Hebrew]

Chiesa, Bruno. 1979. *Emergence of Hebrew Biblical Pointing: The Indirect Sources*. Frankfurt: Peter Lang.

Dotan, Aron. 2005. 'Babylonian Residues in the London Pentateuch Codex'. In *Studies in Bible and Exegesis* 7, edited by Shmuel Vargon, Yosef Ofer, Jordan S. Penkower, and Jacob Klein, 33–40. Ramat Gan: Bar-Ilan University Press. [Hebrew]

Dukan, Michèle. 2006. *La Bible hébraïque: Les codices copiés en Orient et dans la zone séfarade avant 1280*. Bibliologia: Elementa Ad Librorum Studia Pertinentia 22. Belgium: Brepols.

Ginsburg, Christian D. 1880. *The Massorah Compiled from Manuscripts: Alphabetically and Lexically Arranged*. 4 vols. London. [Hebrew]

Gottheil, Richard. 1905. 'Some Hebrew Manuscripts in Cairo'. *Jewish Quarterly Review* 17/4: 609–55.

Kahle, Paul. 1902. *Der Masoretische Text des Alten Testaments nach der Überlieferung der Babylonischen Juden*. Leipzig: J.C. Hinrichs'sche Buchhandlung.

———. 1913. *Masoreten des Ostens: Die Ältesten Punktierten Handschriften des Alten Testaments und der Targume*. Beiträge zur Wissenschaft vom Alten Testament 15. Leipzig: J.C. Hinrichs'sche Buchhandlung.

Khan, Geoffrey. 2020. *The Tiberian Pronunciation Tradition of Biblical Hebrew*. 2 vols. Cambridge: Open Book Publishers and the Faculty of Asian and Middle Eastern Studies.

Morgenstern, Matthew. 2011. *Studies in Jewish Babylonian Aramaic: Based on Early Eastern Manuscripts*. Harvard Semitic Studies 62. Winona Lake, IN: Eisenbrauns.

Ofer, Yosef. 1992. 'The Babylonian Masorah to the Pentateuch in a Tiberian Recension'. *Leshonenu* 56: 269–83. [Hebrew]

———. 2001. *The Babylonian Masora of the Pentateuch: Its Principles and Methods*. The Academy of the Hebrew Language Sources and Studies 6. Jerusalem: The Hebrew University Magnes Press. [Hebrew]

———. 2011. 'An Old Manuscript with Babylonian Vocalization of the Hagiographa'. In *Israel: Linguistic Studies in the Memory of Israel Yeivin*, edited by Rafael I. (Singer) Zer and Yosef Ofer, 129–54. Publications of the Hebrew University Bible Project 6. Jerusalem: Hebrew University Magnes Press. [Hebrew]

———. 2019. *The Masora on Scripture and Its Methods*. Fontes et Subsidia ad Bibliam Pertinentes 7. Berlin: de Gruyter.

Penkower, Jordan S. 2020. 'The Biblical Variants between Sura and Nehardea: Text, Vocalization, Open and Closed Sections'. *Jewish Studies Internet Journal* 18. [Hebrew]

Strack, Hermann L. 1897. 'Über Verloren Gegangene Handschriften des Alten Testaments'. In *Semitic Studies in Memory of Rev. Dr. Alexander Kohut*, edited by George Alexander Kohut, 560–72. Berlin: S. Calvary & Co.

Weil, Gerard E. 1963. 'La Massorah Magna Babylonienne des Prophetes'. *Textus* 3/1: 163–70.

Yeivin, Israel. 1966. 'Two Terms of the Babylonian Masora to the Bible'. *Leshonenu* 30/1: 25–28. [Hebrew]

———. 1968. *The Aleppo Codex of the Bible: A Study of its Vocalization and Accentuation*. Publications of the Hebrew University Bible Project 3. Jerusalem: Magnes Press, The Hebrew University. [Hebrew]

———. 1973. 'More on the Traditional Babylonian Term בע'. *Leshonenu* 37: 154–56. [Hebrew]

———. 1985. *The Hebrew Language Tradition as Reflected in the Babylonian Vocalization*. 2 vols. Jerusalem: The Academy of the Hebrew Language. [Hebrew]

———. 2003. *The Biblical Masorah*. Studies in Language 3. Jerusalem: The Academy of the Hebrew Language. [Hebrew]

THE MARGINAL *NUN/ZAYIN*: MEANING, PURPOSE, LOCALISATION[1]

Vincent D. Beiler

In some early masoretic Bible codices, a large letter resembling *nun* or *zayin* may occur in the margin, often in conjunction with the marking of *qere/ketiv*.[2] The Aleppo Codex does not have this marking even once, while another illustrious codex, the Cairo Codex of the Prophets (C), has the marking more than 500 times on about as many pages (Martín-Contreras 2015, 81). This large letter is generally absent or infrequent in codices long cited by scholars (with the already noted exception of C).[3] For example, there are only 76 such letters in the Leningrad Codex (Martín-Contreras 2015, 88–90) and 42 in Heb.24°5702 (formerly known as Sassoon 507) (Himbaza 2000, 175). To the best of my knowledge, no such markings occur in either British Library Or.

[1] Special thanks to Joseph Habib, for his critical comments and encouragement, and to Elvira Martín-Contreras, for her willingness to interact with and critique my ideas—the paper is better for it.

[2] For purposes of convenience, I group together all possible types of *qere* marking (i.e., *qere*, *ketiv we-la qere*, *qere we-la ketiv*, and *ketiv*), and shall refer to them to simply as *qere/ketiv*. See Yeivin (1980, 56–59).

[3] Cf. Breuer (1976, 14) for commonly cited codices.

 https://doi.org/10.11647/OBP.0330.03

4445 or JUD 002 (formerly Sassoon 1053).[4] It has been suggested that the marking is ancient, perhaps predating the remainder of the *masora magna* and *parva* (e.g., Yeivin 1980, 52). Its distribution appears to be widespread, being found in Tiberian, Babylonian, and Palestinian manuscripts—this being the primary reason that the mark is thought to predate the remaining *masora* (Ofer 2019, 89–91). Yeivin (1980, 52) notes that the letter generally fell out of use after the 12th century, although Penkower finds limited instances of the letter in later codices and scrolls (2019).

Scholars of the past and present have offered their opinions regarding both this signifier and what it might signify. If *nun*, perhaps the letter stands for קריין 'what is read' (Kahle[5]) or נסחא 'variant' (*BH*[3], 51). If *zayin*, perhaps the letter stands for זיטימא 'uncertain' (Yeivin 1980, 52). The letter could even be a simple marking and not a letter at all (again Yeivin). After examining seventeen diverse codices containing the letter, Himbaza argues that the sign was probably a *nun* (2000, 173).

As this sign occurs most frequently in conjunction with *qere/ketiv* notes, the letter may signal the existence of an alternate tradition to the reader. The letter does not accompany *qere*

---

[4] The full name of what was formerly known as Sassoon 1053 is Geneva, Jacqui E. Safra, JUD 002. Special thanks to Nehemia Gordon, who kindly provided me with the colour images, and to Jolanda van Nijen of the Jacqui E. Safra Judaica Collection, who has been instrumental in permitting scholars access to said images.

[5] As quoted by Yeivin (1980, 52); Himbaza (2000); Martín-Contreras (2015). None of these scholars, however, indicate where Kahle is purported to have said this—nor have I yet succeeded in finding it.

notes in all instances, however, nor do *qere* markings—either explicitly or implicitly—always appear to accompany it (e.g., EVR II B 1233, 2 Kgs 19.13). In some early scrolls and Ashkenazi and Italian codices—but not in Oriental codices—the marker denotes section divisions on which there is disagreement (Penkower, 2019).

Himbaza suggests that the marginal letter serves to alert the reader to a textual problem (2000, 174). Martín-Contreras argues that (in the Cairo Codex) the letter is a warning marker, alerting the reader to an issue in the consonantal text without explaining it (2015, 88). Penkower (2019) notes that the marginal letter is employed to mark points of dispute.

A related, but distinctly different sign, נון מנוזרת *nun menuzeret* 'isolated *nun*', also known as נון הפוכה *nun hafukha* 'inverted *nun*', appears in Bible codices at Num. 10.35–36 (2x) and Ps. 107.23–28, 40 (7x).[6] While the meaning of this 'isolated *nun*' is debated, it may indicate that a portion of text is out of place (b. *Shabbat* 115b–116a). Lieberman (1962, 38–46) finds a parallel with certain Greek texts that use an *antisigma*, i.e., reverse *sigma*, to indicate misplaced text (cf. Yeivin 1980, 46–47). Tov (2001, 54–55) believes that the use of the *sigma* and *antisigma* pair (what became our modern-day parentheses) can be seen in 11QpaleoLev[a], indicating the long-standing use of the notation in Hebrew texts to mark wrongly placed verses. It is possible that our marginal letter is a later outgrowth of the 'isolated *nun*'. How-

[6] Not all codices are in agreement regarding the exact verses in Psalm 107 where the 'inverted *nun*' should appear.

ever, as the two signs are never confused with one another—despite a potential overlap of meaning—there is no evidence to support such an assertion. Perhaps the signs are only accidentally similar.

I shall propose that the purpose of the letter, possibly a *zayin*, was (or became) practical: a means of avoiding certain types of copyist mistakes when recording *qere/ketiv* notes. Because the sign occurs in certain script types more than others, I will also argue that the notation can function as something of a regional identifier, although I leave that region to be identified by others. The explanations offered here are generally compatible with, but independent from, the explanations cited above.

1.0. Description of Corpus

The data for the present paper are drawn from a database of ca. 15,000 Masorah parva (Mp) notes, taken from 38 early (the 12th century and prior) codices containing the Former Prophets. The study is larger than 38 isolated classmarks, however. Apart from the original 38, there are as many as 43 additional classmarks containing leaves from one of the original 38.[7] To the best of my

[7] Some of the joins are obvious: the reference ranges, the number of lines, and the script similarities prevent other conclusions. Other joins are less certain. The complete list of the 38 classmarks, along with the potential joins for each, are as follows (a plus sign following a classmark indicates the presence of possible joins; the join suggestions are listed in parentheses following the listing of the main classmark; 'I' = First Firkovich collection; 'II' = 2nd Firkovich collection): the Aleppo Codex, the Cairo Codex, the Leningrad Codex, JUD 002, I Bibl. 13/80, I Bibl. 68, II B 24+(II B 1184, II B 1323, II B 1335, note that several folios of

knowledge, the study includes all early manuscripts for which I was able to access images.[8]

I examined the big four codices as pertains to the Former Prophets (Aleppo, Leningrad, Cairo, and JUD 002), plus two lesser-known codices of the First Firkovitch collection, I Bibl. 13/80 and I Bibl. 68 of the library at St Petersburg. The remainder are all St Petersburg II B classmarks (that is, from the Second Firkovitch collection). Every codex from the I Bibl. or the II B collection was examined, provided it contained at least one of the predetermined reference ranges (listed below), was sufficiently 'early' in appearance (e.g., left justification method did not include significant letter elongation; see Beit-Arié 2021, 472, nn. 30, 31), and had three columns.[9] All codices fall under the rubric

II B 24 do not belong), II B 25 + (II B 145, parts of II B 210, II B 223, II B 1197), II B 35, II B 39 + (II B 217), II B 43, II B 50 + (II B 1298, II B 1349, II B 1379), II B 55, II B 56 + (II B 211, parts of II B 81, most of II B 71, II B 216), II B 63, II B 70 + (II B 212), II B 71(two folios belong with II B 56 +), II B 77 (one section of II B 210, parts of II B 1328, II B 1345), II B 86 + (II B 1405, II B 1406), II B 90, II B 94, II B 99 + (II B 219, II B 1269, II B 1325, II B 1326, II B 1339, II B 224, II B 1278), II B 124, II B 206, II B 927, II B 1160 + (II B 1159, II B 1157, II B 1162, II B 1248, II B 1280, II B 1286), II B 1166 + (II B 207, II B 1247), II B 1167, II B 1169, II B 1180 + (II B 1211, II B 1235), II B 1233, II B 1243 + (II B 1255), II B 1270, II B 1272 + (II B 1328), II B 1275, II B 1281 + (II B 1337), II B 1285 + (II B 1474), II B 1378 + (one section of II B 24, last half of II B 81, II B 134, II B 1336).

[8] For example, Gottheil 27 (Breuer's Codex Lm of the Former Prophets), of the pen of Samuel ben Jacob, has not been digitised.

[9] There is one exception. EVR II B 124 is two-column, but exceptionally early, the colophon (if believed) dating to 946 CE. Regarding the forging

of Oriental,[10] broadly speaking, and have Tiberian vocalisation. Despite these unifying characteristics, the scripts of the manuscripts show considerable variety.

The collation was limited to *masora parva* notes that fall within four reference ranges (Jdg. 3–6, 1 Sam. 16–19, 1 Kgs 8–10, and 2 Kgs 17–20).[11] *Masora parva* notes falling outside of these ranges were not considered. For this reason, there are doubtless manuscripts with instances of the marginal letter that I did not record. In such manuscripts, however, occurrences of the marginal letter are demonstrably infrequent. The conclusions drawn in this paper, therefore, fit best with codices containing frequent occurrences of the marginal *zayin/nun*.

1.1. Manuscripts that Use the Marginal Letter

The marginal letter was observed in fifteen of the 38 codices examined. In only thirteen of the fifteen codices does the marginal letter occur with high frequency (i.e., the letter occurs adjacent to an explicitly marked *qere/ketiv* note in the majority of *q/k* instances); we will focus on these thirteen.[12] For the purpose of

---

hand of Firkovich in the colophon of this codex, see Beit-Arié (2020, 202–3). According to Beit-Arié, the actual date is somewhere between 946 and 1036.

[10] For a description of Oriental scripts, see Olszowy-Schlanger (2015, *14–20); Beit-Arié et al. (1987, 1–51).*

[11] The data are taken from my larger PhD thesis project (2022), where manuscripts are compared according to their *masora parva* note collocations.

[12] These thirteen high-frequency-inclusion codices include: II B 24+, II B 35, II B 43, II B 50+, II B 71+, II B 927, II B 1166+, II B 1167, II B

analysis, I have arranged the thirteen manuscripts into three subtypes, based primarily upon whole-page comparisons of the manuscripts.

In the first six manuscripts, labelled Script A, the folios are generally crowded, leaving only small inter-column 'margin' spaces between the words and lines. The width of the strokes is proportionally wide when compared against letter height and width. Despite the wide stroke marks of the calamus, the script still manages to be slightly calligraphic, as can be observed particularly in the first three examples (calligraphic: i.e., the presence of serifs and the use of a calamus with an angled tip).

There is some similarity of Script A with what Olszowy-Schlanger (2014, 279–99; 2015, 14–20) has labelled 'South-Western Oriental', i.e., Egypt especially, but the similarity is only partial.[13] There is likewise some similarity of these manuscripts with what Engel (2013, 486–87) refers to as 'proto-square script',

---

1233, II B 1243+, II B 1270, II B 1285+, and the Cairo Codex. The two remaining codices where the marginal letter occurs with lower frequency are II B 63 and II B 1160+.

[13] The lack of congruence does not, however, rule out the possibility that 'Script A' is Egyptian. It merely shows that the script is not wholly similar to those identified by Olszowy-Schlanger as SW Oriental (Olszowy-Schlanger, personal communication, December 2021). It should also be noted that the MSS examined by Olszowy-Schlanger are less formal in appearance than those I examined (in my case, three-column Bible manuscripts containing full *masora parva* and *magna*). To my mind, this limits the value of a full comparison of the scripts. Similarly, the corpus of MSS identified as SW Oriental by Olszowy-Schlanger is small, again limiting full comparisons.

which Engel describes as "(d)ense texture composed of small letters and small spaces between words and lines.... There are random ornamental characteristics, such as stylised tags on the horizontal lines and a decorative curl of the verticals." As with the 'South-Western Oriental' descriptor, however, the similarity of 'proto-square script' and the present Script A is only partial. For these reasons, I will not attempt to pinpoint the likely point of origin for these MSS (but see below, §5.3).[14]

Figure 1: Script A

EVR II B 1270, p. 15

EVR II B 35, p. 103

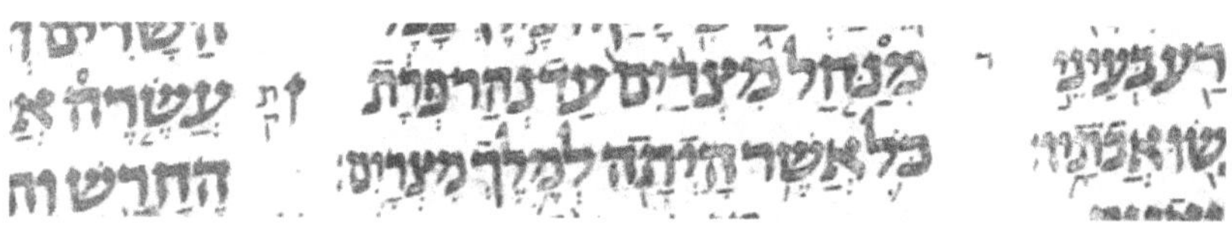

EVR II B 1243+, p. 10

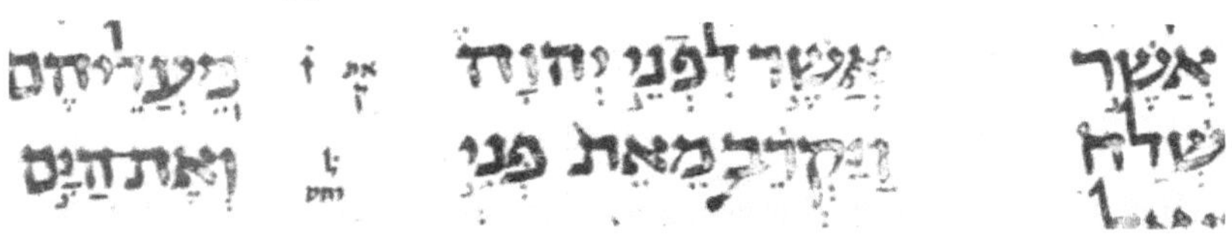

[14] It should also be noted that my descriptions are necessarily cursory—and thus provisional; palaeography is complex, and each script type, as I have identified them (especially Scripts A, B, and D) deserves a much longer treatment than I am able to provide in this article.

EVR II B 1285+ (here, of II B 1474), p. 5

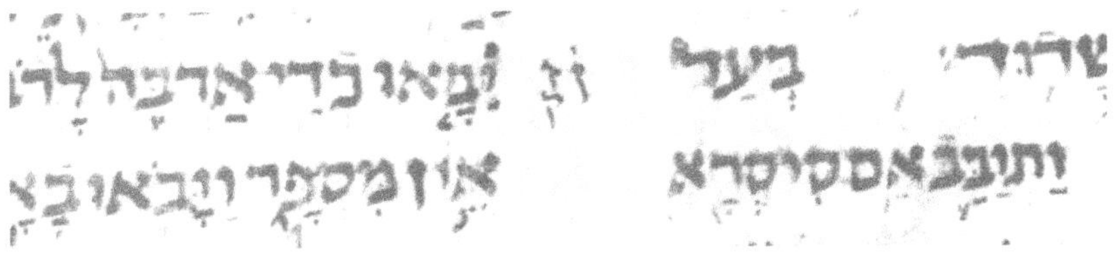

EVR II B 927, p. 51

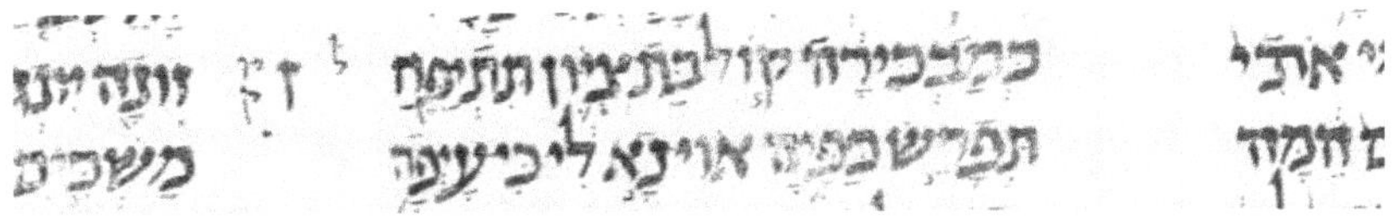

EVR II B 1233, p. 20

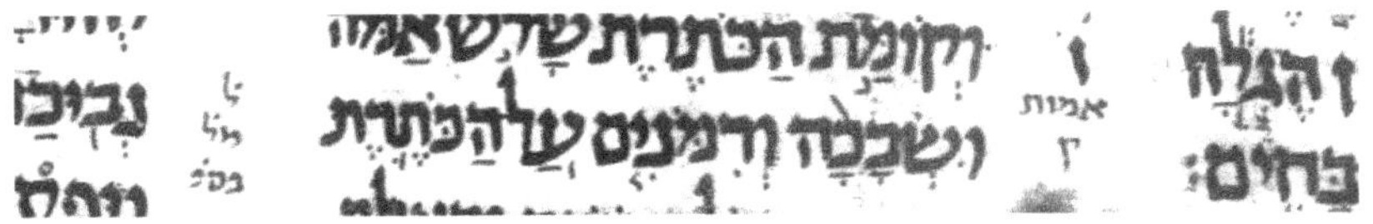

Script B,[15] containing four examples, shows a similarly wide letter stroke in keeping with that of Script A, but, rather than appearing wide throughout, the horizontal lines tend to be wide, and the vertical lines narrow. The letters in Script B are larger than in Script A, and are of the sort that one encounters in especially "heroic" productions (the first three examples especially).

[15] As the present data set yields only four codices for Script B, it may be helpful to note other codices of this script type, so that the alert reader may compare the various codices. These include the Washington Pentateuch, II B 19, II B 20, and II B 1021—all contain the marginal letter and have at least 60 pages (30 leaves) preserved. Classmarks of Script B that are too short to find *qere/ketiv* type notes include II B 1064, II B 1065, II B 1067, II B 1070, II B 1296. Extensively preserved codices appearing to belong to Script B, but that I have not had opportunity to examine beyond a single leaf, include Gottheil 6/Ms. FR 9-005 (note that Ms. FR 9-005 combines Gottheil 5 with Gottheil 6) and Gottheil 18/C3.

In many respects the script of these four examples is similar to Script D (below, in due course), with the exception of the wide horizontal strokes.

When comparing paratextual features, however, the similarities between Scripts A and B are especially marked (e.g., *sedarim* markers are similarly formed; the *masora parva gimel* is often triple-dotted[16]), suggesting that the scripts may have similarities that extend beyond the presence of the marginal letter[17] and the wide letter strokes. The marginal *nun/zayin* in these MSS is very similar in appearance to that in II B 1270, II B 1233, and II B 1243+ of Script A, again suggesting some overlap in their centre(s) of production.

---

[16] The *supra* triple-dotting of the *masora parva gimel*, on which nothing, to my knowledge, has been written, appears to be an alternate form for marking 3x. In some MSS, only the *masora parva gimel* is triple-dotted. In other MSS, the triple-dotting feature sees wider distribution, particularly with letters having a flat roof, such as *heh* or *bet*, or in two-digit numerals (e.g., יד or כה). The feature is not necessarily ubiquitous within a given MS, but the triple-dotted *gimel* and the single-dotted *gimel* generally appear to have been formed by the same hand. Sometimes *gimels* of identical shape appear on the same page, one triple-dotted and one single-dotted. Double-dotting over single letters, a much rarer feature, is generally equally distributed over all letters (cf. BL Or. 9880; Oxford MS heb. b.17/1).

[17] Cf. Penkower's (2021, 160–61) article comparing codicological and palaeographical similarities between the Washington Pentateuch and the Cairo Codex.

Figure 2: Script B

Cairo Codex, p. 273

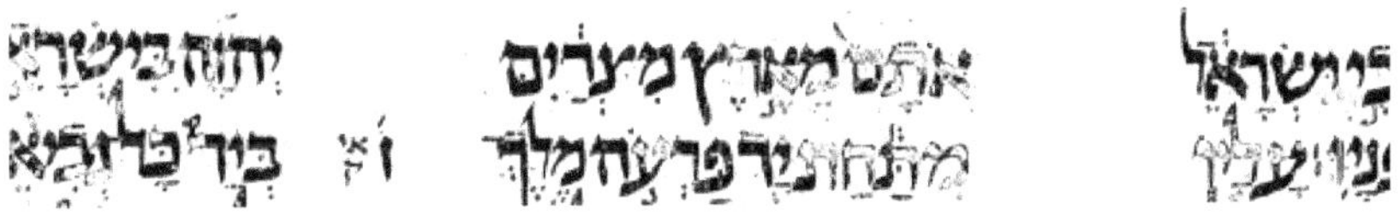

EVR II B 50 +, p. 26

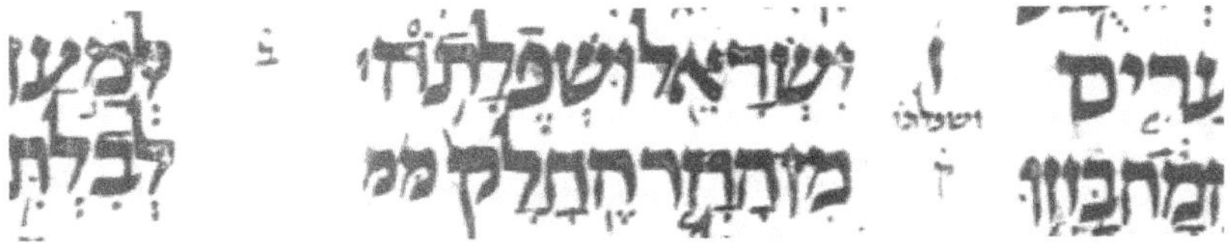

EVR II B 24 +, p. 130

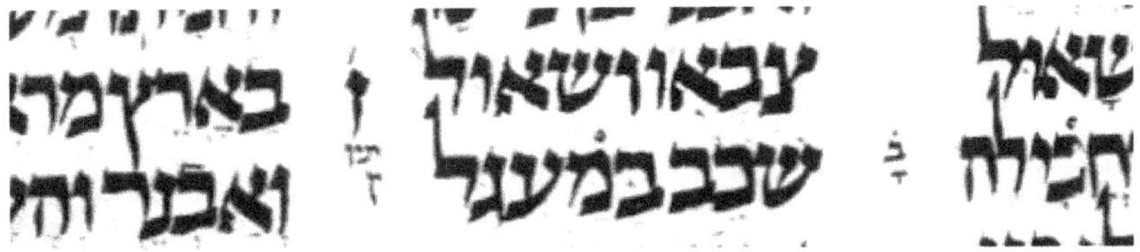

EVR II B 1166 +, p. 8

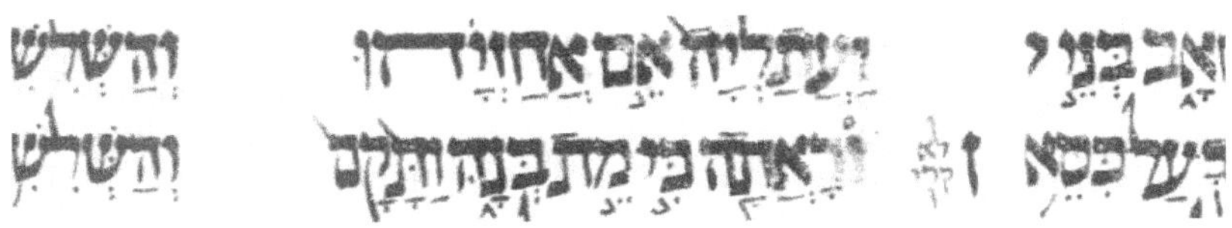

There remain three manuscripts where the marginal letter occurs frequently. I see little in these scripts from a paratextual or script standpoint that link them to Script A or Script B in any meaningful way—or to one another. Nonetheless, the marginal letter appears in these manuscripts with regularity, and I record that fact here.

Figure 3: Script C

EVR II B 1167, p. 6

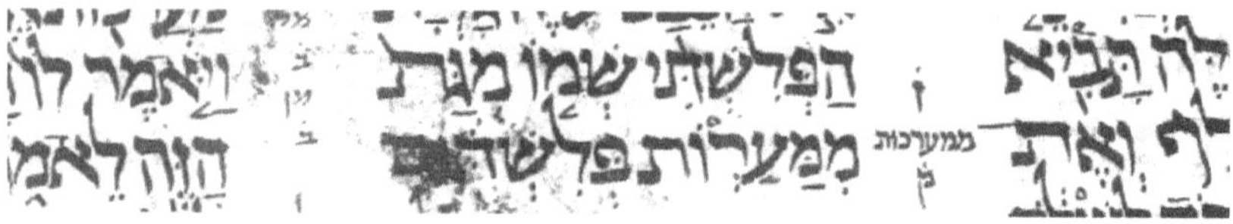

EVR II B 43, p. 24

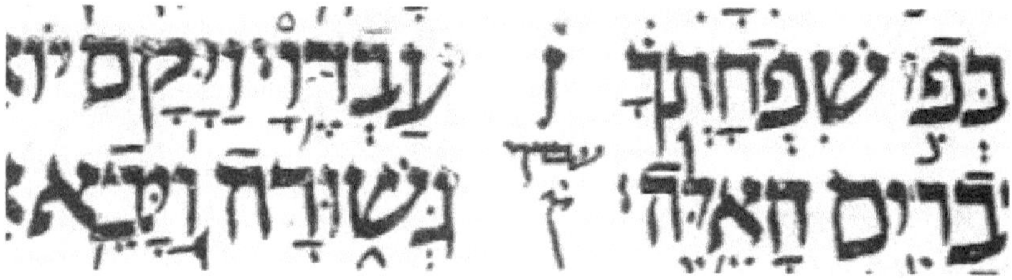

EVR II B 71 +, p. 103

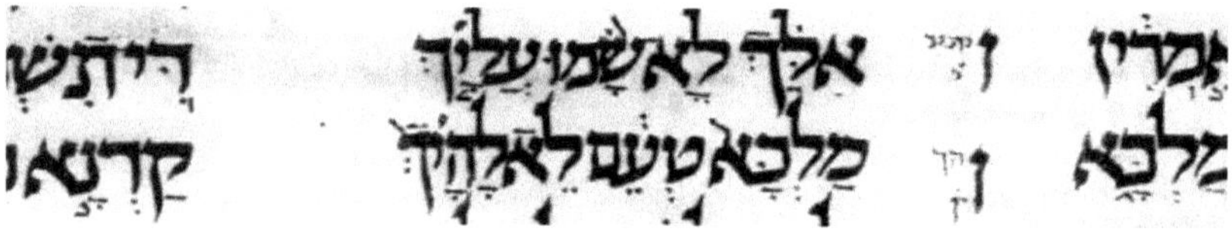

1.2. Manuscripts that Do Not Use the Marginal Letter

Our large, marginal letter was not found in 23 of the 38 manuscripts (Figures 4 and 5).[18] Although the manuscripts lacking the marginal *nun/zayin* show script variations, certain trends are readily observed. Most notably, fourteen codices contain a script

[18] NB, some of these 23 MSS still may contain infrequent occurrences of the marginal letter (e.g., the Leningrad Codex) not found within the stated reference ranges (Jdg. 3–6, 1 Sam. 16–19, 1 Kgs 8–10, and 2 Kgs 17–20). One should distinguish between studies where the letter occurs or does not occur with high frequency (the salient point of difference in the current paper) and MSS where the letter does or does not occur full stop (cf. Himbaza 2000).

style found in some of the earliest dated Bible codices in our possession, e.g., EVR II B 17 (930 CE), EVR II B 10 (946 CE), and EVR II B 39 (989 CE).[19] Many scholars will recognise this script due its congruity with the Aleppo Codex. The fourteen manuscripts are included below as Script D.

Figure 4: Script D

Aleppo Codex

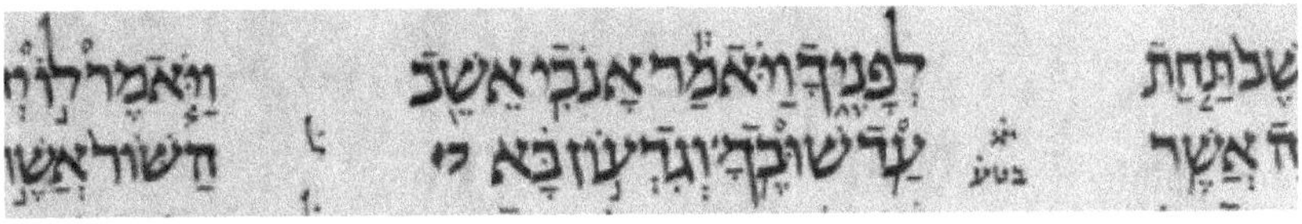

EVR II B 39+, p. 10

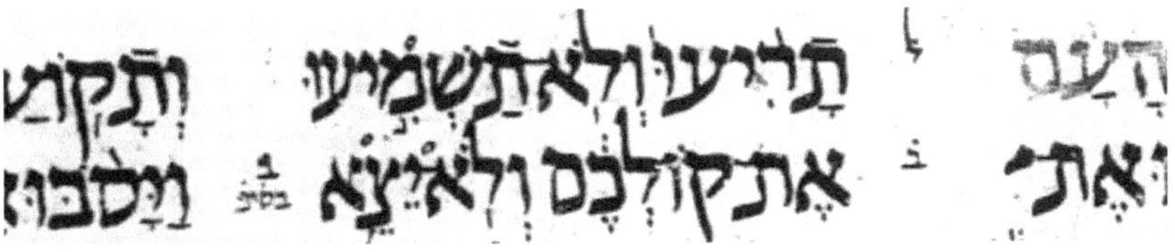

EVR II B 25+, p. 22

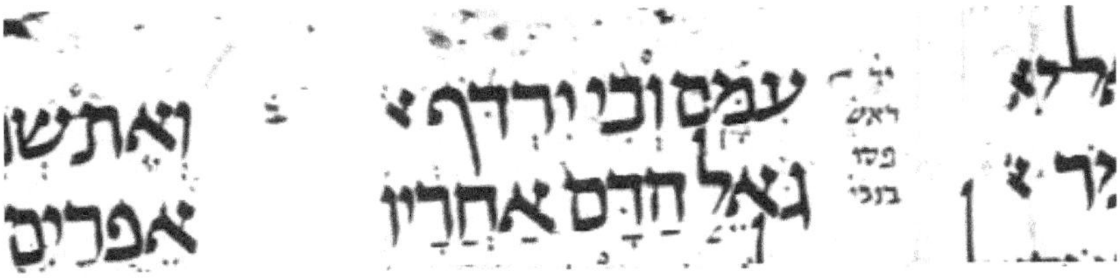

[19] Dated examples of this script type, some already mentioned above, may be found in Beit-Arié's *Specimens of Mediaeval Hebrew Scripts, Volume I: Oriental and Yemenite Scripts* (1988: esp. plates 4, 5, 10, 11, 12, 15, 16, 19).

EVR II B 99+, p. 34

EVR II B 70+, p. 6

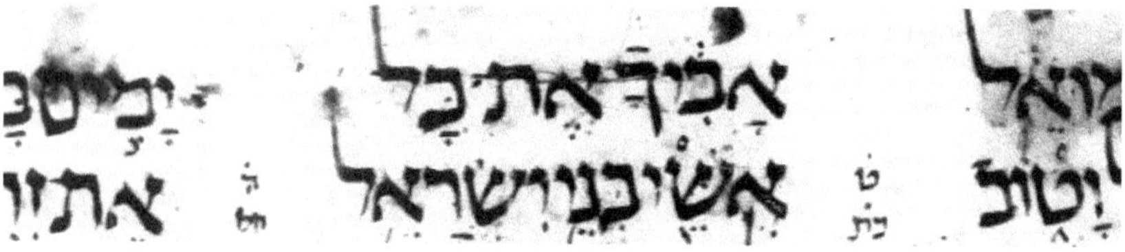

EVR I Bible 13/80, p. 19

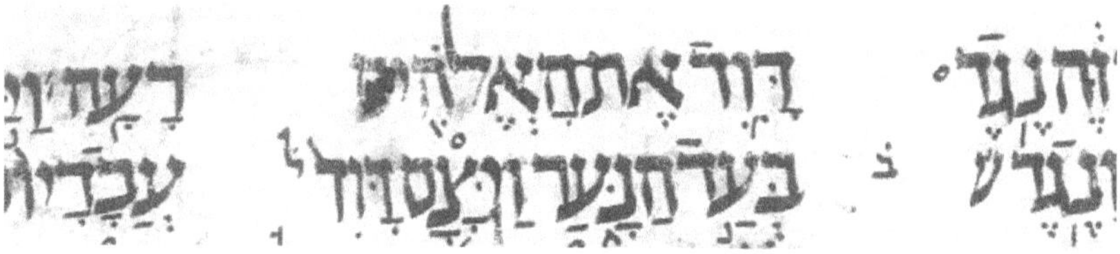

EVR II B 77+, p. 20

EVR II B 1272+, p. 6

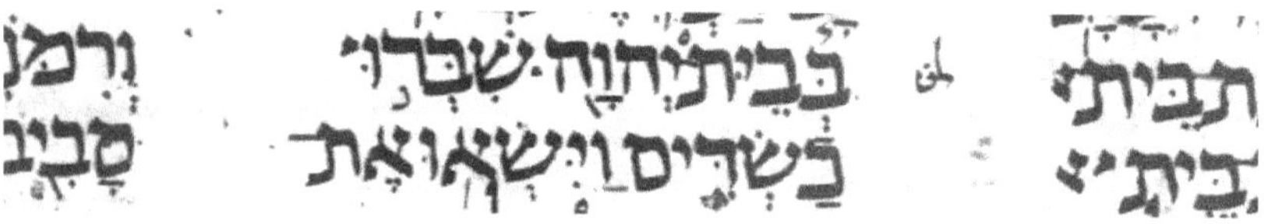

EVR II B 1378 +, p. 19

EVR II B 1169, p. 6

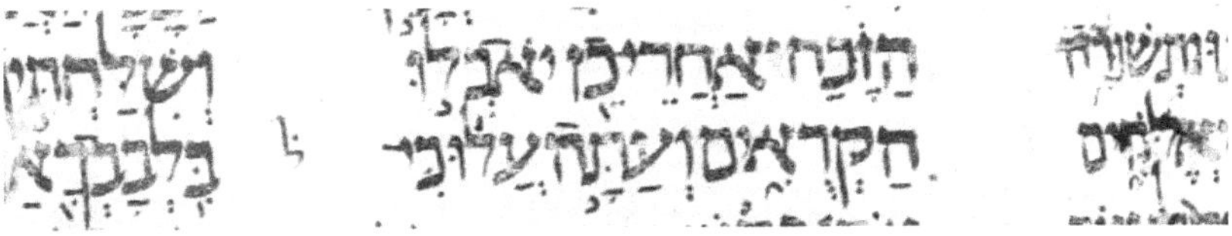

EVR II B 55 +, p. 7

EVR II B 56 +, p. 14

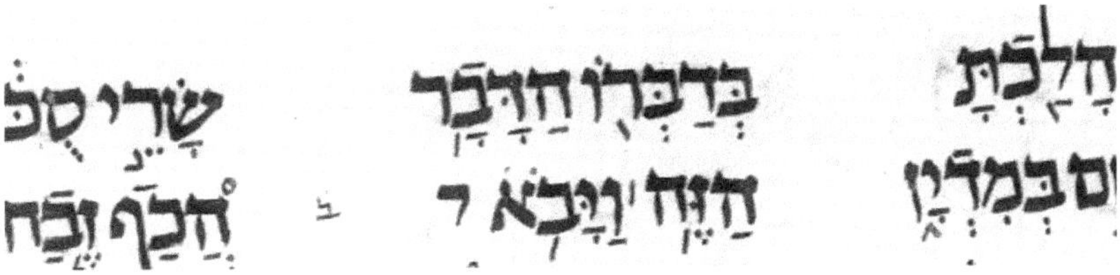

EVR Bibl. I 19a/Leningrad Codex

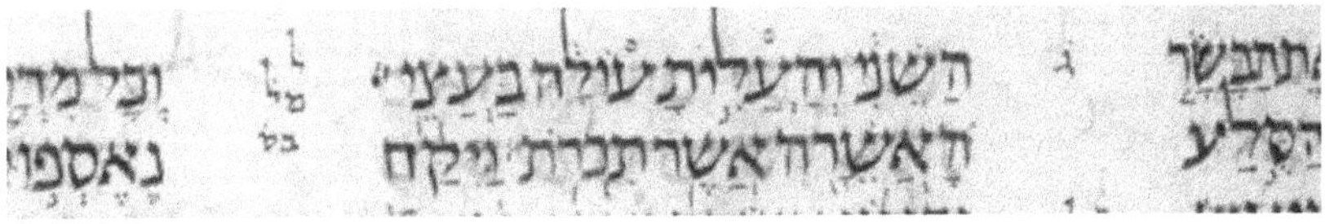

EVR II B 86 +, p. 8

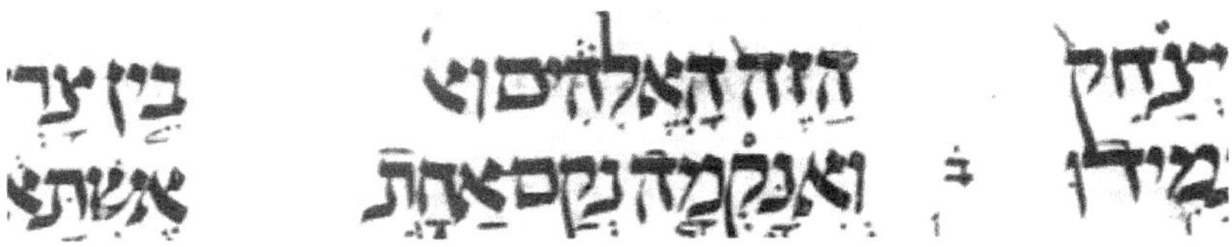

The final three of the above manuscripts do not fit into the Script D category as neatly as the others, but their similarities to the foregoing eleven are nonetheless remarkable. In sum, the above fourteen manuscripts show considerable congruence, presenting a script subtype that has not appeared in manuscripts with frequent attestations of the large, marginal letter (Scripts A–C).

There remain nine manuscripts (Figure 5, below), which do not employ the large, marginal letter. These MSS are of several types. One classmark, EVR II B 90, shows Sephardi influence mixed with some similarity to Script D. Several manuscripts have very small and fine writing (e.g., I Bibl. 68, II B 206, II B 94, JUD 002), making script comparison less productive. EVR II B 1275 is similar to Script A. Clearly, neither script categories nor scribal practices were entirely fixed. These final nine manuscripts are listed below.

Figure 5: Final nine codices without the marginal letter

II B 124, p. 17

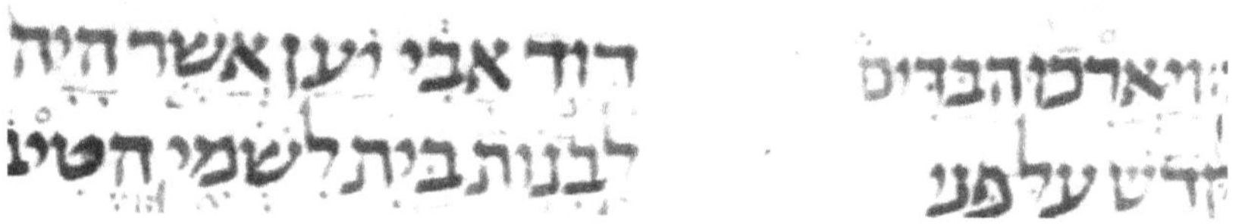

II B 1281+, p. 8

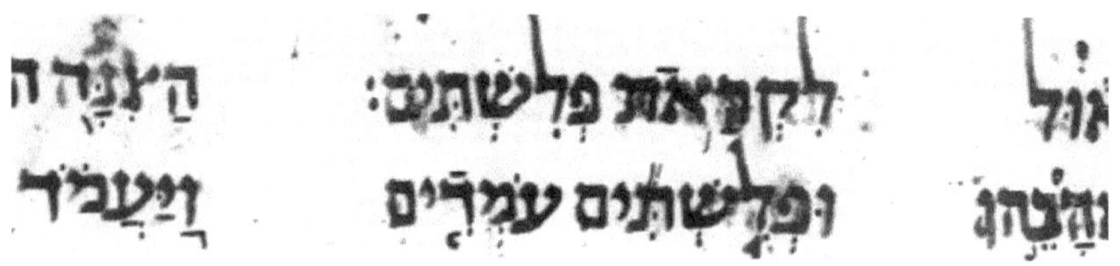

I Bibl. 68, p. 5

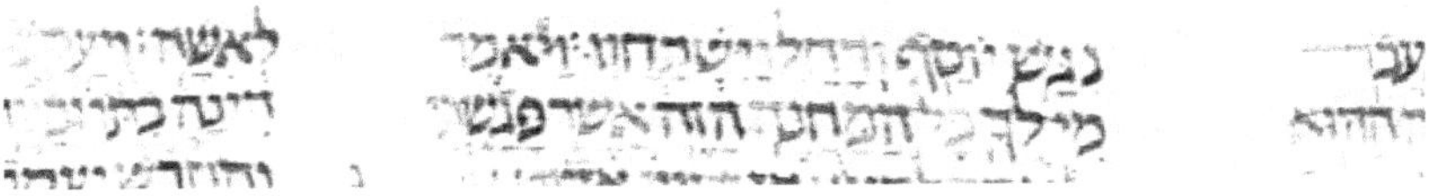

JUD 002 (formerly Sassoon 1053)

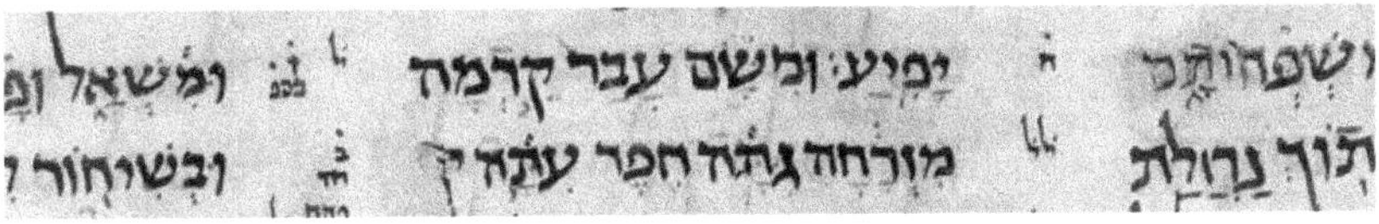

II B 206, p. 6

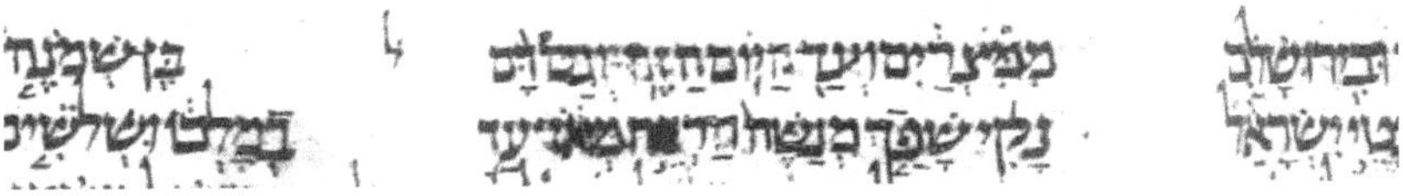

II B 94, p. 9

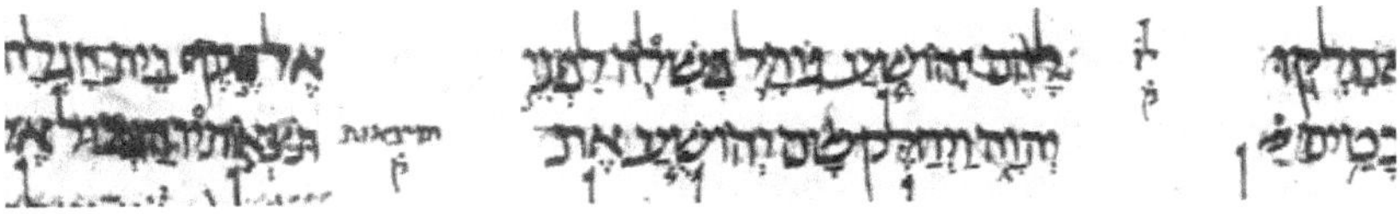

II B 90, p. 6

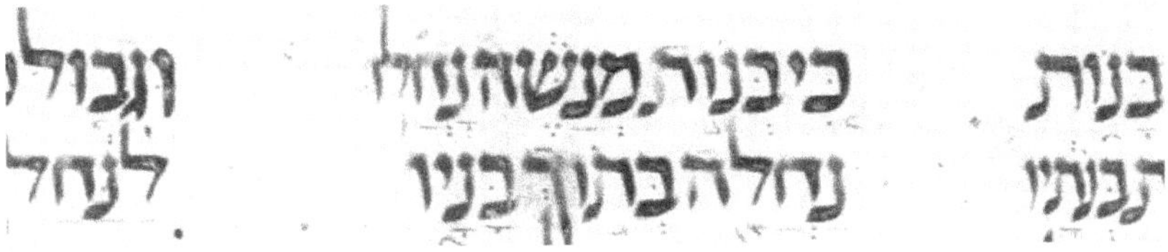

II B 1275, p. 6

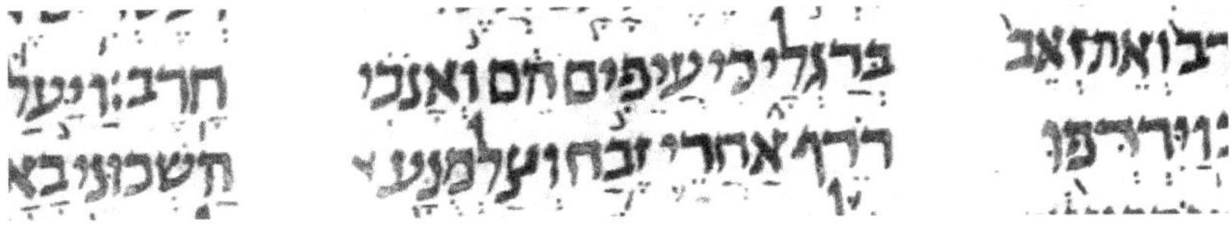

II B 1180+, p. 9

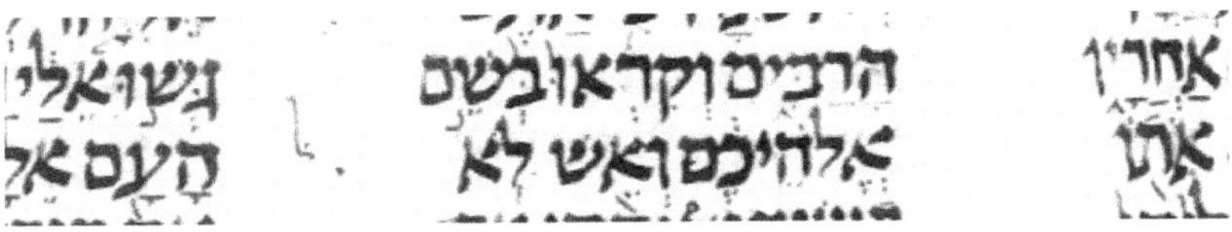

Although the above descriptions provide only the briefest of an overview, we are left with some unmistakable patterns. First, codices of the script style of the Aleppo Codex et al. (Script D) are unlikely to have the marginal letter with any frequency. Secondly, in the majority of instances, the scripts with the marginal letter contain paratextual features not found in Script D. These data support, for example, the argument that the Cairo Codex was not from a ben Asher centre of production (cf. Penkower 1990; Beit-Arié et al. 1997, 28–29).

2.0. Is the Large, Marginal Letter a Final *Nun*?

In a visual inspection of the present codices, it is difficult to decide if the marginal letter is a *zayin* or a final *nun*. In the main text, context, rather than letter shape, is frequently determinative. As there are no other large letters in the margin against which our letter may be assessed—and because the large letter is not part of a word—we must rely upon minor differences of sometimes questionable significance. On the basis of the codices that Himbaza (2000, 174) examined, he concluded that the marginal letter was a *nun*. Likewise, in the manuscripts surveyed by Penkower (2019) a *nun* seemed likely. However, the present evidence is only in partial agreement with those assessments. To my eye, in only nine of the fifteen manuscripts does the marginal letter appear more likely to be *nun* than *zayin*. My readings are open to debate, admittedly, and we lack the space to do extensive comparative work in each manuscript. Still, the letter is not necessarily a *nun*—or, perhaps, was not considered to be a *nun* at all times or in all regions.

Table 1: Final *nun* and *zayin* comparison

ID	**Marginal letter**	**Final *nun***	***zayin***	**Most resembles**
II B 63 (p. 81)				*nun*
II B 50+ (pp. 146, 149)				*zayin?*
II B 24 (pp. 103, 110)		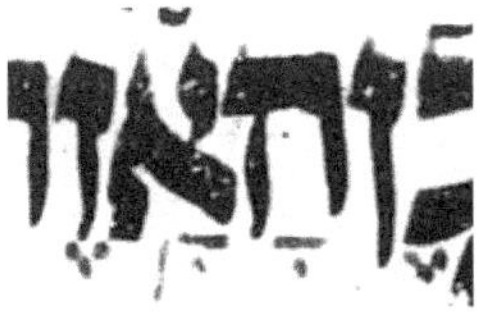 *Zayin* ↑	*Nun* ↑	*zayin?*
II B 1167 (p. 6)				*zayin*
II B 35 (p. 92)	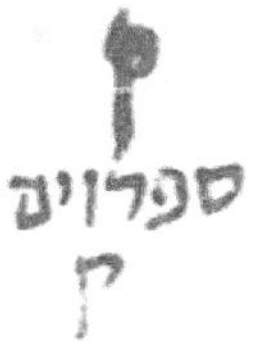			*zayin* (*nun* in main text is markedly longer)

II B 43 (p. 5)		*nun*?
II B 1270 (p. 5)		*zayin*?
II B 1233 (p. 5)		*nun*
II B 1243+ (pp. 5, 9)		*nun*?
II B 927 (p. 35)	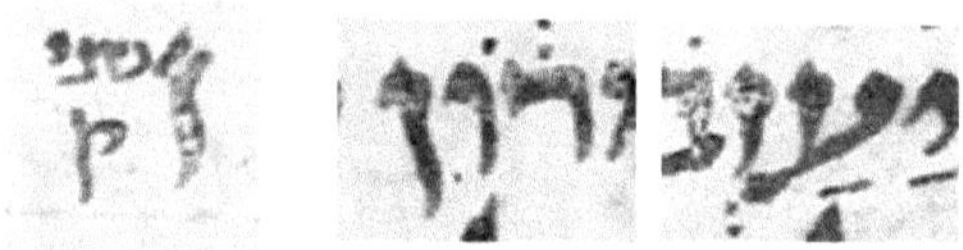	*nun*
II B 1160+ (here, of II B 1248) (p. 11)		*nun*
II B 1166+ (p. 17)	 *nun*↑ ↑*zayin*	*nun*

II B 1285+ (1474) (p. 5)		*nun*
II B 71+ (p. 91)	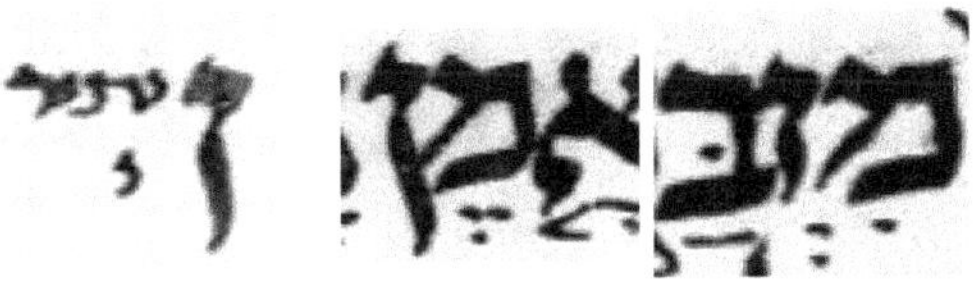	*nun* (letter is obviously long)
Cairo Codex (p. 273)		*zayin*

Left unaddressed in the *nun* or *zayin* discussion is a rather troublesome question. Namely, if the letter is a *nun*, why should the final form be used to mark an abbreviation? Why not simply use a non-final *nun* as one would do to indicate the number fifty? As noted above, Kahle suggested that the final *nun* stood for קריין, a solution which Yeivin dismissed as “astonishing” (1980, 52). I would tend to agree. To the best of my knowledge, there is no precedent for the use of a final form to indicate a non-final letter within the *masora parva*. For example, the abbreviation for פסוקין ‘verses’ is פ̇, never ף̇; the abbreviation for מן ‘from’ is מ̇, never ם̇.[20]

The exception to this rule occurs only in mnemonics. In Deut. 30.16, the proper sequence for the three-word phrase מִצְוֺתָיו וְחֻקֹּתָיו וּמִשְׁפָּטָיו ‘commandments, and statutes, and judgements’ is indicated by BHS as צ̇ק̇פ̇. In manuscripts, however, the *pe* is always

[20] Instances of מ̇ indicating ‘from’ can be found in virtually every codex. Instances of בפ̇ indicating ‘in the verses’ are less frequent—but see, for example, the Cairo Codex: Jdg. 5.13 (2x), 23, 30 (2x).

written in its final form, namely צקֹף.[21] Similarly, the mnemonic לאׄזׄןׄ appears at Ps. 25.7 in the Leningrad Codex. Here, אׄ = אני or אלה, זׄ = זאת; ןׄ = נא. Once again, a non-final letter is written as a final letter. In both cases, the reason the final letter of the three-word mnemonic takes the final form is due to its position within the mnemonic. As a stand-alone abbreviation, however, there is no reason for a non-final letter to be written as a final letter.

The most reasonable path in identifying the marginal letter, then, is to assume that it cannot be a *nun* and is therefore either a *zayin* or simply a marker of unknown meaning which happens to resemble a final *nun*. With this in mind, we turn to an angle of the problem that has not received treatment in the literature.

3.0. *Masora parva* Notation as a Two-Step Process

Although our marginal letter is often the same size as the main text, there are a minority of instances where the letter is more nearly the smaller size of the surrounding *masora parva*. In some codices (e.g., EVR II B 1167), the marginal letter is characteristically small. In others, the size varies from instance to instance (e.g., EVR II B 43, EVR II B 973, EVR II B 1243+, EVR II B 1285+). These codices with variable-sized marginal letters provide us with an important bit of insight regarding the order of operations in the writing of a codex. Namely, when our letter is large, its central position in the margin indicates it was added at

---

[21] In my database of Torah MSS at Deut. 30.16, a final *pe* is written 9x: Washington Pentateuch (later additions), JUD 002, II B 10, Vat.evr.448, II B 59, II B 96, II B 74, II B 18, and II B 158. No occurrences of a non-final *pe* were observed.

a point prior to the *qere* note and/or the surrounding *masora parva* notes. When the marginal letter is more nearly the size of the remaining *masora parva*, however, its position indicates that it was added at the same time as the surrounding *masora parva* notes. These statements can be proven through a careful examination of the following images.

3.1. Letter Size as Evidence of a Two-Step Process

Figure 6: II B 927, p. 41

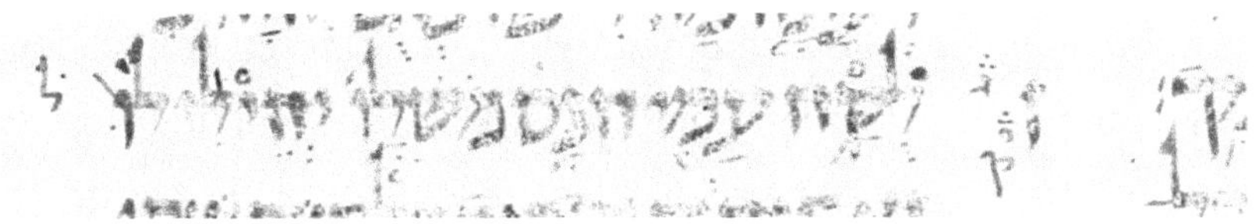

In the above image are three *masora parva* notes. They concern, in verse order, the words לֻקַּח ‘is taken’, משלו/מֹשְׁלָיו ‘their rulers’, and יְהֵילִילוּ ‘make them howl’ (Isa. 52.5). In situations such as this, where multiple *masora parva* notes occur on the same line, the *masora parva* comments generally are organised according to verse order. This means that the *masora parva* note for לֻקַּח should occur farthest to the right, the *masora parva* note for יְהֵילִילוּ should occur farthest to the left, and the *masora parva* note for משלו/מֹשְׁלָיו should occur somewhere between the above two.

In the present instance, however, there are some problems. Our large letter occurs farthest to the right, and its associated *qere* comment (י׳ ק), is squeezed alongside, below and to the left. The *gimel* associated with לֻקַּח, rather than occurring farthest right, now occupies the second spot. The explanation for this reversal in the order of *masora parva* notes is not hard to find: the large letter was written prior to and without regard for the remaining notes. Rather than erase the large letter and start over, the scribe of the smaller *masora parva* notes elected to place the *gimel* in the second place instead of the first. An alert reader would perhaps have had no trouble sorting out these comments. The fact remains that this reverse ordering of the notes is highly atypical in the present corpus.

Contrast the above example with the following one, also from EVR II B 927, where the marginal letter is the size of the remaining *masora parva* comment. Here, one can see how the entire comment is integrated, our marginal letter occurring slightly to right of centre in the margin space, allowing for the comfortable addition of the remaining portion of the note.

Figure 7: II B 927, p. 10

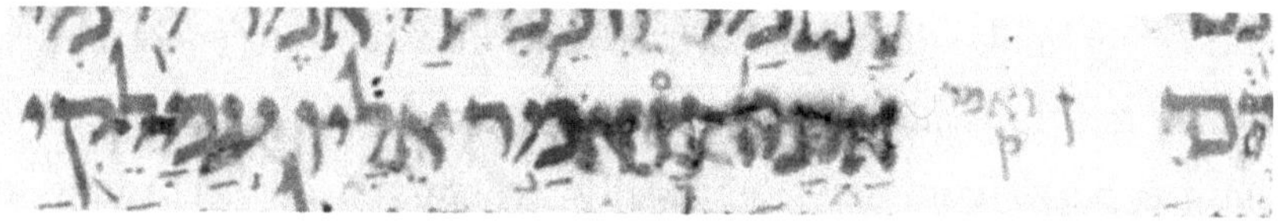

This pattern holds for all codices examined above. Where the marginal letter is large, it tends to occupy pride of place, in the centre of the margin space or slightly to right of centre—perhaps in anticipation of an eventual *qere/ketiv* comment. When the letter is smaller, it is more integrated, space-wise, with surrounding *masora parva* notes.

3.2. Letter Placement as Evidence of a Two-Step Process

In codices where the marginal letter is large, it almost always occurs level with the word(s) being commented upon. That is, the letter is hung from the line in the same way as the main text.

Figure 8: II B 24, p. 130

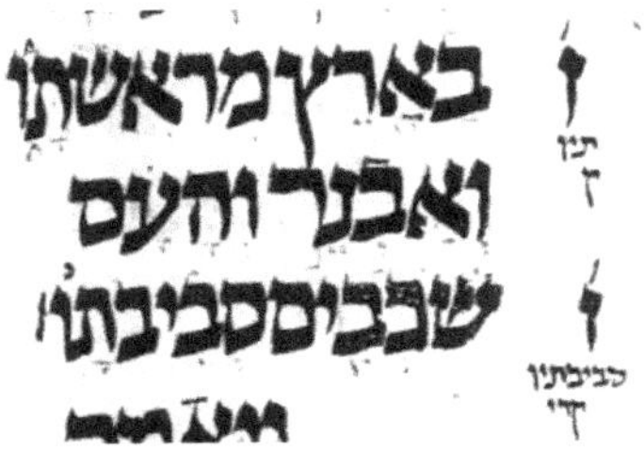

When the marginal letter is smaller, however, it may appear above the line of the main text being commented upon in the following manner:

Figure 9: II B 43, p. 24

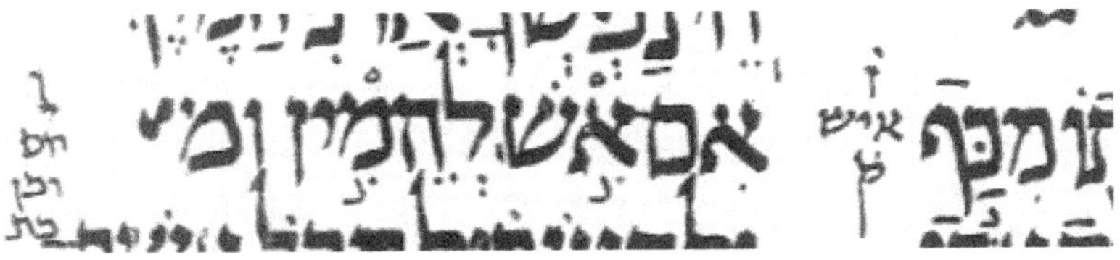

Although the defective spelling of אִשׁ 'man' (2 Sam. 14.19) is being commented upon in the above image, our small marginal letter sits just above the headline of the referent, rather than hanging just below it. Why? It appears that the scribe, considering the note as a whole, chose to align the centre of the note most nearly with the proper line of the main text. Contrast the above example from Figure 9 with the former example in Figure 8, where the large marginal letter was written level with the main text with no regard for eventual placement of smaller *masora parva* notes. Once again, in codices that contain the large, marginal letter, the writing of the *masora parva* appears to have been a process consisting of at least two steps.[22]

[22] An exception may be found, for example, in the Cairo Codex at 1 Sam. 17.23. In this instance, the *qere* note ממערכות ק was written first and our

3.3. Ink Differences as Evidence of a Two-Step Process[23]

We can reach a similar conclusion when comparing the ink of the large, marginal letter with the remaining *masora parva* note.

Figure 10: Washington Pentateuch, Exod. 22.26

letter, of small size, is squeezed in beside the *qere* comment, almost as an afterthought. This example, nonetheless, proves the general rule: a large *nun/zayin* is written prior while a small *nun/zayin* is written later.

[23] NB, images of the Washington Pentateuch and Schøyen 1630 were chosen due to the availability of colour images; they are *not* part of the current data set, which are comprised of black and white images with only three exceptions (Aleppo, Jud 002, Leningrad, the first two of which contain no instances of the marginal letter). Also note that 75 of the 76 occurrences of the marginal letter in Leningrad occur in the Writings, the sole exception appearing in Jdg. 20.13 (Martín-Contreras 2015, 88–89). The lopsided distribution of the marginal letter in Leningrad remains unexplained, although the presence of a secondary scribe (or scribes) seems likely (cf. Himbaza 2017, 355–68).

Figure 11: Leningrad Codex, Job 26.12

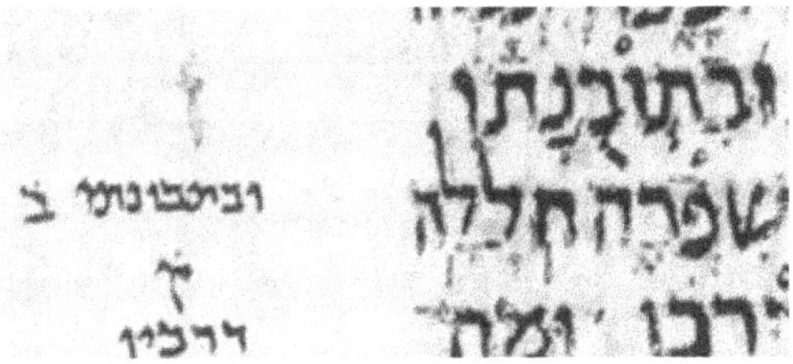

In the Washington Pentateuch, the ink of the large letter is in relatively good condition, matching the ink of the main text. The *qere* comment, by contrast, appears to have flaked off. In the case of the Leningrad Codex, the reverse has occurred. The main text and the marginal letter are dim (the main text obviously has been reinked) while the ink of the smaller *masora parva* hand remains intact.

Something similar has happened with Schøyen 1630. Although the image quality is poor, one can still see a black ink used for main text and the large, marginal letters. A (now) reddish ink was used for the remaining Mp notes, including those accompanying the marginal letter.

Figure 12: Schøyen 1630, Zech. 14

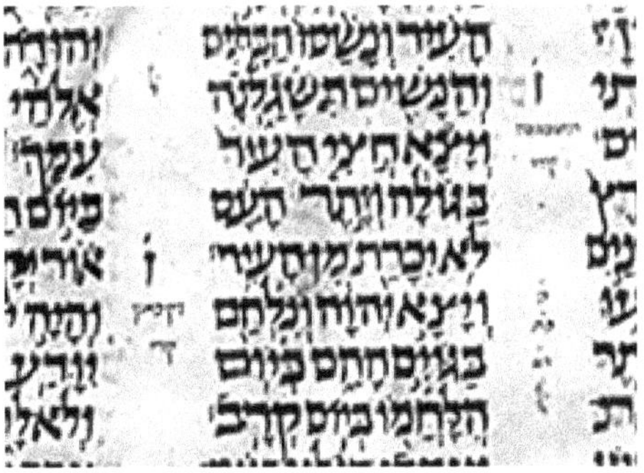

In sum, it appears that the marking of the *masora parva* notes was a process of at least two stages. First, probably at the time of writing of the main text, a large letter was recorded in the margin at *qere/ketiv*-type instances. Secondly, at a time after the large letter had been inserted, the remaining *masora parva* was written. In instances where the large marginal letter was initially 'missed', the later scribe sometimes still elected to write it in the margin, albeit now with the hand size of the remaining *masora parva* notes.

4.0. Does the Large, Marginal Letter Always Indicate *qere/ketiv*?

It is the view of Martín-Contreras that in C the marginal letter does not necessarily indicate *qere/ketiv*. Supporting this claim are 90 instances in C where the marginal letter appears without a *qere/ketiv* type note alongside (2015, 83–89).[24] However, the assertion of Martín-Contreras regarding the putative independence

[24] My calculations are based upon the data of Martín-Contreras (2015, 83–87). To arrive at 90 occurrences, I omitted instances said to be marked for *ketiv* or *qere* or some combination of the two. This yielded 93 occurrences. Of these 93, three appear to have been entered in error (marginal letter not visible: Jdg. 21.20; *qere* note present but marked as not present: 2 Sam. 22.23; 2 Kgs 11.1), bringing the number of instances to 90. The references are as follows. From §1, 2x: 1 Sam. 9.26; 2 Sam. 14.11. From §2.1, 12x: 1 Sam. 24.19; 25.3, 8; 2 Sam. 3.3; 1 Kgs 21.21; 2 Kgs 13.6; Jer. 19.15; 32.35; 39.16; Ezek. 16.25; 23.43; Mic 1.15. From §2.2, 75x: Josh. 6.7; 7.21; Jdg. 9.8, 12; 13.17; 17.2; 1 Sam. 15.16; 24.5; 25.34; 28.8; 2 Sam. 1.16; 10.9, 17; 11.1, 24; 12.1, 13.8; 14.11; 21.9; 23.20; 1 Kgs 1.27; 2.24; 6.16; 8.26; 9.25; 12.3, 21; 18.36; 22.13; 2 Kgs 7.12; 8.21; 11.15; 14.2; Isa. 23.12; 26.20; 42.24; Jer. 1.5; 2.33; 3.4; 4.19; 5.7; 10.17; 15.16; 22.23; 31.21, 39; 34.11; 41.17; 42.20; 46.11; 48.44; 49.28; 51.13; Ezek. 4.6; 9.5, 8; 16.13, 18, 22, 31, 31, 43, 47, 51;

of the marginal letter appears less certain when comparing C to other early codices. Of the 90 instances where C contains a marginal letter but does not mark *qere/ketiv* (see above, n. 24), 79 of them are explicitly marked as *qere* in the Leningrad Codex.[25] Of the remaining eleven, I was able to find explicit *qere* marking in eight instances,[26] leaving only three examples[27] where a *qere* marking was not found. In other words, even if a note is not *qere/ketiv* in C, this is not to say that the note was not considered to be so by masoretic scribes more generally.

Moreover, 75 of the above 90 instances in C where the marginal letter occurs without explicit marking of *qere* occur in conjunction with יתיר 'superfluous', a term regarded by Yeivin as occurring in "*qere/ketiv* situations" (1980, 94).

Penkower (2019) provides numerous examples, primarily in Torah scrolls, where the marginal letter was not intended to preserve *qere/ketiv*, but instead marked section division disagree-

---

18.28; 23.14, 42; 27.3; 29.4; 36.16; Hos. 4.6; 10.14; Mic. 1.3, 10, Zech. 1.4. From §§2.3–2.6, 0x. From §2.7, 1x: 2 Kgs 5.25.

[25] The eleven instances not marked as *qere* in either L or C are: 1 Sam. 25.3, 8; 2 Sam. 10.17; 11.1; 12.1; 1 Kgs 9.25; 2 Kgs 8.21; Ezek. 9.8; Hos. 4.6; 10.14; Mic. 1.15.

[26] 1 Sam. 28.8 (I Bibl. 68); 2 Sam. 11.1 (II B 43); 2 Sam. 12.1 (II B 1255–part of II B 1243 +); 1 Kgs 9.25 (II B 35); 2 Kgs 8.21 (II B 35); Ezek. 9.8 (II B 24); Hos. 4.6 (II B 50); Hos. 10.14 (II B 50).

[27] No *qere* note found: אֲבִגָ֑יִל 'Abigail' (1 Sam. 25.3); חֵלָ֑אמָה 'to Helam' (2 Sam. 10.17); אָבִ֣י 'I will bring' (Mic. 1.15). There may be codices where *qere* is marked at these locations; I have not yet succeeded in finding them.

ments. The few codices cited by Penkower, however, are (a) entirely Ashkenazi or Italian and (b) generally later than the present corpus. As the use of the large marginal letter to indicate disputed section divisions was not found in the present study focusing on Oriental codices, it appears that the letter's meaning could have varied from region to region (Ashkenazi vs. Oriental) or medium to medium (Torah scrolls vs. codices). It is also possible that the signs, although visually similar, were not understood by the scribes who wrote them as being identical.

In the present corpus, the marginal letter is almost wholly associated with *qere/ketiv*. Where the letter appears without the explicit mention of *qere* in a given codex, the word has a *qere* marking at the same reference in a codex elsewhere within the corpus.

There are also instances where the *qere* is implicitly present, even when no mention of it is made in the margin. For example, in EVR II B 50 at Jdg. 4.11, the marginal letter appears by itself; there is no *qere* marking in evidence. The word being commented upon, בצענים/בְּצַעֲנַנִּים 'at Zaanaim', has the *ketiv* spelling, but the *qere* vocalisation. This indicates that the *qere*, although perhaps not explicitly marked, was certainly known to the scribe who wrote the note. These data point towards a usage of the large marginal letter in Oriental codices that is wholly focused on *qere/ketiv*.

5.0. Suggestions Regarding the Letter's Meaning, Use, and Localisation

5.1. The Marginal Letter as *Zayin*

As demonstrated above, there is insufficient evidence to decide if the marginal letter is a symbol or an actual letter. If the marginal letter began its existence as an actual letter with an actual meaning, however, we should take a fresh look at possibilities that begin with the letter *zayin.*[28] Yeivin has suggested זיטימא 'uncertain', based upon a comment found in EVR II B 10:

> אליין מלייא באורייתא דכתיבן לבר מן דפא זׄ/ן ומנקדון מירום מילתא או מירום אתא ואינון זיטימא ומחלוקת ופליגין עליהון .
>
> These are the words in the Torah where זׄ/ן is written beside the column, and a dot is marked above a word or letter. That word or letter is uncertain, and there are different opinions on it.[29]

Penkower notes, however, that the ensuing list of catchwords in EVR II B 10 pertain to space break disagreements for Torah scrolls (2019, 145; cf. Dotan 2007, 616). In other words, the comment in EVR II B 10 does not appear relevant when considering

[28] There are numerous instances where the letter is undoubtedly final *nun*-like (cf. Penkower 2019), but as these manuscripts are generally later, one should be careful before assuming that the meaning of the letter remained static while the shape of the letter underwent modifications.

[29] The identity of the symbol in this example is not clear-cut, necessitating the dual entry of the note as זׄ/ן.

non-space break type usages such as those found in the present corpus.

We might also consider other options, such as זכר 'remember!' or זוגא/זוגין 'pair/pairs', either of which would serve as a reminder to the reader that what is on the page is different from what should be read. This latter suggestion is especially consonant with the masoretic ethos, being part and parcel of the masoretic project as seen most famously in *Sefer Okhlah ve-Okhlah*. It is also precisely the kind of note one would expect in a text where a known difference (*ketiv* and *qere*) could be found.

5.2. Why Was the Marginal Letter Large?

Why was the marginal letter large, especially in codices where the marginal letter occurred the most frequently? Here, I would suggest two reasons, one historical and the other practical.

The consensus is that the marginal letter is early, that is, probably predating the remaining *masora parva* notes (e.g., Ofer 2019, 89–91). For scribes at this stage of transmission (now lost to us), there was little reason for the letter to be small. The scribe simply wrote the letter in the margin using the calamus he, or she, was already using, establishing the pattern that the letter be large.

As time went on, *masora parva* comments and *qere/ketiv* comments also were added to the margins of Bible codices. This made the marginal letter somewhat redundant (Penkower 2019). That is, the marginal letter was merely signalling what the *qere* made explicit; it did not serve an additional function. The writing of the letter continued to serve a practical purpose, however, which may have extended its use.

Scribes recording the *masora* enjoyed freedom to include whichever notes they preferred (i.e., Yeivin's Rule). The only exception was where the traditions for *ketiv* and *qere* differed. In these situations, both traditions, if known, must necessarily be recorded. To ensure that these differences were not missed, it was convenient to write our letter at the time when the consonants of the main text were written. This would provide practically fail-safe assurance that the location of the 'pair'—or whatever the sign meant—would receive comment by the later scribe(s) when the smaller *masora parva* notes were written.

Of course, instances would have arisen where the large letter was inadvertently missed, or where a later scribe judged that the large letter should not have been written in the first place. This is to be expected, as the exact assemblage of *qere* notes varies from codex to codex (cf. Ofer 2008; 2019, 92–93). In instances where the marginal letter was not included during the initial entry process, scribes of the remaining *masora parva* did not necessarily feel compelled to write this letter, its primary usefulness having already passed.[30]

---

[30] There is an additional explanation for the letter's size which merits consideration. Namely, since one likely use of a model codex was to ensure an accurate public reading in the synagogue, the presence of the marginal letter (particularly if it was of a size that could be readily spotted) would assist the proofer in correcting the reader at the very point where the reader was most likely to go wrong: the pronunciation of the *qere*. Many thanks to Estara Arrant for this suggestion.

5.3. The Marginal Letter and Localisation

Finally, we arrive at the issue of localisation. There are some tantalising clues to suggest centres of scribal activity where the marginal letter was more likely to occur. In the manuscripts with colophons that Himbaza (2000, 187) examined, an Egyptian origin seemed the most likely. In the manuscripts I examined, it was observed that several manuscripts show some similarity in their features with SW Oriental scripts. Recognizing that uncertainties remain, I do not insist upon this association, but suggest it as a line of inquiry that merits further research.

Regardless, it remains abundantly clear that scripts resembling that of the Aleppo Codex and manuscripts like it are the least likely of all codices to have the large marginal letter with any frequency. This provides us with, at minimum, a negative definition. Namely, codices that contain frequent attestations of the large marginal letter are not from centres of production associated with NE Oriental script of the 'Tiberian' type (i.e., Script D, above).

In the present corpus, the only manuscript with the marginal letter containing a colophon is the Cairo Codex—whose colophon claims that it was written in Tiberias.[31] As the Cairo Codex shows some significant differences in paratextual features—not to mention vocalisation differences (cf. Yeivin 2003, 13–19) with

[31] As stated above, the Leningrad Codex is here excluded, as its sparing use of the marginal letter does not occur with the reference ranges under examination (for the occurrences in L with references, see Martín-Contreras 2015; Himbaza 2000).

other codices known to have originated in Tiberias and Jerusalem—it remains possible that Egypt is more probable for the writing of C than Palestine. But, as a large number of 10th–12th-century Bible manuscripts that have survived to the present originated in, passed through, or ended up in Egypt, suggesting an Egyptian origin is not entirely illuminating. As Olszowy-Schlanger (2015, 14–20) notes, competing intellectual centres may sometimes be found within the same city (cf. Engel 2013, 488). A more fruitful line of inquiry may be to identify paratextual feature distributions, which, in turn, could suggest scribal schools. Once the 'schools' become better understood, we will be in a firmer position to posit likely localisation—or to discuss it in a more meaningful manner.[32]

Despite these necessary qualifiers, it remains likely that the writing of the marginal letter, for the time period of the manuscripts in question (10th–12th century), was a scribal practice more associated with Egypt than elsewhere. It may even be that the letter fell out of use precisely due to the increased prestige of the Aleppo Codex and codices similar to it.

---

[32] For example, script sub-type, the large marginal letter, the triple-dotting of certain *masora parva* notes, and the use of the marginal יפה 'well/good/correct' with no additional qualifiers tend to occur in tandem. Prima facie, this would indicate localisation. For other paratextual features that may occur in tandem, see Penkower (2021, 160–61).

6.0. Summary

The present article considers the recurrent use (or absence) of a particular marginal letter in 38 early Bible codices. In these codices, the use of the letter is limited to certain script subtypes, suggesting that regional difference and/or scribal school heavily influenced the letter's usage, particularly in the codices where the letter appears with high frequency. The placement and size of the letter suggest a two-stage method of *masora parva* note entry (first the large letter, and later the smaller writing). Finally, it may be unhelpful to identify the symbol as a final *nun*. Instead, the letter may be better understood as a scribal sign (either *zayin* or a sign of unknown meaning) written to indicate an alternate tradition (*qere/ketiv*) that the scribe of the main text was at special pains to record.

References

Beit-Arie, Malachi. 2020. 'Supplement: The Forgery of Colophons and Ownership of Hebrew Codices and Scrolls by Abraham Firkowicz'. *Fakes and Forgeries of Written Artifacts from Ancient Mesopotamia to Modern China*, edited by Cécile Michel and Michael Friedrich, 195–205. Berlin-Boston: De Gruyter.

———. 2021. *Hebrew Codicology: Historical and Comparative Typology of Medieval Hebrew Codices Based on the Documentation of the Extant Dated Manuscripts until 1540 Using a Quantitative Approach*. Jerusalem: The Israel Academy of Sciences and Humanities.

Beit-Arié, Malachi, Colette Sirat, and Mordecai Glatzer. 1997. *Codices hebraicis letteris exarati quo tempore scripti fuerint exhibentes*, Vol. I. Turnhout: Brepols.

Beit-Arié, Malachi, Edna Engel, and Ada Yardeni. 1987. *Specimens of Mediaeval Hebrew Scripts, Vol. 1: Oriental and Yemenite Scripts*. Jerusalem: The Israel Academy of Sciences. [Hebrew]

Breuer, Mordechai. 1976. *The Aleppo Codex and the Accepted Text of the Bible*. Jerusalem: Mosad Harav Kook. [Hebrew]

Dotan, Aron. 2007. 'Masorah'. *Encyclopaedia Judaica*, 2nd edition, edited by Fred Skolnik, et al., XIII:604–56. Jerusalem: Keter Publishing House.

Engel, Edna. 1998. 'Style of the Hebrew Script in the Tenth and Eleventh Centuries in the Light of Dated and Datable Genizah Documents'. *Teʿuda* 15: 365–410. [Hebrew]

———. 2013. 'Script, History of Development'. In *Encyclopedia of Hebrew Language and Linguistics*, edited by Geoffrey Khan, et al., III:485–502. Leiden: Brill.

Ginsburg, Christian D. 1880. *The Massorah Compiled from Manuscripts*. 3 vols. London: no publisher.

Himbaza, Innocent. 2000. 'Le *Nûn* Marginal et la Petite Massore'. *Textus* 20: 173–91.

———. 2017. 'La diversité des sources du manuscrit de Leningrad B19a'. *Semitica* 59: 355–68.

Kahle, Paul. 1927. *Masoreten des Westens*. Stuttgart: Kohlhammer.

Kelly, Page H., Daniel S. Mynatt, and Timothy G. Crawford. 1998. *The Masorah of Biblia Hebraica Stuttgartensia*. Grand Rapids, MI: William B. Eerdmans.

Lieberman, Saul. 1962. Hellenism in Jewish Palestine: Studies in *the Literary Transmission, Beliefs, and Manners of Palestine in the I Century B.C.E.–IV Century C.E.,* 2nd edition. New York: Jewish Theological Seminary of America.

Martín-Contreras, Elvira. 2015. 'The Marginal *Nun* in the Masora of the Cairo Codex of the Prophets: Use and Function'. *Vetus Testamentum* 65: 81–90.

Ofer, Yosef. 2008. 'Ketiv and Qere: The Phenomenon, Its Notations, and Its Reflection in Early Rabbinic Literature'. *Leshonenu* 70: 55–73. [Hebrew]

———. 2019. *The Masora on Scripture and Its Methods.* Fontes et Subsidia ad Bibliam pertinentes 7. Berlin: De Gruyter.

Olszowy-Schlanger, Judith. 2014. 'On the Hebrew Script of the Greek-Hebrew Palimpsests from the Cairo Genizah'. In *The Jewish-Greek Tradition in Antiquity and the Byzantine Empire,* edited by James Aitken and J. Carleton Paget, 279–99. Cambridge: Cambridge University Press.

———. 2015. 'Manuscrits hébreux et judéo-arabes médiévaux'. *Annuaire de l'École pratique des hautes études (EPHE), Section des sciences historiques et philologiques* 146: 14–20.

Penkower, Jordan. 1990. 'A Pentateuch Fragment of the Tenth Century Attributed to Moses Ben-Asher (MS Firkovicz B 188)'. *Tarbiz* 60: 355–70. [Hebrew]

———. 2019. 'The 12th–13th-Century Torah Scroll in Bologna: How It Differs from Contemporary Scrolls'. In *The Ancient Sefer Torah of Bologna: Features and History,* edited by Mauro Perani, 135–66. 'European Genizah': Text and Studies 59. Leiden: Brill.

———. 2021. 'An Eleventh-Century Eastern Masoretic Codex of the Pentateuch'. *Textus* 30: 152–70.

Tov, Emmanuel. 2001. *Textual Criticism of the Hebrew Bible,* 2nd edition. Minneapolis, MN: Augsburg Fortress-Assen: Koninklijke Van Gorcum.

Yeivin, Israel. 1980. *Introduction to the Tiberian Masorah.* Translated and edited by E. J. Revell. Masoretic Studies 5. Missoula, MT: Scholars Press.

———. 2003. *The Biblical Masorah.* Jerusalem: The Hebrew Academy of Language. [Hebrew]

TIBERIAN *KETIV-QERE* AND THE COMBINED SAMARITAN WRITTEN-READING TRADITION: POINTS OF CONTACT AND CONTRAST

Aaron D. Hornkohl

The phenomenon of *ketiv-qere* is the clearest indication of the composite nature of the Tiberian biblical tradition. Against the backdrop of the normally harmonious relationship between the tradition's written (i.e., consonantal, orthographic) and pronunciation (i.e., vocalisation, recitation) components, such acknowledged cases of written-reading dissonance are clear evidence of divergence (see Khan 2013a; 2020, I:33–49).

Crucially, however, beyond this, the phenomenon is opaque. The *ketiv-qere* mechanism signals, but does not explain, discord within the tradition, which is left for scholars to illuminate. It is sometimes assumed that the pronunciation tradition 'protects' or 'corrects' readings that have become garbled in the written tradition. While this may occasionally be the case (especially in cases of possible conflation of *waw* and *yod*, relevant in more than one case below), the view that it is the norm fails to do justice to the relationship between the *ketiv* and the *qere*. In many cases, both represent plausible readings. It is thus simplest

 https://doi.org/10.11647/OBP.0330.04

and most appropriate to think of the two components as transmitted artifacts that represent related but distinct traditions of pronunciation and interpretation—a major difference being that the written component only partially and ambiguously reflects how it was ever orally realised, whereas the pronunciation component does so more comprehensively and precisely. In sum, throughout the vast majority of the biblical text, there is no evidence to suggest anything other than harmony between the two components of the tradition; but in a not insignificant minority, the two clearly diverge.

In a number of cases in which the *ketiv* and *qere* offer synonymous linguistic alternatives, the *qere* reflects the characteristically later option. This is consistent with the view that the oral development of the Tiberian reading tradition, which was ultimately recorded in the vowel signs superimposed on medieval consonantal manuscripts, was largely complete by the end of Second Temple times. Having crystallised in the late antique period, it was something of a mixed linguistic system, regularly preserving features of more ancient Hebrew and simultaneously incorporating later secondary features. It should come as no surprise, then, that instances in which the reading component diverges from its written counterpart—whether or not explicitly acknowledged in masoretic sources—often show signs of secondary linguistic development (Khan 2013b; 2020, I:56–85; Hornkohl 2018, 86–91; 2020a, 248–57, 263–64; 2020b, 420–22).

For its part, the Samaritan biblical tradition is also composite, comprising related but independent written and recitation components that blend First and Second Temple traits. Letter shapes, word-separation dots, content, and much in the way of linguistic data hark back to the Iron Age, suggesting antiquity. The orthography and some minority linguistic features, on the other hand, display much in common with Hebrew and Aramaic sources that date from the end of the Second Temple period (Ben-Ḥayyim 2000, 3–4, §0.4; Tal and Florentin 2010, 25–28). This tallies with Tov's (2012, 79) summary, which emphasises that many features considered distinctively or especially Samaritan already distinguish proto-Samaritan manuscripts from proto-Masoretic material at Qumran, indicating that "the ש-group reflects a popular textual tradition of the Torah that circulated in ancient Israel in the last centuries BCE, in addition to the 𝔐-group and other texts." Some very late developments in the Samaritan reading tradition (see, e.g., the Samaritan phonology in §3.0 below) are due to contact with Arabic (see, e.g., Ben-Ḥayyim 2000, 29, §1.0.1, 32–33, §1.1.4).

There is no exact Samaritan counterpart to the Tiberian *ketiv-qere* mechanism. Even so, due in part to the chronological distance between the respective linguistic traditions embodied in the written and reading components of the Samaritan Pentateuch, dissonance between the two is commonplace. It is far more frequent than in the combined Tiberian written-reading tradition, with the Samaritan recitation tradition regularly 'updating' the oral realisation ostensibly reflected in the consonantal text—which, to be sure, itself shows occasional contemporisations in accord with Second Temple conventions (Hornkohl 2021, 8–9; see also §11.0, below). Additionally, it is also important to bear in mind the Samaritan biblical tradition's penchant for harmonisation, a characteristic that extends from the ironing out of perceived discrepancies in content to grammatical levelling and the imposition of morphosemantic order (Ben-Ḥayyim 2000, 121–22, §2.2.1.1.5; Tal and Florentin 2010, 28–34; Tov 2012, 80–86; Hornkohl 2021).

The present study examines a selection of verb-centred *ketiv-qere* instances in the Tiberian Pentateuch (based primarily on L, with comparison to A where possible and appropriate).[1] In the following discussions, an attempt is made to explain cases of Masoretic *ketiv-qere* dissonance, to compare the relevant Samaritan written form and oral realisation, and to contextualise all within broader historical linguistic trends.

1.0. *Qere* הַיְצֵא || *ketiv* הוצא (Gen. 8.17)

Throughout the MT, *hifʿil* הוֹצִיא 'bring out, take out' presents the following imperatival forms:

[1] 1 = first person; 2 = second person; 3 = third person; A = Aleppo Codex; BA = Biblical Aramaic; BH = Biblical Hebrew; C = common (gender); CBH = Classical Biblical Hebrew; CGT = Cairo Geniza Targum; DL = dual; F = feminine; FT = Fragment Targums; K = *ketiv*; L = Leningrad Codex (Firkovich B 19 A); M = masculine; MT = Masoretic Textual Tradition; PL = plural; Q = *qere*; QA = Qumran Aramaic; QH = Qumran RH = Rabbinic Hebrew; S = singular; SAT = Samaritan Arabic Translation; SP = Samaritan Pentateuch; ST = Samaritan Targum; t. = Tosefta; TN = Targum Neofiti; TO = Targum Onkelos; tr. = transitive; TY = Targum Yerushalmi (i.e., Targum Pseudo-Jonathan); y. = Talmud Yerushalmi.

MS: הוֹצִיא-/הוֹצֵא (Gen. 8.17 *ketiv*; 19.5, 12; Exod. 3.10; Lev. 24.14; Judg. 6.30; 19.22; 1 Kgs 22.34; 2 Kgs 10.22; Isa. 43.8; Ezek. 24.6; Ps. 25.17; 142.8)

FS: הֽוֹצִיאִי (Josh. 2.3)

MPL: הוֹצִיאֻ-/הוֹצִיאוּ-/הוֹצִיאוּ (Gen. 38.24; 45.1; Exod. 6.26; Josh. 6.22; 10.22; 2 Sam. 13.9; 1 Kgs 21.10; 2 Kgs 11.15; Isa. 48.20; 2 Chron. 23.14; 29.5)

The lone exception is *qere* הַיְצֵא || *ketiv* הוצא in (1).

(1) כָּל־הַחַיָּ֨ה אֲשֶׁר־אִתְּךָ֜ מִכָּל־בָּשָׂ֗ר בָּע֧וֹף וּבַבְּהֵמָ֛ה וּבְכָל־הָרֶ֛מֶשׂ הָרֹמֵ֥שׂ עַל־הָאָ֖רֶץ **הוצא** (K) **הַיְצֵ֣א** (Q) אִתָּ֑ךְ וְשָֽׁרְצ֣וּ בָאָ֔רֶץ וּפָר֥וּ וְרָב֖וּ עַל־הָאָֽרֶץ׃
'Every living thing that is with you of all flesh—birds and animals and every creeping thing that creeps on the earth—**bring out** with you, that they may swarm in the earth, and be fruitful and multiply on the earth.' (Gen. 8.17)

Depending on one's expectations of the *ketiv-qere* phenomenon, this instance may be surprising. It is not uncommon in cases of written-reading dissonance for the *qere* to reflect a usage more conventional than that reflected in the *ketiv*. Here, however, the situation is reversed. *Ketiv* הוצא matches the form that occurs in the 24 other occurrences of this verb's imperative, whereas the *qere* is unique.

A well-known Hebrew feature is the merger of original I-*w* and I-*y* verbs, especially the shift from I-*w* to I-*y* in syllable-initial position, e.g., *qal* יָלַד 'give birth' (cf. Arabic ولد; Blau 2010, 104, §3.4.8.6–9, 245–46, §4.3.8.4.4–8n). The original *w* seems to have fared better in other environments, e.g., as the offglide of a diphthong, but even there it frequently loses consonantal force due to monophthongisation, e.g., *nifʿal* נוֹלַד < **nawlad* 'be born' (Blau

2010, 228, §4.3.5.3.2), *hifʿil* הוֹלִיד < **hawlid* 'beget' (Blau 2010, 235–36, §4.3.5.7.5). The shift I-*y* to I-*w*, restricted chiefly to non-word-initial *y*, is also known, e.g., יָבֵשׁ 'be/become dry' (cf. Arabic يبس), but *hifʿil* הוֹבִישׁ 'dry (tr.)'. Of special relevance in this connection is the case of *ketiv* הושר *qere* הַיְשַׁר 'make level! (MS) (Ps. 5.9). In this *ketiv-qere* instance, it would seem that the orthography reflects a tradition in which an original I-*y* form was realised as if it were I-*w* due to analogical pressure of the majority shift *y* > *w* (as sometimes in Aramaic, in the case of this root; see *CAL*, s.v.). The *qere*, conversely, is in accord with the conventional I-*y* *hifʿil* form as evidenced elsewhere in the combined Tiberian written-reading tradition as well as in other ancient Hebrew sources (including the DSS and Ben Sira).

In the case of the root ו/יצ"א, on the other hand, the Semitic evidence (e.g., Ethiopic *waḍʾa*, Old South Arabic *wḍʾ* or *wẓʾ*) seems to indicate an original I-*w* form, which secondarily shifted to I-*y* in Northwest Semitic (Hebrew, Aramaic, Phoenician, Ugaritic).

As the expected form, the *ketiv* requires no explanation. For the *qere* there are various explanations. It may reflect truly ancient phonological diversity that was generally levelled in favour of the dominant *y* > *w* shift (cf. the related Aramaic *shafʿel* שיצי, which also preserves the *y*). Along these lines, Cohen (2007, 53–54) has suggested that the reading tradition exploited the option of an exceptional I-*y* form in Gen. 8.17 in the interests of aural euphonic repetition, הַיְצֵא 'bring out' (v. 17), וַיֵּצֵא־ 'and (Noah) came out' (v. 18), יָצְאוּ 'came out (MPL)' (v. 19). Alternatively, it is not impossible that the *qere* here stems from a written tradition in which an ambiguous *waw* was misinterpreted as a *yod*. This would suggest that at least some cases of *qere* might stem from the reading of manuscripts, rather constituting a purely oral endeavour.[2]

For its part, the combined written-reading Samaritan tradition at Gen. 8.17 has הוציא *ūṣi*. The long *u*-vowel is standard in Samaritan I-*w hifʿil* verbs (as the open-syllable equivalent of closed-syllable short *o*; Ben-Ḥayyim 2000, 44, §1.2.0), as is the *i*-vowel in the open second syllable of verbs III-ʾ. Given the SP's penchant for levelling and harmonisation, its presentation of a standard imperative here is not unexpected, though in this case it also occasions the rather rare agreement of the Samaritan tradition with the Tiberian *ketiv*.

2.0. *Qere* וַיּוּשַׂם || *ketiv* ויישם (Gen. 24.33)

An acknowledged feature of late antique Hebrew involves shifts of G- to C-stem, i.e., *qal* to *hifʿil*, with no accompanying semantic change. The shift appears to have been especially frequent in, though by no means exclusive to, hollow, i.e., II-*w/y*, verbs, e.g., dcrivations of בי"ן 'understand', זי"ד 'act arrogantly', קי"א 'vomit', רי"ב 'quarrel', לי"ץ 'scoff' (Hornkohl f.c.).

While the Tiberian reading tradition is opaque with regard to the analysis of II-*w/y* prefix conjugation (*yiqṭol*) verbal forms, i.e., whether they are *qal* or *hifʿil* (as opposed to suffix conjugation [*qaṭal*] forms, participles, and infinitives), this is not the case with *hofʿal* forms. Based on regular sound changes, the expected *qal* passive *wayyiqṭol* form of the verb שָׂם 'put' is וַיִּישֶׂם 'and it was

[2] I am grateful to Geoffrey Khan for raising this possibility.

put', on which the Tiberian written and reading traditions agree at Gen. 50.26; see example (2).[3]

(2) וַיָּ֣מָת יוֹסֵ֔ף בֶּן־מֵאָ֥ה וָעֶ֖שֶׂר שָׁנִ֑ים וַיַּחַנְט֣וּ אֹת֔וֹ **וַיִּ֥ישֶׂם** בָּאָר֖וֹן בְּמִצְרָֽיִם׃
'So Joseph died, being 110 years old. They embalmed him, **and he was put** in a coffin in Egypt.' (Gen. 50.26)

This is precisely the orthography one finds in the *ketiv* ויישם (Gen. 24.33), but the corresponding *qere* וַיּוּשַׂם 'and it was put' is *hofʿal* (Cohen 2007, 63–64; Blau 2010, 97, §3.4.3.3; cf. GKC 148, 284; Bergsträsser 1918–1929, I:459); see example (3).

(3) **ויישם** (K) **וַיּוּשַׂ֤ם** (Q) לְפָנָיו֙ לֶֽאֱכֹ֔ל וַיֹּ֙אמֶר֙ לֹ֣א אֹכַ֔ל עַ֥ד אִם־דִּבַּ֖רְתִּי דְּבָרָ֑י וַיֹּ֖אמֶר דַּבֵּֽר׃
'Then food **was set** before him to eat. But he said, "I will not eat until I have said what I have to say." He said, "Speak on."' (Gen. 24.33)

This evidently reflects three related secondary developments: (1) passive formation of II-*w/y* verbs on the analogy of I-*w/y*, (2) the well-known decline of the *qal* internal passive, and, since *hofʿal* represents the internal passive of *hifʿil*, (3) hifilisation, i.e., the broad movement from *qal* to *hifʿil* with no corresponding semantic shift (Blau 2010, 97, §3.4.3.3). In other words, a realisation such as *qere* וַיּוּשַׂם implies the existence of *hifʿil* הֵשִׂים, as seen occasionally in the Tiberian written tradition (Ezek. 14.8; 21.21; Job 4.20) and more commonly in late antique extra-biblical Hebrew (SirA 4v.22 = Sir. 11.30; t. Giṭṭin 7.13; Sifre Devarim 315; y. Sanhedrin 1.1; frequently in the Babylonian Talmud).

---

[3] According to Blau (2010, 97, §3.4.3.3), the expected resolution of the diphthong *uy* is contraction to *ī*, thus *wayyī́śɛm* < **wayyúyśɛm*.

The Samaritan form that corresponds to Tiberian *ketiv* ויישם *qere* וַיּוּשַׂם (Gen. 24.33), as well as to Tiberian וַיִּישֶׂם (Gen. 50.26), is ויושם *wyuwwāšåm*. The written form might conceivably reflect the same *qal* internal passive > *hofʿal* shift as seen above in the Tiberian *ketiv-qere*. Indeed, Ben-Ḥayyim (1977, 271) formally classifies the form as *hifʿil* passive. Crucially, however, the form realised in the Samaritan pronunciation tradition does not reflect the *hofʿal* stem, i.e., the internal passive of *hifʿil*, but an external passive, in this case most probably Gt, with assimilation of the infix -*t*-, in the following manner: *yuwwaśem* < *yiwwaśem* < *yitwaśem* (alternatively, Dt, with assimilation of the infix -*t*- and simplification of middle-radical gemination; Ben-Ḥayyim 2000, 178, §2.10.4). And, of course, this may well underlie the Samaritan written form, as well. Thus, like the Tiberian reading tradition in the *ketiv-qere* in Gen. 24.33, the Samaritan reading tradition replaces the archaic *qal* internal passive with a secondary and more contemporary alternative. While the Tiberian *qere* tallies with rather common *hofʿal* use throughout the combined Tiberian written-reading tradition, the Samaritan recourse to Gt forms, especially with assimilated -*t*- (or to Dt forms with assimilated -*t*-) smacks of late Aramaic linguistic practices uncharacteristic of the early Hebrew linguistic sources.

3.0. *Qere* וְיִֽשְׁתַּחֲוּוּ || *ketiv* וישתחו (Gen. 27.29; 43.28)

Twice in the MT, *ketiv-qere* discord focuses on *yiqṭol* forms of the verb הִשְׁתַּחֲוָה 'bow down'; see examples (4) and (5).

(4) יַֽעַבְד֣וּךָ עַמִּ֗ים וישתחו (K) וְיִֽשְׁתַּחֲו֤וּ (Q) לְךָ֙ לְאֻמִּ֔ים הֱוֵ֤ה גְבִיר֙ לְאַחֶ֔יךָ
וְיִשְׁתַּחֲו֥וּ לְךָ֖ בְּנֵ֣י אִמֶּ֑ךָ אֹרְרֶ֣יךָ אָר֔וּר וּֽמְבָרְכֶ֖יךָ בָּרֽוּךְ׃
'Let peoples serve you, and nations **bow down** to you. Be lord over your brothers, and may your mother's sons bow down to you. Cursed be everyone who curses you, and blessed be everyone who blesses you!' (Gen. 27.29)

(5) וַיֹּאמְר֗וּ שָׁל֛וֹם לְעַבְדְּךָ֥ לְאָבִ֖ינוּ עוֹדֶ֣נּוּ חָ֑י וַֽיִּקְּד֖וּ וישתחו (K) וַיִּֽשְׁתַּחֲוּֽוּ׃ (Q)
'They said, "Your servant our father is well; he is still alive." And they bowed their heads **and prostrated themselves**.' (Gen. 43.28)

In Tiberian Hebrew, the 3MS prefix conjugation form of this verb is unique, in that it ends with *-ū*, יִשְׁתַּחוּ 'he bowed down', cf. MPL יִשְׁתַּחֲוּוּ 'they bowed down'.[4] Since the *ketiv* form resembles the relevant 3MS *yiqṭol* form, it may at first glance be tempting to argue that the *ketiv* simply construes as singular what the *qere* construes as plural. Given the context in both cases, however, this seems unlikely. Both passages include other clear instances of 3MPL *yiqṭol* forms in proximity, including, in example (4), explicitly 3MPL וְיִשְׁתַּחֲוּוּ later in the verse.

If the solution is not morphosemantic, perhaps it is phonological. 3MS יִשְׁתַּחוּ *yištaḥū* and the reconstructed precursor of 3MPL יִשְׁתַּחֲווּ *yištaḥăwū* < **yištaḥwū* are distinguished by only the

---

[4] The unique form would appear to be a natural consequence of the syllable structure of short a prefix conjugation (*yiqṭol*) *hishtafʿel* form from root חו"י/חו"ו, *yištaḥū* < *yištaḥu* < *yištaḥw*, in which the vowelless radical *w* of the word-final consonant cluster *ḥw* could be preserved only as a long *u*-vowel (for analysis as a derivation of שח"ו see Blau 2010, 237, §4.3.6.1).

onglide in the diphthong *-wū*. In the absence of an epenthetic *ḥaṭef* vowel to resolve the *-ḥw-* consonant cluster, the *w* would have been extremely vulnerable to syncope and, presumably, graphic non-representation.

Another possibility, raised by Cohen (2007, 18), is that in these cases, as well as those of *ketiv* ויצו || *qere* וַיְצַוּ֯וּ ‘and they commanded’ (Jdg. 21.20), *ketiv* ויאמר || *qere* וַיֹּאמְר֯וּ ‘and they said’ (1 Sam. 12.10), and *ketiv* וידבר || *qere* וַיְדַבְּר֯וּ ‘and they spoke’ (1 Kgs 12.7), the *ketiv* represents rare defective spelling of the word-final plural morpheme.

And, of course, in all of the above cases there is the possibility of simple textual corruption, i.e., the accidental graphic omission of the expected *waw*.

Whatever the most compelling explanation for the relevant Tiberian *ketiv-qere*, the SP shows no trace of dissonance. Both the written component of the tradition and its reading counterpart reflect standard 3MPL forms: וישתחוו *wyištā̄bbu*. The spelling reveals no disharmony between these plural forms and others in the vicinity nor between these plural forms and other plural forms of this verb.

The Samaritan pronunciation deserves special comment. Evidence indicates that the early realisation of Samaritan *waw*, namely *w*, shifted to *v* in the Second Temple period and that later, due to coalescence of *v* < *w* and *v* < *b*, most cases of *v (< w)* were included in the general *b* < *v* shift due to Arabic. The doubled middle radical may, as in Tiberian Hebrew, reflect pattern gemination, but it is also possible that it derives from regular assimilation of the guttural *ḥ*, i.e., *-bb-* < *-ww-* < *-ʾw-* < *-ḥw-*. Samaritan Hebrew also more conspicuously distinguishes between singular ישתחוי *yištā̊bbi* and plural ישתחוו *yištā̊bbu*, the singular realised as a standard, rather than short, III-*y* prefix conjugation (*yiqṭol*) form. It should be noted that all of the above developments in the Samaritan tradition are secondary features that reflect phenomena that typologically post-date the form of the Tiberian *qere*.

4.0. *Qere* בָּ֣א גָ֑ד || *ketiv* בגד (Gen. 30.11)

(6) וַתֹּ֥אמֶר לֵאָ֖ה בגד (K) בָּ֣א גָ֑ד (Q) וַתִּקְרָ֥א אֶת־שְׁמ֖וֹ גָּֽד׃
'And Leah said, **"Good fortune has come!"** so she called his name Gad.' (Gen. 30.11)

Though it has been suggested that the Tiberian *ketiv* and *qere* in (6) are mere phonological variants reflecting a single common exegetical tradition (Cohen 2007, 42–43), the testimony of ancient witnesses arguably indicates otherwise, i.e., that they reflect diverging interpretations. *Ketiv* בגד is taken as an adverbial in the sense of 'with good fortune'; cf. LXX Ἐν τύχῃ 'with luck'; Vulgate *feliciter* 'happily'. *Qere* בָּ֣א גָ֑ד,[5] on the other hand, is a verb-subject verbal clause; cf. Peshiṭta ܐܬܐ ܓܕܐ 'fortune has come'; TO אתא גד 'fortune has come'; TY אתא מזלא טבא 'good luck has come'; TN/FT/CGT אתא גדה טבא 'good fortune has come'. The *ketiv* and *qere* variants are of approximately equal plausibility and

---

[5] In L, the marginal *qere* notation is especially detailed, including not just the conventional information of consonants and word separation (with בא and גד on separate lines), but also vocalisation (minus the *dagesh* in the *bet* of בא and the *rafe* over the *gimel* of גד) and accentuation.

each enjoys support, both ancient and medieval (on the latter, see Habib 2020, 318).[6]

The combined Samaritan written-reading tradition has בגד *afgåd*, which the ST renders בסור 'tidings, news', apparently in line with the Tiberian *qere*. Cf. the SAT, which renders جاء عسكر 'an army has come', which rather corresponds to the Tiberian *ketiv*. Despite the diachronic proximity of the Tiberian *qere* (and reading tradition, more generally) and the Samaritan reading tradition, the latter sometimes agrees with the Tiberian *ketiv*. This appears to be such a case.

5.0. *Qere* וַיִּלֹּ֫ונוּ || *ketiv* וילינו (Exod. 16.2); *qere* וַיַּלִּ֫ינוּ/תַלִּ֫ינוּ || *ketiv* וילונו/תלונו (Exod. 16.7; Num. 14.36; 16.11)

In Tiberian Hebrew, the root לי"ן/לו"ן II 'grumble, complain' is represented by largely synonymous *nifʿal* and *hifʿil* forms. Beyond the written-reading deviation at issue here (which is not necessarily limited to the acknowledged instances of *ketiv-qere*), several additional factors combine to complicate the Tiberian paradigm of לי"ן/לו"ן II: (a) potential conflation of II-*w* and II-*y* forms (at both linguistic and textual levels); (b) partial homophony with forms of לי"ן/לו"ן I 'lodge, spend the night' (against which problem, secondary morphological gemination developed in some forms of לי"ן/לו"ן II; (c) the morphosemantic challenge of the formal distinction between intransitive, transitive, and causative

[6] In L, a note in the bottom margin of the page including (6) (fol. 17v) lists cases of single-word *ketiv* versus two-word *qere* and vice versa.

senses; (d) broad morphosemantic movement away from *qal* in favour of morphology perceived to have greater semantic iconicity.

As reflected in the Tiberian reading tradition, the fourteen occurrences of לי"ן/לו"ן II 'grumble, complain' seem to comprise a suppletive paradigm with notable outliers. See Table 1.

Table 1: Tiberian forms of לי"ן/לו"ן II by TAM form and stem (*binyan*)

TAM form	Case (reference)	Stem (*binyan*)
qaṭal forms and participles	תְּלֻנֹּתֵיכֶם אֲשֶׁר־אַתֶּם מַלִּינִם עָלָיו (Exod. 16.8)	*hifʿil*
	מַלִּינִים (Num. 14.27a)	
	תְּלֻנּוֹת בְּנֵי יִשְׂרָאֵל אֲשֶׁר הֵמָּה מַלִּינִים עָלַי (Num. 14.27b)	
	הֲלִינֹתֶם (Num. 14.29)	
	תְּלֻנּוֹת בְּנֵי יִשְׂרָאֵל אֲשֶׁר הֵם מַלִּינִם עֲלֵיכֶם (Num. 17.20)	
(way)yiqṭol forms	תַלִּינוּ (Exod. 16.7 *qere*; *ketiv* תלונו)	
	וַיָּלֶן (Exod. 17.3)	
	וַיַּלִּינוּ (Num. 14.36 *qere*; *ketiv* וילונו)	
	תַלִּינוּ (Num. 16.11 *qere*; *ketiv* תלונו)	
	וַיִּלֹּנוּ (Exod. 15.24)	*nifʿal*
	וַיִּלּוֹנוּ (Exod. 16.2 *qere*; *ketiv* וילינו)	
	וַיִּלֹּנוּ (Num. 14.2)	
	וַיִּלֹּנוּ (Num. 17.6)	
	וַיִּלֹּנוּ (Josh. 9.18)	

The lone suffix conjugation form (Num. 14.29) and all participles (Exod. 16.8; Num. 14.27a, 27b; 17.20) are consonantally unambiguous *hifʿil* forms. It may, however, be significant that three of these forms—and no others—are explicitly transitive, taking as direct object a form of תְּלֻנָּה 'complaint' (Exod. 16.8; Num. 14.27b; 17.20), while the remaining two forms (Num. 14.27a, 29) occur in the same context. The lone causative prefix conjugation form (Num. 14.36) is also *hifʿil* (and, critically, one of the cases of *ketiv-qere* discord). Of the eight remaining prefix conjugation forms, three are *hifʿil* (Exod. 16.7 *qere*; 17.3; Num. 16.11 *qere*; two involve *ketiv-qere* dissonance), and five are *nifʿal* (Exod. 15.24; 16.2 *qere*; Num. 14.2; 17.6; Josh. 9.18; one involves *ketiv-qere* dissonance). It may be significant that all *yiqtol* forms in the reading tradition are *hifʿil*, whereas, with two notable exceptions, *wayyiqtol* forms are *nifʿal*: the exceptions are וַיָּ֫לֶן (Exod. 17.3) and the causative *qere* וַיַּלִּ֫ינוּ (Num. 14.36) (on both of which see below). For another perspective consider Table 2.

Table 2: Tiberian forms of ל"י/לו"ן II in canonical order

Reference	Form in context	Stem	Semantics	Source
Exod. 15.24	וַיִּלֹּ֧נוּ הָעָ֛ם עַל־מֹשֶׁ֖ה	N	intr.	J
Exod. 16.2Q	וַיִּלֹּ֜ונוּ כָּל־עֲדַ֧ת בְּנֵי־יִשְׂרָאֵ֛ל עַל־מֹשֶׁ֥ה וְעַֽל־אַהֲרֹ֖ן	N	intr.	P
2K	וילינו כָּל־עֲדַת בְּנֵי־יִשְׂרָאֵל עַל־מֹשֶׁה וְעַל־אַהֲרֹן	H	?	
7Q	כִּ֥י תַלִּ֖ינוּ עָלֵֽינוּ	H	tr.?	P
7K	כִּי תלונו עָלֵינוּ	N	?	
8	תְּלֻנֹּתֵיכֶ֔ם אֲשֶׁר־אַתֶּ֥ם מַלִּינִ֖ם עָלָֽיו	H	tr.	P
Exod. 17.3	וַיָּ֤לֶן הָעָם֙ עַל־מֹשֶׁ֔ה	H	?	E
Num. 14.2	וַיִּלֹּ֨נוּ֙ עַל־מֹשֶׁ֣ה וְעַֽל־אַהֲרֹ֔ן כֹּ֖ל בְּנֵ֥י יִשְׂרָאֵֽל	N	intr.	P
27a	הֵ֛מָּה מַלִּינִ֥ים עָלָֽי	H	tr.?	P
27b	תְּלֻנּ֞וֹת בְּנֵ֣י יִשְׂרָאֵ֗ל אֲשֶׁ֨ר הֵ֧מָּה מַלִּינִ֛ם עָלַ֖י	H	tr.	P
29	אֲשֶׁ֥ר הֲלִֽינֹתֶ֖ם עָלָֽי	H	tr.?	P
36Q	וַיַּלִּ֤ינוּ עָלָיו֙ אֶת־כָּל־הָ֣עֵדָ֔ה	H	caus.	P
36K	וילונו עָלָיו אֶת־כָּל־הָעֵדָה	N	intr.	
Num. 16.11Q	כִּ֥י תַלִּ֖ינוּ עָלָֽיו	H	?	P
11K	כִּי תלונו עָלָיו	N	?	
Num. 17.6	וַיִּלֹּ֜נוּ כָּל־עֲדַ֤ת בְּנֵֽי־יִשְׂרָאֵל֙... עַל־מֹשֶׁ֥ה וְעַֽל־	N	intr.	P
20	תְּלֻנּ֞וֹת בְּנֵ֣י יִשְׂרָאֵ֗ל אֲשֶׁ֨ר הֵ֛ם מַלִּינִ֖ם עֲלֵיכֶֽם	H	tr.	P
Josh. 9.18	וַיִּלֹּ֥נוּ כָל־הָעֵדָ֖ה עַל־הַנְּשִׂיאִֽים	N	intr.	

It is difficult to conceive of an exhaustively satisfying account of the particular constellation of forms as reflected in either the orthographic or the recitation tradition, including the four acknowledge *ketiv-qere* cases, since a comprehensive morphosemantic rationale for the use of *hifʿil* versus *nifʿal* (*way*)*yiqtol* forms is elusive. Neither does recourse to putative Pentateuchal source provide clarification. It is, of course, possible that graphic confusion between *waw* and *yod* is relevant in some cases. It may also be that the *hifʿil* and *nifʿal* forms are, at least to some extent, synonymous and grammatically interchangeable—though distributional differences—especially the exclusive use of *hifʿil* for unequivocally transitive cases—militate against this. Another factor worthy of consideration is contextual proximity. Note that in three pericopes with multiple forms, i.e., Exod. 16, Num. 14, and Num. 17, the initial grumbling is indicated via an apparently intransitive *nifʿal*, whereas the use of *hifʿil* forms ensues only in the immediate vicinity of another explicitly transitive *hifʿil* (Exod. 16.8; Num. 14.27b; Num. 17.20). It seems reasonable to postulate that these forms were realised as *hifʿil*, whether due to attraction or to analysis as genuine, if elliptical, transitives (noted by 'tr.?' in Table 2). *Wayyiqṭol* forms are generally *nifʿal*, unless causative—though וַיָּלֶן (Exod. 17.3) remains an outlier.[7]

Moving to the specific cases of *ketiv-qere* dissonance, graphic and/or linguistic conflation of II-*w* and II-*y* may be applicable in any or all cases (Cohen 2007, 72–73).[8] Without definitively ruling out these possibilities, the following discussions will consider alternative hypotheses.

---

[7] Though pure conjecture, it is possible that the apparently *hifʿil* וַיָּלֶן is in reality an old intransitive *qal* II-*y* form. While other intransitives were realised as *nifʿal*, this case may have retained its realisation due to similarity with *hifʿil* forms.

[8] Textually, the graphic similarity—or, in some cases, identity—between *waw* and *yod* requires no elaboration. On the linguistic level, consider the

Perhaps the most straightforward case involves the causative in (7).

(7) וְהָאֲנָשִׁ֔ים אֲשֶׁר־שָׁלַ֥ח מֹשֶׁ֖ה לָת֣וּר אֶת־הָאָ֑רֶץ וַיָּשֻׁ֗בוּ וילונו (K) וַיַּלִּ֤ינוּ (Q) עָלָיו֙ אֶת־כָּל־הָ֣עֵדָ֔ה...

'And the men whom Moses sent to spy out the land—they returned, **and they made** all the congregation **grumble** against him...' (Num. 14.36)

Here the *hifʿil* form seems especially fitting for the double-transitive causative semantics. The *ketiv* may reflect local exegesis different from that represented by the *qere*, according to which the words וילונו עָלָיו֙ אֶת־כָּל־הָ֣עֵדָ֔ה were understood to mean not what the returning spies did *to* the people, but what they did *with* the people: 'and they grumbled with the congregation' (rather than 'and they made the congregation grumble').[9]

Turning to example (8):

(8) וילינו (K) וַיִּלּ֜וֹנוּ (Q) כָּל־עֲדַ֧ת בְּנֵֽי־יִשְׂרָאֵ֛ל עַל־מֹשֶׁ֥ה וְעַֽל־אַהֲרֹ֖ן בַּמִּדְבָּֽר׃

'**And** the whole congregation of the people of Israel **grumbled** against Moses and Aaron...' (Exod. 16.2)

If not a simple corruption or synonymous linguistic variant, the *hifʿil ketiv* morphology in example (8) is consistent with the nearby *hifʿil* participle at Exod. 16.7—though, admittedly, at odds with the *nifʿal ketiv* morphology in the neighbouring verse

regular pairing of *qal yiqṭol* יָשִׂים and infinitival (לָ)שׂוּם 'put' and of *qal yiqṭol* יָלִין and infinitival לָלוּן 'lodge'. Further examples could be adduced.

[9] Cf. LXX διεγόγγυσαν κατ' αὐτῆς πρὸς τὴν συναγωγὴν '(they) murmured against it [i.e., the land] to the assembly', in which, to be sure, the sense is neither causative nor comitative.

in example (9), below. The *nifʿal qere* is consistent both with other *nifʿal* intransitive forms—contrasting with transitive or causative *hifʿil* morphology—and with the *nifʿal* majority of *way-yiqṭol* forms.

Examples (9) and (10) reflect the same *ketiv-qere* dissonance in very similar usages.

(9) ...וְנַ֣חְנוּ מָ֔ה כִּ֥י **תלונו** (K) **תַלִּ֖ינוּ** (Q) עָלֵֽינוּ׃

‘...For what are we, that **you grumble** against us?’ (Exod. 16.7)[10]

(10) ...וְאַהֲרֹ֣ן מַה־ה֔וּא כִּ֥י **תלונו** (K) **תַלִּ֖ינוּ** (Q) עָלָֽיו׃

‘...And Aaron, what is he that **you grumble** against him?’ (Num. 16.11)

Due to the verbal similarity, i.e., near parallel structures comprising כִּי + תלו/ינו + עַל, it is no surprise that the *yiqṭol* forms have matching stems within the Tiberian reading and written traditions, respectively. There seems to be logic to both alternatives. The *hifʿil qere* in (9) is consistent with the explicitly transitive *hifʿil* participle in the following verse. Conceivably, the *hifʿil qere* in (10) was also deemed transitive, or was simply read as *hifʿil*,

---

10 In L, the *ketiv-qere* instance at Exod. 16.7 is signalled by means of a *circellus* above the *ketiv*, which is vocalised and accented according to the reading תַלִּ֖ינוּ, as well as by an intercolumnal notation reading קרי ׳. Upon close inspection, however, L’s *ketiv* does not unambiguously read תלונו. The ostensible first *waw* is noticeably shorter than the second and is more similar in shape to the *yod* in the next word, עָלֵֽינוּ. Cf. the *waws* and *yods* in the surrounding context. It is possible that the *qere* orthography has actually found its way into the written tradition here, though it has been furnished with a *ketiv-qere* note consistent with the *masora*.

on the basis of its similarity to (9). At any rate, according to the *qere*, all forms except *wayyiqṭol* are *hifʿil*. As for the *ketiv*—it is conceivable that the influence worked in the opposite direction, i.e., the *yiqṭol* form in example (10) was deemed an intransitive *nifʿal* and verbal similarity determined the *nifʿal* realisation of the near parallel instance in (9), all of which resulted in consistently *nifʿal yiqṭol* forms in the orthographical tradition, contrasting with *hifʿil-nifʿal* diversity in the case of *wayyiqṭol* forms.

Having attempted to clarify the complex situation in the Tiberian tradition, we may turn to the rather simpler situation in the SP. Here, as in Tiberian Hebrew, *qaṭal* and participial forms are *hifʿil*, e.g., הלנתם *allentimma* and מלנים *mallēnəm*, respectively. Unlike in the MT, however, all prefix conjugation forms—whether *yiqṭol* or *wayyiqṭol*, and no matter their semantics—are *qal*, e.g., וילן *wyillån*, וילנו *wyillā̊nu*, תלנו *tillā̊nu*. Whether *qal* or *hifʿil*, forms consistently reflect geminate analysis (i.e., לנ"ן), which in Samaritan Hebrew routinely involves gemination of the first radical, on the I-*n* pattern (see Ben-Ḥayyim 1977, 154; 2000, 156, §2.7.6). While the Samaritan derivation and stem arrangement show no morphological distinction between intransitive and causative semantics,[11] thanks to the geminate derivation, there is no chance of homophony with forms of לי"ן/לו"ן I 'lodge, spend the night', which—whether *qal* or *hifʿil*—in Samaritan Hebrew has the form of a *hifʿil* with gemination of the first radical וילן *wyallən*, וילינו *wyallīnu*, תלין *tallən* (Ben-Ḥayyim 2000, 152, §2.6.13).

---

[11] Against the SP's equivalence of intransitive and causative forms, the ST's syntax in ורנו עליו ית כל כנשתה reveals a causative reading of the verb.

Two further points seem relevant. First, it is noteworthy that both the Tiberian and Samaritan recitation traditions exhibit what must be considered secondary gemination in the case of forms of לי"ן/לו"ן II ‘grumble, complain’. Though the explanations for gemination in each tradition differ—lexeme-specific semantic disambiguation in Tiberian (Yeivin 1980, 362; Khan 2020, I:524) and broader paradigmatic pattern suppletion in Samaritan—the mere fact of the shared trait arguably points to its early, pre-schism development.

Second, there is the matter of stem morphology in both traditions. Given the dissonance and uncertainties discussed above, the antiquity of the *hifʿil-nifʿal* Tiberian arrangement may be questioned. The Samaritan *hifʿil-qal* arrangement adds to the uncertainty. Is it possible that the Tiberian *nifʿal* goes back to an earlier *qal*, which was preserved in the Samaritan tradition? The secondary nifalisation of original *qal* verbs with intransitive and middle semantics is a feature of the evolution of ancient Hebrew as seen in the extant sources, especially relevant to Second Temple chronolects, e.g., the Tiberian LBH orthographical tradition, the Tiberian biblical recitation tradition more broadly, and the Samaritan biblical tradition (Hornkohl 2021). Regarding the latter, it should be borne in mind that, (a) Samaritan לי"ן/לו"ן II ‘grumble, complain’ is analysed as a geminate verb; (b) Samaritan geminate verbs are routinely realised as I-*n* forms with assimilated *nun*; (c) Samaritan I-*n* forms with assimilated *nun* (and similarly realised geminate forms) are ineligible for *nifʿal* analysis;[12]

[12] The same is true of Tiberian Hebrew; cf. יִנָּקֵם (Exod. 21.20) versus the preservation of *qal* internal passive יֻקַּם (Exod. 21.21), both ‘he must be

and (d) the Samaritan *qal* vowel pattern is that of the dominant *yiqtål* template rather than that expected of II-*w*/*y* forms. Thus, a speculative, though not implausible hypothesis is that an original *qal* underwent nifalisation in Tiberian Hebrew but was preserved, albeit with secondary gemination and vocalism, in Samaritan Hebrew (see Hornkohl 2021, 9–10).

6.0. *Qere* קְרוּאֵי || *ketiv* קריאי (Num. 1.16); *qere* קְרִיאֵי || *ketiv* קרואי (Num. 26.9)

The cases of *ketiv-qere* dissonance in (11) and (12) are mirror images.[13]

(11) אֵלֶּה קריאי (K) קְרוּאֵי (Q) הָעֵדָה נְשִׂיאֵי מַטּוֹת אֲבוֹתָם רָאשֵׁי אַלְפֵי יִשְׂרָאֵל הֵם׃

‘These were the **ones chosen from** the congregation, the chiefs of their ancestral tribes, the heads of the clans of Israel.’ (Num. 1.16)

(12) וּבְנֵי אֱלִיאָב נְמוּאֵל וְדָתָן וַאֲבִירָם הוּא־דָתָן וַאֲבִירָם קרואי (K) קְרִיאֵי (Q) הָעֵדָה אֲשֶׁר הִצּוּ עַל־מֹשֶׁה וְעַל־אַהֲרֹן בַּעֲדַת־קֹרַח בְּהַצֹּתָם עַל־יְהוָה׃

‘The sons of Eliab: Nemuel, Dathan, and Abiram. These are the Dathan and Abiram, **chosen from** the congregation, who contended against Moses and Aaron in the company of Korah, when they contended against the LORD’ (Num. 26.9)

---

avenged’. Ineligible for *nifʿal* analysis and realisation, the latter retained its *qal* passive vocalism, though it may also have been identified as *hofʿal*.

[13] In L, a masoretic note at the bottom of the page that includes (11) (fol. 74r) lists *ketiv-qere* instances involving interchanges of *waw* and *yod*.

Both involve substantives related to the verb קָרָא 'call, read', in the *qå̄ṭīl* and *qå̄ṭūl* nominal patterns. The former is common, but not systematically productive in ancient Hebrew "for stative or passive actant nouns, mostly adjectives, but also with secondary substantive meaning, especially for the passive ones" (Fox 2003, 192; Huehnergard 2007). For its part, *qå̄ṭūl* in ancient Hebrew "is a completely productive patiens participle, serving for the object of transitive verbs" (Fox 2003, 201). While no historical phase of Hebrew lacks *qå̄ṭīl* or related *qəṭīl* forms, specific lexemes are limited to, or especially characteristic of, late Hebrew chronolects. This is possibly due in part to contact with Aramaic, in which the related *qəṭīl* template is fully productive as the G-stem passive participle (Fox 2003, 195). Examples include: נָתִין 'temple servant' (LBH; QH; RH; Samaritan Hebrew), שָׁלִיחַ 'messenger' (RH; cf. BA; QA; TA), חֲסִין 'strong' (1x in BH; various Aramaic dialects), and פָּקִיד 'official' (CBH [rare]; LBH; QH; Samaritan Hebrew; cf. Egyptian Aramaic).

In (11) and (12) above, the two terms have the general sense of 'leaders'. Some have sought a semantic distinction between קְרוּאֵי הָעֵדָה and קְרִיאֵי הָעֵדָה, but Cohen (2007, 197–98) adduces arguments and references against such an approach. Significantly, the *ketiv* in one place confirms the validity of the *qere* in the other and vice versa. Additionally, each form is also found in a similar context elsewhere in biblical literature, where the written and reading components of the tradition apparently coincide: cf. נְשִׂיאֵ֥י עֵדָ֛ה קְרִאֵ֥י מוֹעֵ֖ד 'chiefs of the congregation, chosen from the assembly' (Num. 16.2) and בַּחוּרֵ֤י חֶ֙מֶד֙ פַּח֣וֹת וּסְגָנִ֣ים כֻּלָּ֔ם שָׁלִשִׁ֣ים וּקְרוּאִ֔ים 'desirable young men, governors and commanders all of them, officers and men of renown' (Ezek. 23.23). Each of the components of the combined Tiberian tradition seems to bear witness to a situation of genuine lexical diversity, differing only with respect to the proper context for the respective forms.[14]

In the SP, the forms in examples (11) and (12) are both written and read קריאי *qaryā'i* (< **qaryāy* < **qariyyāy* < **qārī'āy*, from the *qatīl* template + Aramaic gentilic *-āy*; Ben-Ḥayyim 2000, 284, §4.3.8). This is consistent with the form in SP Num. 16.2, where the MT has קְרִאֵ֣י. That the Samaritan tradition should unify forms, and do so in favour of what constitutes the majority form (in Samaritan as well as Tiberian), is not surprising. But there may be more to the story, with the choice of forms being part of a broader preference for late forms characteristic of Aramaic and RH. Ben-Ḥayyim (2000, 199–200, §§2.13.2–4) lists *qā̊ṭol*, *qēṭəl*, and *qā̊ṭəl* as templates for the Samaritan *qal* passive participle, all of which bear marks of post-classical development. The shift from PS *qatūl* to *qā̊ṭol* can be explained in line with regular Samaritan vowel changes, but based on *qā̊ṭol*'s use for the *qal* active participle, one may infer the influence of the *qā̊ṭol nomen agentis* pattern so common in late Aramaic, especially Syriac, and RH (Hornkohl 2013, 148–52). For their part, the Samaritan *qēṭəl* and *qā̊ṭəl* templates may both have developed from PS *qatīl*,

[14] Consider the interchange between the approximately synonymous English *venerable* and *venerated* in "The specimens of the venerated Bede, as given by Colonel Dow before his *History of Hindustan*, exhibit rhyme" (Morgangw 1858, 354) and the more customary appellation, reflecting Catholic soteriology, "the Venerable Bede."

but alternatively reflect Aramaic *qəṭīl* and Hebrew *qå̄ṭīl*, respectively.[15]

7.0. *Qere* וַיּוֹרֶשׁ || *ketiv* ויירש (Num. 21.32)

In Tiberian BH there is a general distinction between *qal* יָרַשׁ and *hifʿil* הוֹרִישׁ, in that the *qal* typically takes an inanimate object and means 'inherit, take possession of', whereas the *hifʿil* tends to take an animate object and to denote the sense of 'dispossess, disinherit, drive out; cause to inherit'. Not infrequently, however, there is semantic and grammatical reversal (see the standard lexicons).

---

[15] Whatever the case, the incidence in the SP of *qå̄ṭəl* and *qēṭəl* for the G-stem passive participle is comparatively greater than in the Tiberian Torah, including: בעילת *bīlåt* 'married (to a husband)' || MT בְּעֻלַת (Gen. 20.3; Deut. 22.22), חגרים *ēgīrəm* 'girded' || MT חֲגֻרִים (Exod. 12.11), וחמישים *wēmīšəm* 'and equipped' || MT וַחֲמֻשִׁים (Exod. 13.18), משחים *må̄'šīm* 'smeared (with oil), anointed' || MT מְשֻׁחִים (Lev. 2.4; 7.12; Num. 3.3; 6.15; 7.10), נגף *nēgəf* 'struck (by plague), defeated' || MT נֶגֶף 'plague' (Num. 8.19; Deut. 28.7, 25), הנשך *annūšək* 'who is bitten' || MT הַנָּשׁוּךְ (Num. 21.8; on the *u*-vowel in Samaritan Hebrew, see Ben-Ḥayyim 2000, 200, §2.3.14 Note), נתנים *nētīnəm* 'given, dedicated' || MT נְתֻנִים (Num. 8.16, 16, 19; 18.6; Deut. 28.31, 32), הפקדים *affēqīdəm* 'those put in charge, the officers' || MT פְּקוּדֵי (Num. 31.14, 48), השבי *aššēbi* 'that was captured' || MT הַשְּׁבִי 'the captivity' (Num. 31.26), ושדיפת *wšådīfot* 'blighted (by the east wind)' || MT וּשְׁדוּפֹת (Gen. 41.6, 23, 27). This comparatively high *qəṭīl*/*qå̄ṭīl* incidence may well be due to the influence of Samaritan Aramaic and of contemporaneous Hebrew dialects, e.g., RH, in which *qəṭīl* and *qå̄ṭīl* served as passives with more regularity than in Tiberian BH. The SP appearance of *qēṭəl* passive forms of פקד and נתן is certainly a striking point of commonality with post-exilic Hebrew.

With this morphosemantic background in mind, it is possible to turn to the instance of *ketiv-qere* in (13).

(13) וַיִּשְׁלַח מֹשֶׁה לְרַגֵּל אֶת־יַעְזֵר וַֽיִּלְכְּדוּ בְּנֹתֶיהָ ויירש (K) וַיּוֹרֶשׁ (Q) אֶת־הָאֱמֹרִי אֲשֶׁר־שָֽׁם׃

'And Moses sent to spy out Jazer, and they captured its villages, **so he dispossessed** the Amorites who were there.' (Num. 21.32)

There are opposing tendencies at work in the broader context of this passage. On the one hand, excluding the verse under discussion, throughout the book of Numbers, the seven cases of *qal* יָרַשׁ (Num. 13.30; 21.24, 35; 27.11; 33.53; 36.8, 8) and the seven cases of *hifʿil* הוֹרִישׁ (Num. 14.12, 24; 32.21, 39; 33.52, 53, 55) occur with their expected semantic and grammatical characteristics, as described above, with the exception of the *hifʿil* form at Num. 14.24. These include the nearly parallel usage to Num. 14.24 in the *hifʿil* with animate object וַיּ֫וֹרֶשׁ אֶת־הָאֱמֹרִי אֲשֶׁר־בָּהּ 'and he dispossessed the Amorite who dwelt therein' (Num. 32.29).

On the other hand, in the immediate context of the *ketiv-qere* dissonance of Num. 21.32—where, with an animate object, one expects a *hifʿil*—come two cases of *qal* יָרַשׁ with inanimate objects: וַיִּירַשׁ אֶת־אַרְצוֹ 'and (Israel) took possession of his land' (Num. 21.24) and וַיִּֽירְשׁוּ אֶת־אַרְצוֹ 'and they took possession of his land' (Num. 21.35). It would seem that the Tiberian *ketiv* reflects a tradition in which the form of יר"ש at Num. 21.32 was read as *qal* in harmony with verbs in close proximity—resulting in a less standard, but acceptable use of the *qal* with an animate object—whereas the *qere* preserves a tradition more strictly observant of the standard semantic and grammatical distinction between *qal* יָרַשׁ and *hifʿil* הוֹרִישׁ.

Turning to the Samaritan tradition, one finds nearly the same distribution of forms as in the Tiberian Torah, the chief difference being a greater number of *qal* forms due mainly to Samaritan textual pluses. Additionally, there are two individual cases of what might be considered typical Samaritan harmonisation. First, the lone Tiberian *piʿʿel* form in 'All your trees and the fruit of your land the הַצְּלָצַל ('locust, cricket'?) will possess (יְיָרֵשׁ)' (Deut. 28.42) is paralleled in the SP by *hifʿil* יורש *jūrəš*. The ostensible *hifʿil* replacement of *piʿʿel* is certainly in line with the SP's penchant for levelling irregular forms, though *hifʿil* is unexpected in the case of an inanimate object (though, to be sure, the non-human subject is also exceptional).16 Second, the irregular Tiberian *hifʿil* with inanimate object suffix יוֹרִשֶׁנָּה '(his seed) will inherit it (i.e., the land)' (Num. 14.24) finds as its Samaritan parallel the more predictable *qal* with inanimate object suffix יירשנה *yīrå̄šinnå*.

With the broader Samaritan picture and these individual examples in mind, it is no surprise that in the case of the Tiberian *ketiv-qere* at Num. 21.32, the SP agrees with the tradition preserved in the Tiberian *qere* וַיּוֹרֶשׁ, albeit with slight adjustment for

16 Ben-Ḥayyim (1977, 130) analyses the form as a *hifʿil* prefix conjugation, but it is equally analysable as a *qal* active participle, which would preserve more conventional semantics and grammar. Incidentally, the Tiberian *piʿʿel* may also be queried. As a *hapax*, one wonders if *piʿʿel* יְיָרֵשׁ developed secondarily in place of *qal* יִירַשׁ due to the unique usage. Alternatively, the agricultural devastation wrought by an insect plague (if that is what is envisioned) suits the 'intensive' semantics often associated with the *piʿʿel* stem.

purposes of number agreement with the closest subject referent, i.e., ויורישו *wyūrīšu* 'and they dispossessed'; cf. the text and translation in example (13), above. The Samaritan imposition of order and harmoniousness is thus conspicuous in several relevant facets.

8.0. *Qere* לְכָה־ || *ketiv* לך (Num. 23.13)

In the span of a few years, Steven Fassberg (1994, 13–35; 1999) and Ahouva Shulman (1996, 65–84, see especially 84, n. 22) independently arrived at similar explanations for BH's so-called 'lengthened imperative': that it denotes action in the direction of the speaker or for the benefit thereof. Its use with such imperatives is not obligatory (see below), but is limited to such, at least in most forms of ancient Hebrew, up to and including Second Temple traditions, though there are sporadic signs of misuse and definite signs of disuse (especially RH).[17]

With specific regard to imperatival forms of *qal* הָלַךְ, Shulman (1996, 75–81) argues convincingly that the short and long forms normally denote, respectively, 'go (away)' and 'come (here)', with the speaker as reference point. Shulman notes that speaker-orientation is inferable from a following preposition with first-person suffix and/or verb form, e.g., inclusive first-person plural cohortatives, first-person singular cohortatives denoting action that can be performed only after the approach of the addressee, and imperatives inviting action on behalf of the speaker. It must be emphasised, though, that while long imperatives consistently

[17] Arguable examples of archaising pseudo-classical misuse may be detected in non-biblical material from Qumran, e.g., 4Q88 10.7, 8, 8; 4Q200 f5.9 (= Tobit 4.9); 4Q416 f4.3; 4Q418 f222.2.

denote speaker-orientation, the morphological marking is not obligatory for this speaker-orientation, e.g., the short form לֵךְ is sometimes followed by prepositions with first-person morphology (e.g., Jdg. 18.19; 1 Kgs 13.15) or by first-person verbs implying speaker-orientation (e.g., Jdg. 4.22; 2 Chron. 25.17 *ketiv*).

We are now positioned to examine the *ketiv-qere* instance in example (14).

(14) וַיֹּ֨אמֶר אֵלָ֜יו בָּלָ֗ק לך־ (K) לְכָה־ (Q) נָּ֣א אִתִּ֗י אֶל־מָק֤וֹם אַחֵר֙ אֲשֶׁ֣ר תִּרְאֶ֣נּוּ מִשָּׁ֔ם אֶ֚פֶס קָצֵ֣הוּ תִרְאֶ֔ה וְכֻלּ֖וֹ לֹ֣א תִרְאֶ֑ה וְקָבְנוֹ־לִ֖י מִשָּֽׁם׃

'And Balak said to him, "Please **come** with me to another place, from which you may see them. You shall see only a fraction of them and shall not see them all. Then curse them for me from there."' (Num. 23.13)

That the imperative לך invites movement in the direction of the speaker is indicated by the following אִתִּי 'with me' and וְקָבְנוֹ־לִי מִשָּׁם 'and curse him for me from there'. Given the examples of speaker-oriented short-imperative לֵךְ, above, the *ketiv* must be seen as an acceptable, if rare, use of the short imperative for expressing movement toward the speaker. The *qere*, conversely, reflects the more common lengthened morphology of the imperative, לְכָה־, in the sense of 'come' (cf. the *ketiv-qere* in 2 Chron. 25.17). The *qere* is also in line with parallel commands in the context (Num. 10.29; 22.6, 11, 17; 23.7, 27; 24.14; cf. the short imperative in cases of ablative movement: Num. 22.20, 35).

The Samaritan situation is complex. On the one hand, where it appears in the SP, use of the lengthened imperative resembles that in the MT. This is to say that the lengthened imperative appears in Samaritan Hebrew in the same grammatical contexts and with the same meaning as in Tiberian Hebrew, i.e., for actions involving motion toward the speaker or for the benefit thereof. Even so, the lengthened imperative is less common in the SP than in the MT Torah. This tallies with the aforementioned disuse of the form in some forms of late antique Hebrew, most notably RH. Indeed, against just four cases in which the SP has a lengthened imperative and the MT does not (Gen. 19.9; Exod. 17.2; Num. 21.6; Num. 23.18), there are twenty or more arguable cases in which the SP has a short form against an MT lengthened one (Gen. 15.9; 19.32; 21.23; 25.33; 27.3, 4, 7; 29.19, 21;[18] 37.13; 43.8; 47.31; Exod. 3.10; 32.10;[19] Num. 10.29; 23.13, 27; 24.14; 27.4; Deut. 26.15; 33.23). Significantly, seven of these latter involve Samaritan לך *lik* || MT לְכָה. Though the combined Samaritan written-reading tradition preserves lengthened imperatives, in general, and the lengthened לכה *līka*, more specifically (Gen. 31.44; Num. 22.6, 11, 17; 23.7, 7), the SP seems to evince a situation in which the perceived distinction between short and lengthened imperatives has undergone a degree of erosion, so that retention of the final ה- *-a* was not deemed vital for the sake of semantic disambiguation.[20]

---

[18] Here הבה is read *ībi* = Tiberian הָבֵא 'bring'.

[19] The SP reads הניחה לי *annīy'yē-lli* (Ben-Ḥayyim 2000, 74, §1.4.10), but it is not clear that the *-ē* suffix is that of the lengthened imperative.

[20] This contrasts markedly with Samaritan use of the lengthened first-person *wayyiqṭol*, i.e., the pseudo-cohortative, which, in line with other Second Temple Hebrew chronolects, is far more common in both the written and reading components of the SP than in the Tiberian Pentateuch (see Hornkohl, f.c.).

Parallel to the Tiberian *ketiv-qere* in Num. 23.13, the SP has unlengthened לך *lik*, in agreement with the Tiberian *ketiv*. This concords with the same form at SP Num. 23.27 and 24.14 (both of which have lengthened imperatives in the MT), but clashes with lengthened לכה *līka* at SP Num. 22.6, 11, 17; 23.7, 7 (which are all lengthened in the MT). Such diversity, especially in a single pericope, is uncharacteristic for the SP.

9.0. *Qere* תְּנִיאוּן || *ketiv* תנואון (Num. 32.7)

(15) וְלָ֣מָּה תנואון (K) תְּנִיא֔וּן (Q) אֶת־לֵ֖ב בְּנֵ֣י יִשְׂרָאֵ֑ל מֵעֲבֹר֙ אֶל־הָאָ֔רֶץ אֲשֶׁר־נָתַ֥ן לָהֶ֖ם יְהוָֽה׃

'Why **will you discourage** the heart of the people of Israel from going over into the land that the LORD has given them?' (Num. 32.7)

Since all other forms of the verb in question in the Tiberian tradition are *hifʿil* (Num. 30.6, 6, 9, 12; 32.9; Ps. 33.10; 141.5)—including consonantally unambiguous *qaṭal* forms (Num. 30.6, 6, 12; Ps. 33.9) and a form in the immediate vicinity in the same idiom וַיָּנִ֗יאוּ אֶת־לֵ֙ב בְּנֵ֣י יִשְׂרָאֵ֔ל 'and they discouraged the hearts of the children of Israel' (Num. 32.9)—it is difficult to view the *ketiv* in example (15) as anything other than a result of conflation of *waw* and *yod*, presumably arising from their graphic similarity.

The verb in the SP is consistently *hifʿil*, with no divergences between the written and reading components of the tradition

(Num. 30.6,[21] 6, 6, 12; 32.7, 9). Thus, in Num. 32.7, SP תניאון *tanniyyon* || MT *qere* תְנִיאוּן.

10.0. *Qere* 3CPL *qaṭal* ו- || *ketiv* 3FPL *qaṭal* ה- (Deut. 21.7; Num. 34.4?)

In the lower margin of L on the page that includes Deut. 21.7 (fol. 111v), the *masora parva* reads:

> יֹדֹ כתֹ הֹ וקרֹ וו לא יקרחה קרחה לא שפכה כי נשברה בעת ההיא עלה עריו נצתה לא נושבה עתה יזנה ולא יהיה עוד שממה שפכה המרמרה עודינה שלה
>
> Fourteen[22] times the *ketiv* is *heh* and the *qere* is *waw*: לֹא־יקרחה קָרְחָה 'they shall not make bald patches' (Lev. 21.5); לֹא שפכה '(our hands) did not spill' (Deut. 21.7); כִּי־נשברה 'for (the ships) were wrecked' (1 Kgs 22.49); בָּעֵת הַהִיא עלה 'at that time (the servants of Nebuchadnezzar king of Babylon) came up' (2 Kgs 24.10); עָרָיו נצתה 'his cities fell to ruin' (Jer. 2.15); לֹא נושבה '(cities that are) not settled' (Jer. 22.6); עַתָּה יזנה 'now they will prostitute'[23] (Ezek. 23.43); וְלֹא־יהיה־עוֹד 'and they will no longer be' (Ezek. 37.22); שממה 'they have been laid desolate' (Ezek. 35.12); שפכה '(my feet) slipped' (Ps. 73.2); חמרמרה '(my face) reddened' (Job. 16.16); עודינה '(our eyes) still' (Lam. 4.17); שלה 'blasphemy' (Dan. 3.29)

---

[21] SP Num.30.6 includes an infinitive absolute הנא *anni* with no parallel in the MT.

[22] The note gives the figure יֹדֹ 'fourteen', but lists just thirteen cases, omitting all five occurrences of והיה תוצאות (see below) as well as צֹאן אֹבְדוֹת היה עַמִּי 'lost sheep have been my people' (Jer. 50.6).

[23] The *ketiv* in this verse is actually עת יזנה, the *qere* עַתָּה יִזְנוּ.

While the forms listed in the masoretic note represent various categories with diverse explanations for the interchange, several involve an apparent 3FS *qaṭal* form and a FPL or FDL subject. There is consensus that the Proto-Semitic suffix conjugation paradigm distinguished between 3MPL and 3FPL endings, the former *-ū* and the latter *-ā* (Huehnergard and Pat-El 2019, 8). A distinction is observed in Akkadian (*-ū* vs. *-ā*; Hasselbach-Andee 2019, 105), Arabic (*-ū* vs. *-na*; Birnstiel 2019, 384), Aramaic (*-u* vs. *-u/a/in*; Kaufman 1998, 126), Syriac ([*-w*] vs. [*-y*]; Pat-El 2019, 663), and Geʿez (*-u* vs. *-a*; Butts 2019, 132). By contrast, in Hebrew, for the most part, dedicated 3FPL *qaṭal* morphology fell out of use in favour of epicene ־וּ. There are some 25 cases in which it has been argued that biblical suffix conjugation forms ending in ־ָה or *ketiv* ־ה with plural subjects represent a form with dedicated 3FPL morphology (see Hornkohl 2013, 142–45 for summary and references). This seems a plausible explanation for the *ketiv* form in example (16) and may also have relevance for (17).

(16) וְעָנ֖וּ וְאָמְר֑וּ יָדֵ֗ינוּ לֹ֤א שפכה (K) שָֽׁפְכוּ֙ (Q) אֶת־הַדָּ֣ם הַזֶּ֔ה וְעֵינֵ֖ינוּ לֹ֥א רָאֽוּ׃
‘and they shall testify, ‘Our hands **did** not **shed** this blood, nor did our eyes see it shed.’ (Deut. 21.7)

In L, intercolumnal notes on יָדֵ֗ינוּ at Deut. 21.7 and יָדֵ֣ינוּ at Jer. 6.24 read ו֗ מל ‘six times *plene*’.[24] This shows, among other things, that the Masoretic Tradition was primarily concerned with the

[24] According to L, there are actually seven such instances: Gen. 5.29; Deut. 21.7; 32.27; Jer. 6.24; Hos. 14.4; Ps. 90.17, 17. However, the masoretic note is confirmed by similar notes in A at Hos. 14.4 and Ps. 90.17 and, most crucially, by A’s defective יָדֵ֣נוּ at Deut. 32.27, which shows that L deviates slightly from its own *masora*.

word's correct orthography, whatever its meaning. In this case, the *ketiv* שפכה can be argued to preserve an archaic 3FPL in agreement with FDL 'our hands', while the *qere* unambiguously represents the more standard 3CPL, effecting harmony with the 3CPL in וְעֵינֵ֖ינוּ לֹ֥א רָאֽוּ 'and our eyes did not see' later in the verse.

The SP not surprisingly adopts the more standard CDL ידינו לא שפכו *yēdīnu lā̊ šā̊fā̊ku* 'our hands did not shed'. This is in keeping with the tradition's quest for consistency. Yet, the Samaritan propensity for levelling unconventional forms does not preclude the possibility of preserved archaisms. Indeed, MT וְעֵינֵ֤י יִשְׂרָאֵל֙ כָּבְד֣וּ 'and Israel's eyes grew heavy (= dim)' (Gen. 48.10) || SP ועיני ישראל כבדה *wīni yišrā̊ʾəl kā̊bā̊da*, where the SP verb is evidently a suffix conjugation (*qaṭal*) form preserving dedicated 3FP morphology.

The above considerations may also apply to example (17).

(17) (Q) וְהָיוּ֙ (K) והיה וְנָסַ֣ב לָכֶם֩ הַגְּב֨וּל מִנֶּ֜גֶב לְמַעֲלֵ֤ה עַקְרַבִּים֙ וְעָ֣בַר צִ֔נָה
תּוֹצְאֹתָ֔יו מִנֶּ֖גֶב לְקָדֵ֣שׁ בַּרְנֵ֑עַ וְיָצָ֥א חֲצַר־אַדָּ֖ר וְעָבַ֥ר עַצְמֹֽנָה׃

'And your border shall turn south of the ascent of Akrabbim, and cross to Zin, **and** its limit **shall be** south of Kadesh-barnea. Then it shall go on to Hazar-addar, and pass along to Azmon.' (Num. 34.4)

In BH, the lexeme תוֹצָאוֹת 'limits, farthest reaches' (25x) is always plural. In (17) it is tempting to attribute the apparent mismatch between *ketiv* והיה and plural subject תּוֹצְאֹתָיו 'its limits' to an alternative syntactic interpretation, according to which והיה functions as a 'discourse marker' rather than a verb proper (see van der Merwe, Naudé, and Kroeze 2017, 427–28). In that case, a corresponding English translation would have a discourse marking 'and it will be' followed by the rendering of a verbless clause 'its limits will be south of....' Yet, it is important to consider this case from a broader perspective. A form of תּוֹצָאוֹת follows a form of הָיָה nineteen times in BH. In eleven of these הָיָה is plural (Num. 34.5, 8, 9, 12; Josh. 15.7, 11; 16.3, 8; 19.14, 22, 29), in three הָיָה is singular (Josh. 17.9, 18; 19.33), and in five the verb is singular in the *ketiv* and a plural in the *qere* (Num. 34.4; Josh. 15.4; 18.12, 14, 19). This means that according to the written component of Tiberian BH, the form תּוֹצָאוֹת is the subject of an apparent singular form of הָיָה nearly as often (8x) as it is the subject of a plural form of the verb (11x). In six of the eight cases of apparently singular הָיָה, the verb is a suffix conjugation form; in the other two, the verb is וַיְהִי (Josh. 17.9; 19.33). It is worth mentioning at this point that though the Tiberian tradition regularly construes תוצאת as a plural via verbal agreement and/or a plural possessive suffix יו- (cf. *ketiv* תצאתו Josh. 16.3), only in a minority of cases is the form explicitly spelled as a plural in ות-. It may be that, alongside the plural form, a singular along the lines of תצאה* or תצאת* was also known (see below), but was secondarily levelled in conformity with the plural at a date sufficiently early that the plurality was sporadically recorded in the spelling tradition.

Whatever the exact explanation for the *ketiv-qere* dissonance in (17) and the other four relevant *ketiv-qere* instances involving היה and תצאות, it is clear that the written component of the Tiberian tradition preserves a situation of singular and plural diversity more extensive than that preserved in the corresponding reading tradition, where plural agreement is greatly, albeit not exclusively, favoured.

Intriguingly, the SP agrees with the Tiberian *ketiv*: והיה *wēyya*. This is in line with the Samaritan convention according to which the noun תוצאיתו *tūṣā̊ʾītu* is treated as singular and consistently paired with 3MS והיה. This may be considered evidence for an originally singular option for consistently plural Tiberian תֹּצָאוֹת (see above).

11.0. *Qere* שָׁכַב || *ketiv* שגל (Deut. 28.30)

The euphemistic employment of שָׁכַב 'lie (down)' in reference to sexual relations is common throughout BH (and is matched by euphemistic renderings in the ancient versions). This usage was also secondarily extended to instances of *ketiv* שג"ל 'rape, ravage', one such case obtaining in example (18) (see also Isa. 13.16; Jer. 3.2; Zech. 14.2).

(18) אִשָּׁה תְאָרֵשׂ וְאִישׁ אַחֵר ישגלנה (K) יִשְׁכָּבֶנָּה (Q) בַּיִת תִּבְנֶה וְלֹא־תֵשֵׁב בּוֹ כֶּרֶם תִּטַּע וְלֹא תְחַלְּלֶנּוּ׃

'You shall betroth a wife, but another man **shall ravish her**. You shall build a house, but you shall not dwell in it. You shall plant a vineyard, but you shall not enjoy its fruit.' (Deut. 28.30)

Cohen (2007, 264) proffers a compelling motivation for such euphemistic *ketiv-qere* cases. Words that were deemed problematic to utter in public, due to perceived impropriety or taboo, were replaced in oral recitation by more appropriate substitutes, but continued to be copied faithfully in the written tradition.

In the case of (18) and similar, the euphemistic substitution could not be effected without certain grammatical modifications.

First, the verb שָׁכַב normally takes one of the comitative prepositions, עִם or אֵת both ‘with’ (Orlinsky 1944). On seven occasions one encounters שָׁכַב אֹת-, i.e., the definite accusative/direct object marker, but in six of the seven only the vocalisation calls for such an analysis.[25] The earlier syntax was more likely with the preposition אֵת ‘with’, its reinterpretation as the direct object marker secondary. In this way, secondary disambiguation was created between originally intransitive שָׁכַב with comitative עִם or אֵת ‘lie with’, on the one hand, and the innovative transitive שָׁכַב with accusative אֵת in the more aggressive sense of ‘forcibly engage in sex’, on the other (cf. the Targumic distinction between שכב עים and שכב ית). Relatedly, the verb שָׁכַב nowhere in BH bears an object suffix *except* where it is read as the *qere* for *ketiv* שגל, as in (18) above. Finally, BH lacks a *nifʿal* נִשְׁכַּב except where it is read instead of apparently *nifʿal* *נשגל, as in Isa. 13.16 and Zech. 14.2. Significantly, unambiguous consonantal *nifʿal* *נשכב is first attested in material in the non-biblical material from Qumran (4Q270 f5.19; 4Q271 f3.12) and persists in RH. Relatedly, no passive *qal* or *puʿʿal* cognate of שָׁכַב is known from ancient Hebrew beyond that in the *qere* of Jer. 3.2 (and no *piʿʿel* is attested at all). All of the above point to the likely secondary development of transitive שָׁכַב אֹת-, perhaps in the early Second Temple period (cf. שָׁכַב אוֹת- with *mater waw* in Ezekiel) (Beuken 2004, 663). In other words, שָׁכַב אֹת- is itself an unmarked case of *ketiv-qere* mismatch in line with the replacement of transitive שג"ל with originally intransitive שכ"ב for purposes of (public) oral recitation.

[25] אֹת-: Gen. 34.2; Lev. 15.18, 24; Num. 5.13, 19; 2 Sam. 13.14; אוֹת-: Ezek. 23.8.

The *qere* form in (18) involves two of the three aforementioned secondary developments: שָׁכַב with transitive semantics and שָׁכַב with an object suffix—both traits that it seems to have inherited due to its substitution for transitive (presumably G-stem) שג"ל.

While *qere* שכ"ב is almost certainly secondary, the evidence seems indicative of rather early replacement. Greek ἕξει αὐτήν 'will have her' and Syriac ܢܣܒܝܗ̇ 'will take her' are ambiguous as evidence of their Hebrew *Vorlage*. Though certainly euphemistic, they do not obviously correspond to either the Tiberian *ketiv* or *qere*. But other ancient versions arguably confirm the antiquity of the *qere* tradition: Vulgate *dormiat cum ea* 'will sleep with her'; Targum Onkelos ישכבינה 'will lie with her'; 1QIsa[a] 11.24 תשׁ֯כ֯בנה || MT Isa. 13.16. Depending on the antiquity of its *plene* spelling, the Tiberian orthographic שכב אות- in Ezek. 23.8 may also testify to the antiquity of the substitution.

For its part, the combined Samaritan written-reading tradition at Deut. 28.30 has ישכב עמה *yiškåb imma* 'will lie with her'. Assuming the primary status of ישגלנה, as in the Tiberian *ketiv*, the Samaritan euphemistic solution goes farther than that of the Tiberian *qere*. It avoids not only an inappropriate word, but tortured grammar, too, resorting to conventional rection for the verb שכב with a transparently comitative preposition. Indeed, Samaritan Hebrew does not know the formulation of transitive שכב with direction object את; Tiberian שָׁכַב אֶת- is consistently paralleled by Samaritan שכב את- *šåkåb itt-* (Gen. 34.2; Lev. 15.18, 24; Num. 5.13, 19), i.e., intransitive verb with comitative preposition. In this case the Samaritan penchant for harmonisation has led to mixed results of development and conservation: on the one hand, modification of the original ישגלנה to more acceptable and grammatical ישכב עמה not only in the recitation tradition, but at the level of the orthography; on the other hand, preservation of שכב with a comitative preposition, in contrast to the innovative Tiberian distinction between neutral שָׁכַב with comitative אִת- 'lie with' and the more explicitly non-consensual שָׁכַב with accusative/direct object אֹת- 'rape, ravish'.

12.0. Conclusion

In the introduction to this study, the diachronic relationship between the various relevant linguistic traditions of the Torah were sketched as follows: an ancient Tiberian orthographic component; a largely harmonious, but somewhat later Tiberian reading component; an ancient Samaritan written component with clear and widespread evidence of Second Temple reworking; and a Samaritan reading component replete with Second Temple and later features. While this broad characterisation may be generally accurate, it finds only partial support in the cases examined above; see Table 3. This fact should inform understanding of the relationship between the Tiberian *ketiv* and *qere* traditions.

A few of the cases discussed in the body of this study exhibit the diachronic progression expected based on the characterisation sketched in the introduction, e.g., archaic Tiberian *ketiv*, standard Tiberian *qere*, and late Samaritan combined tradition: §§10.0 (though the SP elsewhere also preserves such an archaism) and 11.0. Similar is the situation of archaic *ketiv*, late *qere*, and later SP in §2.0 as well as those of the unexplained *ketiv*, standard *qere*, and late SP form in §3.0 and the SP's levelling in favour of a late form in §6.0. The relatively late character of the SP is the most conspicuous diachronic trait, though its preservation of *qal* morphology against Tiberian *qere nifʿal* in the case of §5.0 might be an exception, as may more than one Samaritan feature associated with §10.0.

Table 3: *Ketiv*, *qere*, and Samaritan findings with summary discussions

1.0.	Q: הַיְצֵא	K: הוצא	SP: הוציא *ūṣi*
	qere: non-standard I-*y* (error? euphony?), *ketiv*: standard I-*w*; SP = *ketiv*		
2.0.	Q: וַיּוּשַׂם	K: ויישם	SP: ויושם *wyuwwåšåm*
	qere: late, *ketiv*: archaic; SP: late Aramaic/post-biblical stem		
3.0.	Q: וְיִשְׁתַּחֲווּ	K: וישתחו	SP: ישתחוו *yištåbbu*
	qere: standard plural, *ketiv*: unexplained (?); SP = *qere*, with later phonology		
4.0.	Q: בָּא גָד	K: בגד	SP: בגד *afgåd*
	qere/ketiv: plausible; SP = *ketiv*, ST = *qere*		
5.0.	Q: וַיִּלּוֹנוּ; תַּלִּינוּ; וַיַּלִּינוּ	K: וילינו; תלונו; וילונו	SP: וילנו *wyillånu*; תלנו *tillånu*; וילנו *wyillånu*
	qere/ketiv: complex stem arrangement; SP ≠ *qere/ketiv*; less differentiated arrangement; shared gemination and *qal* vestiges possibly ancient		
6.0.	Q: קְרוּאֵי; קְרִיאֵי	K: קריאי; קרואי	SP: קריאי *qaryāʾi*
	qere and *ketiv* agree on variation, but not location; SP alternately = *ketiv/qere*, unifying according to a late pattern typical of Aramaic/RH		
7.0.	Q: וַיּוֹרֶשׁ	K: ויירש	SP: ויורישו *wyūrīšu*
	qere: global morphosemantic consistency; *ketiv* local harmony; SP ≈ *qere*, with broad morphosemantic consistency		
8.0.	Q: לְכָה־	K: לך	SP: לך *lik*
	qere: standard marked usage, *ketiv*: acceptable unmarked variant; SP = *ketiv*, along with less use of the marked option and local inconsistency		
9.0.	Q: תְּנִיאוֹן	K: תנואון	SP: תניאון *tanniyyon*
	qere: standard, *ketiv*: graphic error (?); SP = *qere*		
10.0.	Q: וְהָיוּ; שָׁפְכוּ	K: והיה; שפכה	SP: שפכו *šåfåku*; והיה *wēyya*
	qere: standard 3CPL ending, *ketiv*: archaic 3FPL ending (frequent with תוצאות); SP = *qere/ketiv*; SP knows the archaic 3FPL		
11.0.	Q: יִשְׁכָּבֶנָּה	K: ישגלנה	SP: ישכב עמה *yiškåb imma*
	qere: late euphemistic replacement, with syntax of *ketiv*, creating distinct sense of שָׁכַב; SP = *qere*, with syntax of substitute lexeme		

Beyond this, it is worth remarking that the SP agrees with the Tiberian *ketiv* nearly as often—five occasions: §§1.0, 4.0 (against the ST), 8.0, 10.0—as it agrees with the Tiberian *qere*—

six occasions: §§3.0, 6.0, 7.0 (with slight modification), 9.0, 10.0, 11.0. This seems due mainly to the Samaritan penchant for consistency and harmony, which often leads to levelling in line with the majority form, which is the *ketiv* in §§1.0 and 10.0 (והיה), but the *qere* in §§3.0, 7.0, 9.0, 10.0 (שפכו), and 11.0. Be that as it may, the SP occasionally exhibits inconsistency and/or a minority form: §8.0. Moreover, the non-uniform character of the Samaritan exegetical tradition is evidenced by the divergent interpretations of the SP and the ST in §4.0.

Turning to the combined Tiberian tradition, while inexplicable forms are occasionally presented by both the *ketiv* and the *qere*, it seems that in the majority of cases the preserved form in each tradition can be justified. More rarely—especially in instances where graphic similarity between *waw* and *yod* may have been at play—it seems likely that the *ketiv* form represents a corruption avoided in the *qere* (§§3.0, 9.0)—though, it has been suggested that an otherwise unexplained *qere* form may have arisen from *waw-yod* conflation: §1.0.

It has been remarked that in most cases the Tiberian *ketiv* and *qere* both represent plausible readings. While this arguably sheds important light on the *ketiv-qere* phenomenon, there is evidence that the traditions differ with respect to more than just natural historical linguistic development. Consider, in particular, the cases discussed in §§7.0 and 11.0. In both cases, the *qere* seems to reflect a linguistic tradition characterised by deliberate care. In §7.0, this manifests in the global morphosemantic consistency of the distinction between nearly synonymous *hifʿil* and *qal* forms. In §11.0, it is seen in secondary disambiguation between intransitive (comitative) שָׁכַב and transitive שָׁכַב. Both developments reflect what in another connection Khan (2021a, 330–31) has described as "a general Second Temple development in the proto-Masoretic reading tradition involving the introduction of strategies to increase… clarity of interpretation."[26]

References

Primary Sources

A= Aleppo Codex: Bar Hama, Adon. 2002. Digitalization of *The Aleppo Codex*. https://barhama.com

Ben Sira: Abegg, Martin G. 2009. *Ben Sira Electronic Database (BENSIRA-C/BENSIRA-M)*. Accordance Modules. Altamonte Springs, FL: OakTree Software, Inc.

Dead Sea Scrolls Biblical Texts: Abegg, Martin G., Jr. 2009a. *Dead Sea Scrolls Bible Canonical/Manuscript Order (DSSB-C/DSSB-M)*. Accordance Modules. Altamonte Springs, FL: OakTree Software, Inc.

Dead Sea Scrolls Non-biblical Texts: Abegg, Martin G., Jr. 2001. *Non-Biblical Dead Sea Scrolls from Qumran (QUMRAN)*. Accordance Module. Altamonte Springs, FL: OakTree Software, Inc.

Egyptian Aramaic: Porten, Bezalel, and Ada Yardeni (eds.). 2007. *Textbook of Aramaic Documents from Ancient Egypt (TAD-T)*.

[26] Khan subsumes such strategies under the general heading of *orthoepy*; see Khan (2018b; 2020, I: 73–85, 99–105).

Accordance Module. Altamonte Springs, FL: OakTree Software, Inc.

L = Leningrad Codex: Zuckerman, Bruce E. 1990. *Leningrad Codex Images*. Included in BibleWorks 10. West Semitic Research Group.

LXX: Taylor, Bernard A., and Dale M. Wheeler (eds.). 2008. *Greek Septuagint Database*. Accordance Module. Altamonte Springs, FL: OakTree Software, Inc. Based on Ralfs, Alfred (ed.). 2006. *Septuaginta*. Revised by Robert Hanhart. Stuttgart: Deutsche Bibelgesellschaft.

Peshiṭta: Abegg, Martin, and Jerome Lund (eds.). 2010. *Syriac Peshitta (Old Testament) (PESHOT-T)*. Accordance Module. Altamonte Springs, FL: OakTree Software, Inc.

RH = Rabbinic Hebrew (Mishna, Tosefta, Talmuds): Maʾagarim Database of the Academy of the Hebrew Language: https://maagarim.hebrew-academy.org.il/Pages/PMain.aspx

Samaritan Arabic Translation: Shehadeh, Haseeb (ed.). 1989–2002. *The Arabic Translation of the Samaritan Pentateuch: Edited from the Manuscripts with an Introductory Volume*. 2 vols. Jerusalem: Israel Academy of Sciences and Humanities. [Arabic and Hebrew]

Samaritan Pentateuch Oral Tradition: Ben-Ḥayyim, Ze'ev. 1977. *The Words of the Pentateuch*. Vol. 4 of *The Literary and Oral Tradition of Hebrew and Aramaic amongst the Samaritans*. Jerusalem: The Academy of the Hebrew Language. [Hebrew]

Samaritan Pentateuch Written Tradition: Tal, Abraham, and Moshe Florentin (eds.). 2010. *The Pentateuch: The Samaritan Version and the Masoretic Version*. Tel-Aviv: The Haim Rubin Tel-Aviv University Press.

Samaritan Targum: Tal, Abraham. 2010. *Samaritan Targum (SAMTARG)*. Accordance Module. Altamonte Springs, FL: OakTree Software, Inc.

Targums: Cook, Edward M. (ed.). 2007a. *Targum Geniza (TARGG-T)*. Accordance Module. Altamonte Springs, FL: OakTree Software, Inc.

———. 2007b. *Targum Fragments (TARGF-T)*. Accordance Module. Altamonte Springs, FL: OakTree Software, Inc.

———. 2008. *Targum (TARG-T)*. Accordance Modules. Altamonte Springs, FL: OakTree Software, Inc.

Vulgate: Fabbri, Marco V. 2008. *Tagged Latin Vulgate (VULG-T)*. Accordance Modules. Altamonte Springs, FL: OakTree Software, Inc. Based on Weber, Robert (ed.). 1994. *Biblia Sacra Iuxta Vulgatem*. 4th edition. Stuttgart: Deutsche Bibelgesellschaft.

Secondary Sources

Ben-Ḥayyim, Ze'ev. 2000. *A Grammar of Samaritan Hebrew: Based on the Recitation of the Law in Comparison with the Tiberian and Other Jewish Traditions*. Revised English edition. Jerusalem: The Hebrew University Magnes Press.

Bergsträsser, Gotthelf. 1918–1929. *Hebräische Grammatik*. 2 vols. Leipzig: Vogel.

Beuken, Willem A. M. 2004. 'שָׁכַב'. In *Theological Dictionary of the Old Testament*, edited by G. Johannes Botterweck, Helmer Ringgren, and Heinz-Josef Fabry, translated by Douglas W. Scott, vol. 14, 659–71. Grand Rapids, MI: Eerdmans.

Birnstiel, Daniel. 2019. 'Classical Arabic'. In *The Semitic Languages*, 2nd edition, edited by John Huehnergard and Na'ama Pat-El, 367–402. London: Routledge Taylor & Frances Group.

Blau, Joshua. 2010. *Phonology and Morphology of Biblical Hebrew*. Linguistic Studies in Ancient West Semitic 2. Winona Lake, IN: Eisenbrauns.

Butts, Aaron Michael. 2019. 'Gəʕəz (Classical Ethiopic)'. In *The Semitic Languages*, 2nd edition, edited by John Huehnergard and Na'ama Pat-El, 117–44. London: Routledge Taylor & Frances Group.

Cohen, Maimon. 2007. *The Kethiḇ and Qeri System in the Biblical Text: A Linguistic Analysis of the Various Traditions Based on the Manuscript 'Keter Aram Tsova'*. Jerusalem: The Hebrew University Magnes Press. [Hebrew]

Fassberg, Steven E. 1994. *Studies in Biblical Syntax*. Jerusalem: The Hebrew University Magnes Press. [Hebrew]

———. 1999. 'The Lengthened Imperative קָטְלָה in Biblical Hebrew'. *Hebrew Studies* 40: 7–13.

Fox, Joshua. 2003. *Semitic Noun Patterns*. Harvard Semitic Studies 52. Winona Lake, IN: Eisenbrauns.

GKC = Kautzch, Emil (ed.). 1910. *Gesenius' Hebrew Grammar*. Translated by Arthur E. Cowley. Oxford: Oxford University Press.

Hasselbach-Andee, Rebecca. 2019. 'Akkadian'. In *The Semitic Languages*, 2nd edition, edited by John Huehnergard and Na'ama Pat-El, 95–116. London: Routledge Taylor & Frances Group.

Hornkohl, Aaron D. 2013. *Ancient Hebrew Periodization and the Language of the Book of Jeremiah*. Studies in Semitic Languages and Linguistics 74. Leiden: Brill.

———. 2018. 'Diachronic Exceptions in the Comparison of Tiberian and Qumran Hebrew: The Preservation of Early Linguistic Features in Dead Sea Scrolls Biblical Hebrew'. In *The Reconfiguration of Hebrew in the Hellenistic Period: Proceedings of the Seventh International Symposium on the Hebrew of the Dead Sea Scrolls and Ben Sira at Strasbourg University, June 2014*, edited by Jan Joosten, Daniel Machiela, and Jean-Sébastien Rey, 61–92. Studies on the Texts of the Desert of Judah 124. Leiden: Brill. https://doi.org/10.1163/9789004366770_006

———. 2020a. 'Discord between the Tiberian Written and Reading Traditions: Two Case Studies'. In *Studies in Semitic Vocalisation*, edited by Aaron D. Hornkohl and Geoffrey Khan, 227–80. Cambridge: University of Cambridge and Open Book Publishers. https://doi.org/10.11647/OBP.0207.07

———. 2020b. 'The Hebrew of the Dead Sea Scrolls and the Tiberian Reading Tradition: Shared Departures from the Masoretic Written Tradition'. *Dead Sea Discoveries* 27/3: 410–25. https://doi.org/10.1163/15685179-bja10012

———. 2021. 'Niphalisation in Ancient Hebrew: A Perspective from the Samaritan Tradition'. *Journal for Semitics* 30/2: 1–17. https://doi.org/10.25159/2663-6573/9207

———. Forthcoming. *Studies in the Historical Depth of the Tiberian Reading Tradition*. Cambridge Semitic Languages and Cultures. Cambridge: The Faculty of Asian and Middle Eastern Studies and Open Book Publishers.

Huehnergard, John. 2007. '*Qāṭīl* and *Qəṭīl* Nouns in Biblical Hebrew'. In *Sha'arei Lashon: Studies in Hebrew, Aramaic, and Jewish Languages Presented to Moshe Bar-Asher*, edited by Aharon Maman, Steven E. Fassberg, and Yochanan Breuer, I:*3–*45. Jerusalem: Bialik Institute.

Huehnergard, John, and Na'ama Pat-El. 2019. 'Introduction to the Semitic Languages and Their History.' In *The Semitic Languages*, 2nd edition, edited by John Huehnergard and Na'ama Pat-El, 1–21. London: Routledge Taylor & Frances Group.

Kaufman, Stephen A. 1998. 'Aramaic'. In *The Semitic Languages*, edited by Robert Hetzron, 114–30. London: Routledge Taylor & Frances Group.

Khan, Geoffrey. 2013a. '*Ketiv* and *Qere*'. In *Encyclopedia of Hebrew Language and Linguistics*, edited by Geoffrey Khan, II: 463–68. Leiden: Brill.

———. 2013b. 'Tiberian Reading Tradition'. In *Encyclopedia of Hebrew Language and Linguistics*, edited by Geoffrey Khan, III: 769–78. Leiden: Brill.

———.2018. 'Orthoepy in the Tiberian Reading Tradition of the Hebrew Bible and Its Historical Roots in the Second Temple Period'. *Vetus Testamentum* 68: 1–24.

———. 2020. *The Tiberian Pronunciation Tradition of Biblical Hebrew*. 2 vols. Cambridge Semitic Languages and Cultures 1.

Cambridge: University of Cambridge and Open Book Publishers. https://doi.org/10.11647/OBP.0194.01

———. 2021. 'The Coding of Discourse Dependency in Biblical Hebrew Consecutive *Weqaṭal* and *Wayyiqṭol*'. In *New Perspectives in Biblical and Rabbinic Hebrew*, edited by Aaron D. Hornkohl and Geoffrey Khan, 299–354. Cambridge Semitic Languages and Cultures 7. Cambridge: University of Cambridge and Open Book Publishers. https://doi.org/10.11647/OBP.0250

Morgangw, Lolo. 1858. 'History of the British Bards: Rhyme, Antiquity of'. *The Cambrian Journal*, 353–63. Published under the auspices of the Cambrian Institute, London: Longmans & Co., J. Russel Smith, and J. Petheram.

Orlinsky, Harry M. 1944. 'The Hebrew Root *ŠKB*'. *Journal of Biblical Literature* 63/1: 19–44.

Pat-El, Na'ama. 2019. 'Syriac'. In *The Semitic Languages*, 2nd edition, edited by John Huehnergard and Na'ama Pat-El, 653–78. London: Routledge Taylor & Frances Group.

Shulman, Ahouva. 1996. 'The Use of Modal Verb Forms in Biblical Hebrew Prose'. PhD dissertation, University of Toronto.

Tov, Emanuel. 2012. *Textual Criticism of the Hebrew Bible*. 3rd revised and expanded edition. Minneapolis, MN: Fortress Press.

van der Merwe, Christo H. J., Jacobus Naudé, and Jan H. Kroeze. 2017. *A Biblical Hebrew Reference Grammar*. 2nd edition. London: T&T Clark, Bloomsbury Publishing.

Yalon, Ḥanoch. 1971. *Pirqe Lashon*. Jerusalem: Bialik.

Yeivin, Israel. 1980. *Introduction to the Tiberian Masorah*. Translated and edited by E. J. Revell. Masoretic Studies 5. Missoula, MT: Scholars Press, for The Society of Biblical Literature and the International Organization for Masoretic Studies.

A FURTHER ANALYSIS OF THE 'BYZANTINE (ITALIAN-LEVANTINE) TRIAD' OF FEATURES IN COMMON TORAH CODICES[1]

Estara J Arrant

In my recent studies on the variation of Tiberian vowel and diacritic signs in medieval Hebrew Bible codices from the Cairo Genizah, I have highlighted, analysed, and contextualised a specific pattern involving the Tiberian signs *shewa* and *dagesh* (Arrant 2020; 2021). This pattern of features, which in this article is called the 'Byzantine Triad' of features,[2] includes the following:

- the placement of a sign resembling *dagesh* in consonantal *ʾalef*, often with a corresponding *rafe* placed over *mater lectionis ʾalef*;[3]

[1] Many thanks to the editors and peer reviewers of this volume for their helpful comments. I thank the Syndics of the Cambridge University Library for permission to use the images of the manuscripts which appear here.

[2] In previous studies (Arrant 2020; 2021), I called this phenomenon the 'Byzantine Trio'.

[3] Typically, this is accompanied by a pattern of *rafe* usage extended to non-*begedkefet* letters, but this is not further discussed here, as variation

 https://doi.org/10.11647/OBP.0330.05

- the placement of *shewa* under otherwise unvocalised word-final *ʿayin* and *ḥet*;
- a pattern of 'extended' use of *dagesh forte* in letters which do not, according to the standard rules of the Tiberian system, require a *dagesh forte*.

These variations have been discussed previously in the context of 'Palestino-Tiberian' vocalisation and 'extended Tiberian' vocalisation and have been identified in famous codices (such as *Codex Reuchlinianus*) (Díez Macho 1956; 1963; Morag 1959; Yeivin 1983; Fassberg 1990; Khan 1991; 2017; 2020; Heijmans 2013; Blapp 2017). However, the discussions are somewhat limited in focus to the developmental chronology of these particular systems of sign usage within the Tiberian Masoretic tradition, treating these features individually, rather than in conjunction with each other.

Prior to Arrant (2020; 2021), the significance of the specific pattern of co-occurrence of these three signs had gone unnoticed in scholarship. In these two studies, I took a contextualising approach to the vocalisation of Geniza Torah codices and, through the use of machine learning algorithms, analysed a large swath of around 1,800 Torah codices with many different kinds of non-standard Tiberian vocalisation. In a sub-group of the corpus, I identified the three features listed above, which co-occur in a distinct pattern (identified on the basis of strong statistical evidence, and further supported by linguistic and codicological findings). In addition to bearing the pattern in their use of the signs, I found

in the use of *rafe* in Bible MSS is a complex issue which deserves separate treatment.

that such MSS often exhibit trends in vowel sign interchange that are reminiscent of, or may even reflect, forms of 'Palestino-Tiberian' vocalisation. As this specific grouping of features appeared to occur in MSS with palaeographies ranging between Italian, Byzantine, and Levantine Oriental, this triad of features was designated 'Byzantine' (to describe the span of regions) (Arrant 2020, 515). The principal contribution of these studies was, therefore, to conceive of manuscripts characterised by the Byzantine Triad of features as a distinctive 'type' of medieval Tiberian Hebrew Bible.

However, a study devoted to the Byzantine Triad of features alone, detailing its exact features within the corpus of Hebrew Bible manuscripts and exploring the impact this grouping of features has upon the reading of the text as a coherent pattern, has not been undertaken. Similarly, no attempt has yet been made to engage with the codicological context(s) in which the Triad appears and to consider its role in the reality of biblical study and ritual use. Finally, Arrant (2021) identified three more fragments that display the Byzantine Triad of features (two of which appear to come from the same codex), which need to be further contextualised with those published in Arrant (2020).

In the present article I seek to study the Byzantine Triad of features on the basis of the broadest array of up-to-date evidence available. I will describe the entire phenomenon in greater depth, paying special attention to its linguistic function and impact upon the text, contextualising the pattern of co-occurrence within its codicological surroundings and suggesting ways in which it may have functioned in practical use. I also discuss the terminology I have used to describe it, including a brief justification for the term 'Byzantine Triad'. All of the MSS studied separately in my previous publication (Arrant 2020, especially 516–19; 2021) will be considered together in context, with the rest of the data being sourced from my PhD thesis (Arrant 2021). The MS fragments are from Cambridge's Taylor-Schechter and Lewis Gibson collections and consist of Torah Bible codices on parchment.[4]

1.0. The 'Byzantine Triad' of Features and Their Purpose

It seems that, when the three aforementioned features co-occur in a MS, they work in unison in an orthoepic manner to preserve and reinforce the Tiberian Masoretic syllable structure of Biblical Hebrew.[5] In this section I will describe the form and presentation of each feature separately, and then analyse how they cooperate to achieve such an effect.

1.1. Individual Feature Analysis

First, I will examine each element of the Byzantine Triad of features alone and seek to understand its independent function.

[4] The eleven MSS currently identified as characterised by the full complement of Byzantine Triad features are: T-S NS 21.6, T-S NS 248.5, T-S NS 248.11, T-S NS 248.12, T-S NS 248.16, T-S NS 248.17, T-S Misc. 2.75, Or.1080 A.4.18, Or.1080 A.4.20, Or.1080 A.4.3, and T-S AS 64.238. The final three were identified as having the Byzantine Triad in Arrant (2021). Or.1080 A.4.20 and T-S AS 64.238 seem to come from the same codex.

[5] On the notion of orthoepy and its relevance to Hebrew Bible reading traditions, see Khan (2018; 2020, I: 73–85, 99–105).

Since there is slight variation in the presentation of these signs from codex to codex, I will also give details of such variations and their significance for our understanding of the element's overall function. Note that throughout this article, all counts of features are approximate: due to damage, an exact number for a given feature cannot be relied upon. The counts do, however, represent the majority of the MS texts and so are reliable as broad indicators of the nature of the texts and their major trends.

1.1.1. *'Dagesh'* in *ʾalef*

In all manuscripts that show the Byzantine Triad of features, a dot appears in *ʾalef*, placed higher than the level of the vowels (so as not to be mistaken for a *ḥireq*), between the midstroke and left 'foot' of the *ʾalef*. For example, וְרָאָ֖ה 'and sees' (Num. 21.8) in T-S NS 21.6:

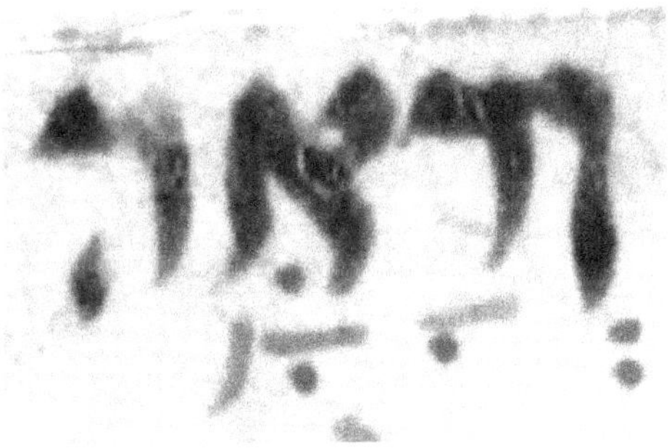

This sign occurs only in consonantal *ʾalef* (i.e., *ʾalef* with a vowel) in the following manuscripts:

- T-S NS 21.6 (~39 identified occurrences), e.g., יִשְׂרָאֵ֑ל 'Israel' (Num. 20.28), אַרְנֹ֖ן 'Arnon' (twice), נַּחֲלִיאֵ֑ל 'Nahaliʾel' (twice);

- T-S NS 248.5 (~14 identified occurrences), e.g., אֶת direct object marker (12 times); אַחַת 'one' (twice);
- T-S NS 248.11 (~26 identified occurrences), e.g., מִטֻּמְאֹת 'from impurity' (Lev. 16.19), אֶת direct object marker (15 times), וְאַחֲרֵי 'and after' (Lev. 16.26);
- T-S NS 248.12 (~95 identified occurrences), e.g., וְאֶת 'and' + direct object marker (41 times); אַהֲרֹן 'Aaron' (three times); וַיִּשָּׂאֻם 'and carried them' (Lev. 10.5);
- T-S NS 248.16 (~42 identified occurrences), e.g., קְרִיאֵי 'representatives of' (Num. 26.9), מֵאוֹת 'hundreds' (5 times), לְשָׁאוּל 'to Saul' (twice);
- T-S NS 248.17 (~19 identified occurrences), e.g., הָאָתוֹן 'the female donkey' (3 times), אֲדַבֵּר 'I speak' (Num. 22.35), מוֹאָב 'Mo'ab' (Num. 22.36);
- T-S Misc.2.75 (~66 identified occurrences), e.g., לְאִישׁ 'to/for a man' (7 times), אֲנָשִׁים 'men' (twice), לְאָחִיו 'to his brother' (three times);
- Or.1080 A.4.18 (~48 occurrences), e.g., הָאֱמֹרִי 'the Amorite' (6 times); אֶת direct object marker (15 times), מוֹאָב 'Mo'ab' (5 times);
- Or.1080 A.4.20 (~82 identified occurrences), e.g., מְאֹד 'very' (twice), אִם 'if' (6 times), תִּירְאוּ 'you (MPL) see' (3 times), and its join T-S AS64.238 (~38 identified occurrences), e.g., הָאֲנָשִׁים 'the men' (twice), וַיַּרְאוּם 'and they (M) showed them' (Num. 13.26), רָאִינוּ 'we saw' (3 times);
- Or.1080 A.4.3 (~28 identified occurrences), e.g., אֲשֶׁר 'that' (twice), תִּירְאוּ 'you (MPL) see' (twice), הָאָרֶץ 'the earth' (3 times).

In general, this marking is consistent and regular; each time a consonantal ʾalef appears in the text, it is marked with the sign.[6] Therefore, it apparently does not serve to mark the occasional *ʾalef* that readers might be prone to forget to pronounce.[7] Furthermore, as is evident from the examples above, the occurrence of the sign is not conditioned by any specific positioning within the word; it occurs in open syllables, closed syllables, and when a vocalic *ʾalef* is the first consonant in the word. Nor is the phenomenon grammatically restricted; it does not occur only in proper nouns, in prepositions, or with particular verbs, etc. It seems, then, that this sign functions to mark, specifically, the consonantal quality of vocalic *ʾalef* and does so as a typical feature of the diacritic system within these manuscripts. The apparent function of this *dagesh*-like sign was to ensure that consonantal *ʾalef* was not elided when the text was read aloud. The intention was to preserve the sound (and, thus, the syllabification).

Further support for this position may be seen in the tendency in these manuscripts to place a *rafe* on quiescent *ʾalef*, thereby explicitly marking that in such cases *ʾalef* is not pronounced as a consonant (Arrant 2020, 516–19).

---

[6] The exception in the present corpus is T-S NS 248.5, in which the sign in question appears in only two words.

[7] Such 'utilitarian' forms of non-standard vocalisation and diacritic use do indeed appear in Geniza Bible manuscripts. They seem to function almost like an *aide memoire* to help the reader pronounce only specific, perhaps troublesome, words correctly; for a discussion of Bible MSS with such utilitarian features, see chs 4 and 5 of Arrant (2021). This phenomenon of a *dagesh*-like sign in consonantal *ʾalef* is too regular for such a function to be the case here.

At this point one may question whether the sign should be considered a *dagesh* or *mappiq*. On the basis of its consistent occurrence within the manuscripts on every consonantal *ʾalef*, together with the frequent simultaneous placement of *rafe* on quiescent *ʾalef*, in a pattern that is not grammatically or semantically conditioned, the sign is more akin to *dagesh* than *mappiq*. A comprehensive discussion of this issue, which compiles relevant external evidence, is found in Khan (2020, I:135–50), who convincingly shows that grammarians of the time considered such a dot a *dagesh forte*, doubling the *ʾalef* to ensure its pronunciation when consonantal.[8]

1.1.2. *Shewa* on a Word-Final Guttural (*ʿayin* or *ḥet*)

The second feature of the Byzantine Triad of features that appears in all manuscripts,[9] is the placing of a *shewa* on word-final, otherwise unvocalised *ʿayin* or *ḥet*, e.g., וַיִּשְׁלַחְ 'and sent' (Num. 21.32) in Or.1080 A.4.18:

---

[8] One should also note, however, that MSS like these (and various related MSS) also extend the use of the *mappiq*: "Mappiq is typically also extended from word-final *heh* to word-initial and word-medial *heh* and has the same function of marking the *heh* as consonantal" (Arrant 2020, 516).

[9] Since words ending with an unvocalised *ʿayin* or *ḥet* are comparatively infrequent and because Geniza Bibles passages are often fragmentary, it may be that there are more Bibles with the Triad than are analysed in this article.

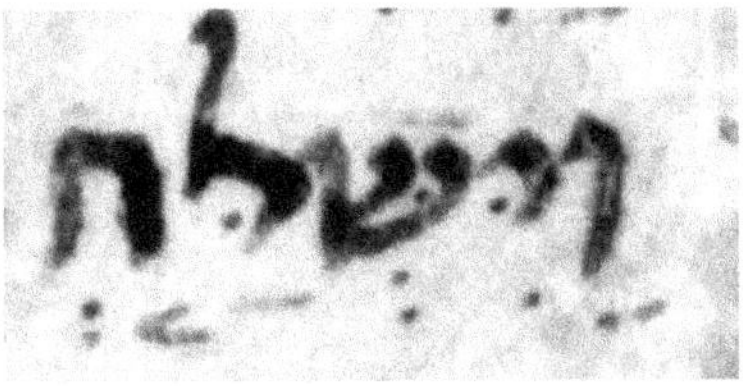

And on ʿ*ayin*, e.g., אֲשֶׁר־נִשְׁבַּעְ 'which swore' (Num. 14.16) in Or.1080 A.4.3:

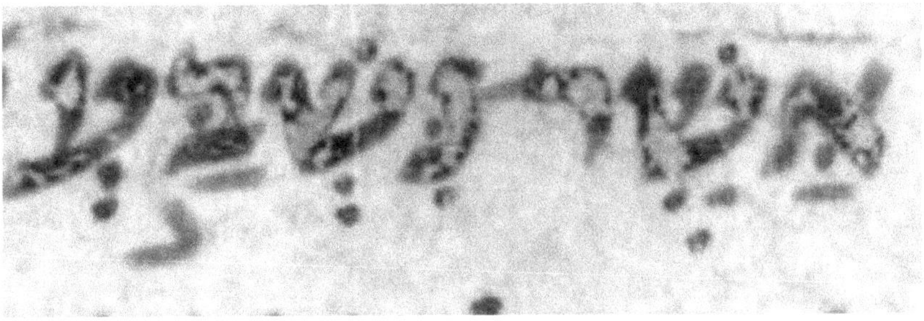

Examples of this vocalisation in manuscripts exhibiting the Triad:[10]

- T-S NS 21.6 (~3 identified occurrences), e.g., וַיִּשְׁמַּעְ 'and he listened' (Num. 21.3), וַיְּשַׁלַּחְ 'and he sent' (twice);
- T-S NS 248.11 (~7 identified occurrences), e.g., וְלָקַחְ 'and he will take' (4 times), לְשַׁלַּחְ 'to send' (twice), שֶׁבַעְ 'seven' (Lev. 16.19);

[10] Note that T-S NS 248.5 is an outlier regarding this feature: it was identified as a Byzantine Triad manuscript in Arrant (2020), but its word-final *shewa* does not occur with a guttural. Instead, it occurs three times in words ending in יו-, for example, עָלָיוְ 'upon it' (Exod. 30.9). I include it in this study because it was analysed in Arrant (2020). I view the *shewa* here as having essentially the same function as *shewa* with a word-final guttural: to signal to the reader that the final letter is consonantal and that the syllable is closed. T-S NS 248.12 also has this feature alongside *shewa* on word-final ʿ*ayin* and *ḥet*.

- T-S NS 248.12 (~26 times, including on word final יו-, see fn. 10), e.g., וַיִּקַּחְ 'and he took' (Lev. 8.27), הַנֹּגֵעְ 'who touches (M)' (4 times);
- T-S NS 248.16 (~9 identified occurrences), e.g., קֹרַחְ 'Koraḥ' (twice), לְשׁוּתֶלַחְ 'to Shuthelaḥ' (twice), לְבֶלַעְ 'to Belaʿ' (Num. 26.38);
- T-S NS 248.17 (~2 identified occurrences), e.g., וַיִּזְבַּחְ 'and he offered' (Num. 22.40), וַיִּשְׁלַחְ 'and he sent' (Num. 22.40);
- T-S Misc.2.75 (~ 2 identified occurrences), e.g., בְּהָנִיַחְ 'in giving rest' (Deut. 25.19, with *pataḥ* under the *yod* and a *shewa* under the *ḥet*) and תִּשְׁכָּחְ 'you (MS) will forget' (Deut. 25.19);
- Or.1080 A.4.18 (~5 identified occurrences), e.g., וַיִּקַחְ 'and he took' (twice), לְרֵיַחְ 'as an aroma' (Num. 28.24), וַיִּשְׁלַּחְ 'and he sent' (Num. 21.32; the *dagesh* in the *lamed* is non-standard as well);
- Or.1080 A.4.20 (once): סְלַחְ־נָא 'forgive please' (Num. 14.19);
- T-S AS 64.238 (~2 identified occurrences), e.g., שָׁלַחְ 'he sent' (Num. 13.16), שֶׁבַעְ 'seven' (Num. 13.21);
- Or.1080 A.4.3 (~3 identified occurrences), e.g., נִשְׁבַּעְ 'he swore' (Num. 14.16), וָפֶשַׁעְ 'and transgression' (Num. 14:18), סְלַחְ־נָא 'forgive please' (Num. 14.19).

Occasionally, a *naqdan* confused furtive *pataḥ* and a *shewa* meant to close a syllable. For example, Or.1080 A.4.18 has an instance where the *naqdan* placed a *shewa* where a furtive *pataḥ* would be expected: נִיחֹחְ (Num. 28.24). The manuscript does not show free interchange of vocalic *shewa* and *pataḥ* except in two places, both instances where the *naqdan* substituted a *pataḥ* or *ḥaṭef pataḥ* for *shewa*, e.g., יַעֲזֵ֗ר for יַעְזֵ֗ר 'Jazer' (Num. 21.32); יַ֫הֲצָה̄ for יַ֫הְצָה 'to Jahaz' (Num. 21.23). In the light of these cases, it appears that the interchange between furtive *pataḥ* and *shewa* here is, strictly speaking, a case not of vowel interchange, but of *shewa* mistakenly placed under a guttural as if it closed a syllable. This interpretation is strengthened by the placement of word-final *shewa* below all other word-final gutturals that close the syllable within this fragment.

This sign is used in an orthoepic manner, serving to preserve the pronunciation of the gutturals and/or the proper syllabification of the text. When unvocalised *ʿayin* or *ḥet* appear at the end of a word, they should invariably close the syllable. In this phonetic environment, especially without a vowel such as furtive *pataḥ*, the guttural is vulnerable to elision from pronunciation, due, it seems, to the weakening of gutturals in the reading tradition of the scribe. This results in the loss of the sound of the final consonant and creates an open syllable. Wherever there is a word-final unvocalised guttural letter, by placing a *shewa* beneath that letter, the *naqdan* cues the reader to stop and close the syllable, and, if possible, to try to pronounce the guttural.

1.1.3. Extended Use of *dagesh forte*

The third member of the Byzantine Triad of features is the placement of *dagesh forte* in letters which are not otherwise geminated according to the standard Tiberian Masoretic tradition. This sign can occur in a range of letters, with the pattern appearing to be idiosyncratic, its extent determined by the judgement of the individual scribe. It occurs with high frequency in each manuscript and has been studied in its own right in multiple pieces of scholarship (Morag 1959; Eldar 1978; Yeivin 1983; Khan 1991; 2017; Blapp 2017).

In this section, I am interested in determining whether there are meaningful details or patterns in the small variations of each scribe's use of extended *dagesh*. The aim is to identify conditioning factors and to assess the degree of variation in usage between MSS.[11] The factors in question are the letters that take extended *dagesh* and their phonological context, i.e., where they appear in the syllable, what sounds precede the geminated consonant, and patterns of accentuation. In this section, I will first present and describe the data, and thereafter engage with the scholarly discussion surrounding the interpretation of this feature.

In the present corpus of eleven MSS, the majority of occurrences of extended *dagesh* occur at word-initial syllable onset. Out of hundreds of cases of extended *dagesh*, only around 25 were found to occur in the middle of a word. Of these word-medial occurrences, the majority were located at syllable onset, after

[11] In some cases, the examination involved a closer look than was previously possible; for damaged MSS I used microscopy at ~50x magnification to help confirm or deny the possibility of the placement of *dagesh*. This proved helpful, in that it allowed for the discovery of more features than I originally found in my PhD research, and it also clarified points where, to the naked eye, a *dagesh* may seem to be present, but in fact the dot was a blemish on the writing surface and not ink. Due to this and to manuscript damage, any counts of the occurrence of this extended *dagesh* are approximations and should not be taken as exact.

both silent and vocalic *shewa*, for example, וְקַשְׂקֶּשֶׂת 'scales' (T-S NS 248.12, twice in the MS), שְׁלַחְתָּנוּ 'you (MS) sent us' (T-S AS 64.238, Num. 13.27). A small minority of these word-medial occurrences of extended *dagesh* were placed at the end of a syllable, for example, in the *samekh* that closes the middle syllable in וּכְנִסְּכָּהּ 'and like its drink offering' (Exod. 29.41, T-S NS 248.5) and in וּסְּעוּ 'and go out' (Num. 14.25, Or.1080 A.4.20). These *dagesh* signs *within* a word appear to be strategically placed where consonants cluster at a syllable juncture so as to avoid the elision of sounds at syllable onset or, rarely, syllable coda. They occur mostly in the consonants *ṭet*, *lamed*, *nun*, and *mem*, and once in *resh*: דֶּרֶּךְ 'way' (Num. 14.24, Or.1080 A.4.20).

Far more commonly, extended *dagesh* is placed in the first consonant of a word, typically when that consonant is *lamed*, *mem*, or *nun*, i.e., sonorant, especially nasal or labial, consonants. Infrequently, the *dagesh* is placed in word-initial *samekh*, *qof*, *ṣade*, and *zayin*. Extended *dagesh* at the beginning of a word appears to be more common when the final consonant of the preceding word is a sonorant (nasal or labial). It appears that the *dagesh* serves to force the reader to stop and pronounce what is effectively a doubled consonant, and to thereby distinguish between two similar (or identical) sounds.

Each manuscript, however, tends to have its own idiosyncratic usage of this sign, which I will now explore. Generally, the MSS discussed here tend to fall into two categories: those that use extended *dagesh* at every opportunity (nearly every word-initial *lamed*, *mem*, or *nun*), and those that are more selective (using extended *dagesh* at particular 'problem points' within the text). In

Table 1 below, I summarise the main consonants in which word-initial *dagesh* occurs, whether there is a trend for it to occur after a disjunctive or conjunctive accent, and whether it occurs after a word that ends in an open or closed syllable. Where a 'slight preference' is present, this indicates that the counts between options are too close (nearly equal), and so a definite preference or cannot be confidently stated given the condition of the MSS. See Table 1.

Table 1's data reveal the following general trends. First, *lamed*, *mem*, and *nun* are universally represented as taking extended *dagesh* in *every* manuscript. Less regularly it appears in sibilants, e.g., *ṣade*, *samekh*, and *zayin*. Second, with the exception of two MSS (with nearly equal representation), extended *dagesh* is more commonly written in word-initial consonants that follow a disjunctive accent. This being the case, the number of times in which word-initial extended *dagesh* is present following a conjunctive accent is sufficiently regular to argue that the type of accentuation in the preceding word is not a major conditioning factor that triggers the presence of extended *dagesh* in these MSS. The same mixed picture holds for word-initial extended *dagesh* following open or closed syllables. While there is a preference for closed syllables in all but one manuscript, this preference is not strong enough for us to definitively say that extended *dagesh* occurs characteristically after a closed syllable and not after open syllables. Therefore, the data appear to show that accentuation and syllable structure are not determinative factors for the placement of the sign.[12]

[12] Arrant (2020, 516ff.; 2021, 489) states that this *dagesh* occurs after a vowelless consonant, summarising the current scholarly consensus on extended *dagesh*. The data here clarify the picture: the relevant *dagesh tends*

Table 1: Use of extended *dagesh* in word-initial consonants

Classmark (description of application)	Consonants	Preference for occurring after disjunctive/ conjunctive accent	Preference for occurring after open/closed syllable
T-S A21.6 (consistently, but not extensively)	mainly: ל, מ, נ; occasionally: ס	disjunctive (slight)	closed (definite: ~21 to ~12)
T-S NS 248.11 (consistently, but not extensively)	mainly: ל, מ; occasionally: ס	disjunctive (slight)	closed (definite: ~15 to ~4)
T-S NS 248.12 (extensively, to a lot of letters, in a wide array of contexts)	mainly: ל, מ, צ; occasionally: ט, נ, ק, ז	disjunctive (strong: ~51 to ~17)	closed (definite: ~48 to ~22)
T-S NS 248.16 (extensively to word-initial ל and מ)	mainly: ל, מ; once: צ, ק	disjunctive (strong: ~71 to 13)	closed (definite: ~50 to ~32)
T-S NS 248.17 (selectively; see discussion below)	mainly: ל, מ; once: נ	disjunctive (slight)	closed (slight)
T-S NS 248.5 (selectively; see discussion below)	twice: ל	disjunctive: 1x conjunctive: 1x	closed: 1x open: 1x
T-S AS 64.238 + Or.1080 A.4.20 (consistently, but not extensively)	mainly: ל, מ, נ; occasionally: ז, ט, ס, צ, ק	disjunctive (slight)	closed (definite: ~19 to ~3)
Or.1080 A.4.3 (consistently, but not extensively)	mainly: ל, מ, נ; occasionally: ס, ק	disjunctive (definite: ~22 to ~13)	closed (slight)
Or.1080 A.4.18 (extensively)	mainly: ל, מ; occasionally: ז (1x), נ, ס, צ, ק (1x)	nearly equal (disjunctive ~25, conjunctive ~22)	equal
Or.1080 A.4.20 (consistently, but not extensively)	mainly: ל, מ, נ; occasionally: ז, ט, ס, צ	disjunctive (slight)	closed (definite: ~28 to ~11)

to occur after a vowelless consonant, but a significant number occur after an open syllable, i.e., one that ends in a vowel.

T-S Misc.2.75 (extensively)	mainly: ל, מ, נ; occasionally: ז, צ	disjunctive (definite: ~25 to ~12)	open (definite: ~25 to ~14)

Given the data above, I would argue that extended *dagesh* is primarily conditioned by consonant clusters involving *lamed*, *mem*, and *nun*, when these letters are the second consonant in a two-consonant cluster. Some manuscripts apply this feature extensively, so that nearly every word-initial *lamed, mem*, or *nun* has a *dagesh*. Some apply it consistently, but not universally. But most telling are those that apply the feature selectively. This is enlightening, as we can see scribal choice at play in the use of the sign. To demonstrate this, I will briefly discuss the two MSS which apply extended *dagesh* only in certain phonological contexts: T-S NS 248.5 and T-S NS 248.17.

T-S NS 248.5

This manuscript has the smallest degree of usage of extended *dagesh*. It occurs word-initially only twice and word-internally once. The word-internal occurrence is וּכְנִסְּכָּהּ for וּכְנִסְכָּהּ 'and like its drink offering' (Exod. 29.41). The *dagesh* here appears to distinguish the *samekh* from the *kaf* and prevent the merging of the sounds or the eliding of the *samekh*. The other two uses of extended *dagesh* in this manuscript are in the *lameds* in the phrase אֲקַדֵּשׁ לְּכַהֵן לִּי 'I will consecrate [them] to minister to me' (Exod. 29.44). Again, the placement in consonant clusters reinforces the distinction between sounds, but it is more noticeable in the second occurrence, where the *dagesh* is placed in a *lamed* that occurs after another sonorant (*nun*). It seems that the *dagesh* was placed in locations that may have been tricky for a reader to pronounce accurately when reading quickly.

T-S NS 248.17

While this manuscript includes this feature to a far greater degree than T-S NS 248.5 (see above), its usage is still comparatively infrequent relative to the other MSS studied in this article. I was able to count only 19 instances of extended *dagesh* in this manuscript, whereas in the other manuscripts the occurrences typically trend up past 50 times. The instances where extended *dagesh* occurs are either where there is vowel harmony (in the case of an open syllable before the extended *dagesh*), or where there are consonants between the two words which have points of articulation that are close to each other (such as a dental following a bilabial). The data can be broken down as follows:

- *dagesh* in word-initial alveolar *lamed*—occurs after *mem* (bilabial): בִּלְעָ֖ם לְּבָלָ֑ק 'Bilʿam to Balak' (Num. 23.3) and בִּלְעָם֙ לְּאָת֔וֹן 'Bilʿam to the donkey' (Num. 22.29); after *taw* and *resh*:[13] לַעֲשׂ֣וֹת לְּךָ֑ 'to do to you' (Num. 22.30), וַיֹּ֖אמֶר לְּֽא, 'and he said "No."' (Num. 22.30); occurs after long vowels in an open syllable (~6 times), e.g., כֻּלּ֖וֹ לְּֽא 'and all of them [you will] not [see]' (Num. 23.13), אֵלֶ֙יךָ֙ לִּקְרֹא '[I sent] to you to invite [you]' (Num. 22.37); occurs after a guttural rein-

[13] We do not know, of course, if this *resh* was realised as an alveolar or uvular. In the example cited, it would have been pronounced as a uvular rhotic in the standard Tiberian pronunciation tradition (Khan 2020, I:223–34).

forced with a *shewa* (once): וַיְשַׁלַּח לְבִלְעָם,'and he sent to Bilʿam' (Num. 22.40);

- *dagesh* in word-initial *mem* (bilabial)—occurs after *resh* and *lamed* (three times): וּדְבַר מַה 'and whatever [is revealed' (Num. 23.3), עַל־מָּה 'why' (Num. 22.32), עִיר מּוֹאָב 'the city of Moab' (Num. 22.36); occurs after a labial (twice): מוֹאָב מֵּהַרְרֵי '...Moab from the hills of...' (Num. 23.7), לְבִלְעָם מֶּה '...to Bilʿam "what..."' (Num. 22.28); occurs after a dorsal consonant (twice): בָלָק מֶּלֶךְ '...Balak king [of Moab]' (Num. 23.7), מֶּלֶךְ־מוֹאָב 'king of Moab' (Num. 23.7); occurs after a diphthong (once): עָלַי מֵּעוֹדְךָ 'upon me, your whole life' (Num. 22.30);
- *dagesh* in word-initial *nun*: occurs after a diphthong (once): יְהוָה נִּצָּב '[the angel of] the LORD standing' (Num. 22.31).

For the most part, these occurrences make sense if conceived in terms of proximity in points of articulation: where there is a cluster of coronal and labial consonants, a *dagesh* is placed to distinguish one consonant from the other.

The absence of this feature in other locations may serve to explain such selectivity—that it is primarily difficult consonant clusters which trigger the placement of extended *dagesh* in select manuscripts. In MSS that use this feature comprehensively, it appears that the usage has become systematic in its application throughout the whole of the text, particularly for *lamed*, *mem*, and *nun*. I would argue that for such comprehensive occurrences, the original intention is still the same, but the feature spread to all occurrences as a normalising function of the diacritic.[14]

These data offer some modifications to the scholarly discussion on extended *dagesh*. Yeivin (1983, 297) and Khan (2017, 267) discuss extended *dagesh* at word-initial syllable onset as typically occurring after a closed syllable, and at word-medial syllable onset as typically following silent shewa (Khan 2017, 267) and/or differentiating between two similar letters (Yeivin 1983, 297). Khan (2017, 267–69) describes cases of extended *dagesh* also occurring in a *deḥiq* structure, i.e., a *dagesh* placed word-initially following a word with a conjunctive accent ending in an unstressed open syllable. Moreover, scholars debate the phonetic function of the sign, with Morag arguing that these signs break syllable boundaries, and Eldar (1978, 125–43) terming the sign דגש מפריד 'separative *dagesh*', and Khan concluding that the sign is a *dagesh forte* functioning orthoepically to distinguish syllable and consonant divisions.

These astute observations are not contradicted by the Byzantine Triad MSS presented here. I would argue, however, that the data show some additional trends that may (depending on further research) prove unique to MSS characterised by the Byzantine Triad of features. First, in these latter MSS, extended *dagesh* does not show a strong preference for occurring after a closed syllable, but rather, often occurs after open syllables. Moreover, this goes beyond a classic *deḥiq* structure, in that after

[14] Khan (2017, 267–68) gives an excellent analysis of the phonological impact of this sign to distinguish the syllables and to reinforce the pronunciation of the second element in a syllable division.

an open syllable, the sign can occur regardless of whether the preceding accent is conjunctive or disjunctive and regardless of whether the preceding syllable is stressed or unstressed. Therefore, while MSS seem to show a slight preference for the sign after disjunctive accents and closed syllables, this is by no means the typical presentation of the feature. Indeed, it appears that the majority of these MSS take extended *dagesh* according to the conditioning factors discussed in scholarship, but further extend it, placing it in any word-initial *lamed*, *mem*, or *nun* by default. In the case of those MSS where the feature is selectively placed, the primary conditioning factor is the desire to ensure careful reading at difficult consonant clusters across words, whatever the preceding syllable's status or accentuation. My claim, therefore, is that these MSS represent one *type* of extended *dagesh* within the overall phenomenon.[15]

A further observation that has come to light in one of the MSS supports this claim. T-S NS 21.6 adds a *paseq* between the last two words of וַיִּדַּ֨ר יִשְׂרָאֵ֥ל נֶ֛דֶר 'and Israel made a vow' (Num. 21.2):

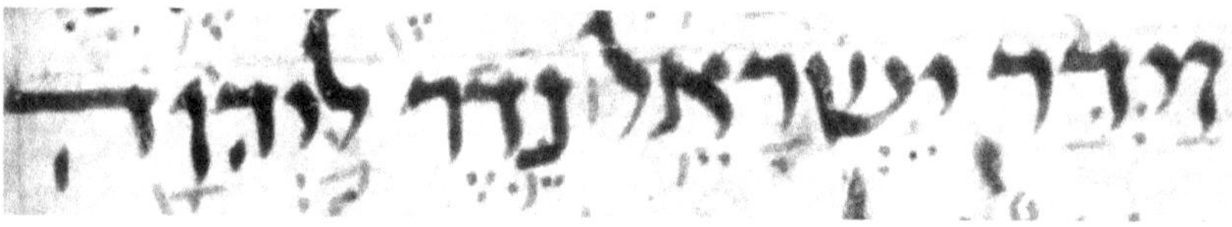

This sign is not attested in BHS/L at this location, but it is clearly a *paseq*, since the sign is identical to other instances of *paseq* within the MS. Here its function appears to be to enhance further

[15] It is to be noted that Yeivin (1983) and Khan (2017) both acknowledge that within the patterns they describe, there are many forms of variation and exceptions. The case of these MSS appears to be such an instance.

the distinction between the *lamed* and the *nun*, forcing the reader to stop and pronounce the words separately. This instance of non-standard accentuation clearly correlates with other orthoepic functions of the *dagesh* in the oral reading of the text.

1.2. The Features in Tandem

We have seen in the above sections the individual presentation of each component of the Byzantine Triad of features. As these features co-occur in the manuscripts, however, they should be seen as complementing one another. In this sense, the Triad appears to be an attempt to preserve accuracy in the reading, particularly by reinforcing correct syllabification. The insertion of a *dagesh* preserves the pronunciation of vocalic *ʾalef* by making the reader pause, and thereby ensures that the syllable remains intact. By marking word-final unvocalised gutturals, the *shewa* reminds the reader that the syllable is closed (and also helps to preserve the pronunciation, however weak, of the guttural). Finally, by placing a *dagesh* in consonant clusters that are particularly vulnerable, the syllabification both within words and between words is preserved by signalling to the reader to pronounce with added force consonants at risk of being slurred over during reading.

It is noteworthy that the vocalisers of these texts made creative use of the Tiberian system of signs to encourage correct syllabification through extending the rules of their placement. None of the signs are technically used incorrectly with regards to its essential function: the *dagesh forte* sign is used here, as it is in masoretic codices, to geminate the consonant. Likewise, silent *shewa* here closes syllables according to its standard function. Indeed, even *dagesh* in *ʾalef* is attested in masoretic codices, something Khan discusses extensively (2020, I:135–50). What appears to have happened in Bibles with the Byzantine Triad of features is that the function of the signs is used creatively, with non-standard placement, to promote a more careful, masoretic reading.[16]

1.3. Vowel Sign Interchange Patterns Associated with the Byzantine Triad of Features

Manuscripts with the Byzantine Triad of features described above were found in Arrant (2020; 2021) to have important distinctions when compared with a large number of Bibles from the same corpus. A characteristic phenomenon in many 'near-model' and 'common' Bibles from the Cairo Geniza is the presence of a dizzying array of vowel sign interchanges in seemingly idiosyncratic ways from manuscript to manuscript. Especially in Arrant (2021), it was established that such interchanges are neither random nor meaningless. Different patterns of vowel sign inter-

[16] There are a few other non-standard features that characterise these manuscripts, but not at the consistent level of a pattern: there are occasional irregularities in *begedkefet* notation; many of these Byzantine Triad MSS (along with other MSS with close palaeographies) place the *shin* dot within the *shin* (or even double the dot, with a dot inside the *shin* and a dot atop the *shin*); at times the *dagesh* in the *zayin* of הזה 'this' is dropped. These features deserve further exploration outside of the current study.

change correlate statistically with codicological features, regional distinctions in palaeography, and each other in distinct patterns that are linguistically meaningful.[17]

Arrant (2020) gives an overview of the Triad features and vowel sign interchanges of eight MSS discussed in the present study: T-S NS 21.6, T-S NS 248.5, T-S NS 248.11, T-S NS 248.12, T-S NS 248.16, T-S NS 248.17, T-S Misc.2.75, and Or.1080 A.4.18. As the present study examines an additional three MSS—T-S AS 64.238, Or.1080 A.4.20, and Or.1080 A.4.3—it provides an updated picture of the vowel sign interchange data available for Bibles with the Byzantine Triad of features.

Arrant (2020, 514) notes that the MSS analysed in that study presented interchange patterns fitting Schema Patterns X, Y, 1, and 1a. To review:

- Pattern X: MSS with this pattern have regular interchange of *shewa* (usually vocalic) with *pataḥ*, indicating that the MSS belong to a tradition which pronounced *shewa* as [a].
- Pattern Y: MSS with this pattern feature a three-way interchange of *shewa*, *ḥireq*, and *ṣere*, probably reflecting raising of the quality of vocalic *shewa*.
- Pattern 1: in MSS with this pattern, *pataḥ* and *qameṣ* freely interchange, on the one hand, and *ṣere* and *segol* freely interchange, on the other. There is no exchange between *a*-

[17] The statistical backing for this correlation is strong; approximately 409 codices (out of around 1400 codices comprising 1851 leaves) in the corpus of Arrant (2020; 2021) had such 'non-standard' Tiberian vocalisation and, so, can be considered sufficient for a representative sample. Cf. Arrant (2021, 29–63) for the statistical methodology.

and *e*-class vowels. This effectively reduces the vowel inventory to five, with single /a/ and /e/ vowels.

- Pattern 1a: related to, but unlike Pattern 1, in this pattern *qameṣ* and *pataḥ* remain distinct (so that there are two realisations *a*-class vowels), but *ṣere* and *segol* have merged into a single *e*-class vowel (as indicated by their free interchange throughout the manuscript in question).

In Arrant (2020; 2021), patterns X and Y were described as 'notational' interchanges, where vocalic *shewa* was simply replaced with the vowel sign of the equivalent vocalic quality, i.e., *pataḥ*, *ṣere*, or *ḥireq*, depending on the pattern.[18] Patterns 1 and 1a consist of true phonological interchanges of vowels, reflecting a vowel system in the Hebrew pronunciation of the MSS that differed from that of the standard Tiberian pronunciation. Such an inventory has been identified as 'Palestinian' in quality (Heijmans 2013). Thus, it appears that the vocalisers of these MSS sought to preserve syllable structure according to the rules of the Tiberian Masoretic system, though their individual phonological profile differed along the trend of realising vocalic *shewa* as a raised vowel, and in some MSS, of reducing the vocalic inventory to that of a five-vowel system of pronunciation, which is characteristic of the Palestinian pronunciation tradition.

---

[18] It is important to distinguish the two: the interchange between *ṣere* and *segol* is a true vowel interchange, where the two /e/ vowels have merged into one pronunciation. The interchange of high vowels with *shewa*—which in these Bibles had an /e/ realisation (rather than the /a/ realisation of Pattern X)—is a notational, rather than a phonetic, distinction.

The MSS analysed in Arrant (2020) were of professional codicological quality. Their diacritic differences show striving towards the preservation of the syllabification and pronunciation of the consonants, while their vowel sign interchanges may reflect the realities of Hebrew pronunciation in the region(s) in which they were copied and used. As mentioned above, they range in palaeography from Italian to Levantine Oriental, and their vowel sign interchange (with its Palestinian Hebrew associations) appears to go in hand with such regional designations. In this study we have added three additional fragments (two of which are related) which appear to be codicologically and palaeographically similar to the MSS studied in Arrant (2020), with the exception of one (discussed below). However, they are less formal than the MSS studied in Arrant (2020); for example, they lack *masora*, and one is smaller and has only one column. The three fragments here (T-S AS 64.238, Or.1080 A.4.20, and Or.1080 A.4.3), therefore, represent a slight expansion in terms of codicological features from the originally identified Byzantine Triad group. Here, therefore, we explore whether there is a slightly wider profile of vocalic interchange present alongside a slightly wider codicological and palaeographic range.[19]

[19] One may notice here my reticence to mention palaeographic dating. I am hesitant to ascribe dates to manuscript fragments, mainly because both script styles and linguistic features can become fossilised and persist for quite some time. While I do give tentative dating estimates below, it is more meaningful here, in my opinion, to show relationships between objectively verifiable features (such as similarity of script or vowel sign interchange), than to make an argument for trends based on

Table 2 summarises the vowel interchanges in the 2020 case study contrasted with those of the three additional manuscripts included in this study.

Table 2: Comparative summary of vowel interchanges in MSS studied in Arrant (2020; 2021); NI = notational interchange; VSI = vowel sign interchange reflecting deviation from Tiberian pronunciation; numbers in parentheses indicate count of occurrences

2020 Case Study 'Near-Model' Torahs
Or.1080 A.4.18: Patterns X, Y, 1 NI: *pataḥ/ḥaṭef pataḥ* and (silent) *shewa* (1) VSI: *pataḥ* for *qameṣ* (2); *qameṣ* for *pataḥ* (9); *segol* for *ṣere* (2); *ṣere* for *segol* (1); *ṣere* for *ḥireq* (1); *ṣere* for *pataḥ** (1) *Note minimal interchange between *ṣere* and *pataḥ*, violating Pattern 1.
T-S NS 248.11: Patterns X, 1 NI: *pataḥ* for *ḥaṭef pataḥ* (5) VSI: *segol* for *ḥaṭef pataḥ** (1); *shewa* for *pataḥ* (1); *segol* for *ṣere* (1); *ṣere* for *segol* (1); *pataḥ* for *qameṣ* (1) *כַּאֶשֶׁר for כַּאֲשֶׁר (Lev. 16.15) appears to be a unique case of vowel harmony; every other instance of אֲשֶׁר in the MS is vocalised with *pataḥ* instead of *ḥaṭef pataḥ* (and no *pataḥ-segol* interchange).
T-S NS 248.17: Pattern 1?* VSI: *ḥireq* for *pataḥ* (1): מִלְאַךְ for מַלְאַךְ (Num. 22.35); *qameṣ* for *pataḥ* (1) וַיִּזְבָּח for וַיִּזְבַּח (Num. 22.40) *This manuscript is an outlier; unlike most of the other manuscripts, it does not have any notational interchange, and its vowel interchanges are very minimal.
T-S NS 21.6: Patterns 1, Y* VSI: *pataḥ* for *qameṣ* (1); *shewa* for *ḥireq* (5); *ṣere* for *segol* (2) *Like T-S NS 248.17, this manuscript has no notational interchange.
T-S Misc.2.75: Patterns X, 1a[20] VSI: *shewa* for *qameṣ* (1); *ṣere* for *segol* (1)

palaeographic dating (though this does not reduce my estimation of the usefulness of palaeographic dating in other scientific contexts).

[20] Contrary to my 2020 article that identified it erroneously as Pattern Y, the MS does not interchange *shewa*, *ḥireq*, and *segol*.

T-S NS 248.5: Patterns X, 2a NI: *ḥaṭef pataḥ* for *pataḥ* (1); *ḥaṭef qameṣ* for *qameṣ* (1) VSI: *qameṣ* for *pataḥ* (1); *qameṣ* for *segol* (1); *segol* for *ṣere* (1); *shewa* for *pataḥ* (4); *shewa* for *segol* (1)
T-S NS 248.12: Pattern Y? VSI: *shewa* for *segol* (2)
T-S NS 248.16: Patterns Y NI: *ḥaṭef pataḥ* for *shewa* (1); *ḥaṭef qameṣ* for *qameṣ* (1) VSI: *ḥireq* for *shewa* (1); *ḥireq* for *shureq* (1), *pataḥ* for *qameṣ** (1) *Some minimal indication of Pattern 1, but incomplete.
2021 PhD Torahs (with basic codicological information)
T-S AS64.238 (+ join with OR.1080 A.4.20; two-column parchment codex, portrait format,[21] no Masoretic notes): Pattern X NI: *pataḥ* for *ḥaṭef pataḥ* (6); *pataḥ* for *shewa* (1); *shewa* for furtive *pataḥ* (1); *shewa* for *ḥaṭef pataḥ* (4) VSI: *qameṣ* for *pataḥ** (1) **Some minimal indication of Pattern 1, but incomplete.
Or.1080 A.4.20 (two-column parchment codex, portrait format, no Masoretic notes): Patterns X, 2a NI: *ḥaṭef pataḥ* for *pataḥ* (1); *pataḥ* for *ḥaṭef pataḥ* (9); *shewa* for *pataḥ* (2); *segol* for *ḥaṭef segol* (1); *shureq* for *qubbuṣ* (2); *shureq* for *shewa** (1) VSI: *pataḥ* for *segol* (1); *qameṣ* for *pataḥ* (1) *The *shureq* for *shewa* occurs once, on וּזַרְעוֹ for וְזַרְעוֹ (Num. 14.24).
Or.1080 A.4.3 (1 column parchment codex, landscape format, no Masoretic notes) **Patterns X, 2b** NI: *ḥaṭef pataḥ* for *pataḥ* (6); *shewa* for furtive *pataḥ* (2); *shewa* for *ḥaṭef pataḥ* (3) VSI: *pataḥ* for *segol* (1); *segol* for *ṣere* (1); *ṣere* for *segol* (2)

The table above indicates a trend of interchange consistent with Patterns X, Y, 1, and 1a. A minority of MSS in the 2020 case study have vowel sign interchange patterns that are typically seen in Bibles where the vowel inventory is reduced under (presumably) Arabic phonological influence (specifically, patterns 2a and 2b) (see Arrant 2021, 157ff.). Two of the additional three MSS included in the present study also have 2a/2b.

---

[21] Portrait format = length (of a page) > width; landscape format: width > length.

The defining feature of these MSS as a whole seems to be the rarity of interchange phenomena; when vowel sign interchanges occur, they are not pervasive, but usually occur only once or twice. Notational interchanges tend to happen with greater frequency than vowel sign interchanges. There seems to be no meaningful difference between the MSS in the 2020 case study and the additional three MSS in terms of vowel sign or notational interchanges.

Therefore, the profile of Byzantine Triad Bibles seems to be a tendency for:

- frequent notational interchange between *ḥaṭef* vowels, *pataḥ*, and *shewa*;
- relative infrequency of vowel sign interchanges indicative of 'Palestinian' Hebrew phonology (Patterns Y, 1, 1a);
- outliers with very minimal interchanges indicative of a reduced vowel inventory (in Patterns 2a and 2b).

This picture is consistent, then, with a general 'Palestino-Tiberian' association of linguistic phenomena regarding vocalisation.

2.0. The 'Book-Type' of the Byzantine Triad of Features

As Arrant (2020; 2021) has demonstrated that vocalisation and codicological features are mutually informative and that patterns between vocalisation and codicology often correlate, only a few cursory observations about the codicology of Byzantine Triad Bibles are necessary. Arrant (2020) contextualised the 'near-model' Byzantine Triad MSS (two–three columns, on parchment, with partial masoretic notes) among other 'near-model' Bibles lacking the Byzantine Triad. Arrant (2021) dealt with the three additional, 'non-model' Byzantine Triad MSS within the context of other Bibles without the Triad, but with a similar codicology.[22] Because Bible codices with the Byzantine Triad of features share codicological styles with Bibles that lack these features, they are not completely codicologically distinct from Bibles with standard and non-standard Tiberian vocalisation. However, their codicilogy is still informative as to the contexts in which they were used. In this section I will discuss the codicological relationship between 'near-model' and 'non-model' Bibles with the Triad features, give observations on their palaeographic range, and make inferences about their practical function(s).

2.1. Near-Model Byzantine Triad Codices

The codices examined in Arrant (2020) were 'near-model': all are written on parchment and have partial masoretic notes. The first observation of note is that all but one of these Byzantine Triad codices (T-S NS 248.12) has two columns rather than three and, so, are by default smaller and less grandiose than full, exemplary, three-column Masoretic Bibles. They are ruled, tend to be pricked on the outside margin (T-S Misc.2.75 is pricked on both margins, while Or.1080 A.4.20 and T-S AS 64.238 are not pricked at all). They are plain, with no illumination or ornate decoration. Their script is smaller than that seen in the grandiose Oriental exemplary codices (though this is expected, as smaller script is typical of Italian, Byzantine, and Southwestern Oriental script types). All

[22] See Arrant (2021, chs. 3–4) for a contextualised discussion of Byzantine 'Trio' Bibles within the larger corpus.

of them have *masora parva*, but not *masora magna*. They range in size from 18.4–31.7 cm long x 15.65–25.3 cm wide, i.e., on the smaller side of Bible codices.[23] They all have a portrait format (length greater than width). They have a range of 19–27 lines per page. Indeed, the combination of their general minimalist appearance, skilled writing, careful vocalisation, and small size seems to indicate that these codices were carefully written, yet intended for practical use.

They have the following palaeographic and codicological ranges:

- T-S Misc.2.75: two columns, 26.6 x 22.7 cm, 26 lines, Italian, 12th or 13th c.
- T-S NS 21.6: two columns, 21 x 19.8 cm, 20 lines, Italian-Byzantine, probably 12th c.
- Or.1080 A.4.18: two columns, 18.4 x 15.6 cm, 19 lines, Italian, 12th c.
- T-S NS 248.5: two columns, 22.2 x 9.2 cm, 21 lines, Levantine Oriental-Byzantine (from the Levant; Syria-Palestine, but not an earlier calligraphic hand such as seen in the Aleppo Codex; appears to have some scattered 'Byzantine' features).
- T-S NS 248.11: two columns, 21.4 x 19 cm, 23 lines, Levantine Oriental-Byzantine.

[23] For example, Arrant (2020) discusses a type of Bible there termed 'Large Monumental Levantine Codex', which ranges in size from 35–38.2 cm long and 32–35 cm wide, and had 25–30 lines. Multiple groups are discussed in Arrant (2020; 2021), all of which are significantly larger than the eleven MSS studied here.

Figure 1: Near-Model Byzantine Triad Codices: T-S Misc.2.75r (top left), T-S NS 248.11r (top right), Or.1080 A.4.18v (bottom)

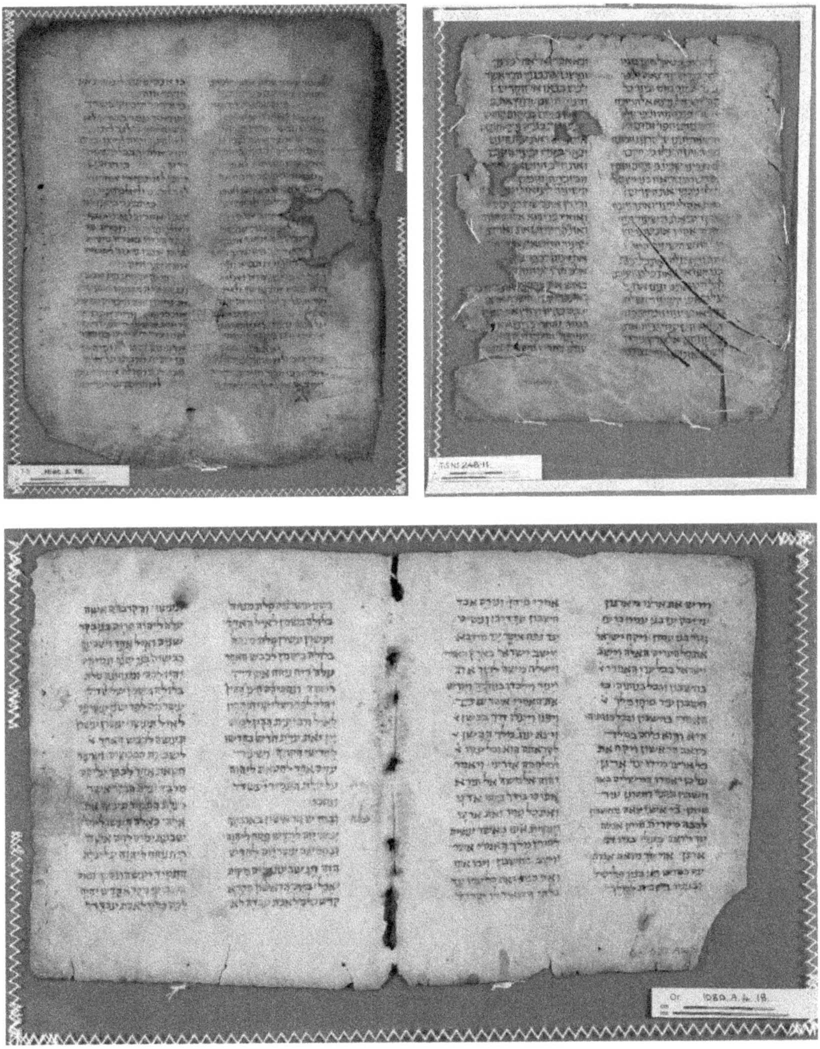

- T-S NS 248.17: two columns, 24.3 x 19.3 cm, 23 lines, Levantine Oriental-Byzantine.
- T-S NS 248.12: two columns, 31.7 x 25.3 cm, 27 lines, Levantine Oriental-Byzantine.
- T-S NS 248.16: two columns, 21.7 x 23.1 cm, 20 lines, Italian-Byzantine.

2.2. 'Non-Model' Byzantine Triad Codices

The three additional codices studied here were analysed in Arrant (2021). As the thesis did not study any 'near-model' codices, these are slightly distinct from the group above. Two of the fragments are similar to the above 'near-model' group in terms of size, column number, and number of lines:

- Or.1080 A.4.20: two columns. 22.2 x 19.3 cm, 23 lines, Levantine Oriental to Byzantine
- T-S AS 64.238: two columns. 20.7 x 18.9 cm, 23 lines, Levantine Oriental to Byzantine

Further analysis of the handwriting and the fact that they have consecutive passages (T-S AS 64.238 has Num. 13.7–14.6, Or.1080 A.4.20 Num. 14.7–35) indicates that they are in fact two leaves from the same Bible codex. Visually, they are nearly identical to the MSS of the above group, except that they lack masoretic notation.

Our final Bible, Or.1080 A.4.3, is unique. It is a single-column parchment codex in landscape format (12.5 cm long x 16.1 cm wide). It appears to have Italian (circa 12th c.) palaeography. Unlike the other two Bibles here or those in the near-model

Figure 2: 'Non-Model' Byzantine Triad Codices: Or.1080 A.4.20r (top left), T-S AS 64.238r (top right), and Or.1080 A.4.3v (bottom)

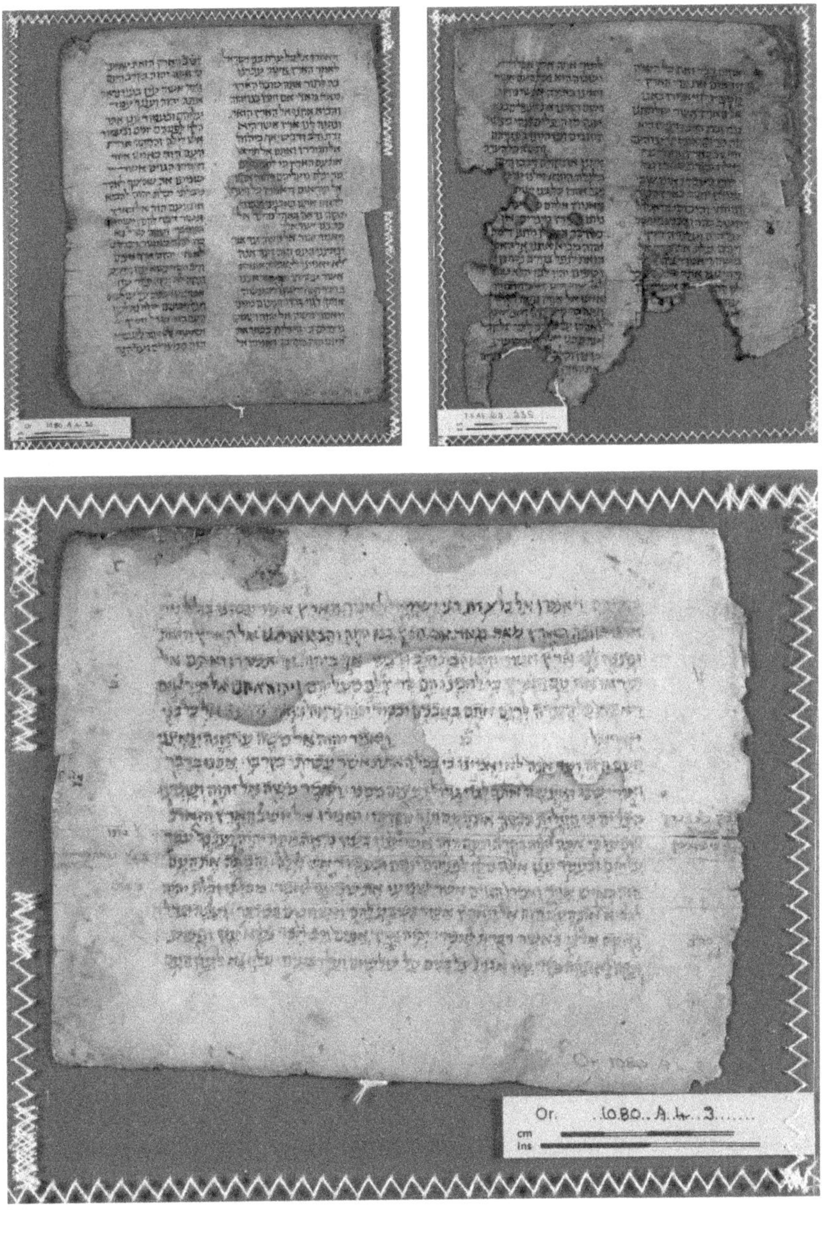

group, it has only 15 lines per page. Its compact size, small writing, wide margins, and format make it appear informal, but the quality of the script is exquisite.

It appears that, with the exception of Or.1080 A.4.3 (because of its landscape format), the Bibles with the Byzantine Triad of features are very similar in appearance and come from a restricted range of palaeographic regions.

Given their features, what can we infer about their purpose? We must remember the careful vocalisation which seeks to ensure correct syllabification and pronunciation of gutturals. Such usage of the signs appears to indicate that these manuscripts were read aloud, as the signs themselves have no independent grammatical meaning except to ensure the prescribed syllable pronunciation. One could read the text silently without these signs and still grasp the correct grammar and understand the content. When read aloud these signs fulfil their purpose.

The small size of these Bibles indicates that they were not grandiose endeavours and were not meant to be perfect specimens of an elaborate, beautiful, masoretic work. They are carefully made and vocalised, yet still have an informal character. While we can only guess as to whether they were read at home, or in the synagogue, or both, we can clearly see that they were to be studied and read aloud. The rewriting on T-S AS 64.238, indicates that it was used for quite some time and may have needed repair. I propose that they may have been made for the purpose of study and preparation for reading the Torah aloud in a didactic setting (whether a synagogue service or at home) and, therefore, are 'personal', yet ritualistic. They are small enough to be easily carried and held, yet written with sufficient care to be professional, skilful, aesthetically pleasing, and textually reliable.

3.0. Conclusions

This article has assessed eleven Bible codices from the Geniza which are strongly similar on linguistic and codicological grounds. In conclusion, I will briefly discuss their diacritic, codicological, and palaeographic connections to other kinds of Bibles, and finally, the terminology we may choose to use to describe them.

3.1. Vocalisation: Connections to 'Extended Tiberian'

These Bibles have many of the features that scholars have come to associate with 'Extended Tiberian' vocalisation, to the degree that they may be considered an integral part of that phenomenon. However, they are a distinctive subgroup of the extended Tiberian tradition in their manifestation of particular features. These include their regular application of *shewa* to word-final gutturals, the further extension of what we typically consider 'extended *dagesh*' to cover nearly all instances where a sonorant, especially nasal or labial, consonant begins a word (regardless of the syllable or accentuation status of the preceding word), and their placement of *dagesh* in consonantal *ʾalef*. This subtype of Extended Tiberian is closely related to Palestino-Tiberian, with its close association with Palestinian pronunciation. Further research may be necessary to distinguish any other patterns within such MSS.

3.2. Codicology and Palaeography: Connections from the Levant to Italy

The Bibles in this study have been assessed codicologically in terms of functional implications. We have also noted that they seem to represent a palaeographic range from the Levant up to Italy. The book type represented has connections to other Bibles studied in Arrant (2020, esp. 536; 2021, esp. 220) from Italy, and the handwriting and extended vocalisation is very similar to that of *Codex Reuchlinianus*, for example. Though they are few, I would argue that such coherence is potentially evidence of scribal connections through regions, from the Levant, through Syria and Greece, into Italy, and then up into Ashkenaz.[24]

3.3. A 'Byzantine' Triad of Features?

The final aspect of these Bibles that I will address here is the adjective which I have used to describe them: 'Byzantine'. It is simultaneously accurate, and in some ways also misleading. It is true that the script type of these Bibles ranges from Italian, to Italian-Byzantine, to Levantine Oriental-Byzantine. The original motivation for calling them Byzantine was because this range of representation covers the region of Western Asia Minor and slightly beyond, up to Italy and down to Palestine. Therefore, 'Italian-

[24] Note that Khan and other scholars also trace the features of Extended Tiberian from Italy up into Ashkenaz (cf. Khan, 2017, 270). The importance of this observation for our understanding of the history of the transmission of the Hebrew Bible in the medieval period will be explored further in the future expanded and updated publication of my PhD thesis.

Levantine' is also an accurate descriptor. However, this is only a palaeographic factor. Their unique pattern of vocalisation also can be described in ways other than three chosen features; for example, these three features do not cover the extensive placement of *rafe*, or the vowel sign interchanges involved.[25] Classification on the bases of these three features also does not indicate the inherent connections these Bibles have to the Extended Tiberian tradition. Yet the Byzantine Triad of features was specifically chosen, because Bibles with all three features appear very similar; there are many other kinds of Bibles which have one or two features of the Triad, but differ from these both codicologically and textually. In short, there is no single term perfectly apt for describing these Bibles in all their nuances. I submit that for the time being, Byzantine Triad, or even Italian-Levantine Triad, must suffice. However, it is possible that with further research, additional manuscript fragments with these features will surface, and further analysis on other aspects may turn up more suitable descriptors. This conclusion, therefore, is certainly not the final word on these fascinating Bible manuscripts.

References

Arrant, Estara J. 2020. 'An Exploratory Typology of Near-Model and Non-Standard Tiberian Torah Manuscripts from the Cairo Genizah'. In *Studies in Semitic Vocalisation*, edited by

[25] Nor does it deal with the diverse features mentioned in n. 16, though these do not appear to occur with measurable regularity.

Aaron D. Hornkohl and Geoffrey Khan, 467–548. Cambridge: University of Cambridge and Open Book Publishers. https://doi.org/10.11647/OBP.0207.07

———. 2021. 'A Codicological and Linguistic Typology of Common Torah Codices from the Cairo Genizah'. PhD dissertation, University of Cambridge.

Blapp, Samuel. 2017. 'The Non-Standard Tiberian Hebrew Language Tradition According to Bible Manuscripts from the Cairo Genizah'. PhD dissertation, University of Cambridge.

Díez Macho, Alejandro. 1956. 'Un Manuscrito Hebreo Protomasoretico y Nueva Teoria acerca de los Llamados MSS. Ben-Naftali'. *Estudios biblicos* 15: 187–213.

———.1963. 'A New List of so-called "Ben Naftali" Manuscripts: Preceded by an Inquiry into the True Nature of These Manuscripts.' In *Hebrew and Semitic Studies presented to Godfrey Rolles Driver in Celebration of his Seventieth Birthday*, 16–52. Oxford: Clarendon Press.

Eldar, Ilan. 1978. *The Hebrew Language Tradition in Medieval Ashkenaz (ca. 940–1350 CE)*. Jerusalem: Magnes Press, The Hebrew University of Jerusalem.

Heijmans, Shai. 2013. 'Vocalization, Palestinian'. In *Encyclopedia of Hebrew Language and Linguistics*, edited by Geoffrey Khan et al., III:964–67. Leiden: Brill.

Khan, Geoffrey. 1991. 'The Syllabic Nature of Tiberian Hebrew Vocalization'. In *Semitic Studies: In Honor of Wolf Leslau on the Occasion of His Eighty-fifth Birthday, November 14th, 1991*, edited by Alan S. Kaye, 850–65. Wiesbaden: Harrassowitz.

———.2017. 'The Background of the So-called "Extended Tiberian" Vocalization of Hebrew'. *Journal of Near Eastern Studies* 76/2: 265–73.

———.2018. 'Orthoepy in the Tiberian Reading Tradition of the Hebrew Bible and Its Historical Roots in the Second Temple Period'. *Vetus Testamentum* 68: 1–24.

———. 2020. *The Tiberian Pronunciation Tradition of Biblical Hebrew*. 2 vols. Cambridge Semitic Languages and Cultures 1. Cambridge: University of Cambridge and Open Book Publishers. https://doi.org/10.11647/OBP.0194.01

Morag, Shelomo. 1959 'The Vocalization of Codex Reuchlinianus: Is the "Pre-Masoretic" Bible Pre-Masoretic?'. *Journal of Semitic Studies* 4/3: 216–37.

Yeivin, Israel. 1983. '*Mashmaʿut Siman ha-Dagesh ba-Niqud ha-Ṭavrani ha-Murḥav*.' In *Hebrew Language Studies Presented to Professor Zeev Ben-Ḥayyim*, edited by Moshe Bar-Asher et al., 293–307. Jerusalem: Magnes Press, The Hebrew University of Jerusalem.

HEBREW VOCALISATION SIGNS IN KARAITE TRANSCRIPTIONS OF THE HEBREW BIBLE INTO ARABIC SCRIPT

Geoffrey Khan

1.0. The Karaite Transcriptions

In the 10th and 11th centuries CE many Karaite scribes in the Middle East used Arabic script to write not only the Arabic language, but also the Hebrew language. Such Hebrew texts in Arabic transcription were predominantly Hebrew Bible texts. These were sometimes written as separate manuscripts containing continuous Bible texts. Some manuscripts in Arabic script contain collcctions of biblical verses for liturgical purposes. Arabic transcriptions of verses from the Hebrew Biblical or individual Biblical Hebrew words were in many cases embedded within Karaite Arabic works, mainly of an exegetical nature, but also in works of other intellectual genres. Several Karaite Arabic works also contain Arabic transcriptions of extracts from Rabbinic Hebrew texts (Tirosh-Becker 2011). The Karaites transcribed into Arabic script only texts with an oral reading tradition, as was the case with the Hebrew Bible and rabbinic texts in the Middle Ages. The transcriptions reflect, in principle, these oral traditions. It is for this reason that their transcription of the Hebrew Bible represents

 https://doi.org/10.11647/OBP.0330.06

the *qere* (the orally transmitted reading tradition of the text) rather than the *ketiv* (the written tradition). Other types of Hebrew text that were written by Karaites during the Middle Ages without an oral tradition, e.g., documents, commentaries, law books, were always written in Hebrew script (Khan 1992).

Most of the known manuscripts containing Karaite transcriptions of Hebrew into Arabic script are found in the British Library (Khan 1993), the Firkovitch collections of the National Library of Russia in St. Petersburg (Harviainen 1993), and in the Cairo Geniza collections (Khan 1990). These manuscripts emanate from Palestinian circles of Karaites or Karaites in Egypt who had migrated to Egypt from Palestine after the capture of Jerusalem by the Crusaders in 1099. The majority of them were written in the 10th and 11th centuries.

Most of the transcriptions of Biblical Hebrew reflect the Tiberian reading tradition or an attempt to reflect this tradition.

The Tiberian pronunciation tradition of Biblical Hebrew was regarded as prestigious and authoritative in the medieval Middle East. It is likely that the authoritativeness of the Tiberian tradition had its roots primarily in its association with the Palestinian *Yeshiva* 'Academy', the central body of Jewish communal authority in Palestine, which was based in Tiberias from late antiquity until the Middle Ages. The Masoretes were closely associated with the Palestinian *Yeshiva* (Khan 2020b, I:86). Due to its authority and prestige, the Tiberian pronunciation was the ideal target in the oral reading of the Bible in communities. In such situations, outside the inner circles of the masoretic masters of Tiberias, there was always a risk that the ideal target would have been missed, resulting in an imperfect performance of the Tiberian tradition. In a previous paper (Khan 2020a), I discussed various aspects of the imperfect performance of the Tiberian tradition that are reflected by some of the manuscripts of Karaite transcriptions form the British Library. This imperfect performance was attributed to the impact of the phonological system of the vernacular language of the scribes. In the current paper I shall expand on the previous study by examining reflections of imperfect performance in a wider range of manuscripts from the British Library. I shall discuss aspects of imperfect performance discernible in the distribution of the vocalisation signs that are used in the manuscripts. Many of the Karaite transcriptions have Tiberian vocalisation signs. In several manuscripts these correspond to the distribution of signs in the standard tradition of Tiberian vocalisation, as it appears in the model Tiberian masoretic codices. In many manuscripts, however, some of the signs deviate from this standard distribution. The paper will focus in particular on (i) deviations in the distribution of vowel signs that reflect imperfect performance of Tiberian vowel qualities and (ii) deviations in the distribution of *shewa* and *ḥaṭef* signs that reflect imperfect performance of Tiberian syllable structure. In such manuscripts these types of deviation in the use of signs do not take place in every case and a certain proportion of the marking of signs corresponds to the standard Tiberian usage.

The corpus that has been used for this study includes the following manuscripts (BL = British Library):

BL Or 2539 MS A, fols 56–114
BL Or 2549 MS A, fols 1–140
BL Or 2549 MS B, fols 141–308
BL Or 2551 MS A, fols 1–30
BL Or 2551 MS B fols 31–101

BL Or 2552 MS A, fols 1–89
BL Or 2556
BL Or 2559

2.0. Vowel Quality

The Tiberian vowel signs reflect in principle distinctions in quality (Khan 2020b, I:244–45). Deviations from the standard distribution of the signs could, in principle, reflect either the application of the Tiberian signs to represent a different pronunciation tradition or an inability to distinguish correctly the qualities of the Tiberian vowels. It is the latter explanation that is the most satisfactory for the majority of the cases of deviation in distribution of the vocalisation signs in the corpus of manuscripts studied in this paper.

The deviations that are found in the manuscripts have been classified into the following categories:

(1) *pataḥ* for *segol* (but not vice versa)
(2) *pataḥ-segol* interchange
(3) *pataḥ-segol* interchange, marginal *pataḥ-qameṣ* interchange
(4) *pataḥ-segol* interchange, *pataḥ-qameṣ* interchange

2.1. *Pataḥ* for *segol* (but not vice versa)

BL Or 2559 fols 1–53

نافس (BL Or 2559, fol. 5v, 4) || L[1] נֶ֫פֶשׁ 'corpse' lit. 'soul' (Lev. 22.4)

[1] L = Codex Leningradensis, which is the basis of *BHS* (*Biblia Hebraica Stuttgartensia*). Biblical citations are from *BHS* unless otherwise indicated.

واتّام (BL Or 2559, fol. 6v, 8) || L וְאַתֶּם 'and you (MPL)' (Gen. 9.7)

BL Or 2549 MS A fols 140–41

ولباهمات (BL Or 2549, fol. 58r, 6) || L וּלְבֶהֱמַת 'and for the beast of' (Jer. 7.33)

In this manuscript *ḥaṭef pataḥ* occurs in place of *ḥaṭef segol*:

اعبور (BL Or 2549, fol. 2v, 2) || L אֶעֱבוֹר (*ketiv*: אעבד) 'I will transgress' (Jer. 2.20)

اعسا (BL Or 2549, fol. 22r, 8) || L אֶעֱשֶׂה׃ 'I will (not) make' (Jer. 4.27)

الاهيّا (BL Or 2549, fol. 72r, 14) || L אֱלָהַיָּא 'the gods' (Jer. 10.11)

BL Or 2551 MS A, fols 1–30

ابطح باخ (BL Or 2551 MS A, fol. 21r, 12) || L אֶבְטַח־בָּךְ׃ 'I will trust in you' (Ps. 55.24)

2.2. *Pataḥ-segol* Interchange

BL Or 2552 MS A, fols 1–89

2.2.1. *Pataḥ* for *segol*

ويّحفارو (BL Or 2552 MS A, fol. 12r, 11) || L וַיֶּחְפָּרוּ׃ 'and they were ashamed' (Job 6.20)

يعتار (BL Or 2552 MS A, fol. 52r, 8) || L יֶעְתַּר 'he prays' (Job 33.26)

هاتسناحق-بو (BL Or 2552 MS A, fol. 84v, 11) || L הֲתְשַׂחֶק־בּוֹ

‘will you play with him?’ (Job 40.29)

In this manuscript *ḥaṭef pataḥ* occurs in place of *ḥaṭef segol*:

اعسنا (BL Or 2552 MS A, fol. 36v, 6) || L אֶעֱשֶׂה ‘[What] shall I do?’ (Job 31.14)

اعرّوص (BL Or 2552 MS A, fol. 41r, 5) || L אֶעֱרֽוֹץ ‘I tremble’ (Job 31.34)

يَاحضو (BL Or 2552 MS A, fol. 85r, 3) || L יֶֽחֱצ֣וּהוּ ‘will they divide him?’ (Job 40.30)

2.2.2. *Segol* for *pataḥ*

معباذيهام (BL Or 2552 MS A, fol. 56r, 9) || L מַעְבָּֽדֵיהֶם ‘their works’ (Job 34.25)

2.3. *Pataḥ-segol, pataḥ-qameṣ* (Marginal) Interchange

2.3.1. *Pataḥ* for *segol*

BL Or 2549 MS B fols 141–308

وباحذاشيم (BL Or 2549 MS B, fol. 306r, 8) || L וּבֶחֳדָשִׁים ‘and in the new moons’ (Ezek. 45.17)

BL Or 2551 MS B fols 31–101

هرحب-فيخا (BL Or 2551 MS B, fol. 41r, 4) || L הַרְחֶב־פִּ֗יךָ ‘make wide your mouth!’ (Ps. 81.11)

نامنو (BL Or 2551 MS B, fol. 62r, 14) || L נֶאֶמְנוּ 'they are trustworthy' (Ps. 93.5)

BL Or 2556

باذراع (BL Or 2556, fol. 4r, 9) || L בְּאֶדְרָע 'by force' (Ezra 4.23)

يُنساللخون (*sic* with two *lāms*) (BL Or 2556, fol. 16r, 13) || L יִשְׁאֲלֶנְכוֹן 'requires of you' (Ezra 7.21)

In this manuscript *ḥaṭef pataḥ* occurs in place of *ḥaṭef segol*:

الاهاخ (BL Or 2556, fol. 15v, 12) || L אֱלָהָךְ 'your God' (Ezra 7.19)

وهاعماذنو (BL Or 2556, fol. 69v, 12) || L וְהֶעֱמַדְנוּ 'and we placed' (Neh. 10.33)

هاحطياو (BL Or 2556, fol. 84r, 12) || L הֶחֱטִיאוּ 'made sin (CPL)' (Neh. 13.26)

اعسا-حاسذ (BL Or 2556, fol. 112r, 1) || L אֶעֱשֶׂה־חֶסֶד 'I will deal loyally' (1 Chron. 19.2)

2.3.2. *Segol* for *pataḥ*

BL Or 2549 MS B fols 141–308

هاحشمالا (BL Or 2549 MS B, fol. 169r, 12) || L הַחַשְׁמַלָה: 'gleaming metal' (Ezek. 8.2)

In this manuscript *ḥaṭef segol* occurs in place of *ḥaṭef pataḥ*:

امولا (BL Or 2549 MS B, fol. 234v, 3) || L אֲמֻלָה ‘sick’ (Ezek. 16.30)

BL Or 2551 MS B fols 31–101

واسمورا (BL Or 2551 MS B, fol. 57v, 4) || L וְאַשְׁמוּרָה ‘and a watch’ (Ps. 90.4)

لعزرث (BL Or 2551 MS B, fol. 68v, 1) || L לְעֶזְרַת ‘for the help of’ (commentary on Ps. 102.14)

ممسلتو (BL Or 2551 MS B, fol. 76r, 11) || L מֶמְשַׁלְתּוֹ ‘his dominion’ (Ps. 103.22)

يحراص (BL Or 2551 MS B, fol. 32r, 1) || L יֶחֱרַץ־ ‘he will (not) sharpen’ (Exod. 11.7)

BL Or 2556

اسذذّيوث (BL Or 2556, fol. 83r, 7) || L אַשְׁדֳּדִיּוֹת (*ketiv*: אשדודיות) ‘women of Ashdod’ (Neh. 13.23)

2.3.3. *Qameṣ* for *pataḥ* (Marginal)

BL Or 2549 MS B fols 141–308

خراث (BL Or 2549 MS B, fol. 224v, 16) || L כָּרַּת־ ‘it was [not] cut off’ (Ezek. 16.4)

لاذماث (BL Or 2549 MS B, fol. 159v, 12) || L לְאַדְמַת ‘to the land of’ (Ezek. 7.2)

In this manuscript *ḥaṭef pataḥ* occurs very marginally in place of *ḥaṭef qameṣ*:

وباحذاشيم (BL Or 2549 MS B, fol. 306r, 8) || L וּבֶחֳדָשִׁים 'and in the new moons' (Ezek. 45.17)

BL Or 2551 MS B fols 31–101

تستاتار (BL Or 2551 MS B, fol. 58v, 10) || L תִּסְתַּתָּר׃ 'it will be hidden' (Isa. 29.14)

BL Or 2556

باناين (BL Or 2556, fol. 6v, 2) || L בָּנַיִן 'they are building' (Ezra 5.4)

2.4. *Pataḥ-segol, pataḥ-qameṣ* Interchange

BL Or 2539 MS A, fols 56–114

2.4.1. *Pataḥ* for *segol*

وات (BL Or 2539 MS A, fol. 63r, 6) || L וְאֶת־ 'and + object marker' (Gen. 21.10)

وتيلخ (BL Or 2539 MS A, fol. 63v, 8) || L וַתֵּלֶךְ 'and she went' (Gen. 21.14)

قاسث (BL Or 2539 MS A, fol. 64r, 3) || L קֶשֶׁת 'a bow' (Gen. 21.16)

2.4.2. *Segol* for *pataḥ*

هناعر (BL Or 2539 MS A, fol. 63v, 2) || L הַנַּעַר ‘the boy’ (Gen. 21.12)

وتيلاخنا (BL Or 2539 MS A, fol. 77r, 9) || L וַתֵּלַכְנָה ‘and they (FPL) walked’ (Gen. 24.61)

ناثن لاخ (BL Or 2539 MS A, fol. 95r, 4) || L נָֽתַן־לָֽךְ׃ ‘he gave to you (MS)’ (Deut. 8.10)

2.4.3. *Pataḥ* for *qameṣ*

يَاذَاعْتّي (BL Or 2539 MS A, fol. 67v, 9) || L יָדַעְתִּי ‘I know’ (Gen. 22.12)

ابراهام (BL Or 2539 MS A, fol. 68r, 5) || L אַבְרָהָם ‘Abraham’ (Gen. 22.14)

هاانشا (BL Or 2539 MS A, fol. 70r, 8) || L הָֽאִשָּׁה ‘the woman’ (Gen. 24.5)

دباراي (BL Or 2539 MS A, fol. 84r, 1) || L דְּבָרָ֑י ‘my words’ (Deut. 4.10)

هشامايم (BL Or 2539 MS A, fol. 85v, 6) || L הַשָּׁמָ֑יִם ‘the heavens’ (Deut. 4.19)

2.4.4. *Qameṣ* for *pataḥ*

حالاق (BL Or 2539 MS A, fol. 85v, 4) || L חָלַק ‘he divided’ (Deut. 4.19)

ارباعيم (BL Or 2539 MS A, fol. 94r, 8) || L אַרְבָּעִים 'forty' (Deut. 8.4)

2.5. Discussion

The deviations from the standard distribution of the Tiberian vocalisation signs indicate that the scribes were not copying the signs directly from model Tiberian Bible codices. They must either have been copied from manuscripts with a non-standard distribution of signs or marked independently by the Karaite scribes in an attempt to represent an oral reading tradition of the text. In effect, the cause in both scenarios amounts to the same process. If they were copied from other manuscripts with non-standard Tiberian vocalisation, the non-standard distribution in such manuscripts would itself have been the result of an attempt to represent an oral reading tradition. It can be assumed, therefore, that the phenomenon is the result of the assigning of signs to represent an oral tradition. This oral tradition can be assumed to be the Tiberian pronunciation tradition. The deviation in distribution is most easily explained as the result of imperfect learning and performance of the standard Tiberian tradition rather than the reflection of a different pronunciation tradition, such as the Palestinian or Babylonian pronunciation, or an extended type of Tiberian pronunciation tradition. This is because the vocalisation and transcription of the manuscripts do not reflect distinctive features of these other traditions of pronunciation. These would include features such as the lack of distinction between *segol* and *ṣere*, which is a feature of the Palestinian pronunciation (Revell 1970), distinctive Babylonian syllabic structure (Yeivin 1985,

283–398), or the extended use of *dagesh* to all non-guttural consonants as a marker of syllable onset after a preceding closed syllable, which is characteristic of the extended Tiberian tradition (Morag 1959; Yeivin 1983; Khan 2017).

The various different typologies of deviation in the distribution of the signs from the standard Tiberian vocalisation that are presented above in §§2.1–4 reflect different degrees of imperfect learning and performance of the Tiberian pronunciation tradition. The manuscripts in categories §§2.1–2 exhibit deviations only with regard to the *pataḥ* and *segol* signs. The manuscripts in categories §§2.3–4, however, exhibit deviations with regard to the distribution of *pataḥ*, *segol*, and *qameṣ*. It is important to observe that there is an implicational hierarchy in the typology of the categories. If there are deviations with regard to *qameṣ*, this implies that there are also deviations with regard to *pataḥ* and *segol*. If there are deviations with regard to *pataḥ* and *segol*, however, this does not imply that there is necessarily deviation with regard to *qameṣ*.

This hierarchy corresponds to different degrees of imperfection in the learning and performance of the Tiberian tradition. Manuscripts with deviation only in the distribution of *pataḥ* and *segol* reflect a lesser degree than those with deviations also with regard to *qameṣ*.

It can be safely assumed that the vernacular language of the scribes was Arabic. The fact that some manuscripts reflect deviations only with regards to *pataḥ* and *segol*, which had the qualities [a] and [ɛ] in the Tiberian pronunciation, indicates that the Arabic-speaking scribes had greatest difficulty distinguishing these qualities. This can be explained by the hypothesis that Hebrew [a] and [ɛ] and their respective long counterparts [aː] and [ɛː] were matched by the scribes with the similar sounding Arabic phonemes /a/ and /aː/. This is a recognised process when two languages are in contact. It involves the convergence of phonological systems of the languages, whereby phonetic tokens in one language are matched with a phoneme in a contact language.[2] The Arabic phonemes /a/ and /aː/ would have had a range of allophones, as in the modern Arabic dialects, that included not only the quality of [a] and [aː], but also the higher quality of [ɛ] and [ɛː], by the process of raising (*ʾimāla*), and the back quality [ɑ] by the process of suprasegmental pharyngealisation (*tafkhīm*) (Barkat-Defradas 2011b; 2011a; Levin 2011). This would have facilitated the interchange of the qualities of Tiberian *pataḥ* [a] and [aː] and Tiberian *segol* [ɛ] and [ɛː]. Due to both of these qualities being matched by the Arabic-speaking scribes with the Arabic prototypes [a] and [aː], the speakers had difficulty distinguishing their quality in the reading tradition and so imperfectly applied the standard Tiberian distribution of the signs.

The fact that the scribes were able to maintain the standard Tiberian distribution of the *qameṣ* and make the correct morpholexical contrasts with *pataḥ* could be explained by the assumption that the *qameṣ* phonetic token [ɔː] that was heard in the Tiberian reading was not matched with the /aː/ phoneme of Arabic. This is likely to have been due to its being sufficiently distinct in quality from the phonetic tokens of Arabic /aː/ for it to be kept apart. It is a recognised phenomenon in the research of second language acquisition that learners can more easily acquire a phoneme that is not similar to one in the native language than a phoneme that has phonetic tokens that are similar to those of a phoneme in the

[2] For more details of the process see Blevins (2017).

native language. When there is a high degree of resemblance between distinct sounds in the target and native languages, they are more liable to be wrongly matched.[3] The scribes of manuscripts in categories §§2.1–2, therefore, correctly learnt the distribution of Tiberian *qameṣ* and kept it separate from the vowel system of their Arabic vernacular.

The scribes of manuscripts in categories §§2.3–4, however, not only failed correctly to learn the Tiberian distribution of *pataḥ* and *segol*, but also imperfectly learnt the distribution of *qameṣ*. The vast majority of cases of Tiberian *qameṣ* that are incorrectly vocalised in the manuscripts are long *qameṣ*, but there are a few sporadic examples of short *qameṣ*. This imperfect learning and performance would have come about since the scribes matched also the *qameṣ* with prototypes in the vowel system of their vernacular speech. These, again, would have been Arabic /a/ and /aː/. As remarked, Arabic /a/ and /aː/ were realised with a range of qualities, including [ɛ] and [ɛː], by the raising process of *ʾimāla*, and [ɑ] and [ɑː], by the backing process of *tafkhīm*. The backed allophones [ɑ] and [ɑː] occurred in the environment of the Arabic emphatic, i.e., pharyngealised, consonants, such as /ṣ/ and /ṭ/. The matching of the Hebrew *qameṣ* vowel, which had the quality [ɔ], [ɔː], with Arabic /a/, /aː/, would have been facilitated by the existence of the similar sounding, though not identical, backed allophones [ɑ] and [ɑː] of Arabic /a/ and /aː/.

In order to explain fully the distribution of vowel signs exhibited in the data presented in §§2.1–4, it must be assumed that

[3] See, for example, Eckman and Iverson (2003) and the literature cited there.

the scribes had learnt the correct phonetic realisation of the Tiberian vowel signs (i.e., *pataḥ* [a], [aː], *segol* [ɛ], [ɛː], *qameṣ* [ɔ], [ɔː]). In fact, it is likely that Tiberian *pataḥ* had a back realisation [ɑ] in the environment of emphatic consonants such as *ṭet* and *tsade* (Khan 2020b, I:248), so the scribes would have learnt that the *pataḥ* sign had the range of qualities [a, aː, ɑ, ɑː]. The scribes did not, however, identify perfectly the sounds of the signs with what they heard in the reading tradition.

This assumption is necessary to explain why the *segol* and *pataḥ* signs interchange and the *pataḥ* and *qameṣ* signs interchange, but *segol* and *qameṣ* do not interchange, although all three vowels have been matched with the Arabic prototypes /a/, /aː/.

The realisation of the qualities of the vowel signs in question have the following relative position in the buccal vowel space:

Figure 1: *Segol* [ɛ]—*pataḥ* [a, ɑ]—*qameṣ* [ɔ] in the buccal vowel space

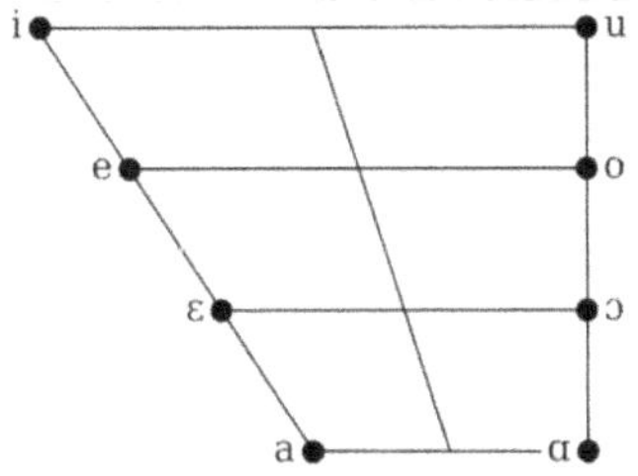

The quality of *segol* [ɛ] was articulated adjacent to the range of *pataḥ* [a, ɑ]. The quality range of *pataḥ* [a, ɑ] was adjacent to both [ɛ] on one side and [ɔ] on the other. The quality of [ɛ], however, was not adjacent to [ɔ]. The qualities of the Tiberian vowel signs that the scribe had learnt were confused with qualities adjacent to them in the reading tradition heard by the scribe. This can be represented as follows:

Table 1: Vowel adjacency and association

	vowel sign	associated sounds in the oral reading tradition
1	*pataḥ* [a, ɑ]	[ɛ], [a, ɑ]
2	*segol* [ɛ]	[ɛ], [a, ɑ]
3	*pataḥ* [a, ɑ]	[ɛ], [a, ɑ], [ɔ]
4	*qameṣ* [ɔ]	[a, ɑ], [ɔ]

In manuscripts in category §2.1 only process 1 is attested. In category §2.2 processes 1 and 2 are attested. In categories §§2.3–4 all four processes are attested.

The fact that manuscripts in category §2.1 exhibit only the marking of *pataḥ* for *segol* and not vice versa, i.e., process 1, may possibly be linked to the relative frequency of *pataḥ* and *segol* in the Tiberian Masoretic Text. *Pataḥ* occurs considerably more frequently than *segol*. A count of the tokens of *pataḥ* and *segol* in the whole Tiberian Masoretic Text using BibleWorks reveals the following statistics:

pataḥ sign	65,067
segol sign	21,874

This statistical dominance of *pataḥ* may have made it easier to confuse *segol* for *pataḥ* than *pataḥ* for *segol*. Process 1, therefore, would be the most liable to occur. The other processes would be increasingly liable to occur as the degree of imperfect learning of the reading tradition increased.

It should be remarked that deviation in vocalisation relating to *qameṣ* is only marginal in manuscripts of category §2.3.

This would reflect, therefore, a lower degree of imperfect learning than is reflected by manuscripts of category §2.4, in which *pataḥ* and *qameṣ* are frequently confused.

3.0. *Shewa* and *ḥaṭef* Signs

The deviations in the corpus from the standard Tiberian marking of *shewa* and *ḥaṭef* signs are presented in various categories below.

3.1. *Shewa* for *ḥaṭef*

3.1.1. *Shewa* for *ḥaṭef pataḥ* on Guttural Consonants

BL Or 2539 MS A

عسنارا (BL Or 2539 MS A, fol. 71r, 2) || L עֲשָׂרָ֔ה 'ten' (Gen. 24.10)

ناهرايم (BL Or 2539 MS A, fol. 71r, 4) || L נַֽהֲרַ֖יִם 'Naharaim' (Gen. 24.10)

واحموريم (BL Or 2539 MS A, fol. 74r, 8) || L וַחֲמֹרִֽים׃ 'and donkeys' (Gen. 24.35)

BL Or 2540

عزبتان (BL Or 2540, fol. 7r, 7) || L עֲזַבְתֶּ֣ן 'you (FPL) have left' (Exod. 2.20)

حثن- (BL Or 2540, fol. 13r, 2) || L חֲתַן־ 'bridegroom of' (Exod. 4.25)

BL Or 2547

وامرتام (BL Or 2547 fol. 4v, 13) || L וַאֲמַרְתֶּם 'and you (MPL) will say' (Josh. 4.7)

هابانيم (BL Or 2547 fol. 5r, 1) || L הָאֲבָנִים 'the stones' (Josh. 4.7)

وهكوهنيم (BL Or 2547 fol. 2r, 2) || L וְהַכֹּהֲנִים 'and the priests' (Josh. 3.14)

ويماهرو (BL Or 2547 fol. 6r, 6) || L וַיְמַהֲרוּ 'and they (MPL) hastened' (Josh. 4.10)

BL Or 2549

ناوم-اذوناي (BL Or 2549, fol. 2r, 1) || L נְאֻם־אֲדֹנָי 'utterance of the Lord' (Jer. 2.19)

ولباهماث (BL Or 2549, fol. 58r, 6) || L וּלְבֶהֱמַת 'and for the beast of' (Jer. 7.33)

لمناضاي (BL Or 2549, fol. 87r, 6) || L לִמְנַאֲצַי 'to those who despise me' (Jer. 23.17)

تلاحمو (BL Or 2549, fol. 95v, 3) || L תִּלָּחֲמוּ 'you will fight' (Jer. 32.5)

BL Or 2551 MS B

حنامال (BL Or 2551 MS B, fol. 31r, 2) || L חֲנָמַל 'frost' (commentary on Ps. 78.47)

BL Or 2552 MS A

واسلّذا (BL Or 2552 MS A, fol. 10r, 12) || L וַאֲסַלְּדָה 'and I shall rejoice' (Job 6.10)

لانسار (BL Or 2552 MS A, fol. 18r, 12) || L לַאֲשֶׁר 'into whose' (Job 12.6)

هغام (BL Or 2552 MS A, fol. 85v, 4) || L הֲגַם 'also?' (Job 41.1)

هييحيا (BL Or 2552 MS A, fol. 23v, 6) || L הֲיִחְיֶה 'will he live?' (Job 14.14)

BL Or 2556

امارنا (BL Or 2556, fol. 6v, 1) || L אֲמַרְנָא 'we said' (Ezra 5.4)

واني (BL Or 2556, fol. 19v, 5) || L וַאֲנִי 'and I' (Ezra 7.28)

واهوات (BL Or 2556, fol. 4v, 2) || L וַהֲוָת 'and it was' (Ezra 4.24)

كاهنّيا (BL Or 2556, fol. 12r, 9) || L כָּהֲנַיָּא 'the priests' (Ezra 6.16)

3.1.2. *Shewa* for *ḥaṭef pataḥ* on Non-guttural Consonants in L

BL Or 2549 MS B

توخلانّو (BL Or 2549 MS B, fol. 148r, 14) || L תֹּאכְלֶנּוּ׃ 'you (MS) will eat it' (Ezek. 4.9)

ونيشار (BL Or 2549 MS B, fol. 177v, 8) || L וָֽאֵשָּׁאֵ֣ר ‘(I) was left’ (Ezek. 9.8)

BL Or 2551 MS A

مقرب لي (BL Or 2551 MS A, fol. 19r, 12) || L מִקֲּרָב־לִ֑י ‘and from war against me’ (Ps. 55.20)

وقربلبو (BL Or 2551 MS A, fol. 20r, 10) || L וּֽקֲרָב־לִ֫בּ֥וֹ ‘and war was in his heart’ (Ps. 55.22)

BL Or 2551 MS B

بارخو (BL Or 2551 MS B, fol. 63v, 11) || L בָּרֲכ֥וּ ‘bless! (MPL)’ (Ps. 100.4)

BL Or 2552 MS A

بيرخوني (BL Or 2552 MS A, fol. 37v, 13) || L בֵרֲכ֣וּנִי ‘they (did not) bless us’ (Job 31.20)

اقاربانّو (BL Or 2552 MS A, fol. 42r, 12) || L אֲקָרֲבֶֽנּוּ׃ ‘I will go near to him’ (Job 31.37)

روطفاس (BL Or 2552 MS A, fol. 52r, 4) || L רֻֽטֲפַ֣שׁ ‘it will be fresh’ (Job 33.25)

صيللو (BL Or 2552 MS A, fol. 83v, 4) || L צִֽלֲל֑וֹ ‘his shadow’ (Job 40.22)

BL Or 2556

وللمذام (BL Or 2556, fol. 1r, 6) || L וּֽלֲלַמְּדָ֥ם ‘and to teach them’ (Dan. 1.4)

واشنسقلا (BL Or 2556, fol. 22r, 7) || L וָאֶשְׁקֲלָ֤ה ‘and I weighed out’ (Ezra 8.26)

وايبارخو (BL Or 2556, fol. 75v, 10) || L וַֽיְבָרְכ֖וּ ‘And they (M) blessed’ (Neh. 11.2)

صللوْ (BL Or 2556, fol. 81r, 8) || L צָֽלֲל֞וּ ‘began to be dark (MPL)’ (Neh. 13.9)

3.1.3. *Shewa* for *ḥaṭef segol* on Guttural Consonants

BL Or 2539

هالوهيم (BL Or 2539 MS A, fol. 66v, 6) || L הָֽאֱלֹהִֽים׃ ‘God’ (Gen. 22.3)

BL Or 2547

هاموري (BL Or 2547 fol. 15r, 2) || L הָאֱמֹרִֽי׃ ‘the Amorites’ (Josh. 13.4)

هاريخو (BL Or 2547 fol. 18v, 15) || L הֶאֱרִ֣יכוּ ‘they outlived’ (Judg. 2.7)

اذوم (BL Or 2547 fol. 29v, 16) || L אֱד֗וֹם ׀ ‘Edom’ (Judg. 11.17)

BL Or 2552 MS A

اليهو (BL Or 2552 MS A, fol. 43v, 5) || L אֱלִיה֤וּא 'Elihu' (Job 32.2)

لانوس (BL Or 2552 MS A, fol. 52r, 9) || L לֶאֱנ֑וֹשׁ 'to man' (Job 33.26)

هاعويثي (BL Or 2552 MS A, fol. 52v, 7) || L הֶעֱוֵ֑יתִי 'I have perverted' (Job 33.27)

هوي (BL Or 2552 MS A, fol. 70r, 5) || L הֱוֵ֫א 'fall!' (Job 37.6)

BL Or 2556

لاهوى (BL Or 2556, fol. 3r, 3) || L לֶהֱוֵ֣א 'will be' (Dan. 2.28)

الاها (BL Or 2556, fol. 4v, 2) || L אֱלָהָ֔א 'the God' (Ezra 4.24)

واداين (BL Or 2556, fol. 6v, 13) || L וֶאֱדַ֫יִן 'and then' (Ezra 5.5)

3.1.4. *Shewa* for *ḥaṭef segol* on Non-guttural Consonants in L

قرى (BL Or 2556, fol. 4r, 7) || L קֱרִ֫י 'was read' (Ezra 4.23)

3.1.5. *Shewa* for *ḥaṭef qameṣ* on Guttural Consonants

BL Or 2552 MS A

اهلي (BL Or 2552 MS A, fol. 40r, 4) || L אָהֳלִ֑י 'my tent' (Job 31.31)

3.1.6. *Shewa* for *ḥaṭef qameṣ* on Non-guttural Consonants in L

BL Or 2556

هقدانسيم (BL Or 2556, fol. 122v, 1) || L הַקֳּדָשִׁים 'the dedicated gifts' (1 Chron. 28.12)

قدم-رحوم (BL Or 2556, fol. 4r, 7) || L קֳדָם־רְחוּם 'before Rehum' (Ezra 4.23)

لاقبيل (BL Or 2556, fol. 11r, 12) || L לָקֳבֵל 'according to' (Ezra 6.13)

كل-قبيل (BL Or 2556, fol. 15r, 11) || L כָּל־קֳבֵל 'in accordance with' (Ezra 7.17)

قذام (BL Or 2556, fol. 14r, 13) || L קֳדָם 'before' (Ezra 7.14)

BL Or 2559

هقّذاشيم (BL Or 2559, fol. 3v, 5) || L הַקֳּדָשִׁים 'the sacred donations' (Lev. 22.3)

بقّذاشيم (BL Or 2559, fol. 5r, 12) || L בַּקֳּדָשִׁים 'of the sacred donations' (Lev. 22.4)

3.2. *Shewa* for Vowel in Unstressed Closed Syllables

Shewa occurs for *pataḥ* in closed unstressed syllables in L:

BL Or 2539 MS A

ويفتاح (BL Or 2539 MS A, fol. 73v, 8) || L וַיְפַתַּח 'and he opened' (Gen. 24.32)

ولاقحتا (BL Or 2539 MS A, fol. 74v, 4) || L וְלָקַחְתָּ 'and you will take' (Gen. 24.38)

بنوقر (BL Or 2539 MS A, fol. 74v, 6) || L בַּבֹּקֶר 'in the morning' (Gen. 24.54)

BL Or 2540

همّراا (BL Or 2540, fol. 8r, 4) || L הַמַּרְאֶה 'the sight' (Exod. 3.3)

ملاخ (BL Or 2540, fol. 8r, 2) || L מַלְאַךְ 'the angel of' (Exod. 3.2)

BL Or 2551 MS B

وياخ (BL Or 2551 MS B, fol. 32r, 6) || L וַיַּךְ 'and he smote' (Ps. 78.51)

وهمملاخا (BL Or 2551 MS B, fol. 39r, 13) || L וְהַמַּמְלָכָה 'and the kingdom' (Isa. 60.12)

ياعمدو مايم (BL Or 2551 MS B, fol. 80v, 4) || L יַעַמְדוּ־מָיִם׃ 'the waters stood' (Ps. 104.6)

BL Or 2556

لمسمّريم (BL Or 2556, fol. 116v, 8) || L לְמִסְמְרִים 'for nails' (1 Chron. 22.3)

3.3. *Ḥaṭef* for *shewa* in L

Ḥaṭef pataḥ occurs for *shewa* on non-guttural consonants in L:

BL Or 2539 MS A

وهناغرا (BL Or 2539 MS A, fol. 71v, 9) || L וְהַֽנַּעֲרָ ‘and the girl’ (Gen. 24.16)

غذولا (BL Or 2539 MS A, fol. 93r, 2) || L גְּדֹלָ֔ה ‘great’ (Deut. 7.23)

BL Or 2549 MS B

كي مالاو (BL Or 2549 MS B, fol. 174v, 10) || L כִּֽי־מָלְא֙וּ ‘because they filled’ (Ezek. 8.17)

بثوخحام (BL Or 2549 MS B, fol. 157r, 1) || L בְּתוֹכְכֶ֑ם ‘in the midst of you’ (Ezek. 6.7)

3.4. *Ḥaṭef* for Vowel in Unstressed Closed Syllables

3.4.1. *Ḥaṭef pataḥ* for *pataḥ* in Unstressed Closed Syllable

BL Or 2539 MS A

ببوقر (BL Or 2539 MS A, fol. 74v, 6) || L בַבֹּ֔קֶר ‘in the morning’ (Gen. 24.54)

ولاقحتا (BL Or 2539 MS A, fol. 74v, 8) || L וְלָקַחְתָּ֥ ‘you (MS) will take’ (Gen. 24.40)

هفيلغسيم (BL Or 2539 MS A, fol. 78v, 5) || L הַפִּֽילַגְשִׁים֙ ‘the concubines’ (Gen. 25.6)

لماعنخام (BL Or 2539 MS A, fol. 81r, 5) || L לְמַֽעַנְכֶ֑ם ‘because of you (MPL)’ (Deut. 3.26)

BL Or 2551 MS B

ياعشقوني (BL Or 2551 MS B, fol. 83v, 1) || L אַל־יַעַשְׁקֻ֥נִי ‘let them [not] oppress me’ (Ps. 119.122)

وثفارتو (BL Or 2551 MS B, fol. 34r, 12) || L וְֽתִפְאַרְתּ֥וֹ ‘and his glory’ (Ps. 78.61)

لاعغ (BL Or 2551 MS B, fol. 38v, 10) || L לַ֥עַג ‘mocking’ (Ps. 79.4)

كاعسخا (BL Or 2551 MS B, fol. 46r, 1) || L כַּעַסְךָ֣ ‘your anger’ (Ps. 85.5)

3.4.2. *Ḥaṭef segol* for *segol* in Unstressed Closed Syllable

BL Or 2551 MS B

عليون (BL Or 2551 MS B, fol. 33r, 13) || L עֶלְי֑וֹן ‘high’ (Ps. 78.56)

ال عمو (BL Or 2551 MS B, fol. 47r, 2) || L אֶל־עַמּ֣וֹ ‘to his people’ (Ps. 85.9)

3.5. *Ḥaṭef* for Vowel in Stressed Closed Syllables

3.5.1. *Ḥaṭef pataḥ* for *pataḥ* in Stressed Closed Syllables

BL Or 2551 MS B

اهابتي (BL Or 2551 MS B, fol. 82v, 4) || L אָהַבְתִּי 'I love' (Ps. 119.119)

3.5.2. *Ḥaṭef qameṣ* for *qameṣ* in Stressed Closed Syllable

BL Or 2551 MS B

اهابتي (BL Or 2551 MS B, fol. 90r, 2) || L אָהָבְתִּי׃ 'I love' (Ps. 119.163)

3.6. Vowel for *shewa*

Pataḥ is marked in place of *shewa* in a number of manuscripts:

BL Or 2539 MS A

ويخرثو (BL Or 2539 MS A, fol. 65v, 3) || L וַיִּכְרְתוּ 'and they (MPL) cut off' (Gen. 21.27)

سر صباو (BL Or 2539 MS A, fol. 66r, 3) || L שַׂר־צְבָאוֹ 'chief of his army' (Gen. 21.32)

فلستيم (BL Or 2539 MS A, fol. 66r, 4) || L פְּלִשְׁתִּים׃ 'Philistines' (Gen. 21.32)

BL Or 2540

مسكنُوث (BL Or 2540, fol. 4r, 7) || L מִסְכְּנוֹת ‘supplies’ (Exod. 1.11)

وايشرصو (BL Or 2540, fol. 3v, 7) || L וַיִּשְׁרְצוּ ‘and they (MPL) swarmed’ (Exod. 1.7)

BL Or 2551 MS B

لا-يدرخو (BL Or 2551 MS B, fol. 35v, 10) || L לֹא־יִדְרְכוּ ‘they will not tread’ (1 Sam. 5.5)

المسوررىم (BL Or 2551 MS B, fol. 55v, 1) || L הַמְשֹׁרְרִים ‘the singers’ (commentary on Ps. 87.7)

BL Or 2559

ونخرثا (BL Or 2559, fol. 3v, 12) || L וְנִכְרְתָה ‘and she shall be cut off’ (Lev. 22.3)

3.7. Vowel for *ḥaṭef*

3.7.1. *Pataḥ* for *ḥaṭef pataḥ* on Guttural Consonants

BL Or 2539 MS A

اماثاخا (BL Or 2539 MS A, fol. 63v, 2) || L אֲמָתְךָ־ ‘your hand-maid’ (Gen. 21.12)

زرعخا (BL Or 2539 MS A, fol. 63v, 5) || L זַרְעֶךָ ‘your seed’ (Gen. 21.13)

كمطاحوي (BL Or 2539 MS A, fol. 64r, 3) || L כִּמְטַחֲוֵי 'like the shots of' (Gen. 21.16)

BL Or 2549

لهشتاحوۏث (BL Or 2549, fol. 47v, 8) || L לְהִֽשְׁתַּחֲוֺת 'to worship' (Jer. 7.2)

BL Or 2551 MS A

واني (BL Or 2551 MS A, fol. 9v, 10) || L וַאֲנִ֥י 'but I' (Ps. 52.10)

راعنان (BL Or 2551 MS A, fol. 9v, 10) || L רַ֭עֲנָן 'green' (Ps. 52.10)

واقوا (BL Or 2551 MS A, fol. 10r, 7) || L וַאֲקַוֶּ֖ה 'and I will wait' (Ps. 52.11)

هيش (BL Or 2551 MS A, fol. 11r, 9) || L הֲיֵ֣שׁ 'is there?' (Ps. 53.3)

BL Or 2551 MS B

ابقاس (BL Or 2551 MS B, fol. 37r, 12) || L אֲבַקֵּשׁ 'I will seek' (Ezek. 34.16)

حخاماو (BL Or 2551 MS B, fol. 58v, 10) || L חֲכָמָ֔יו 'its wise men' (Isa. 29.14)

عسني (BL Or 2551 MS B, fol. 84r, 2) || L עֲשֵׂ֣ה 'act! (MS)' (Ps. 119.124)

هنسيبنو (BL Or 2551 MS B, fol. 39v, 3) || L הֲשִׁיבֵ֑נוּ 'restore us! (MS)' (Ps. 80.20)

BL Or 2559

انسار (BL Or 2559, fol. 6v, 2) || L אֲשֶׁ֣ר 'which' (Lev. 22.5)

3.7.2. *Pataḥ* for *ḥaṭef pataḥ* on Non-guttural Consonants in L

BL Or 2539 MS A

وهشبارخو (BL Or 2539 MS A, fol. 68v, 4) || L וְהִתְבָּרֲכ֣וּ 'and they will bless themselves (MPL)' (Gen. 22.18)

BL Or 2551 MS B

وبارخو (BL Or 2551 MS B, fol. 99r, 1) || L וּבָרֲכוּ 'and bless! (MPL)' (Ps. 134.2)

3.7.3. *Segol* for *ḥaṭef segol* on Guttural Consonants

BL Or 2539 MS A

نااحاز (BL Or 2539 MS A, fol. 68r, 3) || L נֶאֱחַ֥ז 'it was caught' (Gen. 22.13)

BL Or 2540

الُوهيمْ (BL Or 2540, fol. 8v, 6) || L אֱלֹהִ֑ים 'God' (Exod. 3.14)

اعسا (BL Or 2540, fol. 10r, 6) || L אֶעֱשֶׂ֖ה 'I shall do' (Exod. 3.20)

BL Or 2549 MS B

اموري (BL Or 2549 MS B, fol. 238v, 3) || L אֱמֹרִי׃ 'Amorite' (Ezek. 16.45)

BL Or 2551 MS A

الوهيم (BL Or 2551 MS A, fol. 9v, 3) || L אֱלֹהִים 'God' (Ps. 52.9)

هبيشوثا (BL Or 2551 MS A, fol. 12v, 3) || L הֱבִשֹׁתָה 'you put to shame' (Ps. 53.6)

انوش (BL Or 2551 MS A, fol. 17v, 1) || L אֱנ֣וֹשׁ 'man' (Ps. 55.14)

باحوز (BL Or 2551 MS A, fol. 21v, 5) || L בֶּאֱחֹז 'when holding' (Ps. 56.1)

BL Or 2551 MS B

هسيبوثا (BL Or 2551 MS B, fol. 45v, 2) || L הֱשִׁיבוֹתָ 'you caused to return' (Ps. 85.4)

3.7.4. *Qameṣ* for *ḥaṭef qameṣ* on Guttural Consonants

BL Or 2540

عني (BL Or 2540, fol. 8v, 6) || L עֳנִי 'affliction' (Exod. 3.7)

BL Or 2551 MS A

وصاهرايم (BL Or 2551 MS A, fol. 19r, 8) || L וְצָהֳרַיִם 'and noon' (Ps. 55.18)

BL Or 2551 MS B

عقّاايم (BL Or 2551 MS B, fol. 81v, 7) || L עֳפָאיִם 'foliage' (Ps. 104.12)

3.7.5. *Qameṣ* for *ḥaṭef qameṣ* on Non-guttural Consonants in L

BL Or 2556

عمنيّوث (BL Or 2556, fol. 83r, 7) || L עַמֳּנִיּוֹת (*ketiv:* עמוניות) 'women of Ammon' (Neh. 13.23)

3.8. Discussion

In the Tiberian pronunciation tradition, a vocalic *shewa* in principle represents a short vowel in an open syllable (CV).[4] Its quality was by default the same as that of the *pataḥ* vowel sign, i.e., the maximally low vowel [a], e.g.,

תְּכַסֶּה [tʰaχasˈsɛː] 'you (MS) cover' (Job 21.26)
מְדַבְּרִים [maðabbaˈʀiːim] 'speaking' (MPL) (Est. 2.14)

When vocalic *shewa* occurs before a guttural consonant or the letter *yod*, it was realised with different qualities through assimilatory processes. Before a guttural (i.e., א, ה, ח, ע) it was realised as a short vowel with the quality of the vowel on the guttural, e.g.,

בְּעֶרְכְּךָ [bɛʕɛʀkʰaˈχɔː] 'by your evaluation' (Lev. 5.15)
וְהָיָה [vɔhɔːˈjɔː] 'and it became' (Gen. 2.10)
בְּאֵר [beˈʔeːeʀ] 'well'

[4] For further details concerning *shewa* and *ḥaṭef* vowels in the Tiberian pronunciation tradition, see Khan (2020b, I:305–47).

מְאוֹד [moˈʔoːoð] ‘very’

Before *yod,* it was realised as a short vowel with the quality of short *ḥireq* [i], e.g.,

בְּיֽוֹם [biˈjoːom] ‘on the day’ (Gen. 2.17)

לְיִשְׂרָאֵל [lijisr^{ʕ}ɔːˈʔeːel] ‘to Israel (Gen. 46.2)

The *shewa* sign is combined with some of the basic vowel signs to form the so-called *ḥaṭef* signs. In such signs the vocalic reading of the *shewa* as well as its quality are made explicit. The vocalic *shewa* and the *ḥaṭef* vowels were quantitatively equivalent. In all cases they form short open syllables (CV).

In the Tiberian pronunciation the CV of a vocalic *shewa* or a *ḥaṭef* vowel cannot stand alone, but is prosodically dependent on the following syllable, which must be bimoraic (CVV or CVC). The CV syllable is bound with the following syllable in a single metrical foot. It is a metrically weak syllable and the following bimoraic syllable is the strong syllable of the foot. This can be represented thus: (. *), where the brackets enclose the syllables of the foot, the star * represents the strong prominent syllable, and the dot the weak syllable. On a prosodic level, therefore, the phonetic realisation of a word such as תִּסְפְּרֽוּ [t^{h}isp^{h}aˈʀ̟uː] would consist of three syllables parsed into two feet:

[(t^{h}is.) (p^{h}a.ˈʀ̟uː)]

(*) (. *)

This dependent prosodic status of vocalic *shewa* and *ḥaṭef* vowels is associated with the fact that they have the status of epenthetic vowels that break up consonant clusters at syllable onset. On an underlying phonological level, a word such as תִּסְפְּרֽוּ [t^{h}isp^{h}aˈʀ̟uː] would have the form /tispruː/, with the *shewa* [a] as an epenthetic that breaks the onset cluster /pr/ on the phonetic level. The fact that vocalic *shewa* is zero on the phonological level appears to be the reason why the Masoretes marked it with the same sign as they used to mark silent *shewa*. The *ḥaṭef* signs appear to be later developments of the notation system that made the reading of *shewa* as vocalic explicit in certain contexts.

Some of the deviations from the standard Tiberian vocalisation with regard to *shewa* and *ḥaṭef* vowels that are presented above from the Karaite manuscripts may be regarded as reflecting a more primitive stage of the development of the Tiberian vocalisation system. This may apply to the marking of *shewa* instead of a *ḥaṭef* sign on guttural consonants (§3.1), in which the reading of a *shewa* on a guttural was not marked explicitly as vocalic by the addition of a vowel sign next to the *shewa* sign. This phenomenon is found in many Hebrew manuscripts in Hebrew script with Non-Standard Tiberian vocalisation (Khan 2020b, I:340). This may also apply to the marking of *shewa* where L has a *ḥaṭef* sign on a non-guttural consonant (§§3.1.2, 3.1.4, §3.1.6). The model masoretic codices are not consistent in the marking of *ḥaṭef* in this context and some have *shewa* where L has a *ḥaṭef* (Khan 2020b, I:343–46).

The majority of the deviations, however, can be explained as being the result of a reanalysis of the syllable structure in the Tiberian pronunciation. This reanalysis resulted in *shewa* and *ḥaṭef* being interpreted as short vowels on the phonological level rather than phonetic epenthetic vowels. They were, therefore, equivalent to short vowels in closed CVC syllables. This arose since the monomoraic syllable CV with *shewa* or *ḥaṭef* vowels came to be analysed as a legitimate syllable on the phonological level. As is the case with the phonological reanalysis of the quality of vowels, the reanalysis of CV as a legitimate phonological syllable is likely to have been induced by convergence with the phonological system of Arabic, which was the vernacular of the scribes. In Classical Arabic and also in the modern eastern Arabic dialects, such as those of Egypt and the Levant, CV is a legitimate syllable at the phonological level, whether stressed or unstressed, e.g. Modern Cairene Arabic: *ká.tab* 'he wrote', *ka.tábt* 'I/you (ms) wrote' (Mitchell 1962, 26; Watson 2007, 56–58). A word such as תְּסַפְּרוּ [t^{h}asapp^{h}aˈʀ̟uː] in the Tiberian pronunciation would have the phonological syllable structure /tsappruː/. If, however, [t^{h}asapp^{h}aˈʀ̟uː] were parsed according to Arabic syllabic principles, the CV syllables would be analysed as phonological syllables rather than the result of phonetic epenthesis, thus /tasapparuː/. As a result, the /a/ in the open CV syllables /ta/ and /pa/ would be interpreted as having the same phonological status as the /a/ in the closed syllable /sap/. It would follow from this reanalysis that a *shewa* sign and a *pataḥ* sign in a closed syllable represented vowels that were equivalent and this facilitated the interchange of the signs. The same would apply to *ḥaṭef* signs, which, after this syllabic reanalysis according to Arabic principles, would come to be interpreted as representing vowels that were equivalent to the vowel represented by a vowel sign of the same quality that is used to represent a short vowel in unstressed closed syllables, e.g., in a word such as אֲמַרְתֶּם 'you (MPL) spoke' (Gen. 43.27). According to this Arabic type of parsing of syllable structure, the notational distinction between *shewa*, *ḥaṭef*, and full vowel signs lost its original function of distinguishing between phonological vowels and phonetic epenthetics, and so the signs were freely interchanged in open CV and closed CVC syllables.

All cases of *shewa* marked in closed syllables in the corpus are in unstressed closed syllables, in which the vowel would have been short. The vast majority of cases of *ḥaṭef* signs in closed syllables are likewise in unstressed syllables. There are only two cases in stressed syllables, viz.,

BL Or 2551 MS B

اهابتي (BL Or 2551 MS B, fol. 82v, 4) || L אָהֲבְתִּי ‘I loved’ (Ps. 119.119)

BL Or 2551 MS B

اهابتي (BL Or 2551 MS B, fol. 90r, 2) || L אָהֳֽבְתִּי׃ ‘I loved’ (Ps. 119.163)

The practice of marking *shewa* and *ḥaṭef* signs in closed unstressed syllables is sporadically found even in some of the Standard Tiberian Masoretic codices,[5] e.g.

בַּחֲרְטֻמִּם ‘on the magicians’ (L Exod. 9.11)
הָעֲרְבַּיִם ‘the evening’ (L Exod. 30.8)
יֶחֱזְקוּ ‘they are strong’ (L 2 Sam. 10.11)
יַעְכֳּרְךָ ‘he brings trouble on you’ (L Josh. 7.25)
וַהֲרְגְנֻהוּ ‘and we will kill him’ (L Judg. 16.2)
לְמֹּלֶךְ (BL Or. 4445) || L לַמֹּלֶךְ ‘to Molech’ (Lev. 20.3)

[5] Yeivin (1968, 18), Dotan (1985).

This practice in the vocalisation of the model codices may also have been facilitated by contact with Arabic syllable structure, as described above.

4.0. Concluding Remarks

In this paper I have presented various examples of the use of Tiberian vocalisation signs in the Karaite transcriptions of the Hebrew Bible into Arabic script. The focus in the paper has been on cases of vocalisation signs in the manuscripts that deviate from the distribution of the signs that are found in the Standard Tiberian Masoretic tradition. These deviations relate to the distribution of signs representing different vowel qualities and to the distribution of *shewa* and *ḥaṭef* signs. In both sets of cases, it was argued that the deviations can be explained by the hypothesis that the Hebrew of the scribes had undergone a convergence with the phonological structure of their Arabic vernacular. In the case of vowel qualities, this convergence would have resulted in difficulties in distinguishing between some of the Tiberian vowel qualities. In the case of *shewa* and *ḥaṭef* vowels, the convergence resulted in a reanalysis of epenthetic CV syllables of *shewa* and *ḥaṭef* as phonological syllables. It followed that the distinction between *shewa* and *ḥaṭef* signs in open CV syllables and vowel signs in CVC syllables became redundant and the signs, therefore, were interchanged.

References

Barkat-Defradas, Melissa. 2011a. 'Vowel Backing'. In *Encyclopedia of Arabic Language and Linguistics*, edited by Lutz

Edzard and Rudolf de Jong. online: Brill. http://dx.doi.org.ezp.lib.cam.ac.uk/10.1163/1570-6699_eall_EALL_COM_0371.

———. 2011b. 'Vowel Raising'. In *Encyclopedia of Arabic Language and Linguistics*, edited by Lutz Edzard and Rudolf de Jong. online: Brill. http://dx.doi.org.ezp.lib.cam.ac.uk/10.1163/1570-6699_eall_EALL_SIM_0140.

Blevins, Juliette. 2017. 'Areal Sound Patterns: From Perceptual Magnets to Stone Soup'. In *The Cambridge Handbook of Areal Linguistics*, edited by Raymond Hickey, 88–121. Cambridge: Cambridge University Press.

Dotan, Aron. 1985. 'Paṯḥé Ḥaṭfin: A Study in the Evolution of the Tiberian Vocalization'. In *Avraham Even-Shoshan Volume*, edited by Ben-Zion Luria, 157–65. Jerusalem: Kiryath Sepher. [Hebrew]

Eckman, Fred R., Abdullah Elreyes, and Gregory K. Iverson. 2003. 'Some Principles of Second Language Phonology'. *Second Language Research* 19/3: 169–208.

Harviainen, Tapani. 1993. 'Karaite Arabic Transcriptions of Hebrew in the Saltykov-Shchedrin Public Library in St. Petersburg.' In *Estudios Masorericos: En Memoria de Harry M. Orlinsky*, edited by Emilia Fernandez Tejero and María Teresa Ortega Monasterio, 63–72. Textos y Estudios «Cardenal Cisneros» de La Biblia Políglota Matritense 55. Madrid: Consejo Superior de Investigaciones Cientificos.

Khan, Geoffrey. 1990. *Karaite Bible Manuscripts from the Cairo Genizah*. Cambridge University Library Genizah Series 9. Cambridge: Cambridge University Press.

———. 1992. 'The Medieval Karaite Transcriptions of Hebrew in Arabic Script'. *Israel Oriental Studies* 12: 157–76.

———. 1993. 'On the Question of Script in Medieval Karaite Manuscripts: New Evidence from the Genizah'. *Bulletin of the John Rylands University Library of Manchester* 75: 133–41.

———. 2017. 'The Background of the So-Called Extended Tiberian Vocalization of Hebrew'. *Journal of Near Eastern Studies* 76/2: 265–73.

———. 2020a. 'Some Features of the Imperfect Oral Performance of the Tiberian Reading Tradition of Biblical Hebrew in the Middle Ages'. In *Studies in Semitic Vocalisation and Reading Traditions*, edited by Aaron Hornkohl and Geoffrey Khan, 549–92. Cambridge Semitic Languages and Cultures 3. Cambridge: University of Cambridge and Open Book Publishers.

———. 2020b. *The Tiberian Pronunciation Tradition of Biblical Hebrew: Including a Critical Edition and English Translation of the Sections on Consonants and Vowels in the Masoretic Treatise Hidāyat al-Qāriʾ 'Guide for the Reader'*. 2 vols. Cambridge Semitic Languages and Cultures 1. Cambridge: University of Cambridge and Open Book Publishers. doi.org/10.11647/OBP.0163.

Levin, Aryeh. 2011. 'ʾImāla'. In *Encyclopedia of Arabic Language and Linguistics*, edited by Lutz Edzard and Rudolf de Jong. online: Brill. http://dx.doi.org.ezp.lib.cam.ac.uk/10.1163/1570-6699_eall_EALL_SIM_vol2_0022.

Mitchell, Terry F. 1962. *Colloquial Arabic: The Living Language of Egypt*. London: Teach Yourself Books.

Morag, Shelomo. 1959. 'The Vocalization of Codex Reuchlinianus: Is the Pre-Masoretic Bible Pre-Masoretic?' *Journal of Semitic Studies* 4: 216–37.

Revell, E. John. 1970. 'Studies in the Palestinian Vocalization of Hebrew'. In *Essays on the Ancient Semitic World*, edited by John. W. Wevers and Donald. B. Redford, 59–100. Toronto: Toronto University Press.

Tirosh-Becker, Ofra. 2011. *Rabbinic Excerpts in Medieval Karaite Literature*. 2 vols. Jerusalem: Bialik Institute and the Hebrew University. [Hebrew]

Watson, Janet C. E. 2007. *The Phonology and Morphology of Arabic*. Oxford: Oxford University Press.

Yeivin, Israel. 1968. *Aleppo Codex*. Jerusalem: Magnes Press and The Hebrew University of Jerusalem. [Hebrew]

———. 1983. '*Mashmaʿut siman ha-dagesh ba-niqud ha-ṭavrani ha-murḥav*'. In *Hebrew Language Studies Presented to Professor Zeev Ben-Ḥayyim*, edited by Moshe Bar-Asher, Aron Dotan, David Tene, and Gad Ben-Ṣarfatti, 293–307. Jerusalem: Magnes.

———. 1985. *The Hebrew Language Tradition as Reflected in the Babylonian Vocalization*. Jerusalem: The Academy of the Hebrew Language. [Hebrew]

DISSONANCE BETWEEN MASORETIC VOCALISATION AND CANTILLATION IN BIBLICAL VERSE DIVISION

Yochanan Breuer

1.0. Introduction

The *Masora* of the Hebrew Bible rests on three pillars: consonants or written form (*ketiv*), vocalisation (*niqqud*), and cantillation (*ṭeʿamim*) which combine to produce the Masoretic Text.

These three facets are not separate, but inextricably interconnected. It is impossible to vocalise a biblical verse without first clarifying its written form, and it is impossible to cantillate a verse before its vocalisation has been set.

The cantillation depends on the vocalisation, by way of example, in the rules for exchanging of disjunctives and in determining some of the conjunctive cantillations. These all depend on word length —and the precise length of a word can be determined only in accordance with its precise vocalisation. Equally, vocalisation depends on cantillation: for example, in the rules for the pronunciation of the *begadkefat* consonants at the beginning of a word after an open syllable, for which purpose it is important to know whether the preceding word has a disjunctive or a conjunctive cantillation. Similarly, pausal forms depend on the main disjunctive accents.

 https://doi.org/10.11647/OBP.0330.07

When the Masoretes embarked on the task of determining the precise format of the biblical text, they were, accordingly, required to establish this format not in a single aspect, but in all these three aspects together. In each verse, their task was not only to fix the spelling, vocalisation, and cantillation, but also to ask themselves whether these three foundations were consistent. Although the agreement between the three foundations is indeed firm in most cases, there are instances when each of these foundations heads in a different direction.

The most prominent example of dissonance between the different foundations is the phenomenon of the distinction between the written form (*ketiv*) and the form that is read out (*qere*). Dissonance can also be found between the *ketiv* and the cantillation, albeit only in rare instances (M. Breuer 1981). In this article I intend to show this same phenomenon, but this time regarding the connection between the vocalisation and the cantillation. A careful observer of the meaning of the biblical text as indicated by the vocalisation will find that this is not always consistent with the meaning dictated by the cantillation.

For each verse I have attempted to present the disagreements among the biblical commentators regarding its interpretation. This will add to the objectivity of my examination: the two interpretations I propose in each case have not been invented merely to resolve the dissonance between the cantillation and the vocalisation. These differences were present in the exegetical literature. This means that such cases of dissonance are not to be seen as results of artificial masoretic interpretation. Instead, it is an expression of a genuine problem in the interpretation of the verse.[1]

What follows is not an exhaustive list of verses in the Hebrew Bible that display dissonance between vocalisation and cantillation. Instead, the verses below exemplify four different areas in which dissonance occurs:

Absolute versus construct: word groupings that were regarded by the cantillators as construct phrases, but whose words were separated by the vocalisers, or vice versa;

Definiteness: words that were considered definite by the vocalisers, but indefinite by the cantillators;

Pausal versus non-pausal: words that are vocalised as pausal forms, but cantillated with weak disjunctive (or conjunctive) accents, and words vocalised as non-pausal, but cantillated with strong disjunctives;

One word versus two words: words perceived as a single word by the vocalisers, but as two by the cantillators.

2.0. Absolute versus Construct

2.1. Construct in the Vocalisation, Absolute in the Cantillation

(1) מַעֲשֵׂ֨ה חָרַ֟שׁ אֶ֗בֶן פִּתּוּחֵ֣י חֹתָ֒ם תְּפַתַּח֙ אֶת־שְׁתֵּ֣י הָאֲבָנִ֔ים עַל־שְׁמֹ֖ת בְּנֵ֣י יִשְׂרָאֵ֑ל
מֻסַבֹּ֛ת מִשְׁבְּצ֥וֹת זָהָ֖ב תַּעֲשֶׂ֥ה אֹתָֽם׃
'With the work of an engraver in stone, like the engravings of a signet, shalt thou engrave the two stones, according to

[1] The version of the biblical text is according to M. Breuer (1989). The Aramaic *Targum* versions quoted are according to Sperber 1959–1973.

the names of the children of Israel; thou shalt make them to be enclosed in settings of gold.' (Exod. 28.11)[2]

The vocalisation of חרש shows that we have here a construct: חרש-אבן, i.e. "an engraver in stone" or a "stone-engraver." In other words, the onyx stones should be made by a stone-engraver. The division of the vocalised text is therefore:

מעשה חָרַשׁ אבן

Rashi interpreted the verse as follows:

> מעשה חרש אבן - מעשה אומן של אבנים. חרש זה דבוק הוא לתיבה שלאחריו, ולפיכך הוא נקוד פתח בסופו, וכן חרש עצים נטה קו, חרש של עצים. וכן חרש ברזל מעצד, כל אלה דבוקים ופתוחים
>
> The work of a master of stones. This חרש is affixed to the following word, and accordingly its final vowel is a *pataḥ*. Similarly, we have חרש עצים נטה קו (Isa 44:13), "an engraver of wood"; and חרש ברזל מעצד "an engraver of iron" (Isa. 44.12); all these are in the construct and vocalised with a *pataḥ*.

Rabbi Shmuel Ben Meir offered the same commentary.

Yet the cantillation divides the verse differently:

מַעֲשֵׂה חרשׁ אבן

The meaning here is that the onyx stones should be fashioned by an engraver, and that they should be made of stone. Here, then, אֶבֶן 'stone' is a complement of מַעֲשֵׂה 'work'. This same meaning is conveyed by the Aramaic translations: עובד אומן יהויין, מרגלייתא 'the work of an artisan the pearls will be' (Ps.-Jonathan); ܥܒܕܐ

[2] The English translations are taken from the online edition of Mechon Mamre (https://www.mechon-mamre.org/p/pt/pt0.htm).

ܕܐܘܡܢܐ. ܟܐܦ̈ܐ ܚܠܝܦ̈ܬܐ ‘the work of an artisan, engraved stones’ (Pesh.).

Luzzatto sensed the contradiction between the vocalisation and the cantillation in this verse, commenting that the *zarqa* should be on מעשה rather than on חרש (he quotes Rashi on the verse). Since he interpreted the verse according to the vocalisation, he failed to recognise that the cantillation reflects a different interpretation and should not be corrected.

Which interpretation embodies the plain meaning of the verse? It is difficult to determine. Rashi cites חָרַשׁ עֵצִים ‘carpenter’ and חָרַשׁ בַּרְזֶל ‘blacksmith’ in support of the construct form חָרַשׁ אֶבֶן, as indicated by the vocalisation. We should add that it is possible to find constructs that are extremely similar to חָרַשׁ אֶבֶן in:

> וַיִּשְׁלַח חִירָם מֶלֶךְ־צֹר מַלְאָכִים אֶל־דָּוִד וַעֲצֵי אֲרָזִים וְחָרָשֵׁי עֵץ וְחָרָשֵׁי אֶבֶן קִיר וַיִּבְנוּ־בַיִת לְדָוִד׃
>
> ‘and Hiram king of Tyre sent messengers to David, and cedar-trees, and carpenters, and masons—and they built a house for David.’ (2 Sam. 5.11)

In the account of the making of the Tabernacle itself, we find:

> וּבַחֲרֹשֶׁת אֶבֶן לְמַלֹּאת וּבַחֲרֹשֶׁת עֵץ...
>
> ‘and in cutting of stones for setting, and in carving of wood…’ (Exod. 31.5; 35.33)

Accordingly, it is possible that here, too, we have a construct form חרש-אבן.

However, there is another subject that must be examined regarding this verse. The verse includes the root עשה (do, make) and the noun אבן (stone). We must ask what the connection is between the verb עשה, which appears frequently in the description of the building of the Tabernacle, and the material from which the tools of the Tabernacle are made. Is the material connected to the verb עשה, as implied here by the cantillation: מעשה-חרש - אבן, or is it not connected to עשה, in which case the approach is parallel to that of the vocalisation, which does not connect אבן and מעשה. We find divergent practices in this regard.

In some instances, the material is connected to עשה:

> וְעָשִׂ֛יתָ שְׁנַ֥יִם כְּרֻבִ֖ים זָהָ֑ב...
> 'And thou shalt make two cherubim with gold...' (Exod. 25.18)
>
> וְעָשִׂ֥יתָ אֶת־הַמִּזְבֵּ֖חַ עֲצֵ֣י שִׁטִּ֑ים...
> 'And thou shalt make the altar with acacia-wood...' (Exod. 27.1)
>
> וְעָשִׂ֥יתָ אֶת־הַבַּדִּ֖ים עֲצֵ֣י שִׁטִּ֑ים...
> 'And thou shalt make the staves with acacia-wood...' (Exod. 30.5)
>
> וַיַּ֛עַשׂ אֶת־מִזְבַּ֥ח הַקְּטֹ֖רֶת עֲצֵ֣י שִׁטִּ֑ים...
> 'And he made the altar of incense with acacia-wood...' (Exod. 37.25)
>
> וַיַּ֛עַשׂ אֶת־מִזְבַּ֥ח הָעֹלָ֖ה עֲצֵ֣י שִׁטִּ֑ים...
> 'And he made the altar of burnt-offering with acacia-wood...' (Exod. 38.1)

In these verses, each material is clearly connected with עשה.

Elsewhere, however, we find that although the verb עשה and the material appear in the same verse, they are not connected to each other. In these instances, the material is bound to the name of the item being made in a construct phrase:

וְעָשִׂ֕יתָ חֲמִשִּׁ֖ים קַרְסֵ֣י זָהָ֑ב...
'And thou shalt make fifty clasps of gold...' (Exod. 26.6)
וְעָשִׂ֣יתָ עַל־שׁוּלָ֗יו רִמֹּנֵי֙ תְּכֵ֤לֶת וְאַרְגָּמָן֙ וְתוֹלַ֣עַת שָׁנִ֔י...
'And upon the skirts of it thou shalt make pomegranates of blue, and of purple, and of scarlet...' (Exod. 28.33)
וַעֲשֵׂ֤ה לָהֶם֙ מִכְנְסֵי־בָ֔ד...
'And thou shalt make them linen breeches...' (Exod. 28.42)
וַיַּעֲשׂ֥וּ פַעֲמֹנֵ֖י זָהָ֣ב טָה֑וֹר...
'And they made bells of pure gold...' (Exod. 39.25)

In one verse, the text even repeats a noun in order to force the words into a triple construct form:

וְעָשִׂ֤יתָ בַדִּים֙ לַמִּזְבֵּ֔חַ בַּדֵּ֖י עֲצֵ֣י שִׁטִּ֑ים...
'And thou shalt make staves for the altar, staves of acacia-wood...' (Exod. 27.6)

In this case, the second בדי is not necessary; it appears here merely in order to present the material as a complement and not as governed by ועשית.

In the instances presented thus far, the syntactic status of the material is clear from the text itself. Sometimes, however, it is not possible to determine the status on the basis of the text. For example:

וְעָשִׂ֥יתָ כַפֹּ֖רֶת זָהָ֣ב טָה֑וֹר...
'And thou shalt make an ark-cover of/with pure gold...' (Exod. 25.17)
וְעָשִׂ֥יתָ צִּ֖יץ זָהָ֣ב טָה֑וֹר...
'And thou shalt make a plate of/with pure gold...' (Exod. 28.36)

In some cases, the matter was determined by the vocalisers and the cantillators in harmony with one another:

> וְעָשִׂ֗יתָ שְׁתֵּי֙ טַבְּע֣וֹת זָהָ֔ב...
> ‘And thou shalt make two rings of gold…’ (Exod. 28.26, 27)
> וְעָשִׂ֥יתָ לּ֛וֹ זֵ֥ר זָהָ֖ב סָבִֽיב...
> ‘And thou shalt make unto it a crown of gold round about…’ (Exod. 30.3)
> וְעָשִׂ֜יתָ כִּיּ֥וֹר נְחֹ֛שֶׁת וְכַנּ֥וֹ נְחֹ֖שֶׁת לְרָחְצָ֑ה...
> ‘Thou shalt also make a laver of brass and its brass base, …’ (Exod. 30.18)
> וַֽיַּעֲשׂ֗וּ שְׁתֵּי֙ טַבְּעֹ֣ת זָהָ֔ב...
> ‘And they made two rings of gold…’ (Exod. 39.19, 20)

In other instances, the verses appear to unambiguously favour one interpretation, yet despite this both the vocalisers and the cantillators adopted an alternative interpretation:

> וַֽיַּעֲשׂ֛וּ אֶת־הַכָּתְנֹ֥ת שֵׁ֖שׁ מַעֲשֵׂ֣ה אֹרֵ֑ג...
> ‘And they made the tunics of fine linen with woven work…’ (Exod. 28.39)
> וַיַּ֙עַשׂ֙ אֵ֚ת הַכִּיּ֣וֹר נְחֹ֔שֶׁת וְאֵ֖ת כַּנּ֣וֹ נְחֹ֑שֶׁת...
> ‘And he made the laver of brass and its brass base,…’ (Exod. 38.8)
> וְאֵת֙ הַמִּצְנֶ֣פֶת שֵׁ֔שׁ וְאֶת־פַּאֲרֵ֥י הַמִּגְבָּעֹ֖ת שֵׁ֑שׁ...
> ‘And the mitre of/with fine linen, and the goodly head-tires with fine linen…’ (Exod. 39.28)

In these instances, the product is in the definite state while the material is in the indefinite; nevertheless, both the vocalisers and the cantillators perceived the forms as construct forms, contrary to conventional grammar.

In some cases, verses that are virtually identical are treated differently. The differences take the form of alternate readings of the biblical text itself or of the vocalisation or cantillation. Compare the following verses:

> וַיַּ֥עַשׂ אֶת־הַמְּנֹרָ֖ה זָהָ֣ב טָה֑וֹר...
>
> 'And he made the candlestick with pure gold…' (Exod. 37.17)
>
> וְעָשִׂ֥יתָ מְנֹרַ֖ת זָהָ֣ב טָה֑וֹר...
>
> 'And thou shalt make a candlestick of pure gold' (Exod. 25.31)
>
> וְעָשִׂ֥יתָ בְרִיחִ֖ם עֲצֵ֣י שִׁטִּ֑ים...
>
> 'And thou shalt make bars with acacia-wood' (Exod. 26.26)
>
> וַיַּ֥עַשׂ בְּרִיחֵ֖י עֲצֵ֣י שִׁטִּ֑ים...
>
> 'And he made bars of acacia-wood…' (Exod. 36.31)

In the above sets of verses, the alternatives in each pair are explicit in the form of the text itself. Elsewhere, the differences are manifest only in the cantillation:

> וַֽ֠יַּעֲשׂוּ שְׁתֵּ֤י מִשְׁבְּצֹת֙ זָהָ֔ב...
>
> 'And they made two settings of gold…' (Exod. 39.16)
>
> וְעָשִׂ֥יתָ מִשְׁבְּצֹ֖ת זָהָֽב...
>
> 'And thou shalt make settings with gold…' (Exod. 28.13)

In other instances, the alternatives are only in the vocalisation:

> וַיַּ֥עַשׂ אֶת־הַשֻּׁלְחָ֖ן עֲצֵ֣י שִׁטִּ֑ים...
>
> 'And he made the table with acacia-wood…' (Exod. 37.10)
>
> וְעָשִׂ֥יתָ שֻׁלְחָ֖ן עֲצֵ֣י שִׁטִּ֑ים..
>
> 'And thou shalt make a table with acacia-wood…' (Exod. 25.23)
>
> וַיַּ֧עַשׂ בְּצַלְאֵ֛ל אֶת־הָאָרֹ֖ן עֲצֵ֣י שִׁטִּ֑ים...
>
> 'And Bezalel made the ark with acacia-wood…' (Exod. 37.1)

> וְעָשׂ֖וּ אֲר֣וֹן עֲצֵ֣י שִׁטִּ֑ים...
>
> ‘And they shall make an ark of acacia-wood...’ (Exod. 25.10)

The word שֻׁלְחָן ‘table’ appears consistently as an independent word in Exod 37.10 and 25.23. By contrast, אָרוֹן ‘ark’ is presented in the construct state in 25.10. Although it is impossible to determine the matter by cantillation, the vocalisers decided that the form is a construct state. The net result is that this verse differs both from the analogous verse about the ark and the similar verses about the table.

In summary: the verb עשה is very common in verses describing the construction of the Tabernacle, and it appears alongside the material from which the relevant item in the Tabernacle is made: wood, copper, gold, or marble. We find two customs regarding the relationship between עשה and the material: sometimes they appear as complements and in other cases not. The distinctions between these two approaches are sometimes reflected in the biblical text itself, while elsewhere they are implied by the vocalisation or cantillation. The custom of attaching the material to עשה as a complement follows the approach of the cantillators in our case: מַעֲשֵׂה־חָרַשׁ אֶבֶן ‘an engraver’s work in stone’. The alternative custom mirrors the approach of the vocalisers here: מעשה חרש-אבן ‘the work of a stone-engraver’. The only difference between this verse and others is that in this instance, the Masora presents both approaches in a single verse, through the vocalisation, on the one hand, and the cantillation, on the other.

(2) הֵ֥ן עֵ֛ד לְאוּמִּ֖ים נְתַתִּ֑יו נָגִ֥יד וּמְצַוֵּ֖ה לְאֻמִּֽים׃
‘Behold, I have given him for a witness to the peoples, a prince and commander to the peoples.’ (Isa. 55.4)

The cantillation here establishes the following division:

נגִ֥יד ומצוֹ֖ה   לאמִ֥ים

According to this division, לְאֻמִּים ‘peoples’ is not part of a construct, but complements the verb נְתַתִּ֑יו ‘I have given him’. The word must then be analysed as the preposition -לְ before the noun אֻמִּים ‘peoples’, reflecting the plural not of לְאֹם, but of אֻמָּה. Accordingly, neither נָגִיד nor וּמְצַוֵּה are construct forms.

However, the vocalisers pointed וּמְצַוֵּה with a *ṣere*, reflecting the construct state. According to this approach, the division is:

נָגִ֥יד   וּמְצַוֵּ֖ה לְאֻמִּ֥ים

In this case, לְאֻמִּים does not represent -לְ + אֻמִּים, but is the plural form of לְאֹם.

The Aramaic translations appear to analyse the verse in the same way as the cantillators: הא רב לעממיא מניתיה, מלך ושליט על כל מלכותא ‘Behold, a leader for peoples I appointed him, a king and ruler over all the kingdoms’ (TJ); ܗܐ ܣܗܕܐ ܠܥܡ̈ܡܐ ܝܗܒܬܗ. ܫܠܝܛܐ ܘܡܕܒܪܢܐ ܠܐܡ̈ܘܬܐ. ‘Behold, a witness to peoples I made him, a ruler and leader to peoples’ (Pesh.). The change here in the second word (מלכותא or ܐܡ̈ܘܬܐ, rather than עממיא/ܥܡ̈ܡܐ) implies that they read -לְ + אֻמִּים, as does the cantillation.

Qimḥi also follows the cantillation, and accordingly questions the vocalisation: ומצוה בצר"י, שלא כמנהג ‘ומצוה with a *ṣere*, contrary to custom’. Luzzatto is more ambivalent:

> הראשון נראה לי משורש לאום... והשני משורש אמם, נגיד ומצוה נתתיו לעמים, ומלת ומצוה בלתי סמוכה, וראויה לסגול; וגם ייתכן שיהיו שניהם משורש לאם או משניהם משורש אמם
>
> The first instance appears to me to be from the root לאם... and the second from the root אמם, i.e., I have given him a prince and commander to the peoples; the word ומצוה is not in the construct state and should properly have a *segol*; but it is also possible that both of them come from the root לאם or that both come from the root אמם.

Neither of these commentators mentions the fact that both these possibilities are present before us in the masoretic form: one in the vocalisation and the other in the cantillation.[3]

It is difficult to decide which reading represents the correct interpretation of this verse. It only remains to add that according to the division reflected by the cantillation, the two legs of the parallelism contain two different words pronounced identically (לְאֻמִּים and לְ+אֻמִּים), and this may be regarded as poetic refinement and elevation. This consideration is not decisive, but it adds credence to the division of the cantillators.

(3) כִּֽי־שֹׁדֵ֤ד ה' אֶת־בָּבֶ֔ל וְאִבַּ֥ד מִמֶּ֖נָּה ק֣וֹל גָּד֑וֹל וְהָמ֤וּ גַלֵּיהֶם֙ כְּמַ֣יִם רַבִּ֔ים נִתַּ֖ן שְׁא֥וֹן קוֹלָֽם׃

'For the LORD spoileth Babylon, and destroyeth out of her the great voice; and their waves roar like many waters, the noise of their voice is uttered.' (Jer. 51.55)

שְׁא֥וֹן 'noise' is vocalised here as a construct form, and the vocalisation presupposes the following division:

נתן   שְׁאוֹן קולם

[3] See also M. Breuer (1982, 386); Ḥakham (1984, 590, n. 23).

The subject is 'the noise of their voice', and as Rashi interprets נשמע קול צעקתם 'the sound of their shouting was heard'.

However, the cantillation presents a different division:

נתְן שאֹון   קוֹלָם

The division in the cantillation guides us to the reading שָׁאוֹן*, in the absolute state. Accordingly, the subject is קוֹלָם 'their voice' alone, while שָׁאוֹן* is not part of the subject, but an adverb complementing נִתַּן 'is uttered'. According to the cantillation, the meaning of the phrase is 'their voice is uttered noisily', that is 'their voice rose in volume', or, as Qimḥi explained: והיה כמו שאון קולם 'And their voice was like a noise'. The Targum follows a similar approach: וירימון באתרגושא קלהון 'and they raise with noise their voice'. קלהון is the object, while באתרגושא translates שאון. Again, therefore, שאון serves as an adverb, as implied by the division in the cantillation.[4]

The difference between the two interpretations of this verse centres on the question as to whether קול and שאון have identical meanings. If they do, their combination may be regarded as an instance of hendiadys—שאון־קול; the inverse version of this combination—קול־שאון—appears elsewhere in the Bible (Isa. 13.4; 66.6). The vocalisers (and those who follow their approach) interpret our verse in this manner. If the meanings of the two words are not identical, however, then we do not have a single phrase here. Since they are not identical, the sound (קול) can be understood to be made in a manner similar to a שאון. In this reading,

---

[4] Wickes (1887, 68) rearranges the cantillation marks to suit the construct form; see also Ginsburg (1926a, 207).

שאון carries its own distinct semantic weight that is capable of both describing קול and adding to it something it does not carry on its own.

2.2. Absolute in the Vocalisation, Construct in the Cantillation

(4) כִּֽי־כֹ֣ה ׀ אָמַ֣ר ה' הִנְנִ֣י נֹטֶֽה־אֵ֠לֶיהָ כְּנָהָ֨ר שָׁל֜וֹם וּכְנַ֧חַל שׁוֹטֵ֛ף כְּב֥וֹד גּוֹיִ֖ם וִינַקְתֶּ֑ם עַל־צַד֙ תִּנָּשֵׂ֔אוּ וְעַל־בִּרְכַּ֖יִם תְּשָׁעֳשָֽׁעוּ׃

'For thus saith the LORD: Behold, I will extend peace to her like a river, and the glory of the nations like an overflowing stream, and ye shall suck thereof: Ye shall be borne upon the side, and shall be dandled upon the knees.' (Isa. 66.12)

The prevailing interpretation among the commentators is 'behold, I will extend to her like a river—peace; and like an overflowing stream—the glory of the nations'. According to this approach, 'like a river' is a description parallel to 'like an overflowing stream', while 'peace' is an object parallel to 'the glory of the nations'. Accordingly, this interpretation adopts the following division:

כנהר – שלום   וכנחל שוטף – כבוד גוים

This division is followed, for example, in the Peshitta: ܗܐ ܪܡܐ ܐܢܐ ܥܠܝܗ̇ ܫܠܡܐ ܐܝܟ ܢܗܪܐ. 'Behold I cast upon her peace like a river'. The Sages appear to have shared this understanding: השולמית – אומה שאני עתיד לנטות אליה שלום, הה"ד כה אמר ה' הנני נוטה אליה כנהר שלום 'השולמית – refers to the nation to which I shall extend peace, as it is written: 'thus saith the LORD: "Behold, I will extend peace to her like a river"' (Genesis Rabbah 66.2).

However, Luzzatto already noted that the cantillation does not lead to this interpretation. According to the above reading, שלום should have carried an accent of the third degree (*tevir*), which in this position would have been stronger than the *tevir* on שוטף. The *geresh* over שלום shows that the cantillation actually adopts the following division:

כנה֙ר של֜וֹם וכנ֫חל שוט֤ף   כב֖וד גוי֖ם

According to this division, there is only one object in this verse: כבוד גוים. שלום is not an object, but describes נהר, and the two images we have here are 'as a peaceful river' and 'as an overflowing stream'.

This is certainly the meaning intended by the cantillators; it remains for us to ask only what the vocalisers intended. In other words, which of the two above-mentioned meanings is implied by the vocalised text before us: כְּנָהָר שלום?

Since שלום is a noun, and not an adjective, whenever it describes the preceding noun it must form part of a construct. For example: דִּבְרֵ֥י שָׁל֖וֹם 'words of peace' (Deut. 2.26); מַלְאֲכֵ֣י שָׁל֔וֹם 'messengers of peace' (Isa. 33.7); וַעֲצַ֣ת שָׁל֔וֹם 'and the counsel of peace' (Zech. 6.13). And to quote examples when the construct state is dependent on the vocalisation: בִּנְוֵ֣ה שָׁל֑וֹם 'in a peaceable habitation' (Isa. 32.18); מַחְשְׁב֤וֹת שָׁלוֹם֙ 'thoughts of peace' (Jer. 29.11); חֲז֣וֹן שָׁלֹ֑ם 'vision of peace' (Ezek. 13.16); וּמִשְׁפַּ֣ט שָׁל֔וֹם 'and judgment of peace' (Zech. 8.16). Accordingly, if שלום indeed describes נהר, the proper vocalisation here would be כִּנְהַר שלום; the vocalised form כְּנָהָר שלום is, therefore, not a possible reflection of this interpretation.

Accordingly, the vocalised text before us—כְּנָהָר שָׁלוֹם—clearly indicates that this is not a phrase consisting of a noun and an adjective, but rather an adverb and an object. In other words, and in keeping with the opinion of the commentators as we quoted at the beginning of our discussion:

כְּנָהָר – שלום וכנחל שוטף – כבוד גוים

Thus, we see that the difference between the vocalisers' approach and that of the cantillators centres on the interpretation of שלום, and hence also of כנהר. The vocalisers read כְּנָהָר שלום and regard שלום as an object, i.e., 'I will extend peace to her like a river'; the cantillators read כְּנְהַר שלום and understand 'peace' as describing 'river', i.e., 'I will extend to her as a river of peace'.

(5) מַתָּ֣ן אָ֭דָם יַרְחִ֣יב ל֑וֹ וְלִפְנֵ֖י גְדֹלִ֣ים יַנְחֶֽנּוּ׃
'A man's gift maketh room for him, and bringeth him before great men.' (Prov. 18.16)

According to the cantillation, the division here is:

מַתָּ֣ן אָ֭דָם יַרְחִ֣יב ל֑וֹ

The meaning is that a man's gift will expand him or make room for him. This is reflected in the Targum: מוהבתיה דבר נשא מרוחא ליה, and Ibn Ezra also interpreted these words in the same manner.

However, מַתָּ֣ן is vocalised with a *qamets,* indicating the absolute rather than construct state. Accordingly, the vocalisers did not see a construct here, but rather interpreted מַתָּ֣ן as focal. Accordingly, their division is:

מַתָּ֣ן אדם ירחיב לו

And the meaning can be represented with a cleft sentence: 'it is a *gift* that makes room for a man' (Eichel 1790, first introduction).

3.0. Definiteness

(6) פָּ֣תַח צ֭וּר וַיָּז֣וּבוּ מָ֑יִם הָ֝לְכ֗וּ בַּצִּיּ֥וֹת נָהָֽר׃

'He opened the rock, and waters gushed out; they ran, a river in the dry places.' (Ps. 105.41)

The most probable division is that proposed by the vocalisation:

הלכו בַצִּיּוֹת   נהר

The commentators understood the verse according to this division. However, this creates a disagreement between the singular subject נָהָר 'river' and the predicate's plural verb הָלְכוּ 'ran'. Various solutions can be proposed in this respect. Some commentators suggested that the noun מָיִם 'water' (plural in Hebrew) also governs the second part of the verse, so that the meaning would be הָלְכוּ בַּצִּיּוֹת מֵי נָהָר 'the waters of the river flowed in the dry places' (Ibn Ezra). Others argued that the singular 'river' here actually stands for a plural, so that the meaning is 'the rivers flowed in the dry places' (Rashi). Still others opined that the meaning is '(the above-mentioned waters) flowed in the dry places *like* a river', e.g., הליכו בצחותא היך נהרא (Targum). In any case, this interpretation clearly understands צִיּוֹת as the plural of צִיָּה 'a wilderness' (the only occurrence of a plural form of this word in the Hebrew Bible).

The cantillation, however, divides the verse in a different manner:

הָ֝לְכ֗וּ   בצִיּ֥וֹת נהָֽר

What meaning is implied by this division? It would seem to be founded on an interpretation proposed by the Sages, who suggest that צִיּוֹת is not the plural of צִיָּה, but rather of צִי ‘ship’. The Tosefta comments: והיא נעשית נחלים גדולים... הן יושבין באיספקאות ובאין זה אצל זה, שנ' הלכו בציות נהר ‘And it becomes mighty rivers... they sit in ships and come to each other, as it is written: הלכו בציות נהר’ (t. Sukkah 3.12); and more explicitly in Bemidbar Rabba: אשה שהיתה צריכה לילך אצל חברתה מדגל לדגל היתה מהלכת בספינה, שנא' הלכו בציות נהר, ואין ציות אלא ספינות, שנא' וצי אדיר לא יעברנו ‘a woman who needed to go to her friend from a tribe to another tribe would go by ship, as it is said הלכו בציות נהר, and ציות means ships, as it is written: וצי אדיר לא יעברנו ‘a mighty ship cannot cross it’ (Bemidbar Rabba 19.26).[5] According to this interpretation, ציות נהר is a construct chain, and the meaning of הלכו בציות נהר is ‘they went in riverboats’.

However, according to this interpretation, צִיּוֹת cannot be definite. In other words, the interpretation implied by the cantillation requires a *bet* vocalised with *shewa*, rather than the *pataḥ* reflecting the definite article according to the received vocalisation (Ḥakham 1981, 277).

(7) הֲֽלֹא־בַ֭בֶּטֶן עֹשֵׂ֣נִי עָשָׂ֑הוּ וַ֝יְכֻנֶ֗נּוּ בָּרֶ֥חֶם אֶחָֽד׃
‘Did not He that made me in the womb make him? And did not One fashion us in the womb?’ (Job 31.15)

The cantillation establishes the following division:

וַ֝יְכֻנֶ֗נּוּ   בָּרֶ֥חֶם אֶחָֽד

[5] See also Tanḥuma Ḥuqat 21. And see Ben-Yehuda (1908–1958, 5646a, n. 1).

According to this division, the phrase here is רֶ֫חֶם אֶחָד 'one womb', whereby 'one' describes 'womb'. Since אֶחָד is not definite, רֶ֫חֶם must also be construed as indefinite, and accordingly the cantillation requires the reading בְּרחם, with *bet* vocalised with *shewa*. Several commentators interpreted the verse in this manner, including the translator of the Peshitta: ܘܩܢܢ. ܡܪܒܥܐ ܬܩܢ.

However, the vocalisation gives us the definite form בָּרחם, thereby establishing that we do not have a single phrase here. According to the vocalisation, the division is as follows:

ויכננו בָּרֶ֫חֶם   אחד

This interpretation makes אחד the subject of the sentence, rather than a complement of רחם, as interpreted by Ibn Ezra, among others: ויכננו ברחם אל אחד 'One God fashioned us in the womb' (Norzi 1742–1744, VI:50a; Ḥakham 1970, 238, n. 91; Qafih 1973, 263).

(8) נִתַּ֣ן הַסֶּ֔כֶל בַּמְּרוֹמִ֖ים רַבִּ֑ים וַעֲשִׁירִ֖ים בַּשֵּׁ֥פֶל יֵשֵֽׁבוּ׃
'Folly is set on great heights, and the rich sit in a low place' (Eccl. 10.6)

The division according to the cantillation is:

נתַ֣ן הסֶּ֔כל במרומִ֖ים רבִּ֑ים   ועשירִ֖ים בשֵּׁ֥פל ישֵֽׁבו

Here מרומים רבים is a phrase ('great heights') whereby רבים describes במרומים. This interpretation was followed by Rashi, for example: שניתן השטות והרשע במרומי גובה 'For foolishness and evil was placed at a great height'. Once again, the syntactic difficulty is glaring: the noun is definite while its adjective is not. However, the definite character of בַּמרומים is indicated not in the written text itself, but in the vocalisation. Therefore, it seems that the cantillators read בִּמְרוֹמִים רבים, as an indefinite construction.

By establishing the definite vocalisation בַּמְּרוֹמִים, the vocalisers disconnected the two words, resulting in the following division:

נתן הסכל בַּמְּרוֹמִים   רבים ועשירים בשפל ישבו

According to this interpretation, רבים is not an adjective complementing במרומים, but rather joins the second half of the verse, alongside ועשירים. Ibn Ezra accordingly comments: ופירוש רבים כמו גדולים 'And the meaning of רבים is like (that of) גדולים "great ones"' (Yalon 1971, 331).

Lauha (1978, 183) adopted a similar line: "Nach masoretischer Akzentuierung Gehört רבים zu V. 6a, aber wegen seiner Artikellosigkeit kann es nicht als Attrubut zu במרומים gehören und muss mit V 6b kominiert werden" ('According to the cantillation, רבים belongs to the first part of the verse. However, since רבים is indefinite, it cannot serve as an adjective of במרומים and must join the second part of the verse').

These comments are very pertinent but require a slight correction. The indefinite character of רבים indeed disconnects it from במרומים—if that word is definite. But its definite character is conveyed solely by the vocalisation. It is thus evident that by joining the two words together, the cantillators read not בַּמְּרוֹמִים, but rather בִּמְרוֹמִים, and according to this reading there is no difficulty in connecting the two words. The dissonance here, then, is not one between the cantillation and the rules of grammar, as

Lauha's comments may imply, but merely one between the cantillation and the vocalisation (see also Zer-Kavod 1973, 63, n. 15).

4.0. Pausal versus Non-pausal

4.1. Introduction

This section will discuss exceptions to the usual rules concerning pausal and non-pausal forms in the Bible. As a general rule, pausal forms appear with strong disjunctives, while non-pausal forms accompany weaker disjunctives and conjunctives. Clear exceptions to these rules can sometimes be found, however, and these can be explained according to the underlying message of this article: the vocalisation may be exceptional because it is fixed according to a different division.

In order to do so, we should mention some basic fundamentals regarding pausal and non-pausal forms:

(1) A vowel that stems from an original *i* vowel does not change in pause, as זָקַ֫נְתִּי 'I am old' (Gen. 27.2); אַט 'softly' (1 Kgs 21.27); כְּבַ֫ת 'as a daughter' (2 Sam. 12.3) (Breuer 1980, 244–46; Blau 1981). Sometimes a vowel does not change when its origin is not certain, such as מִזַּ֖ן אֶ֑ל־זַ֑ן 'all kinds of stuff' (Ps. 144.13); הַמֶּלְצַ֑ר 'the steward' (Dan. 1.11); מִיכַ֑ל 'Michal' (1 Sam. 14.49). Such forms cannot be considered non-pausal forms, as they do not change in pause.

(2) Pausal forms may appear with accents other than the chief disjunctives, e.g., וְיַֽעֲשׂ֧וּ בְנֵֽי־יִשְׂרָאֵ֛ל אֶת־הַפָּ֖סַח בְּמוֹעֲדֽוֹ 'let the children of Israel keep the **Passover** in its appointed season' (Num. 9.2). Consider, for example:

בִּנְיָמִין֙ זְאֵ֣ב יִטְרָ֔ף בַּבֹּ֖קֶר יֹ֣אכַל עַ֑ד   וְלָעֶ֖רֶב יְחַלֵּ֥ק שָׁלָֽל׃
'Benjamin is a wolf that raveneth; in the morning he devoureth the prey, and at even he divideth the spoil.' (Gen. 49.27)

We may be tempted, according to the forms, to propose a different division:

בנימין זאב יִטְרָף   בבקר יאכל עַד ולערב יחלק שלל

While this division may indeed be more plausible, we cannot reach this conclusion due to the considerations discussed above. On the one hand, a pausal form of the type found here—יִטְרָ֔ף—may appear with a strong disjunctive, such as the first *zaqef* in a verse. On the other hand, it is doubtful whether עַד is truly a non-pausal form, since there is no instance of this word vocalised with a *qameṣ* in a pausal context (*pace* Schlesinger 1962, 88–89).

(3) There are various types of pausal forms, and each type behaves differently. Some types readily tend to adopt the pausal form, while others do so only with the chief disjunctives. Let us take the following example (the division here follows the cantillation):

בְּשִׁבְתְּךָ֤ בְּבֵיתֶ֙ךָ֙ וּבְלֶכְתְּךָ֣ בַדֶּ֔רֶךְ   וּֽבְשָׁכְבְּךָ֖ וּבְקוּמֶֽךָ
'When thou sittest in **thy house**, and when thou walkest by **the way**, and when thou liest down, and when thou risest up' (Deut. 6.7)

It is clear that the only reasonable division of this verse is according to the cantillation. However, we should not compare the pair of forms בֵּיתְךָ/בֵּיתֶךָ with the pair דַּרְכְּךָ/דֶּרֶךְ, since the tendency to the pausal form is extremely weak in the latter type.

The situation is further illustrated by the following example:

נַעְבְּרָה־נָּ֣א בְאַרְצֶ֗ךָ לֹ֤א נַעֲבֹר֙ בְּשָׂדֶ֣ה וּבְכֶ֔רֶם   וְלֹ֥א נִשְׁתֶּ֖ה מֵ֣י בְאֵ֑ר

'Let us pass, I pray thee, through **thy land**; we will not pass through field or through **vineyard**, neither will we drink of the water of the wells.' (Num. 20.17)

Based on the forms in this verse, we should ostensibly depart from the cantillation and divide this verse as follows:

נעברה־נא בְאַרְצְךָ   לא נעבר בשדה וּבְכֶרֶם ולא נשתה מי באר

Here, too, although this is a more plausible division than that established by the cantillation, we cannot claim that it is dictated by the vocalisation. The pair אַרְצֶךָ/אַרְצְךָ cannot be compared to the pair כָּרֶם/כֶּרֶם, since the former is far more prone to adopt the pausal form than the latter (Ben-David 1995, 8–9).

Accordingly, when comparing pausal and non-pausal forms in the same verse, we must draw conclusions only if the compared forms belong to the same type.

4.2. Pausal Form in Context

(9) וָאֹמַ֤ר לָהֶם֙ לְמִ֣י זָהָ֔ב הִתְפָּרָ֖קוּ וַיִּתְּנוּ־לִ֑י וָאַשְׁלִכֵ֣הוּ בָאֵ֔שׁ וַיֵּצֵ֖א הָעֵ֥גֶל הַזֶּֽה׃

'And I said unto them: "Whosoever hath any gold, let them break it off; so they gave it me; and I cast it into the fire, and there came out this calf.' (Exod. 32.24)

In this story, Aaron tells Moses about the sequence of events that ultimately led to the sin of the Golden Calf. His speech includes an ambiguous verbal form הִתְפָּרָקוּ. This word can be understood in two ways, both grammatically and contextually: either as an imperative form or as a third person plural past tense. If it is an imperative, then it is part of Aaron's words to the people that are being quoted here, as he tells them 'whosoever hath any gold—

break it off'. Thus Aaron is repeating his comments as reported earlier in the story itself: וַיֹּאמֶר אֲלֵהֶם אַהֲרֹן פָּרְקוּ נִזְמֵי הַזָּהָב אֲשֶׁר בְּאָזְנֵי נְשֵׁיכֶם בְּנֵיכֶם וּבְנֹתֵיכֶם וְהָבִיאוּ אֵלָי׃ 'And Aaron said unto them: "Break off the golden rings, which are in the ears of your wives, of your sons, and of your daughters, and bring them unto me"' (Exod. 32.2). If this is a third person past tense form, then לְמִי זָהָב 'whosoever hath any gold' are the only words here that Aaron actually spoke at the time of the event, while the following section—הִתְפָּרָקוּ וַיִּתְּנוּ־לִי—describes the people's resulting action: 'they broke off and gave it to me'—paralleling the content of the story itself: וַיִּתְפָּרְקוּ כָּל־הָעָם אֶת־נִזְמֵי הַזָּהָב אֲשֶׁר בְּאָזְנֵיהֶם וַיָּבִיאוּ אֶל־אַהֲרֹן׃ 'And all the people broke off the golden rings which were in their ears, and brought them unto Aaron' (Exod. 32.3).

According to the cantillation, the division of the verse is as follows:

ואמר להם למי זהב   התפרקו ויתנו־לי

The meaning according to this division is clear: Aaron's speech is short, and confined solely to the words לְמִי זָהָב, while הִתְפָּרָקוּ is a past tense form describing the people's actions, and combined in the division of the verse with the adjacent וַיִּתְּנוּ־לִי. Rashi followed this interpretation: ואמר להם – דבר אחד: 'למי זהב', לבד; והם מהרו והתפרקו ויתנו לי 'And I told them – one thing only: "Who has gold?" And they hurried and broke [it] off and gave [it] to me'.

This interpretation reflects a desire to limit Aaron's speech during this affair to the minimum, thereby also mitigating his sin: he spoke only two words, and did not himself tell the people to break off their gold. The main sin is that of the people, who broke off their gold without having been told to do so. The desire to limit Aaron's speech is not confined to the exegesis, however, and can be seen in Aaron's words as reported. Even if we extend his speech to include the word הִתְפָּרָקוּ, this is still markedly concise by comparison to his words as quoted in the story itself: פָּרְקוּ֙ נִזְמֵ֣י הַזָּהָ֔ב אֲשֶׁר֙ בְּאָזְנֵ֣י נְשֵׁיכֶ֔ם בְּנֵיכֶ֖ם וּבְנֹתֵיכֶ֑ם וְהָבִ֖יאוּ אֵלָֽי׃ 'Break off the golden rings, which are in the ears of your wives, of your sons, and of your daughters, and bring them unto me' (Exod. 32.2). Accordingly, even setting aside exegesis, it seems that Aaron was eager to shorten his speech, for understandable reasons. The commentators followed this trend, truncating Aaron's quoted speech still further.

However, the vocalisers pointed הִתְפָּרָקוּ as a pausal form. A pausal form in this context, with a *ṭippeḥa* after a *zaqef* (which is the second king in a verse that also includes an *ʾatnaḥ*) is an unusual occurrence. Accordingly, they appear to have divided the verse differently:

ואמר להם למי זהב הִתְפָּרָקוּ   ויתנו לי

According to this division, הִתְפָּרָקוּ is included in the quote of Aaron's speech: 'whosoever hath gold—break it off!' The people's actions are now confined to וַיִּתְּנוּ־לִי 'and they gave it me'. This interpretation also has support among the commentators. Avarbanel, for example, explains: ולכן אמרתי אליהם: למי זהב—התפרקו! רוצה לומר: כל אחד יתן מהזהב כפי מה שיש לו, הרב ירבה מתנתו והמעט ימעיט '...And so I told them: whoever has gold—take it off! That is to say: each person will give gold according to how much they have, those with much will give more and those with less, less'.

As noted, the thrust of Aaron's comments leaves room for both these interpretations. The same is true of the comparison to the original story in the text, which includes both an imperative form פָּֽרְק֑וּ and the past form וַיִּֽתְפָּֽרְק֑וּ; the form here may be considered to mirror either of these. If we turn to the plain meaning of the verse, however, there seems to be no alternative but to read הִתְפָּרָ֑קוּ as an imperative form, for a simple reason. A past tense form would be expected to appear in an inverted tense form, as is usual in a narrative chunk and in keeping with the surrounding past forms: וָאֹמַ֤ר לָהֶם֙... וַיִּתְּנוּ־... וָאַשְׁלִכֵ֣הוּ... וַיֵּצֵ֖א 'and I said to them... and they gave... and I cast it... and (this calf) came out...' (Exod. 32.24). The exceptional form here shows that this is an imperative concluding Aaron's words.

For our purposes, what is important is not the original interpretation of the form, but the interpretation adopted by the vocalisers and the cantillators, and in this respect they were divided: the vocalisers interpreted התפרקו as an imperative, while the cantillators saw it as a third person past form.

4.3. Pausal Forms in Non-Pausal Contexts and Vice-Versa

(10) וְ֠הֵבִיא אַ֣יִל תָּמִ֧ים מִן־הַצֹּ֛אן בְּעֶרְכְּךָ֥ לְאָשָׁ֖ם אֶל־הַכֹּהֵ֑ן וְכִפֶּר֩ עָלָ֨יו הַכֹּהֵ֜ן עַ֣ל שִׁגְגָת֧וֹ אֲשֶׁר־שָׁגָ֛ג וְה֥וּא לֹא־יָדַ֖ע וְנִסְלַ֥ח לֽוֹ׃

'And he shall bring a ram without blemish out of the flock, according to thy valuation, for a guilt-offering, unto the priest; and the priest shall make atonement for him concerning the error which **he committed**, though **he knew** it not, and he shall be forgiven.' (Lev. 5.18)

This verse describes the sacrifice known by the Sages as אשם תלוי 'contingent guilt offering'. The cantillation establishes the following division:

עַ֫ל שגגתֹ֥ו אשר־שגַ֛ג והֻ֥וא לֹֽא־יָדַ֖ע ונסלַ֥ח לֹֽו

The first part of this clause includes two grammatically similar verb forms: שגג and ידע. As noted above, such a situation is optimal for purposes of comparison, since in such a case the forms are equally prone to pausal formation and they occur within a single verse. Yet as we see, the pausal form appears on the weaker cantillation mark, while the principal mark carries a non-pausal form. Accordingly, the vocalisation implies a different division:

על שגגתו אשר שָׁגָג   והוא לא יָדַע ונסלח לו

Thus the cantillation and the vocalisation disagree as to whether the intermediate section וְהֽוּא לֹא־יָדָע is to be attached to the first part of this clause or to the second (Ben-David 1995, 154, n. 146). What is the background to this uncertainty?

We should firstly note that the words וְהֽוּא לֹא־יָדָע stand out here, since they do not appear in the analogous verses concerning other sacrifices, such as:

...וְכִפֶּ֨ר עָלָ֧יו הַכֹּהֵ֛ן מֵחַטָּאתֹ֖ו וְנִסְלַ֥ח לֹֽו׃

'...and the priest shall make atonement for him as concerning his sin, and he shall be forgiven.' (Lev. 4.26)

...וְכִפֶּ֨ר עָלָ֧יו הַכֹּהֵ֛ן עַל־חַטָּאתֹ֥ו אֲשֶׁר־חָטָ֖א וְנִסְלַ֥ח לֹֽו׃

'...and the priest shall make atonement for him as touching his sin that he hath sinned, and he shall be forgiven.' (Lev. 4.35)

Accordingly, the inclusion of these words here is inherently problematic. On the one hand, it is possible to assume quite simply that והוא לא ידע is merely a reiteration in different words of שגגתו אשר שגג. This is surely the understanding implied by the cantillation in combining these two phrases.

However, the Sages saw in these words a specific reference to the special law concerning this sacrifice, the contingent guilt offering. They explain that contingent guilt occurs only when a person is not certain that he has committed a sin. This offering cannot atone for a sin unless the sinner is unaware of his sin and as far as he does not have certainty. Even after making this offering, if he learns that he indeed sinned, he is obliged to make a new sacrifice—the sin offering (חַטָּאת)—like a regular sinner: וזהו הנקרא אשם תלוי—מפני שהוא מכפר על הספק ותולה לו עד שיודע לו בודאי שחטא בשגגה ויקריב חטאתו 'And this is what is known as the contingent guilt [offering]—since it atones for doubt and remains pending until he knows with certainty that he sinned in error and he makes his sin offering" (Maimonides, *Mishneh Torah, Shegagot* 5.1). Sifra (Finkelstein, 1983, 209) explains: והוא לא ידע ונסלח לו, הא אילו ידע אינו מיתכפר לו, הא למה זה דומה לעגלה ערופה, אף על פי שנערפה ואחר כך נמצא ההורג הרי זה יהריג '"And he knew it not and is forgiven"'—implies that if he did know it, he is not atoned. What does this resemble? The red heifer, that if the murderer was found after the heifer's neck had been broken, he will be executed'. In these comments, the expression וְהוּא לֹא־יָדָע 'and he knew it not' clearly refers to the post factum situation, and if he later learns that he indeed sinned, his atonement is nullified, as Rashi explains here: הא אם ידע לאחר זמן, לא נתכפר לו באשם זה עד

שיביא חטאת 'Yet if he knew later, he is not atoned for this guilt until he has brought a sin offering'. According to the Sages, then, forgiveness depends and is conditioned on the sinner not having been aware of his sin; as soon as he becomes aware of it, the atonement is nullified. This would seem to explain why the vocalisers formed the unit וְהוּא לֹא־יָדַע וְנִסְלַח לוֹ, to emphasise that he is only forgiven for as long as he is unaware.

(11) וַיֹּאמֶר יְהוֹנָתָן לְדָוִד לֵךְ לְשָׁלוֹם אֲשֶׁר נִשְׁבַּעְנוּ שְׁנֵינוּ אֲנַחְנוּ בְּשֵׁם ה' לֵאמֹר ה' יִהְיֶה׀ בֵּינִי וּבֵינֶךָ וּבֵין זַרְעִי וּבֵין זַרְעֲךָ עַד־עוֹלָם׃

'And Jonathan said to David: "Go in peace, forasmuch as we have sworn both of us in the name of the Lord, saying: 'The Lord shall be between me and **thee**, and between my seed and **thy seed**, forever.'"' (1 Sam. 20.42)

The cantillation establishes the following division:

ה' יִהְיֶה׀ בֵּינִי ובינך ובין זרעי ובין זרעך   עד־עולם

However, the vocalisation of the forms here challenges this division, since וּבֵינֶךָ is vocalised as a pausal form, while זַרְעֲךָ appears in a non-pausal form. Here, too, the two words belong to the same category (*shewa* in the non-pausal form versus *segol* in the pausal form in a second person masculine singular pronominal suffix), and again they appear in a single verse. According to the vocalisers, then, the division is:

ה' יהיה ביני וּבֵינֶךָ   ובין זרעי ובין זַרְעֲךָ עד־עולם

The vocalisers and the cantillators disagreed as to whether עד עולם in this verse is attached solely to בין זרעי ובין זרעך (as the vocalisation dictates), or also to ביני ובינך (as the cantillation implies) (Ben-David 1995, 72, n. 110).

The question whether עד עולם properly describes only the following generations or also the current one arises in numerous verses. In several places in the Bible, we find the emphatic particle עולם used to strengthen זֶרַע 'seed'. The following is one example of such a verse: ...וְנָתַתִּי אֶת־הָאָרֶץ הַזֹּאת לְזַרְעֲךָ אַחֲרֶיךָ אֲחֻזַּת עוֹלָם: '...and I will give this land to thy seed after thee for an everlasting possession.' (Gen. 48.4)

Conversely, עולם sometimes undoubtedly also refers to the current generation, as in the verse shortly before the one we are discussing here: ...הִנֵּה ה' בֵּינִי וּבֵינְךָ עַד־עוֹלָם: '...behold, the LORD is between me and thee forever.' (1 Sam. 20.23)

In several verses, however, the question involves the division of the verse, and the commentator or cantillator must decide what is complemented by the word עולם. This is the case in our verse, where the cantillation determined that עולם refers to this generation, as well as future ones. The same is true in the following verses:

...בֵּינִי וּבֵינֶךָ וּבֵין זַרְעֲךָ אַחֲרֶיךָ לְדֹרֹתָם   לִבְרִית עוֹלָם...

'...between Me and thee and thy seed after thee throughout their generations for an everlasting covenant...' (Gen. 17.7)

...לְמַעַן יִיטַב לָהֶם וְלִבְנֵיהֶם   לְעֹלָם:

'...that it might be well with them, and with their children forever.' (Deut. 5.25)

...וְעֹשֶׂה־חֶסֶד לִמְשִׁיחוֹ לְדָוִד וּלְזַרְעוֹ   עַד־עוֹלָם:

'...and showeth mercy to His anointed, to David and to his seed, for evermore.' (2 Sam. 22.51)

...מִפִּיךָ וּמִפִּי זַרְעֲךָ וּמִפִּי זֶרַע זַרְעֲךָ אָמַר ה'   מֵעַתָּה וְעַד־עוֹלָם:

'...(they will not depart) out of thy mouth, nor out of the mouth of thy seed, nor out of the mouth of thy seed's seed, saith the Lord, from henceforth and forever.' (Isa. 59.21)

However, we also find a different pattern of division, whereby the cantillation establishes that עולם refers solely to the seed:

כִּ֧י אֶת־כָּל־הָאָ֛רֶץ אֲשֶׁר־אַתָּ֥ה רֹאֶ֖ה לְךָ֣ אֶתְּנֶ֑נָּה   וּֽלְזַרְעֲךָ֖ עַד־עוֹלָֽם׃

'for all the land which thou seest, to thee will I give it, and to thy seed forever.' (Gen. 13.15)

וְהָי֣וּ בְךָ֔ לְא֖וֹת וּלְמוֹפֵ֑ת   וּֽבְזַרְעֲךָ֖ עַד־עוֹלָֽם׃

'and they shall be upon thee for a sign and for a wonder, and upon thy seed forever.' (Deut. 28.46)

וְשָׁ֤בוּ דְמֵיהֶם֙ בְּרֹ֣אשׁ יוֹאָ֔ב   וּבְרֹ֥אשׁ זַרְע֖וֹ לְעֹלָ֑ם...

'so shall their blood return upon the head of Joab, and upon the head of his seed forever...' (1 Kgs 2.33)

וְצָרַ֤עַת נַעֲמָן֙ תִּדְבַּק־בְּךָ֔   וּֽבְזַרְעֲךָ֖ לְעוֹלָ֑ם...

'the leprosy therefore of Naaman shall cleave unto thee, and unto thy seed forever...' (2 Kgs 5.27)

It emerges that the cantillation itself follows two approaches, sometimes establishing that עולם relates solely to the coming generations and sometimes includes this generation. Accordingly, it is hardly surprising that in our verse, too, the Masoretes disagreed regarding the division, though in this instance the disagreement was between the cantillators, on the one side, and the vocalisers, on the other.

5.0. One Word or Two?

5.1. מאפליה, שלהבתיה

(12) הַדּ֗וֹר אַתֶּם֙ רְא֣וּ דְבַר־ה' הֲמִדְבָּ֤ר הָיִ֙יתִי֙ לְיִשְׂרָאֵ֔ל אִ֛ם אֶ֥רֶץ מַאְפֵּ֖לְיָ֑ה מַדּ֜וּעַ
אָמְר֤וּ עַמִּי֙ רַ֔דְנוּ ל֥וֹא־נָב֛וֹא ע֖וֹד אֵלֶֽיךָ׃

‘O generation, see ye the word of the LORD: have I been a wilderness unto Israel? or a land of **thick darkness**? Wherefore say My people: “We roam at large; we will come no more unto Thee”?’ (Jer. 2.31)

(13) שִׂימֵ֨נִי כַֽחוֹתָ֜ם עַל־לִבֶּ֗ךָ כַּֽחוֹתָם֙ עַל־זְרוֹעֶ֔ךָ כִּֽי־עַזָּ֤ה כַמָּ֙וֶת֙ אַהֲבָ֔ה קָשָׁ֥ה כִשְׁא֖וֹל
קִנְאָ֑ה רְשָׁפֶ֕יהָ רִשְׁפֵּ֕י אֵ֖שׁ שַׁלְהֶ֥בֶתְיָֽה׃

‘Set me as a seal upon thy heart, as a seal upon thine arm; for love is strong as death, jealousy is cruel as the grave; the flashes thereof are flashes of fire, **a very flame of the Lord**.’ (Song 8.6)

The two words we shall discuss here, מאפליה and שלהבתיה, are similar in two respects: (A) They both end with the same *-yah* suffix; (B) The first part of the word, before the suffix, is also found in the Bible as an independent word: מאפל (Josh 24:7), שלהבת (Ezek 21:3; Job 15:30). Needless to say, the suffix יה is also well-known as an independent word. Accordingly, the obvious question regarding each of these two words is whether they constitute a single word, lengthened by the suffix, or two separate words joined as a construct form.

מאפליה: this form is usually considered a single word. Opinion is divided as to its precise meaning—‘darkness’ or ‘wilderness’—and regarding its vocalisation—מְאַפליה or מַאְפליה (see, for example, Ginsburg 1880–1885, 602). However, there appears to be a consensus that this is indeed a single word. The cantillation mark under the *pe* is not a *ṭippeḥa* and cannot be considered such, since a disjunctive can never occur in the word of another disjunctive. This mark is considered a *meʾayla*, and so it is recorded in the *Masora Magna* at Num. 28.26 (Breuer 1982, 106, n. 39). The *meʾayla* has the same appearance as the *ṭippeḥa*, but marks the place of secondary stress in the word and only ever appears in words marked with *silluq* or *ʾatnaḥ*.

שלהבתיה: some of the commentators and translators regard this as a single word, such as the Peshitta: ܫܠܗܒܝܬܐ. Others read two words here; the Targum, for example, has: דמין לגומרין דאישתא דגהינם דברא יתיה ה' 'they are like coals of the fire of hell which God created'. Ibn Ezra commented: מחלוקת בין אנשי המסרה אם היא מלה אחת או שתים. והקרוב שהיא שתים, וסמיכ' השם כמו כהררי אל 'There is a dispute between the Masoretes as to whether this is one word or two. Most probably it is two, and the construct form with the Divine name is as in כהררי אל'. See below for other testimonies concerning this word (Ginsburg 1926b, 574).

These two words resemble others that raise a similar problem. We will briefly review what is known about these other words from the writings of the Sages. The sources for the discussions about these words are of three types: (a) lists prepared by the various Masoretes; (b) the Masora of the Targum; (c) the Talmudic discussion (b. *Pesaḥim* 117a).

The following are the disputed words, with the identification of the disagreeing parties:

כסיה 'throne of the Lord' (Exod. 17.16 [L]): Western/Eastern (Ginsburg 1880–1885, I:592, 709,

III:191; Yeivin 1968, 80–82); School of Sura/School of Neharde‘a (Yeivin 1968, 80–82; 1980, 121–22); Amoraim in the Talmud

ידידיה 'Jedidiah' (2 Sam. 12.25 [L]): Western/Eastern (Ginsburg 1880–1885, I:593; Yeivin 1968, 80–82); Amoraim in the Talmud

הללויה 'hallelujah' (Ps. 104.35 [L]): School of Sura/School of Neharde‘a (Norzi 1742–1744, IV:22b–23a [Ps. 104.35]; Ginsburg 1880–1885, I:709–10; Yeivin 1968, 80–82)

במרחביה 'with great enlargement' (Ps. 118.5 [L]): School of Sura/School of Neharde‘a (Ginsburg 1880–1885, III:191; Yeivin 1968, 80–82)

שלהבתיה 'a very flame of the Lord' (Song 8.6): Ben-Asher/Ben-Naftali (Ginsburg 1880–1885, III:191; Lipschütz 1965, 53)

Thus we have located five words where there is disagreement as to whether we should read one or two words (Yeivin 1968, 80–82). In addition to the sources quoted above, we must now consider how these words were presented in the biblical text (Ginsburg 1966, Introduction, 375ff; Yeivin 1968, 80–82):

כֵּ֣ס יָ֔הּ / כֵּ֣סְיָ֔הּ

יְדִֽידְיָֽהּ

הַֽלְלוּ־יָֽהּ

בַּמֶּרְחָ֥ב יָֽהּ

שַׁלְהֶ֥בֶתְיָֽה

If we look at these words as presented here, we can discern three different sources of opinion for the manner in which they are to be perceived: spelling, vocalisation, and cantillation. In regard to the spelling, is the word written as one connected word or as two separate ones? In regard to the vocalisation, does the *he* have a *mappiq* (implying that the latter part is perceived as the Divine name and hence the entire form is two words) or does it lack a *mappiq* (in which case the latter part is not perceived as the Divine name and the form is considered a single word)? In regard to the cantillation, does the word carry one cantillation mark or two? The following are the perceptions of these words according to these three sources:

Tradition	One word	Two words
Spelling	כסיה (?)	כס יה (?)
	ידידיה	הללו יה
	שלהבתיה	במרחב יה
Vocalisation	שַׁלְהֶבֶתְיָה	כֵּס יָהּ
		יְדִידְיָהּ
		הַלְלוּ יָהּ
		בַּמֶּרְחָב יָהּ
Cantillation		כ֣ס י֔ה
		יד֣ידי֑ה
		הללו־י֥ה
		במרח֣ב י֥ה
		שלה֣בתי֥ה

Thus, we can see that the doubts detailed above were not settled in a uniform manner in the final form of the biblical text. The varying approaches led to the emergence of a mixed system, including not only differences between the words, but also between the three foundations—spelling, vocalisation, and cantillation. It may be worth adding that the cantillation is the only one of these three foundations that adopts a consistent approach to all five forms, interpreting them as two words in each case.

From the standpoint of our subject here—dissonance between the vocalisation and the cantillation—only one of the words is relevant: שלהבתיה. As discussed here, the vocalisers followed the spelling in reading a single word, and accordingly there is no *mappiq* in the *he*. The cantillators clearly took the position that this form constitutes two words, and accordingly it bears two cantillation marks.

We may now turn to the second of the words on our list: מאפליה (Jer. 2.31). This form is not mentioned in the various disagreements between the Masoretes, and ostensibly all agree that it constitutes a single word. This is supported by the above explanation, that this form bears the rare cantillation mark *meʾayla*, which only appears in a word accented with a chief disjunctive. However, we must raise some questions in this regard. Firstly, even if we have not found disagreement among the Masoretes regarding this form, is it really impossible to understand it as constituting two words? After all, and as explained, this form also visibly comprises two words that exist independently in the Bible. And more than one commentator has indeed sensed that while this is one word (according to their perception and as determined by the spelling), it actually comprises two words:

> אבל ארץ מאפליה בירמיה ב'—בכל הספרי' היא מלה אחת, אף על פי שענינה ב' מלות, כלומר מאפל יה, על דרך הררי אל ודומ'
>
> But ארץ מאפליה in Jeremiah 2—in all the books it is a single word, despite the fact that its meaning is as two words, vis. מאפל יה, similar to הררי אל and so forth. (*Sefer Shewaʿ Shemot*, in Ginsburg 1880–1885, III:191)
>
> ובכל הספרים היא מלה אחת וענינה שתי מלות, וכן שלהבתיה. וסמך מאפל אל השם יתברך מרוב האפל, כמו שסמך שלהבתיה מרוב

> השלהבת. וכן כל דבר שרוצה להגדילו סומך אותו אל השם, כמו כהררי אל, עיר גדולה לאלהים, ותהי לחרדת אלהים, נפתולי אלהים, גבר ציד לפני ה'
>
> And in all the books this is a single word, though its meaning is as two words, and the same is true of שלהבתיה. And the construct of מאפל with the Divine name emphasises the darkness, just as the construct שלהבתיה emphasises the flame. And thus when one wishes to amplify anything it is placed in construct with the Divine name, such as כהררי אל 'as mighty mountains', עיר גדולה לאלהים 'an exceeding great city', ותהי לחרדת אלהים 'so it grew into a great terror', נפתולי אלהים 'mighty wrestlings', גבר ציד לפני ה' 'a mighty hunter'. (Qimḥi, in Biesenthal and Lebrecht, 1847, 25, discussing the root אפ"ל)

Secondly, we must note the unusual cantillation here: this is the only place in the Bible where the *me᾽ayla* is preceded by a *tevir* and a *merekha*, accents that are usually subordinate to a *ṭippeḥa* (Breuer 1982, 106). This abnormality may ostensibly be resolved by noting that a *me᾽ayla* also behaves like a *ṭippeḥa* in an additional respect: in several instances it is preceded by a *zaqef* as the ultimate king before the chief disjunctive, and there is no *ṭippeḥa* at all. An example of this is וּבְי֣וֹם הַבִּכּוּרִ֗ים בְּהַקְרִ֤יבְכֶ֨ם מִנְחָ֤ה חֲדָשָׁה֙ לַֽה' בְּשָׁבֻֽעֹתֵיכֶ֑ם 'also in the day of the first-fruits, when ye bring a new meal-offering unto the Lord in your feast of weeks' (Num. 28.26). This phenomenon is found solely before a *me᾽ayla*. As has already been observed (Breuer 1982, 106), the melody was surely similar to that of the *ṭippeḥa* (as the graphic form also implies), and so it was possible to place a *zaqef* before it by way of a final king, despite the fact that the final king is always a *ṭippeḥa*.

However, this deviation is not particularly serious. A *zaqef* serving as a final king is subordinate to the chief disjunctive, as befits a king. The issue is only that it has not become a *ṭippeḥa* as is expected with the final king. The quandary may be resolved by means of the musical cantillation. Since the melody of the *meʾayla* already provides a fine preparation for the *ʾatnaḥ*, there is no longer any need to replace the *zaqef* with a *ṭippeḥa*. In other words, the *zaqef* and the *ṭippeḥa* enjoy equal status, and the distinction between them is a purely melodic one. Accordingly, exchanges between these two marks may be explained on melodic grounds.

In our current case, however, the quandary is vastly more serious, since we have here a serious deviation in the basic rules of the cantillation. The dominion of the *ʾatnaḥ* contains only a single disjunctive, namely a *tevir*, so the dominion of the first-degree disjunctive is divided by a third-degree disjunctive. Yet the basic rule of cantillation, from which all the other rules and details derive, is that the dominion of the disjunctive is divided by means of a disjunctive which is one rank lower. To the best of my knowledge, there is no other example of such a deviation in the Bible—regarding not only *ʾatnaḥ*, but all the cantillation marks.

Above all, however, we must pose the following question: How can we be sure that this cantillation mark is indeed a *meʾayla* and not a *ṭippeḥa*? Let us recall that the sole evidence that this is indeed a *meʾayla* and not a *ṭippeḥa* is the fact that it appears on the word of the chief disjunctive, and we can find no other *ṭippeḥa* in this slot. However, the assumption that the cantillation mark indeed appears here on the chief disjunctive word depends on the assumption that this is indeed a single word. If we assume that these are two separate words—מַאְפֵּל יָהּ—then this mark does not appear on the last word, and, accordingly, must be a *ṭippeḥa* and not a *meʾayla,* since a *meʾayla* appears solely on the last word. Thus, the interpretation of this mark as a *meʾayla* and the interpretation of this form as a single word are mutually dependent: those who regard the form as a single word must argue that the cantillation mark is a *meʾayla* and vice versa; and those who perceive the form as two words must assert that the mark is a *ṭippeḥa* and vice versa.

If we recall our comment above that the cantillators consistently regarded all the words discussed here as two separate words, it is not difficult to hypothesise that here, too, the cantillators were faithful to their method. They perceived this form as two words and marked it with a *ṭippeḥa* and an *ʾatnaḥ*, which are preceded by marks customarily subservient to a *ṭippeḥa*.

As the masoretic form took shape, a situation emerged whereby this word, like others, reflected a blending of contradicttory approaches: in this instance, spelling and vocalisation as one word, on the one hand, and cantillation as two words, on the other. Later Masoretes who saw this as a single word (under the influence of the spelling and vocalisation) could now only define the cantillation mark here as a *meʾayla,* since a disjunctive never appears in the same word with another disjunctive.

If we accept this assumption, all that remains is for us to discuss the meaning of this verse according to the cantillation. First, we must discuss all the words perceived (by anyone) as two words. Even if the word is perceived as two words, the second component—יה—may be in construct with the preceding word, so that the difference in terms of the reading is not great. This is the case, for example, with the words ידיד יה, כס יה, and שלהבת יה. However, once the form is perceived as two words, this creates the possibility of a different verse division, and of regarding יה not as a suffix, but as filling some other grammatical role. This is what happened with the word מרחביה:

> מִֽן־הַ֭מֵּצַר קָרָ֣אתִי יָּ֑הּ עָנָ֖נִי בַמֶּרְחָ֣ב יָֽהּ׃
>
> 'Out of my straits I called upon the Lord; He answered me with great enlargement.' (Ps. 118.5)

Those who perceive מרחביה as a single word will, naturally, regard the entire phrase as a descriptive complement. Those who regard the form as two words may also interpret it as a construct filling the same role, in which case the division remains the same. However, since they regarded the form as two words, the cantillators went one step further, understanding *yah* as the subject of the sentence, so that the division is:

ענני במרחב   יה

rather than

ענני   במרחב יה

What happened in our verse? Here, too, we may regard the form as comprising two words, but in a construct form, as Qimḥi notes in his commentary: ולהגדיל האפל סמך אותו למלת י"ה, וכן שלהבת י"ה, כהררי אל, עיר גדולה לאלהים, ותהי לחרדת אלהים 'And to magnify the [concept of] darkness, he attached it to the word יה, as in שלהבת יה, כהררי אל, עיר גדולה לאלהים, ותהי לחרדת אלהים'. However, the cantillators placed the *ṭippeḥa* (as we see it) on מאפל. Accordingly, their division is:

הַמִּדְבָּ֤ר הָיִ֙יתִי֙ לְיִשְׂרָאֵ֔ל

אִ֛ם אֶ֥רֶץ מַאְפֵּ֖ליָ֑ה

The meaning is thus: 'Have I been like a wilderness to Israel? Or is the Lord a dark land?' In other words, יה here is not in construct with מאפל, but is the subject of the sentence, paralleling הייתי in the first part of the verse.

5.2. ונבזביתך

(14) בֵּאדַ֜יִן עָנֵ֣ה דָנִיֵּ֗אל וְאָמַר֮ קֳדָ֣ם מַלְכָּא֒ מַתְּנָתָךְ֙ לָ֣ךְ לֶהֶוְיָ֔ן וּנְבָ֣זְבְּיָתָ֔ךְ לְאָחֳרָ֣ן הַ֑ב בְּרַם֙ כְּתָבָא֙ אֶקְרֵ֣א לְמַלְכָּ֔א וּפִשְׁרָ֖א אֲהוֹדְעִנֵּֽהּ׃

'Then Daniel answered and said before the king: "Let thy gifts be to thyself, and give thy rewards to another; nevertheless, I will read the writing unto the king, and make known to him the interpretation."' (Dan. 5.17)

ונבזביתך is vocalised as the plural form of נְבִזְבָּה, which appears once in Biblical Aramaic in a similar context: מַתְּנָן וּנְבִזְבָּה וִיקָר שַׂגִּיא 'gifts and rewards and great honour' (Dan. 2.6). However, our word appears with two cantillation marks, a pattern that is not found in similar circumstances. Accordingly, this cantillation would seem to be appropriate for those translations that see two words here, such as the Peshitta: ואיקר ביתך. However, this reading requires a division into two words and a change in the vocalisation: וּנְבָז בַּיְתָךְ.

Thus, the cantillation and the vocalisation disagreed here. The vocalisation understands a single word—the plural form of נבזבה; the cantillators see here two words—נְבָז־בַּיְתָךְ.

6.0. Conclusion

The Masoretic Text of the Hebrew Bible was consolidated after many years of inspection and examination, and the Masoretes laboured tirelessly to clarify and shape its form. They were required to resolve numerous disagreements, some of which remained unresolved even toward the end of the masoretic era.

These disagreements emerge before us in the masoretic lists or as textual variants. Sometimes, however, these disagreements can be discerned within the final masoretic text. The *qere-ketiv* alternates are the most prominent example of this phenomenon, generally representing two ancient versions. The written and recited forms were not finalised simultaneously, and we accordingly find two different versions reflected in a single biblical form.

In this article, I have attempted to show that a similar phenomenon exists between the vocalisation and the cantillation: two different words or interpretations found their way into the biblical text before us and survived in their original forms. We find them before us now in a single version, one in the vocalisation and the other in the cantillation.

The precise explanation for this phenomenon is not entirely clear. We may assume that there were from very early on two different traditions, each with its own vocalisation and cantillation. The different methods and numerous disagreements led to the blending of these distinct traditions as reflected in the final Masoretic Text. However, it may be that the cantillators were acquainted with the vocalised form as we have it, yet nevertheless cantillated the text differently.

Even if the precise reasons behind this phenomenon have not yet been fully clarified, its recognition is nevertheless important. First, in regard to the interpretation of the verses, commentators who strive to utilise all the tools in their possession must not only consider the vocalisation and the cantillation together, but must also examine each separately and determine whether they are compatible. Second, in regard to the study of the relations between the vocalisation and the cantillation, anyone who wishes to examine the history of the crystallisation of the vocalisation and cantillation systems as we know them must also address the phenomenon of the dissonance that is sometimes found between this vocalisation and this cantillation.

References

Ben-David, I. 1995. *Contextual and Pausal Forms in Biblical Hebrew: Syntax and Accentuation*. Jerusalem: Magnes Press. [Hebrew]

Ben-Yehuda, Eliezer. 1908–1958. *The Complete Dictionary of Ancient and Modern Hebrew*. Jerusalem: Langenscheidt. [Hebrew]

Biesenthal, Johann H., and F. Lebrecht (eds). 1847. *Sefer ha-Shorashim le-Rabi David ben Yosef Qimḥi ha-Sfaradi, ʿim ha-Nimuqim me-Rabi ʾEliyhu ha-Levi, ha-Ashkenazi* (Rabbi Davidis Kimhi Radicum liber sive Hebraeum bibliorum lexicon: Xum animadversionibus Eliae Levitae). Jerusalem: no publisher. [Hebrew; Latin]

Blau, Joshua. 1981. 'On Pausal Lengthening, Pausal Stress Shift, Philippi's Law and Rule Ordering in Biblical Hebrew'. *Hebrew Annual Review* 5:1–13.

Breuer, Mordekhai. 1980. 'Le-veruran shel Sugyot be-ṭaʿame ha-Miqra u-v-Niqudo, 3: Hilufe ha-Niqud ben Ben-Asher le-Ven Naftali'. *Leshonenu* 44: 243–62.

———. 1981. 'KĔṮIV, QĔRÉ AND ṬĕʾIM (written, read and chanted)'. *Leshonenu* 41: 260–69.

———. 1982. *Ṭaʿame ha-Miqra be-Khaf ʾAlef Sefarim u-ve-Sifre ʾEmet*. Jerusalem: Mikhlala.

———. 1989. *Torah, Neviʾim, Ketuvim ʿal pi ha-nusaḥ ve-ha-mesorah shel Keter ʾAram Tsovah ve-khitve yad ha-qrovim lo, b-ide Mordekhai Breuer*. Jerusalem: Mossad Harav Kook.

Eichel, I. A. 1790. *Sefer Mishle ʿim Targum ʾAshkenazi u-Veʾur*. Berlin: Chevrat Neʿarim.

Finkelstein, Louis (ed.). 1983. *Sifra on Leviticus: According to Vatican Manuscript Assemani 66*. New York: Jewish Theological Seminary of America.

Ginsburg, Christian David. 1880–1885. *The Massorah*. London: Fromme.

———. 1926a. *The Later Prophets*. London: British and Foreign Bible Society.

———. 1926b. *The Writings*. London: British and Foreign Bible Society.

———. 1966. *Introduction to the Massoretico-critical edition of the Hebrew Bible*. With a prolegomenon by Harry M. Orlinsky. New York: Ktav.

Ḥakham, Amos. 1970. *Sefer Iyyov*. Daʿat Miqra. Jerusalem: Mossad Ha-Rav Kook.

———. 1981. *Sefer Tehillim*. Daʿat Miqra. Jerusalem: Mossad Ha-Rav Kook.

———. 1984. *Sefer Yeshaʿyahu*. Daʿat Miqra. Jerusalem: Mossad Harav Kook.

Lipschütz, Lazar (ed.). 1965. *Mishael ben Uzziel's Treatise on the Differences between Ben Asher and Ben Naphtali*. Jerusalem: Magnes. [Hebrew]

Norzi, Y. S. 1742–1744. *Minkhat Shai*. Mantua: Refael Chayim.

Qafih, Y. 1973. *Iyyov ʿim Tirgum u-Ferush ha-Gaʾon Saʿadiya ben Yosef Piyumi*. Jerusalem: Hamaqor.

Schlesinger, A. 1962. *Researches in the Exegesis and Language of the Bible*. Jerusalem: Ha-Ḥevra le-Ḥeqer ha-Miqra be-Yisraʾel. [Hebrew]

Sperber, Alexander (ed.). 1959–1973. *The Bible in Aramaic*. 5 vols. Leiden: Brill.

Wickes, William. 1887. *A Treatise on the Accentuation of the Twenty-One So-Called Prose Books of the Old Testament*. Oxford: Clarendon Press.

Yalon, Ḥanoch. 1971. *Studies in the Hebrew Language*. Jerusalem: Bialik. [Hebrew]

Yeivin, Israel. 1968. *The Aleppo Codex*. Jerusalem: Magnes Press. [Hebrew]

———. 1980. *Introduction to the Tiberian Masorah*. Translated and edited by E. J. Revell. Masoretic Studies 5. Missoula, MT: Scholars Press, for the Society of Biblical Literature and the International Organization for Masoretic Studies.

Zer-Kavod, A. 1973. *Qohelet*. Daʿat Miqra. Jerusalem: Mossad Ha-Rav Kook.

WHY ARE THERE TWO SYSTEMS OF TIBERIAN ṬEʿAMIM?

Daniel J. Crowther

Unlike their Palestinian and Babylonian cousins, the Tiberian *ṭeʿamim*[1] are found in two self-contained systems: one system for Psalms, Proverbs, and most of Job, and another system for the other books of the Hebrew Bible.[2] By convention, the *ṭeʿamim* unique to Psalms, Proverbs, and Job are referred to as the *ṭeʿamim* of the Three and the *ṭeʿamim* used in the rest of the Hebrew Bible

[1] In this paper, the Hebrew term טעמים is used to denote the diacritical marks that are variously referred to in the literature as 'cantillation marks', 'biblical accents', and 'masoretic punctuation', alongside many other variations of these names. The transliterated Hebrew *ṭeʿamim* is preferred as it suggestive of all the functions of these marks. The English terms refer to more specific and limited functions, such as the marking of stress (accentuation), chant (cantillation), and syntax (punctuation), all of which can be included in a broad understanding of 'the sense (*ṭaʿam*) of the text' (Jacobson 2002, 3–24).

[2] There are many different forms of Palestinian and many different forms of Babylonian *ṭeʿamim* found in the manuscripts (and fragments of manuscripts). These texts bear witness not only to two traditions (beside the Tiberian) of marks for the *ṭeʿamim*, but also to a process of development of the technology of *ṭeʿamim* (Heijmans 2013; Shoshany 2013).

 https://doi.org/10.11647/OBP.0330.08

are referred to as the *ṭeʿamim* of the Twenty-One.[3] This paper addresses three questions:

1. Why are there two kinds of Tiberian *ṭeʿamim*?
2. What are the features of the books of Psalms, Proverbs, and (most of) Job that might best explain why these three books alone have been selected for a different system of *ṭeʿamim*?
3. What is the essential feature of the system of the *ṭeʿamim* in the Three that distinguishes it from the system of the *ṭeʿamim* in the Twenty-One?

1.0. The Absence of Answers in Masoretic Treatises

Extant masoretic treatises that refer to the *ṭeʿamim* are few in number and limited in the degree to which they can be used to answer any of the above questions. In so far as they do address the *ṭeʿamim*, these works appear to focus on the oral performance of the biblical text and so the function and workings of the *ṭeʿamim* tend to be presumed rather than explained.[4] In regard to

[3] Following the tradition of counting the total number of books in the Hebrew Bible as 24, as exemplified in, for example, b. Bava Batra 14b.

[4] The world of early masoretic treatises is a unique place of particular interests. Much of the discussion focuses on the observation of minor grammatical variations in Hebrew that prove rules also observed in Arabic linguistics. A second significant focus appears to have been the preservation of the correct pronunciation of the biblical text with its Tiberian markings, whether or not it seemed to follow these rules (Khan 2000, 5–25; 2013).

the *ṭeʿamim*, the two most important masoretic treatises are the tenth-century *Sefer Diqduqe ha-Ṭeʿamim* ('The Book of the Fine Details of the *Ṭeʿamim*', in Hebrew) by Aaron ben Asher; and the eleventh-century *Hidāyat al-Qāriʾ* ('Guidance for the Reader', in Arabic) by the Karaite grammarian Abū al-Faraj Hārūn.

1.1. *Sefer Diqduqe ha-Ṭeʿamim*

The earliest copy of this work is found in the appendices of the Leningrad Codex, the opening folio of which dates the completion of the whole codex to 1008/9 CE.[5] In the centre of an ornate and colourful end-folio (479r), the scribe reveals himself to be Samuel ben Jacob and declares himself to be a student of Aaron ben Moshe ben Asher (the author of *Sefer Diqduqe ha-Ṭeʿamim*). There is no reason to doubt these declarations—indeed the accuracy of the biblical text of the codex rather tends to support it. In the Leningrad Codex, Samuel ben Jacob's copy of *Sefer Diqduqe ha-Ṭeʿamim* extends to ten folios (479v–488r).[6] The material found in these ten folios can be summarised as follows:

[5] The text of *Sefer Diqduqe ha-Ṭeʿamim* appears to be in the same hand as the rest of the Codex.

[6] The text of *Sefer Diqduqe ha-Ṭeʿamim* is available in facsimile copies of Codex L. Many later copies are found in other codices, but there is much variation in their material, some of which is found in Baer and Strack 1970 (1879). Aron Dotan (1963) produced a critical edition from the many variants. The resultant text is much more concise than that found in Codex L and so contains even less information pertinent to our question.

1. An introduction that offers various blessings and relates scripture to the twenty-two letters of the Hebrew alphabet (479v–480r).
2. Two *piyyuṭim* (liturgical poems) in which the *nequddot*[7] and *ṭeʿamim* are described and praised (480r–481v).
3. The main bulk of the work comprises lists of words that have the same consonants, but varied pronunciation according to variations in their *nequddot* and *ṭeʿamim* (481v–488r).

From this evidence it can be concluded that *Sefer Diqduqe ha-Ṭeʿamim* was not written to explain the workings of the *ṭeʿamim.* Information about the form and nature of the *ṭeʿamim* is, in fact, limited to that found in its two *piyyuṭim,* of which one praises the beauty and efficacy of the *ṭeʿamim* of the Twenty-One and the other praises the beauty and efficacy of the *ṭeʿamim* of the Three.[8] These two devotional poems include word-plays made out of the names of the *ṭeʿamim.* These word-plays describe the form and function of each *ṭaʿam* in a way presumably designed to amuse the reader already familiar with this form and function. For example, the *ṭaʿam* of the Twenty-One commonly known as *geresh* is called in the first *piyyuṭ* by the alternative name *ṭeres* (טֶרֶס), which is likened in form to a net (פֶּרֶס *peres*) or a hook (קֶרֶס *qeres*),

[7] This is the way the *naqdan* of this text (presumably Samuel ben Jacob) refers to what is often, by convention, referred to as *niqqud* by many scholars today.

[8] For a translation of these *piyyuṭim* and a discussion of their contents see Crowther (2015, 48–65).

and these can be connected to one another without any destruction (הֶרֶס *heres*). To enjoy this riddle one must know that *geresh* is written as a supra-linear angled line (a hook), that the symbol has a variant, *gershayim*, which is written as two lines (a net) and that two *geresh* signs, or even a *geresh* and *gershayim*, are allowed by the grammar of the *ṭeʿamim* to follow one another without either of them being transformed (that is, without הֶרֶס, destruction). All of this is most helpful and quite entertaining to the initiated, especially when the *piyyuṭ* is vocalised by the person reading it, for it is in this way (and perhaps this way alone) that it connects the oral to the visual in an oral mnemonic. These oral-visual mnemonics are, however, rather lost on the uninitiated and of little, if any, use in understanding why it might be that there are two systems of Tiberian *ṭeʿamim.*

This summary begs the question as to why this treatise should be entitled *Sefer Diqduqe ha-Ṭeʿamim* when so much of its contents concern the *nequddot.* The answer to this question appears to be that the *ṭeʿamim* are understood in masoretic writings to be the determinants of the *nequddot* (and not vice versa). Therefore, it is the *ṭeʿamim* that are understood to be the ultimate embodiment of the wonders of the oral reading tradition.

1.2. *Hidāyat al-Qāriʾ*

Many different parts of this Judaeo-Arabic treatise were translated into Hebrew in the medieval period in order to be added to the appendices of various codices of the Hebrew Bible.[9] The focus of the treatise is the correct (Tiberian) pronunciation of letters and vowels, for example, in words with *ṭaʿam milleʿel* (penultimate stress) and *ṭaʿam milleraʿ* (ultimate stress). The translation of the section relating these issues to the *ṭeʿamim* was variously copied and came to be known as a treatise in its own right: *Sefer Ṭaʿame ha-Miqra*. The paragraphs that directly concern the *ṭeʿamim*, however, are limited. These paragraphs simply list the names of twelve *ṭeʿamim* of the Twenty-One (here understood in the sense of disjunctive *ṭeʿamim*)[10] and their eight 'servants' (which we would call conjunctive *ṭeʿamim*).[11] The discussion of the *ṭeʿamim* concludes with a list of which 'servant' (conjunctive *ṭaʿam*) is associated with which (disjunctive) *ṭaʿam*.[12] Wickes (1881, 104, n. 11) concludes that the name *Sefer Ṭaʿame ha-Miqra*

[9] Translations of select parts from *Hidāyat al-Qāriʾ* have been copied from various codices and published under a number of names: for example, *Sefer Ṭaʿame ha-Miqra* (Mercerus 1565, repr. 1978); *Manuel du lecteur, d'un auteur inconnu publié d'après un manuscrit venu du Yémen et accompagné de notes* (Derenbourg 1871). For the first convincing argument that *Hidāyat al-Qāriʾ* is the source of these works, see Eldar (1992, 33–42). Regarding the relevance of this work to the *ṭeʿamim*, see Eldar and Ofer (2018).

[10] In the Derenbourg manuscript these names are highly recognisable: *pazer qaṭon, telisha gedola, ṭeres (geresh), yetiv, zaqef, ʾatnaḥta, zarqa, legarmeh, tevir, reviaʿ, ṭifḥa*, and *silluq* (1871, 72).

[11] *Shofar munaḥ, telisha qeṭanna, ʾazla, merkha, darga, mayela*, and *galgal.*

[12] The discussion in Mercerus (1978, 38–44) focuses on five *ṭeʿamim*: namely, *zarqa, legarmeh, reviaʿ, tevir*, and *silluq*.

is "a *misnomer*, for the greater part of the work is not taken up with the טעמים, but with the נקודים."

The reproduction of *Sefer Diqduqe ha-Ṭeʿamim* and *Hidāyat al-Qāriʾ* in the appendices of biblical codices testifies to both to the high regard in which the *ṭeʿamim* were held by the medieval Jewish community and the scarcity of masoretic source texts that describe their function. These two treatises present a simple hierarchical understanding of the grammar of the *ṭeʿamim*, in which disjunctive *ṭeʿamim* are understood to be emperors, kings, dukes, and lords, each served by an appropriate conjunctive servant. Neither of these treatises, nor any other extant masoretic treatise, makes any attempt to explain the rationale behind the Tiberian *ṭeʿamim*, that is, whether they are primarily accents, or primarily punctuation marks, or primarily cantillation marks (or all of these or something more), let alone why there should be two systems of Tiberian *ṭeʿamim*.

2.0. A First Answer: Poetics

According to James Kugel (1981, 109–16), during the late medieval and early-modern period, the *ṭeʿamim* of the Three were widely identified as representing the essence of Biblical Hebrew poetry. This, according to Kugel, led to the "forgetting of parallelism" as the mainstay of biblical poetics. Thus Job 1.1–3.1 and 42.7–17 came to be understood to have been marked with the *ṭeʿamim* of the Twenty-One because they were 'essentially' prose in form, whilst Job 3.2–42.6 were understood to have been marked with the *ṭeʿamim* of the Three because these chapters were poetic in form. There are, however, good reasons to doubt that this approach was ever predominant in rabbinic thought, even if it did successfully infiltrate much of the thinking of early-modern Christian Hebraists.

First, the understanding of the *ṭeʿamim* of the Three as essentially poetic and of the Twenty-One as essentially prosaic is not found in any masoretic treatises. The rabbinic readers of these treatises, therefore, should have been aware that all the extant masoretic treatises and *piyyuṭim* declare both systems of *ṭeʿamim* to give (poetically) enlightened performances of the texts in which they are found.

Second, it is hard to imagine that any Jewish rabbi could have been unaware either that there are important poetic texts in the Torah (notably Gen. 49, Exod. 15, and Deut. 32) or that these texts are presented with the *ṭeʿamim* of the Twenty-One.

Third, the Decalogue is presented in masoretic codices with two sets of *ṭeʿamim*: one for the high (poetic?) cantillation of the trained reader on feast-day and one for the low cantillation of household readings (Cohen and Freedman 1974, 7–19). The high cantillation is presented with the *ṭeʿamim* of the Twenty-One, not the Three.

Fourth, there are many poetic texts outside the Torah presented with the *ṭeʿamim* of the Twenty-One (notably Judg. 5, 2 Sam. 22, and 1 Chron. 16). Any rabbi who proposed that Job switches between the two systems for reasons of poetry and prose would have also needed to provide some cogent explanation of why other books of the Hebrew Bible do not also switch systems of *ṭeʿamim* when their texts also switch from prose to poetry (and back again).

Fifth, the title Song of Songs (*shir ha-shirim*) declares it to be a poetic work, as does one of the rabbinic titles of the book of Lamentations (*qinot*). If it is held that the *ṭeʿamim* of the Three are the poetic *ṭe'amim*, it is far from clear why these two books have been given poetic titles when they are presented with the *ṭeʿamim* of the Twenty-One.

Sixth, consistent with all the above, the authoritative sixteenth-century work *Masoret ha-Masora* by Elijah Levita (Eliyahu Baḥur ha-Levi) praises the poetical virtues of both systems of *ṭeʿamim*, not just the *ṭeʿamim* of the Three and does not refer to the *ṭeʿamim* of the Three as being essentially 'poetic' (Elijah Levita in Ginsburg [ed.] 1867).[13]

3.0. A Second Answer: Verse Length

The titles of William Wickes's two works on the *ṭeʿamim* refer to the "so-called poetic books" (1881) and the "so-called prose books" (1887), both acknowledging the terminology that by the nineteenth century had become conventional and casting doubt upon it.[14] To counter this misnomer, Wickes refers to the eleventh-century writings of Rabbi Yehuda ben Bilʿam (Sephardi) and the twelfth-century *tosafot* of Rabbi Isaac ben Meir (ben Yokheved bat Rashi). Both these works understand verse length,

[13] According to Ginsburg, all his other works are similarly descriptive rather than explicative, including Levita (1538). Nevertheless, in his introduction to the work, Ginsburg (1867, 65, n. 71) himself does refer to the *ṭeʿamim* of the Three as the 'poetic accents'.

[14] Cf. also Davidson's (1861) nineteenth-century introductory work *Outlines of Hebrew Accentuation, Prose and Poetical*.

not poetics, to be the distinguishing mark of the *ṭeʿamim* of the Three. According to Wickes (1881, 8–9): "The idea seems to have been to compensate for *the shortness of the verses* (which is the marked characteristic of the greater part of these books) by a finer and fuller, more artificial and impressive melody."

Table 1: The average number of words per verse in each book of the Hebrew Bible

Book	**Word Total**	**Verse Total**	**Words/ Verse**	**Book**	**Word Total**	**Verse Total**	**Words/ Verse**
Prov.	7034	915	7.7	Amos	2060	146	14.1
Ps.	19642	2527	7.8	Jon.	690	48	14.4
Job	8428	1070	7.9	Zeph.	774	53	14.6
Lam.	1650	154	10.7	Ezek.	19033	1273	15.0
Song	1270	117	10.9	Zech.	3166	211	15.0
1 Chron.	10962	943	11.6	Deut.	14465	959	15.1
Nah.	565	47	12.0	Josh.	10035	658	15.3
Hab.	677	56	12.1	Ruth	1303	85	15.3
Hos.	2391	197	12.1	Hag.	607	38	16.0
Num.	16540	1289	12.8	Mal.	883	55	16.1
Neh.	5428	405	13.4	Judg.	9922	618	16.1
Mic.	1411	105	13.4	2 Sam.	11206	695	16.1
Joel	964	73	13.2	1 Kgs	13234	817	16.2
Isa.	17157	1291	13.3	Jer.	22230	1364	16.3
Gen.	20632	1533	13.5	2 Chron.	13474	822	16.4
Eccl.	3000	222	13.5	1 Sam.	13447	811	16.6
Obad.	292	21	13.9	Dan.	6054	357	17.0
Exod.	16880	1213	13.9	2 Kgs	12389	719	17.2
Ezra	3911	280	14.0	Est.	3078	167	18.4
Lev.	12058	859	14.0				

Three books of the Hebrew Bible average less than eight words per verse: Psalms (7.7), Proverbs (7.8), and Job (7.9). All other books have average verse lengths of twelve words or more, except Lamentations (10.7), Song of Songs (10.9) and 1 Chronicles (11.6).[15] The latter three contain significant sections of short-verse text alongside other sections with long verses. Table 1, therefore, shows that there are two kinds of books in the Hebrew Bible: short-verse books (with less than eight words per verse) and long-verse books (with more than twelve words per verse). According to Wickes, the *ṭeʿamim* of the Three were a practical Tiberian response to the challenge of punctuating (or cantillating) two different kinds of text: short verse texts as against long verse texts.

The credibility of the long-verse/short-verse explanation rests on two foundations. First, whether or not verse lengths were determined prior to the time of the Tiberian Masoretes—only if they were, could verse length have led to the creation of two systems of *ṭeʿamim* (and not vice versa). Second, how one also might explain cases like Lamentations, Song of Songs, and 1 Chronicles: that is, texts that contain clearly defined sections of short verse material that is presented with the *ṭeʿamim* of the Twenty-One.

3.1. The Priority of the Tradition of Verse Division

For Wickes, the existence of an established tradition of verse division prior to the Tiberian Masoretes was suggested by the mention of *pesuqe ha-tora* 'verses of the Torah' and *pesuqe ha-ṭeʿamim*

---

[15] 1 Chron. and 2 Chron are presented in this table as two books to highlight the variations of verse length within the two halves of one work (Chronicles). The same logic was extended to Samuel and Kings. 2 Sam. contains two lengthy poems, without which its average verse length would have exceeded that of 1 Sam.

'verses of the *ṭeʿamim*' in the Mishna (Megillah 4.4.) and Talmud (b. Berakot 19a; 62a–b; b. Qiddushin 32b; b. Yoma 52a–b; b. Nedarim 37b). Whilst it is far from certain that the verse divisions mentioned in the Mishna and the Talmud are identical to those of masoretic tradition (Blau 1896; 1897), a number of texts in the Dead Sea Scrolls do have spaces that indicate traditions of paragraph, section, and even verse division. The first-century CE Isaiah Scroll (1QIsa[a]), for example, has many paragraph and section divisions that are consistent with the later masoretic tradition and the first-century CE Great Psalm Scroll (11QPs[a]) has end-verse spaces which are entirely consistent with the later Masoretic traditions for Ps.119 and 145 (but less so for other psalms) (Burrows, Trever, and Brownlee 1965). Furthermore, the many hundreds of biblical texts with Palestinian and Babylonian *ṭeʿamim* recovered from the Ben Ezra Synagogue, Fustat, Old Cairo ('the Cairo Genizah') display verse divisions (nearly) identical to those found in the later standard (Tiberian) Masoretic Text (Kahle 1927; 1966; Revell 1970, 157–99). In other words, whilst the tradition of verse divisions for many books of the Hebrew Bible may not have been finalised until after the time of the Mishna, and perhaps not even until after the period of the Talmud, we can be confident that the Tiberian Masoretes were the recipients, not the creators, of the versification of the biblical text.

3.2. Lamentations

In BHS, all the verses of the first two chapters of Lamentations are presented as three poetic lines (except 1.7 and 2.19, which are presented as four) (Elliger et al. [eds.] 1977, 1354–67). Whilst the division of each of these verses into stichs is a matter of some debate, it is indisputable that all of these verses are long. They vary between fourteen and twenty words in length. The verses in ch. 4 are not so long. In BHS they are presented as two poetic lines (typically with four stichs) and they vary between eight and seventeen words in length.[16] The verses in chs 3 and 5 are, in comparison, shorter. All of the 66 verses in ch. 3 have fewer than eight words (bar one verse);[17] and all bar two of the 22 verses in ch. 5 have fewer than nine words.[18] Unlike chs 1, 2, and 4, the number of poetic lines found in these verses is indisputable: they must be read as single poetic lines, typically with two stichs each.

If the system of *ṭeʿamim* employed had been determined by line length alone, one might expect the *ṭeʿamim* of Lamentations to switch between the two Tiberian systems, just as in Job. In the case of Job, however, the switch from the *ṭeʿamim* of the Twenty-One to the *ṭeʿamim* of the Three at Job 3.2, and then back at 42.7, follows not only verse length, but also the literary style and content of the text. This switch of *ṭeʿamim* in Job, therefore, presents the book of Job with an introduction, a central discourse, and a conclusion. In the case of Lamentations, the switches between long verse length (chs 1 and 2), short verse length (ch. 3), medium verse length (ch. 4), and short verse length (ch. 5) do not

[16] Lam. 4.13 has eight word-units and 4.5 and 4.14 have nine word-units.

[17] Lam. 3.22 has nine word-units.

[18] Lam. 5.1 and 5.17 have nine word-units.

mark any changes in literary content or style (other than line length). A switch between the systems of *ṭeʿamim* in Lamentations may have thus undermined its unity of style and content.

The use of the *ṭeʿamim* of the Twenty-One for long verses and short verses in Lamentations indicates that the *ṭeʿamim* of the Twenty-One can be used for short verses when they are called upon so to do. There are, however, some problems generated when the *ṭeʿamim* of the Twenty-One are so employed—an issue to which we will return.

3.3. Song of Songs

Song of Songs is presented with 24 short verses and 83 long verses. Unlike Lamentations, these short verses are interspersed between the long verses. The argument for the exclusive use of one form of *ṭeʿamim* (by default, that of the Twenty-One) is thus even more compelling. The use of the *ṭeʿamim* of the Twenty-One for the short verses of Song of Songs again confirms that the *ṭeʿamim* of the Twenty-One can be used for short verses when they are called upon so to do.

3.4. 1 Chronicles

The low average verse length of the half-book 1 Chronicles (the sixth lowest, with 11.6 words per verse) is at odds with that of its other half, 2 Chronicles, which has the fifth highest (16.4). This anomaly is explained by the many short-verse genealogical lists that dominate 13 of the 29 chapters in 1 Chronicles (1 Chron. 1.1–9.44; 11.26–47; 12.24–37; 24.7–18; and 25.9–31). 1 Chron. 16 also contains an extensive quotation of short-verse material that is parallel (near identical) to the text of three psalms.[19] Since both the genealogical and the Psalm material is distinct in style and content from the surrounding narrative, presumably this material could have been presented with the *ṭeʿamim* of the Three. The fact that it is not suggests that there was more involved in the decision to employ the *ṭeʿamim* of the Three than verse length.

In the genealogical lists of 1 Chronicles, many of the verses have five or fewer words and many others are short verses of eight or fewer words. In most of these verses, an *ʾatnaḥ* is found at the point of its most significant semantic division. The grammar (rules) of the *ṭeʿamim* of the Twenty-One require a disjunctive *ṭifḥa* to precede an *ʾatnaḥ* on one of the two word-units before the word with *ʾatnaḥ* (Wickes 1887, 69; Price 1990, 58–61).[20] A similar rule requires a *ṭifḥa* to occur on one of the two words before a *silluq* (Wickes 1887, 62; Price 1990, 54–57). As a result of these two rules, four disjunctive *ṭeʿamim* (that is, *ṭifḥa–ʾatnaḥ–ṭifḥa–silluq*) must be used in every verse presented with *ʾatnaḥ*, even if the verse itself contains a total of only five, six, or seven words. Consequently, on verses of fewer than eight words, the rules of the *ṭeʿamim* of the Twenty-One produce a most predictable pattern of recitation. When these short verses occur consecutively, for example in short-verse poetry or in genealogical lists,

[19] 1 Chron. 16.8–36. The material follows Ps. 105.1–15; 95.1–13; and 106.1, 47–48. The dependency of 1 Chronicles on the Psalter is here presumed for the sake of simplicity. The discussion here regarding the use of different kinds of *ṭeʿamim* is not affected by this presumption.

[20] This is a general rule with the exceptions of *mayela* (16 cases) and when both words preceding *ʾatnaḥ* are monosyllabic (31 cases). See Yeivin and Revell 1979, 177–81; Jacobson 2002, 69–71.

this predictability will cause the recitation to sound repetitive. In the case of many literary genres, such as the psalm material in 1 Chron. 16.8–36, a repetitive recitation may be considered problematic. In the case of the genealogical lists, such as those found in 1 Chron. 1.1–9.44, a predictable and repetitive recitation may be considered most appropriate. It is striking, therefore, that whilst the short-verse poetic material quoted in 1 Chron. 16.8–36 does not use any *ʾatnaḥ ṭeʿamim* to delimit the parallel stichs, most of the short-verse material in 1 Chron. 1.1–9.44 does.

In the Psalter itself, however, all the material quoted in 1 Chron. 16.8–36 does employ *ʾatnaḥ ṭeʿamim*. This does not result in a repetitive recitation, because under the rules of the Three, an *ʾatnaḥ* does not require a disjunctive *ṭaʿam* to precede it. Furthermore, the rules of the Three forbid the occurrence of a disjunctive *ṭaʿam* too close to the *ʾatnaḥ* or *silluq*; that is, two full syllables must separate the syllable with *ʾatnaḥ* or *silluq* and the syllable with the preceding disjunctive *ṭaʿam* (Wickes 1887, 60, 69, 75; Price 1990, 209–13, 234–38).

In 1 Chron. 16, when the Psalms material is quoted, *zaqef ṭeʿamim* are employed where *ʾatnaḥ ṭeʿamim* are found in the Psalter. This is because *zaqef ṭeʿamim* in the Twenty-One, like *ʾatnaḥ ṭeʿamim* in the Three, do not require a preceding disjunctive *ṭaʿam*. This observation has led some commentators to declare that an *ʾatnaḥ* in the Three is equivalent (in pausal effect) to a *zaqef* in the Twenty-One. Before rushing to this imperfect conclusion,[21] however, it would be wise to cast our net a little further and examine, first, the presentation of other poetic texts in the Twenty-One and, second, other texts in the Three that are paralleled by texts in the Twenty-One.

3.5. Short-Verse Poetic Texts with the *Ṭeʿamim* of the Twenty-One

All the short verses of Lamentations chs 3 and 5 are presented as poetic lines with two stichs (that is, as parallelism). In ch. 5, these stichs are delimited by *zaqef ṭeʿamim*: (and *ʾatnaḥ* is not used in any of the verses). In ch. 3, the delimitation of the stichs is a little more complex: *zaqef ṭeʿamim* are used in forty-seven of its sixty-six verses; *ʾatnaḥ* is used once (Lam. 3.56, for a division so unusual, it is not recognised by the stichography of BHK, BHS, or BHQ; see Kittel et al. [eds.] 1937, 1238; Elliger et al. [eds.], 1977, 1367; Jan de Waard 2004); in the remaining eighteen verses *ṭifḥa ṭeʿamim* delimit the first stich.[22] The use of *ṭifḥa* to delimit the first stich is interesting. It allows the second stich (the stich delimited by *silluq*) to be without more smoothly. If *zaqef ṭeʿamim* had been used in these verses, then a *ṭifḥa* would have been required before

[21] It is clear that this conclusion is imperfect since *zaqef ṭeʿamim* do not prohibit a disjunctive *ṭaʿam* occurring closer than two full syllables before them whilst the *ʾatnaḥ* of the Three does. In other words, whilst *zaqef ṭeʿamim* in the Twenty-One *can* perform in a similar way to *ʾatnaḥ ṭeʿamim* in the Three, their identity and function is defined by the system of the Twenty-One and this system is different to that of the Three.

[22] Vv. 2, 3, 5, 7, 11, 15, 17, 19, 21, 30, 31(?), 45, 46, 47, 49, 52, 54, 58, and 64.

the *silluq* (by the rules of the Twenty-One) and this would have added a (presumably unwanted) "pause" to the second stich.[23]

According to Price (1990, 72), the reason why *zaqef ṭeʿamim* are used to delimit the stich of poetic texts in the Twenty-One is because "the domain of *Little Zaqef* is the most complex and flexible of all the other accents." In practice what this means is that *zaqef* can repeat to give one, two, three, or four stichs and can occur without a preceding lesser disjunctive *taʿam*. This flexibility is not unlimited: if there are more than two word-units in the clause of *zaqef*, either a *pashṭa* or *yetiv* disjunctive is required. Even here, however, the judicial use of *maqqefim* can ensure that the "pauses" in each stich are determined solely by poetics and not the grammar of the *ṭeʿamim*.[24]

The book of Lamentations can thus be understood as providing the paradigm for two kinds of presentation for poetic texts of the Twenty-One:

---

[23] As the proponents of prosody have rightly observed, oral segmentation is achieved by multiple means including intonation, stress, emphasis, and melody. For simplicity, these multiple tools are referenced here as "pause". The intended sense of "pause" here is the delimitation markers of oral segmentation. Whether or not there is any period of cessation or silence (a literal pause) would, of course, be determined by the readers chosen method of orally performing the text. The relevance of this to the study of the *ṭe῾amim* is particularly clear in Pitcher 2021.

[24] *Zaqef ṭeʿamim* are used without any *ʾatnaḥ ṭeʿamim* in eight of the 110 verses of 1 Chron. 1–2 (1.14, 28, 30; 2.12, 14, 20, 37, 41, 51). It is interesting to note that when the lists of 1 Chron. 24.7–18 and 25.9–31 do employ *zaqef ṭeʿamim* in this way, the *pashṭa* is never lacking. This is in accord with the poetics of a list. It creates a clear and repetitive recitation.

Presentation 1 [P1]: short verses (nine words or less) with one poetic line of two-stich classic parallelism. In these short verses, *ʾatnaḥ ṭeʿamim* are absent and either *zaqef* or *ṭifḥa ṭeʿamim* delimit the first stich.

Presentation 2 [P2]: long verses (nine words or more) that contain more than two stichs. In these longer multi-stich verses, more complex forms of parallelism may be observed and a combination of *ʾatnaḥ* and *zaqef ṭeʿamim* (alongside other disjunctive *ṭeʿamim*) will be employed to delimit each verse into these stichs.[25]

As previously mentioned, in the Song of Songs (unlike Lamentations), long and short verses are interspersed amongst its eight chapters. In 23 of the 25 verses with eight or fewer word-units, the accentuation follows the first presentation above [P1],[26] whilst all those of nine word-units or more follow the second [P2]. The two exceptions are Song 2.5 and 4.15. These are exceptions that prove the rule. For whilst these two verses do both have eight word-units, both can be read (with the stichography of BHK; see Kittel et al. [eds.] 1977, 1202, 1206) as having three stichs, the first of which is delimited by a *zaqef* and the second by an *ʾatnaḥ*.

Outside of Lamentations, Song of Songs, and 1 Chronicles, two-stich short verses of poetry are observed with *ʾatnaḥ ṭeʿamim*

---

[25] This observation is self-evident, but I have not found it explicitly stated elsewhere.

[26] The 23 verses are Song 1.1, 2, 1.9–2.2, 4, 6; 3.9; 4.7; 5.10; 6.3; 7.7–8, and 11. Strictly speaking, the stichs of these verses are delimited by *zaqef* and *silluq ṭeʿamim.*

delimiting their first stichs—that is, with the kind of presentation observed in the genealogical lists of 1 Chronicles. The crucial observation here, however, is that these poetic verses do not occur in a consecutive run of short verses (which would make the recitation repetitive) in all cases bar one. Once again, this text can be understood to be the exception that proves the rule. The text in question is the Song of David at 2 Sam. 22, which parallels the text of Ps. 18 with strikingly similar, but rarely identical, content. In 2 Sam. 22, 41 of its 51 verses are short verses of eight words or fewer.[27] All of these short verses are presented as two stichs and all of these 41 short verses are delimited by *ʾatnaḥ ṭeʿamim.* The method in 2 Sam. 22 can be taken, therefore, to describe a third method of presenting poetry with the *ṭeʿamim* of the Twenty-One:

> Presentation 3 [P3]: short verses (eight words or less) of two-stich parallelism that employ *ʾatnaḥ ṭeʿamim* to delimit their first stich.

Table 2 observes the employment of these three presentations for twelve of the most widely-recognised poetic texts in the Twenty-One and four prophetic texts also widely considered to be founded upon the poetics of parallelism.

[27] Vv. 1–2 are exceptional, v. 1 forms the title of the poem, v. 2 the opening 'and he said'. Vv. 3, 7, and 16 are read here as a quatrains. Vv. 8, 9, 31, 44, 49, and 51 are read as three stichs.

Table 2: Poetic Texts in the Twenty-One (see Appendix for details)

Passage	Number of verses [stichs]	P1 Short verses delimited by *zaqef* [stichs]	P2 Long verses with *zaqef* + *ʾatnaḥ* [stichs]	% stichs delimited as P1 or P2	P3 Short verses delimited by *ʾatnaḥ* [stichs]	% stichs delimited as P3
Gen. 49.2–27	26 [80]	0	17 [62]	77%	9 [18]	23%
Exod. 15.1–18	18 [60]	3 [6]	12 [48]	90%	3 [6]	10%
Num. 6.24–26	3 [6]	3 [6]	0	100%	0	0
Deut. 32.1–43	43 [140]	0	26 [106]	75%	17 [34]	25%
Judg. 5.2–30	29 [121]	0	26 [115]	93%	4 [8]	7%
1 Sam. 2.1–10	10 [36]	0	7 [30]	83%	3 [6]	17%
2 Sam. 1.19–27	9 [40]	1 [2]	8 [38]	100%	0	0
2 Sam. 22.2–50	49 [109]	0	8 [27]	25%	41 [82]	75%
2 Sam. 23.1–7	7 [23]	0	6 [21]	91%	1 [2]	9%
Isa. 5.1–7	7 [37]	0	7 [37]	100%	0	0
Isa. 40.1–31	31 [114]	0	22 [96]	84%	9 [18]	16%
Hab. 3.2–19	18 [64]	0	14 [56]	87%	4 [8]	13%
Jon. **2.3–10**	8 [28]	0	7 [26]	93%	1[2]	7%
Lam.	154 [536]	88 [176]	66 [352]	>99%	1 [2]	<1%
Song	117	24 [48]	87	100%	0	0
1 Chron. 16.8–36	29 [61]	25 [50]	4 [11]	100%	0	0

From Table 2 it can be seen that, apart from Song, Lam. and 1 Chron. 16, the most frequent presentation of the verses of our sixteen chosen texts is the second presentation type [P2], in which the poetry is presented in longer verses with multiple stichs delimited by *ʾatnaḥ* and *zaqef* (alongside other disjunctive *ṭeʿamim*) (Renz 2003). In many texts, however, short verses occur interspersed between long verses, as was observed in Song of

Songs. Unlike Song of Songs, the other poetic texts in the Twenty-One commonly employ *ʾatnaḥ ṭeʿamim* to delimit these stichs [P3]. Since these verses are interspersed within longer verses, the problem of repetitive recitation does not occur—except in regard to 2 Sam. 22.

Table 2 highlights the extent to which 2 Sam. 22 is an exceptional case. Whilst 75 percent of the stichs of 2 Sam. 22 are presented with the third presentation type [P3], no other poetic text in the Twenty-One presents more than 25 percent of its stichs according to this presentation [P3]. Other than 2 Sam. 22, P3 occurs as a minority presentation within the wider context of longer multi-stich verses [P2].

Outside of 2 Sam. 22, only five of the above poetic texts have consecutive short verses delimited by *ʾatnaḥ*:

1. Gen. 49.19–21: three verses listing the blessings of Jacob upon Gad, Asher and Naphtali.
2. Deut. 32.18–19: two verses. Since v. 19 follows from v. 18, the repetition of form is helpful.
3. Deut. 32.33–34: two verses. Since v. 34 responds to v. 33, the repetition of form is helpful.
4. Isa. 40.16–18: three verses with interlinear parallelism. Since v. 17 repeats the content of v. 16 and v. 18 responds to v. 16–17, the repetition of form aids these connections.
5. Isa. 40.29–30: two verses with interlinear parallelism.

It would appear, then, that only Gen. 49.19–21 and 2 Sam. 22.2–51 are presented so as to be recited in the manner of a list. In the first case this is not problematic—the material is a list. In the second, this is puzzling. The Song of David of 2 Sam. 22 is a song of heterogeneous content, passionate emotion, and dramatic salvation. It is not a list, so why should it be presented to be read in such a repetitive manner?

The treatise *Soferim* may be of help in answering this question. The treatise is a compendium of Talmudic wisdom concerning the correct handling of scriptural scrolls. In this compendium, two pairs of parallel texts are given special attention: 2 Kgs 18–20 || Isa. 36–38 and 2 Sam. 22 || Ps. 18 (Cohen 1965).[28] These texts are recognised as being both very similar and yet having important differences. The differences are thus listed in *Soferim* in order to ensure that no scribe—either intentionally or unintentionally—will harmonise the texts of 2 Sam. 22 and Ps. 18. In the context of this Talmudic wisdom, if the Tiberian Masoretes had presented 2 Sam. 22 with *zaqef ṭeʿamim* [presentation P1], the recitation would have had much the same flow of rhythm and "pause" as Ps. 18. The two texts would have been much more likely to suffer amalgamation in the mouths, minds, and, therefore, hands of their scribal custodians. To avoid this risk, it is plausible that the Tiberian Masoretes may have elected to present the short verses of 2 Sam. 22 with *ʾatnaḥ ṭeʿamim* [presentation P3], even though it has many consecutive short verses. This presentation generated a repetitive recitation for 2 Sam. 22 distinct from the recitation of Ps. 18. The extent of its repetitive

[28] *Soferim* (Scribes), Rule One of ch. 8 lists 72 words of 2 Sam. 22, all of which should be guarded from harmonisation with the different but similar wording of Ps. 18. The words of Ps. 18 are not listed. Ironically, some of the vowel letters given as the definitive form of the words of 2 Sam. 22 differ from those found in Codex L.

nature can be seen in the following comprehensive list of all the disjunctive *ṭeʿamim* as they occur in 2 Sam. 22.32–40:

(32) *ṭifḥa – ʾatnaḥ : ṭifḥa – silluq.*

(33) *ṭifḥa – ʾatnaḥ : ṭifḥa – silluq.*

(34) *ṭifḥa – ʾatnaḥ : ṭifḥa – silluq.*

(35) *ṭifḥa – ʾatnaḥ : ṭifḥa – silluq.*

(36) *ṭifḥa – ʾatnaḥ : ṭifḥa – silluq.*

(37) *ṭifḥa – ʾatnaḥ : ṭifḥa – silluq.*

(38) *ṭifḥa – ʾatnaḥ : ṭifḥa – silluq.*

(39) *ṭifḥa – ʾatnaḥ : ṭifḥa – silluq.*

(40) *ṭifḥa – ʾatnaḥ : ṭifḥa – silluq.*

Anyone reciting (or memorising) 2 Sam. 22 according to these *ṭeʿamim* would thus recite vv. 32–40 in a highly repetitive manner. In terms of the dramatic delivery of the varied content of these verses, this is a bit of a disaster.[29] But in terms of textual memorisation, it would act as a significant reminder that, whilst 2 Sam. 22 is very much the Song of David, it is definitely not the Song of David of Ps. 18.

The genius of this presentation of 2 Sam. 22 is that whilst it testifies to the same delimitation of stichs as Ps. 18, it contains 41 additional disjunctive *ṭeʿamim*. Most of these disjunctive *ṭeʿamim* are imposed upon the recitation by its presentation with *ʾatnaḥ ṭeʿamim* [P3], and none impact the delimitation of a stich.

[29] These verses praise God as a refuge, then as a trainer of my hands for battle, before recounting the manner of the revenge I have taken on my enemies.

These extra disjunctive *ṭeʿamim* add many "pauses" and occur in highly predictable places, which thus stretches the recitation out to sound more like a repetitive list than a song of varied praise.

4.0. A Third Answer: The Dilemma of Short-verse Poetry in the Twenty-One

The observed general preference for *zaqef ṭeʿamim* in delimiting poetry in the Twenty-One is based upon their flexibility. This flexibility allows a stich delimited by *zaqef* to be read either without any other disjunctive *ṭeʿamim* (when the poetics so demand) or with one or more disjunctive *ṭeʿamim* in any place in the clause (when this is more appropriate). The flexibility of *zaqef*, however, comes at a cost. Because it is so flexible, it cannot produce the same syntactic clarity that is delivered by *ʾatnaḥ*. For this reason, *ʾatnaḥ ṭeʿamim* are preferred as markers of dichotomy in the short verses that are interspersed throughout Gen. 49 and Deut. 32. In these texts, the majority presentation is the second [P2], so the recitation of the whole is not made to sound repetitive by occasional short verses with the third presentation [P3]. The dilemma, therefore, of presenting short verse poetic texts with the *ṭeʿamim* of the Twenty-One is that whilst the delimitation of their first stichs by *zaqef* provides flexibility at the expense of clarity, the delimitation of the first stichs by *ʾatnaḥ* provides clarity at the expense of flexibility.

A similar dilemma surrounds the use of *ṭifḥa* to delimit the first stich of a short verse in order that the second stich might be free from disjunctive *ṭeʿamim* (see above). Once again, the system of the Twenty-One is shown to be able to present poetry without any unwanted "pauses" generated by the rules of the *ṭeʿamim* of the Twenty-One. Again, however, the cost of this flexibility is a loss of syntactic clarity. The Tiberian solution to this dilemma was to create a secondary system of *ṭeʿamim* with similar principles to those of the Twenty-One, but with more flexible parameters, i.e., a system that employs *ʾatnaḥ ṭeʿamim* that can be preceded by disjunctive *ṭeʿamim*, but do not make such a precedent mandatory.

4.1. A More Flexible Alternative

In the rules of the *ṭeʿamim* of the Three, the *ʾatnaḥ* is preceded by a *deḥi* disjunctive *ṭaʿam* just as an *ʾatnaḥ* is preceded by a disjunctive *ṭifḥa ṭaʿam* in the Twenty-One. Unlike in the Twenty-One, however, a *deḥi ṭaʿam* can be placed anywhere in a colon delimited by *ʾatnaḥ* (not just on one of the two words preceding the *ʾatnaḥ*) and it need not appear at all.

A similar situation describes the stich delimited by *silluq*. A *silluq* in the Three is preceded by a disjunctive *reviaʿ mugrash*, just as a *silluq* is preceded by a disjunctive *ṭifḥa* in the Twenty-One. Unlike in the Twenty-One, however, a *reviaʿ mugrash* can be placed anywhere in the colon delimited by *silluq* (not just on one of the two words preceding the *silluq*) and it need not appear at all.

Wickes (1881, 99–101) expressed his understanding of this situation in terms of various "laws of transformation." These laws explained why his principle of continuous dichotomy was not followed in so many verses of the Three. According to these laws of transformation, a disjunctive *deḥi* is transformed into a conjunctive *munaḥ* whenever it occurred on the word preceding a word with *ʾatnaḥ* and the stress of its word was not separated from the stress of the word with *ʾatnaḥ* by two or more 'full vowel' syllables. A similar law explained the absence of an expected *reviaʿ mugrash* in a colon delimited by *silluq*. Whilst these laws have much explicative value, the cases of transformation of *deḥi ṭeʿamim* are far more extensive than that delivered by Wickes's simple statement of the laws of transformation (see also Price 1990, 36, 209–13, 234–38).

4.2. Ps. 18 as an Example

Deḥi ṭeʿamim are absent in Ps. 18 in 26 (53 percent) of the 49 stichs that are delimited by *ʾatnaḥ*: 5a, 6a, 7c, 8b, 9b, 12b, 13b, 16c, 18a, 19a, 20a, 21a, 23a, 24a, 25a, 26a, 27a, 31b, 36b, 37a, 41a, 42a, 43a, 46a, 48a, and 50a. In 17 (65 percent) of these 26 cases, the absence is well explained by the law of transformation: namely 6a, 7c, 8b, 9b, 12b, 13b, 16c, 21a, 23a, 24a, 25a, 31b, 37a, 41a, 46a, 48a, and 50a.[30] In these cases, the syntax places

[30] Somewhat obscurely Price (1996, V:1196) lists verses with virtual *deḥi* as 1, 6, 7, 8, 9, 12, 18, 21, 23, 24, 25, 37, 41, 43, 48, and 51. His list agrees with the above in regard to twelve verses (6, 7, 8, 9, 12, 21, 23, 24, 25, 37, 41, and 48) and is divergent in regard to four verses (1, 18, 43, and 51): v. 1 has a *deḥi* before the *ʾatnaḥ*, there is a long run of conjunctives before the *reviaʿ mugrash*, but the reason for a transformation is not well explained by the laws of transformation; vv. 18 and 43 are considered above; v. 51 has six disjunctive *ṭeʿamim* on nine word-units, so it is not clear how an additional *deḥi* disjunctive *ṭaʿam* can be considered to be virtually present (and transformed).

the position of a preceding *deḥi* too near to the stress of the word with *ʾatnaḥ*.

Nine cases, however, are not well explained by the ‘Laws of Transformation,’ specifically, 5a, 18a, 19a, 20a, 26a, 27a, 36b, 42a, and 43a. Three of these nine cases could be explained if the vowel *ḥireq* in a *yiqṭol* verb is not considered to constitute a ‘full vowel’ syllable (26a, 27a, and 36b), but this proposal generates more problems than it solves; for survival of the *deḥi* at other places (for example, Ps. 18.17a and elsewhere in the Psalter) would then require further explanation. Four further cases (5a, 19a, 42a, and 43a) could be explained if a *deḥi ṭaʿam* is considered to be transformed when the word with *ʾatnaḥ* has *maqqefim*. But, again, the survival of *deḥi* in other psalms under these conditions would then require explanation (for example, at Ps. 22.18a). At Ps. 18.18a, it is not clear that a *deḥi* should necessarily be expected on מֵאֹיְבִ֥י ‘from my enemy’ before the short word עָ֑ז ‘strong’. The two words are usually read together to mean ‘from my strong enemy’. Although it must be admitted that a definite article would be expected on עָז. Furthermore, ‘you save me, my enemy is strong’ does form a nice parallel with 18b. The case of 20a is clearer. The *ʾatnaḥ* occurs on the last syllable of לַמֶּרְחָ֑ב ‘to the broad place’. This word is long enough to protect a *deḥi* on the preceding word from transformation (וַיּוֹצִיאֵ֥נִי ‘and he brought me out’), but no *deḥi* is found upon it.

A similar situation pertains to the *reviaʿ mugrash*, which is absent in thirteen (25 percent) of the 51 stichs delimited by *silluq*: 2, 5b, 15b, 19b, 28b, 33b, 36c, 40b, 43b, 44c, 48b, 50b, 51c. In eight of these thirteen cases the law of transformation explains the absence of *reviaʿ mugrash*: 5b, 28b, 33b, 36c, 40b, 43b, 48b, and 50b. Three of the remaining five cases have other explanations. The stichs of vv. 2 and 51c may be considered grammatically exceptional. At 15b there is a *mugrash* symbol without a *reviaʿ*. This probably should be read as an alternative representation of *reviaʿ mugrash*: the anomaly occurs elsewhere, it is consistently replicated in many of the best masoretic manuscripts, and it occurs regularly on monosyllabic words (Dotan 2001, xvi). In regard to 19b, however, one is required to argue, against sense, that the syntactic or prosodic dichotomy is expected between לְמִשְׁעָ֣ן and לִ֑י as a support for me' (and not after יְהוָ֣ה 'the LORD'). The absence of *reviaʿ mugrash* at 44c cannot be explained by the laws of transformation at least in their current guise. Despite these observations, it is not argued here that Wickes' laws of transformation cannot be stretched to accommodate these and multiple similar cases.[31] Rather, it is asked whether there is good purpose to this exercise. What is achieved by these ever-more complex explanations is the preservation of a system of rules of

---

[31] Consider, for example, the cases of the transformation of *deḥi* in the first four ssalms of the Psalter. In Ps. 1.3; 2.2; and 3.9 more than two syllables separate the stress of the word with *ʾatnaḥ* and the stress of the preceding word. The transformed *taʿam* preceding the *ʾatnaḥ* in these cases is *merkha* (not *munaḥ*, as per Wickes's Law of Transformation). In Ps. 2.7 and 4.9, the expected positions of their syntactic dichotomies occur on the second word preceding the *ʾatnaḥ* and not the preceding word. In both cases these words also have *merkha* conjunctive *ṭeʿamim*. Further rules are needed to explain these transformations. For various lists of virtual *deḥi ṭeʿamim* see Price (1996, V:1195–210).

the *ṭeʿamim* that has been supposed to explain them. What is frustrated is an observation of the recitation to which the *ṭeʿamim* bear witness (which may in itself provide good explanation for these *ṭeʿamim*). It seems to me intuitively sensible to take the testimony of the Masoretes more seriously when they claim to be attempting to capture an established tradition of recitation with their *ṭeʿamim*, not creating one through the application of an established grammar of the *ṭeʿamim*.

As Dresher (1994, esp. 16–23) has explained, prosodic recitations can be presented as a series of dichotomies, particularly in regard to prose. But as Janis (1987, esp. 23–100) has also shown, however, they need not necessarily be so understood. Janis (1987, 48–53) has also shown that Wickes's insistence that nothing should break the "principle of continuous dichotomy" can put the cart before the horse when it comes to understanding the dynamics of prosody. More recent prosodic enquiry raises new possibilities (Pitcher 2020). As Price (1990, 26–47) has shown, the rules of the accents can explain almost all the observed occurrences of *ṭeʿamim* in the Twenty-One. This predictability extends to the poetic texts presented with the *ṭeʿamim* of the Twenty-One, but it must be admitted that more flexible *zaqef ṭeʿamim* dominate these texts—that is, a *ṭaʿam* with more flexible rules. The system of the Three was most probably created to extend this flexibility to short-verse poetic texts. In these texts, the rules that appear to govern their distribution must either be understood to be very complex (so Wickes and Price) or to be held more lightly—that is, in a position that is secondary to the poetics. In both cases, it seems that the oral dynamics must be placed to the fore if we are to make good sense of the *ṭeʿamim* and that, if so, two different sets of *ṭeʿamim* provide much interesting evidence for the application of different ways of orally performing different kinds of texts.

4.3. Ps. 18.19–20 as an Example

In Ps. 18 and elsewhere, it is possible to formulate a much simpler and intuitive understanding of the *ṭeʿamim*, by considering how they impact the oral performance of the text. In the example of vv. 19–20, for example, the anomalous lack of mid-stich disjunctive *ṭeʿamim* in 19a, 19b, and 20a can be understood simply to reflect a recitation tradition in which these stichs were recited without any mid-stich "pause". This absence thus causes the mid-stich "pause" of 20b to be heard emphatically and so give its (semantically) remarkable last clause a degree of special emphasis:

יְקַדְּמ֥וּנִי בְיוֹם־אֵידִ֑י וַֽיְהִי־יְהוָ֖ה לְמִשְׁעָ֣ן לִֽי׃

וַיּוֹצִיאֵ֣נִי לַמֶּרְחָ֑ב יְ֝חַלְּצֵ֗נִי כִּ֘י חָ֥פֵֽץ בִּֽי׃

This gives an oral sense or, even, an oral taste to the text. In transliteration, the effect can be seen when English punctuation marks are used to represent the 'pauses' of the *ṭeʿamim*:

*yəqaddə**mūnī** bəyōm-ʾē**ḏī** : wayhī-ʾăḏō**nā̊y** ləmiš**ʿā̊n lī**.*

*wayyōṣīʾ**ēnī** lammɛr**ḥā̊ḇ** : yəḥalləṣ**ēnī**—**kī ḥā̊**pēṣ **bī**.*

In English translation such a recitation might therefore be presented as follows:

They confronted me on the day of my trouble:

but the LORD was there for my support.

And He brought me out to the broad place:

He rescued me—because he delighted in me.

5.0. Conclusions

In an attempt to consider why there are two systems of Tiberian *ṭeʿamim* this paper has been compelled to explore a wide range of observations. At this juncture it seems appropriate to draw them together into a narrative that might explain why there are two systems of Tiberian *ṭeʿamim* and how they might relate to one another.

Texts with Palestinian and Babylonian *ṭeʿamim* employ the same system of *ṭeʿamim* for all the books of the Hebrew Bible. The Tiberian use of two systems appears to be a Tiberian innovation and not a phenomenon that was inherited by them. Early masoretic grammatical treatises consistently describe and praise the Tiberian *nequddot* and *ṭeʿamim* as recording, preserving and passing on an outstanding oral performance of the text. They do not represent the *ṭeʿamim* as a system of punctuation imposed upon the text, but rather a way of presenting an outstanding oral recitation of the text. A significant number of poetic texts in the Hebrew Bible are presented with the *ṭeʿamim* of the Twenty-One, most notably the books of Lamentations and Song of Songs. These books evidence a modified use of the *ṭeʿamim* of the Twenty-One. The three books Psalms, Proverbs and Job stand apart as being founded on parallelism and having significantly shorter verses. The creation of a separate system of *ṭeʿamim* was a response to the combination of both the different oral dynamics of the recitation of short verses and the different oral dynamics of the recitation of poetry. The rules of the *ṭeʿamim* of Three are more flexible than those of the Twenty-One: simpler in general description, but far more difficult to formulate in detail.[32] The mysteries of the rules of the *ṭeʿamim* of the Three only therefore appear to resoluble when the focus is turned away from the rules of the *ṭeʿamim* and towards the dynamics of the recitation.

It has been found to be insightful to approach the *ṭeʿamim* of the Twenty-One as indicators of prosody as defined by linguistics (suprasegmental phonology) in Pitcher (2020). The challenge then remains before us to approach the *ṭeʿamim* of the Three as indicators of prosody as defined by poetics (which in this case will be parallelism) and then, perhaps, to return to some of the poetic texts of the Twenty-One—and their *ṭeʿamim*—equipped with new insight.

---

[32] Price (1996, 1101) claims that for the *ṭeʿamim* of the Three "Twelve of the rules or auxiliaries operated without a single exception. The remaining rules operated with few exceptions and ranged in accuracy from 94. 13% to 99.91%." These impressive results, however, rely upon his extensive use of 'virtual' *ṭeʿamim.* As discussed above, the rules pertaining to the transformations of 'virtual' *ṭeʿamim* are not clear and the rationale behind lists provided by Price is often very hard to discern.

Appendix

Information relevant to Table 2, §3.5:

- Gen. 49.2–27: Gen. 49.2, 5, 12, 14, 16, 19–21, and 23, [P3]; the rest, [P2] incl. v. 18 (three morphemes, one stich as per BHS).
- Exod. 15.1–18: Exod. 15.3, 5, and 14 [P3]; vv. 4 and 13, four-stich lines delimited by *ʾatnaḥ* and *ṭifḥa* [P2]; vv. 1b–c and 12, two-stich lines delimited by *zaqef* [P1]; v. 18, two-stichs delimited by *ṭifḥa* [P1]; the rest [P2].
- Deut. 32.1–43: Deut. 32.1, 3, 5, 9, 12, 16, 18–19, 23, 26, 28, 29, 31, 33–34, 37, and 40 [P3]; the rest [P2].
- Judg. 5.2–30: Judg. 5.18, 22, 25, 29 [P3]; v. 5, three (plus) stichs delimited by *ʾatnaḥ*, *zaqef*, and *ṭifḥa* [P2]; the rest [P2].
- 1 Sam. 2.1–10: 1 Sam. 2.4, 6, and 7, [P3]; v. 2, three stichs delimited by *ʾatnaḥ* and *ṭifḥa*, [P2]; the rest [P2].
- 2 Sam. 1.19–27: 2 Sam. 1.27, [P1]; the rest, [P2].
- 2 Sam. 22.2–50: 2 Sam. 22.8, 9, 31, 44, and 49, three stichs, [P2]; vv. 3, 7, 16 four stichs, [P2]; the rest [P1]. V. 51 excluded, three stichs delimited by *ʾatnaḥ* and *tevir*?
- Isa. 5.1–7: Isa. 5.3, four stichs delimited by *ʾatnaḥ* and *ṭifḥa*; the rest [P2].
- Isa. 40.1–31: Isa. 40.1, 13, 16–18, 23, 25, and 29–30 two stichs delimited by *ʾatnaḥ*, [P3]; v. 8, four stichs delimited by *ʾatnaḥ* and *ṭifḥa*, [P2]; the rest [P2].
- Hab. 3.2–19: Hab. 2.5, 12, 15, and 18, [P1]; v. 7, three stichs delimited by *zaqef* and *ʾatnaḥ*, [P2]; the rest [P2].
- Jon. 2.3–10: Jon. 2.9 [P3]; the rest [P2].

- Lam.: Lam. 1–2, [P2]; Lam. 3, [P1], Lam. 4, [P2]. Lam. 5, [P1].
- Song: Song: the total stich count of P2 material is a matter of some debate.
- 1 Chron. 16.8–36: 1 Chron. 16.29 and 33, three stichs delimited by *ʾatnaḥ* and *zaqef*, [P2]; vv. 33 and 35–36, four stichs delimited by *atnaḥ* and *zaqef*, [P2].

References

Baer, S., and H. L. Strack (eds.). 1970 (1879). *Dikduke Ha-Ṭeʿamim des Ahron ben Moscheh ben Ascher*. Jerusalem: Maqor (originally published Leipzig: Fernau).

Blau, Ludwig. 1896. 'Massoretic Studies, Part 3: The Division into Verses'. *The Jewish Quarterly Review* 9/1: 122–44.

———. 1897. 'Massoretic Studies, Part 4: The Division into Verses (continued)'. *The Jewish Quarterly Review* 9/3: 471–90.

Burrows, Millar, John C. Trever, and William Hugh Brownlee. 1950. *The Dead Sea Scrolls of St. Mark's Monastery*. New Haven, CT: American Schools of Oriental Research.

Cohen, Abraham. 1965. *The Minor Tractates of the Talmud: Massekhoth Ketannoth Translated into English with Notes, Glossary and Indices*. 2 vols. London: Soncino.

Cohen, Miles B., and David B. Freedman. 1974. 'The Dual Accentuation of the Ten Commandments'. In *Masoretic Studies* 1, 7–19. Missoula, MT: International Organization for Masoretic Studies Society of Biblical Literature.

Crowther, Daniel J. 2015. 'The Relevance of the *Ṭeʿamim* to the Textual Criticism, Delimitation and Interpretation of Biblical Poetic Texts with Special Reference to the Song of David at Psalm 18 and 2 Samuel 22'. PhD dissertation, University of Bristol.

Davidson, A. B. 1861. *Outlines of Hebrew Accentuation, Prose and Poetical*. London: Williams & Norgate.

Derenbourg, Joseph. 1871. *Manuel du lecteur, d'un auteur inconnu publié d'après un manuscrit venu du Yémen et accompagné de notes*. Paris: Imprimerie nationale.

Dotan, Aron (ed.). 1963. *Sefer Diqduqe ha-Ṭeʿamim le-R' Aharon ben-Moshe ben-ʾAsher*. Jerusalem: The Hebrew University of Jerusalem.

——— (ed.). 2001. *Biblia Hebraica Leningradensia*. Peabody, MA: Hendrickson Publishers.

Dresher, B. Elan. 1994. 'The Prosodic Basis of the Tiberian Hebrew System of Accents'. *Language* 70/1: 1–52.

Eldar, Ilan. 1992. 'The Art of Correct Reading of the Bible'. In *Proceedings of the 9th Congress of the International Organization for Masoretic Studies, 1989*, 33–42. Atlanta: Scholars Press.

Eldar, Ilan, and Yosef Ofer. 2018. *The Masoretic Accentuation of the Hebrew Bible According to the Medieval Treatise* Horayat ha-Qore. Jerusalem: Bialik Institute. [Hebrew]

Elliger, Karl, et al. (eds.). 1977. *Biblia Hebraica Stuttgartensia*. Stuttgart: Deutsche Bibelstiftung.

Ginsburg, Christian D. (ed.). 1867. *The* Massoreth ha-Massoreth *of Elias Levita: Being an Exposition of the Massoretic Notes on the Hebrew Bible*. London: Longmans, Green, Reader & Dyer.

Heijmans, Shai. 2013. 'Vocalization, Palestinian'. In *Encyclopedia of Hebrew Language and Linguistics*, edited by Geoffrey Khan, III:964–67. Leiden: Brill.

Jacobson, Joshua R. 2002. *Chanting the Hebrew Bible: The Art of Cantillation*. Philadelphia: Jewish Publication Society.

Kahle, Paul Ernst. 1927. *Masoreten des Westens: Texte und Untersuchungen zur vormasoretischen Grammatik des Hebrischen*. 2 vols. Stuttgart: W. Kohlhammer.

———. 1966. *Masoreten des Ostens: Die altesten punktierten Handschriften des Alten Testaments und der Targume*. Hildesheim: G. Olms.

Khan, Geoffrey. 2000. *The Early Karaite Tradition of Hebrew Grammatical Thought: Including a Critical Edition, Translation and Analysis of the Diqduq of 'Abū Ya'qūb Yūsuf ibn Nūḥ on the Hagiographa*. Leiden: Brill.

———. 2013. 'Masoretic Treatises'. In *Encyclopedia of Hebrew Language and Linguistics*, edited by Geoffrey Khan, II:598–604. Leiden: Brill.

Janis, Norman. 1987. 'A Grammar of the Biblical Accents'. PhD dissertation, Harvard University.

Kittel, Rudolf, et al. (eds.). 1937. *Biblia Hebraica*. 3rd edition. Stuttgart: Württembergische Bibelanstalt.

Kugel, James L. 1981. *The Idea of Biblical Poetry: Parallelism and Its History*. New Haven, CT: Yale University Press.

Levita, Elijah. 1538. *Sefer Ṭov Ṭaʿam*. Venice: Daniel Bomberg.

Mercerus, Joannes. 1565. *Sefer Ṭaʿame ha-Miqra*. Paris: G. Morelius.

Pitcher, Sophia L. 2020. 'A Prosodic Model for Tiberian Hebrew: A Complexit Approach to the Features, Structures, and Functions of the Masoretic Cantillation Accents'. PhD dissertation, University of the Free State, Bloemfontein.

———. 2021. 'Towards a prosodic model for Tiberian Hebrew: An intonation-based analysis. *Stellenbosch Papers in Linguistics Plus* 63/1–27.

Price, James D. 1990. *The Syntax of Masoretic Accents in the Hebrew Bible*. Lewiston, NY: Edwin Mellen Press.

———. 1996. *Concordance of the Hebrew Accents in the Hebrew Bible*. 5 vols. Lewiston, NY: Edwin Mellen Press.

Renz, Thomas. 2003. *Colometry and accentuation in Hebrew prophetic poetry*. Waltrop: Hartmut Senner.

Revell, E. John. 1970. *Hebrew Texts with Palestinian Vocalization*. Toronto: University of Toronto Press.

Sanders, James A. 1965. *The Psalms Scroll of Qumran Cave 1 (11QPs^a)*. Discoveries in the Judaean Desert 4. Oxford: Clarendon Press.

Shoshany, Ronit. 2013. 'Biblical Accents: Babylonian'. In *Encyclopedia of Hebrew Language and Linguistics*, edited by Geoffrey Khan, I:268–75. Leiden: Brill.

de Waard, Jan. 2004. *General Introduction and Megilloth*. Biblia Hebraica Quinta. Stuttgart: Deutsche Bibelgesellschaft.

Wickes, William. 1881. *A Treatise on the Accentuation of the Three So-called Poetical Books of the Old Testament*. Oxford: Clarendon Press.

———. 1887. *A Treatise on the Accentuation of the Twenty-one So-called Prose Books of the Old Testament.* Oxford: Clarendon Press.

Yeivin, Israel, and E. J. Revell. 1979. *Introduction to the Tiberian Masorah.* Missoula, MT: Scholars Press.

“SOME FANCIFUL MIDRASH EXPLANATION”: *DERASH* ON THE *ṬEʿAMIM* IN THE MIDDLE AGES AND EARLY MODERN PERIOD

Benjamin Williams

Among the multitude of *ṭeʿamim* ‘cantillation marks’ that adorn the Masoretic Text of the Hebrew Bible, the accent *shalshelet* attracts attention due to its conspicuous zig-zag shape and its sung recitation as a trill or tremolo. Because of its rarity—it occurs just seven times in the twenty-one prose books of the Hebrew Bible—medieval and modern readers have attributed special significance to the passages in which it appears. In his 1887 treatise on the accentuation, William Wickes related medieval explanations to the effect that the accent conveys information about the events narrated not otherwise explicit in the biblical text, such as the prolonged repetition of a particular action, or even angelic intervention in the proceedings. Such aggadic interpretations were not to the taste of sober-minded Wickes. Fearing that a similar interpretation might underlie the Masoretes’ own use of *shalshelet*, Wickes pronounced that the accent’s original meaning, if it could be recovered, would not be worth the reader’s attention: “For we may be sure that we should have had some fanciful

 https://doi.org/10.11647/OBP.0330.09

Midrash explanation, which we can well afford to dispense with" (Wickes 1887, 85).

The purpose of this study is to examine the history of the idea that the shapes, names, and sounds of the *ṭeʿamim* convey information about biblical narratives. Medieval commentators who relayed the *peshaṭ*, the plain meaning of the text, regularly employed the accents to identify pausal forms, stressed syllables, the relationship between consecutive words, and the structure of the verse. But a number of interpreters, including Tobias ben Eliezer, Joseph ibn Caspi, Baḥya ben Asher, and Moses Alsheikh, also used them to formulate narrative details that are not explicit in the text, including twists and turns in the plot, the thoughts and motivations of the characters, and the manner in which direct speech was delivered. The present study examines this technique first by analysing the midrashic method of deriving such information from the graphic features of the consonantal text of the Hebrew Bible. I will then turn to medieval anthologies of midrash and commentaries that favour the *derash*, where unusual and irregular cantillation marks, including *shalshelet*, are interpreted in a similar way. Finally, examples from the commentaries of Moses Alsheikh of Safed (d. 1593) will show how sixteenth-century Sephardi interpreters not only focused on exceptional *ṭeʿamim*, but treated the masoretic system of accentuation more broadly as a source of information concerning biblical narratives. As will be shown in the conclusion, medieval *derash* on the *ṭeʿamim* has inspired several contemporary expositors of the biblical text. It is hoped that an impartial enquiry into the origins of this exegetical method, which neither defends the interpretations nor dismisses them as "fanciful," will enable an understanding of a distinctive interpretive approach to the Masora that has, once again, become popular.

In Isaac Heinemann's classic study of the midrashic method, *Darkhe ha-ʾAggada*, the significance accorded by the rabbis to the shapes and sounds of the consonantal text of the Hebrew Bible is designated as "creative philological" exegesis. Though Heinemann focused on the interpretation of letters, words, sentences, and sections, he acknowledged that other graphic features of the text, including its division into paragraphs, were also the subject of "philological" exposition (Heinemann 1970, 100). Interpretations of the *puncta extraordinaria* in Sifre Numbers 69 illustrate this exegetical method. Among the passages expounded is the reunion of Jacob and Esau in Gen. 33.4, where Esau fell upon his brother's neck and kissed him. The letters of וַיִּשָּׁקֵהוּ are written with supralinear dots:[1]

(1) וַיָּרָץ עֵשָׂו לִקְרָאתוֹ וַיְחַבְּקֵהוּ וַיִּפֹּל עַל־צַוָּארָו וַיִּשָּׁקֵהוּ וַיִּבְכּוּ׃
'Esau ran to meet him. He embraced him, fell upon his neck, ȧṅḋ k̇iṡṡėḋ ḣiṁ, and they wept. (Gen. 33.4)

The midrash reads as follows:

(2) כיוצא בו וישקהו, שלא נשקו בכל לבו. ר' שמעון בן יוחיי או' והלא בידוע שעשו שונא ליעקב אלא נהפכו רחמיו באותה שעה ונשקו בכל לבו.
'…An analogous case is "and k̇iṡṡėḋ ḣiṁ." [The presence of points above the word indicates] that [Esau] did not kiss [Jacob] wholeheartedly. Rabbi Shimʿon ben Yoḥai said, "Is

[1] Unless otherwise noted, biblical texts are cited from the BHS. The consonants of the *qere* are printed in brackets.

it not certain that Esau hated Jacob? But at that particular moment, his disposition changed and he kissed him wholeheartedly.'" (Sifre Numbers 69, ed. Kahana 2011–2015, I:167)[2]

According to the first interpretation, the dots cast doubt on the sincerity underlying Esau's action. Shimʿon ben Yoḥai, by contrast, suggests that the dots reinforce the significance of Esau's kiss as an indication of a profound change of heart. New insights into the motivations and actions of biblical characters may, according to these views, be disclosed by expounding the text's graphic features. This interpretation illustrates the relationship Heinemann (1970, 13) held to be implicit between "creative philology" and the resulting "creative historiographical" insights into the narrative, since, according to the midrashic method, "the interpretation of documents serves as a basis for the description of history."[3]

Though the exposition of graphic features of the Hebrew Bible's consonantal text is well-attested in rabbinic literature (Fishbane 2013, 17–21), a small number of references to masoretic signs can be found in late *midrashim*. An example comes in the first part of Exodus Rabbah (2.6), which Avigdor Shinan

---

[2] Cf. Genesis Rabba 78.9. Midrash Tanḥuma (printed) *Va-yishlaḥ* 4 explains the insincerity of Esau's action by suggesting that, rather than seeking to kiss Jacob (from the root נש"ק), he wished to bite him (from נש"ך). See also Liebermann 1962, 43–46; Shinan 1994; Martín-Contreras 2003.

[3] The full quotation reads: שני מיני פעילות אלו קשורים זה בזה כבר במדע: פירוש התעודות משמש בסיס לתיאור ההיסטוריה, ורק על רקע הקורות יש להבין את הטכסטים.

(1984, 23) has dated to the tenth century CE. The exposition of Exod. 3.4, when God called Moses from out of the Burning Bush by repeating his name, draws attention to other occasions when patriarchs and prophets were similarly addressed. In the case of Abraham, Jacob, and Samuel, the repeated proper nouns are divided in the pointed Masoretic Text by a vertical bar (*paseq*).[4] The midrash explains why the sign is not used in the case of Moses:

> ויאמר משה משה. את מוצא: אברהם אברהם יש בו פסק, יעקב יעקב יש בו פסק, שמואל שמואל יש בו פסק, אבל משה משה אין בו פסק. למה? כאדם שהוא נתון תחת משאוי גדול וקורא: פלוני פלוני, קרב פרוק משאוי זה מעלי! דבר אחר: עם כל הנביאים הפסיק מלדבר עמהם, ועם משה לא הפסיק כל ימיו.
>
> "And [the Lord] said, 'Moses Moses'" (Exod. 3.4). You find in the case of "Abraham, Abraham" (Gen. 22.11) that there is a *paseq*. Likewise, there is a *paseq* in "Jacob, Jacob" (Gen. 46.2) and also in "Samuel, Samuel" (1 Sam. 3.10). But in the case of "Moses Moses", there is no *paseq*. Why is this so? It is like a man who was laden with a heavy burden and shouted, "So-and-so so-and-so, come over here and take this load from me."
>
> Another interpretation (*davar ʾaḥer*) is that God spoke intermittently with all [other] prophets, but never stopped [speaking] with Moses throughout his whole life. (Exodus Rabbah 2.6, ed. Shinan 1984, 116–17)

---

[4] See also Dotan (2005). An eleventh-century dating of this part of Exodus Rabba has been advanced by Bregman (2003, 171–72). Cf. t. Berakhot 1.14; Sifra *Nedava* parasha 1.12 (Weiss 3d); Genesis Rabba 56.7; Tanḥuma (Buber) *Noaḥ* 1, 6, *Va-yera* 46, *Shemot* 15; Tanḥuma (printed) *Va-yera* 23, *Shemot* 18, *Ṣav* 13.

In good midrashic style, the *darshan* expounds Exod. 3.4 in the light of verses throughout the biblical canon which exhibit a similar syntactic formulation. Alternative explanations are proposed, which, as indicated by the term *davar ʾaḥer* ‘another interpretation’, are not mutually exclusive (Fishbane 2013, 16, 21–23). But, unusually for a midrash, the interpretation refers to the masoretic pointing. The *darshan*’s observations correspond with the text in the Leningrad Codex (dated 1008/9 CE), where a *paseq* divides אַבְרָהָ֣ם ׀ אַבְרָהָ֑ם ‘Abraham, Abraham’ in the account of the Akedah (Gen. 22.11), יַעֲקֹ֣ב ׀ יַעֲקֹ֑ב ‘Jacob, Jacob’ before the migration to Egypt (Gen. 46.2), and שְׁמוּאֵ֣ל ׀ שְׁמוּאֵ֑ל ‘Samuel, Samuel’ when God called to the young prophet at Shiloh (1 Sam. 3.10). The lack of a *paseq* when God called Moses’s name twice in Exod. 3.4, therefore, invites an explanation (Freedman 1998, fols 12a, 28b, 32b, 151b; Khan 2013, 10). According to the first interpretation, the absence of the division that would indicate a slight pause in the recitation means that God addressed Moses as hurriedly as someone shouting for urgent assistance with a heavy load (Yeivin 1980, 216, no. 283). The alternative explanation refers to the primacy of Mosaic prophecy, as Moses alone received divine inspiration without interruption (cf. Leviticus Rabbah 1.14–15; Exodus Rabbah 21.4). By means of these explanations, the *darshan* shows how the nature of the revelation at the Burning Bush can be grasped through the midrashic interpretation of features of the masoretic codex.

Expositions of the cantillation marks as sources of narrative information can be found in the *masora* of tenth- and eleventh-century manuscripts. The *masora magna* of the Aleppo Codex (ca.

930 CE) and of the Leningrad Codex compare the accounts of the capture of two kings of Judah, Amaziah and Zedekiah, in 2 Kgs 14.13 and Jer. 34.21, respectively:

(3) וְאֵת֩ אֲמַצְיָ֨הוּ מֶֽלֶךְ־יְהוּדָ֜ה בֶּן־יְהוֹאָ֣שׁ בֶּן־אֲחַזְיָ֗הוּ תָּפַ֛שׂ יְהוֹאָ֥שׁ מֶֽלֶךְ־יִשְׂרָאֵ֖ל בְּבֵ֣ית שָׁ֑מֶשׁ...

'And as for King Amaziah of Judah son of Jehoash, son of Ahaziah, King Jehoash of Israel captured [him] at Beth-Shemesh…' (2 Kgs 14.13a)

(4) וְאֶת־צִדְקִיָּ֨הוּ מֶֽלֶךְ־יְהוּדָ֜ה וְאֶת־שָׂרָ֗יו אֶתֵּן֙ בְּיַ֣ד אֹֽיְבֵיהֶ֔ם וּבְיַ֖ד מְבַקְשֵׁ֣י נַפְשָׁ֑ם וּבְיַד֙ חֵ֣יל מֶ֣לֶךְ בָּבֶ֔ל הָעֹלִ֖ים מֵעֲלֵיכֶֽם׃

'And as for King Zedekiah of Judah and his officials, I will hand [them] over to their enemies and to those who seek their lives, to the army of the king of Babylon, which has retreated from you. (Jer. 34.21)

Though the first parts of the two verses are similarly worded, the masoretic pointing differs. The initial וְאֵת֩ in the account of Amaziah is pointed with the accent *telisha*. The וְאֶת־ in the prophecy of judgement on Zedekiah, however, is joined by *maqqef* to the following word and so lacks any accent and is pointed with the short vowel *segol* rather than *ṣere*. The masoretic note at 2 Kgs 14.13 in the Leningrad Codex explains the discrepancy by relating Amaziah's fate to the name of the accent *telisha*:

הראשון תלש והשני חטף. הראשון נתלש מן הממלכות וחזר למלכות. צדקיהו נחטף מן המלכות ולא חזר למלכות.

The former [i.e., Amaziah] [God] plucked (*talash*) and the latter [i.e., Zedekiah] [God] snatched quickly. The former was plucked (*nitlash*) from his kingship but returned to the

> kingship. Zedekiah was snatched quickly from the kingship, but did not return to the kingship. (Freedman 1998, fol. 211b)[5]

According to this interpretation, the masoretic pointing communicates an element of the narrative. In 2 Kgs 14.13, the *telisha* indicates that Amaziah was temporarily plucked (*talash, nitlash*) from the throne. In Jeremiah, the short vowel on the word וְאֶת־ and its connection to צִדְקִיָּ֫הוּ ‘Zedekiah’ show that Zedekiah’s downfall was quicker than Amaziah’s, since he was deported to Babylon (2 Kgs 25.6–7) and never restored to the throne (Loewinger 1960, 91–92; 1972, 603; Revell 2000, 72; Dotan 2009, 65–66; Ofer 2019, 261–63).

By the end of the tenth century, therefore, the midrashic exposition of graphic features of the Hebrew Bible was no longer limited to those of the consonantal text. Late *midrashim* interpret masoretic signs, though not, to my knowledge, the names or shapes of *ṭeʿamim*. The *masora* itself derives narrative information from the accents, though the verses discussed above are not expounded in extant *midrashim* (Friedeman 2021). But from the late-eleventh century, certain midrashic anthologies and commentaries developed insights into a small number of biblical narratives by explaining unusual *ṭeʿamim* or anomalous patterns of

---

[5] See also the *masora magna* of the Aleppo Codex at 2 Chron. 25.33, fol. 235b.

accentuation.[6] Several explain the account of Potiphar's wife's attempt to seduce Joseph at Gen. 39.8, which begins with the rare accent *shalshelet:*[7]

(5) וַיְמָאֵ֓ן ׀ וַיֹּ֙אמֶר֙ אֶל־אֵ֣שֶׁת אֲדֹנָ֔יו הֵ֣ן אֲדֹנִ֔י לֹא־יָדַ֥ע אִתִּ֖י מַה־בַּבָּ֑יִת וְכֹ֥ל אֲשֶׁר־
יֶשׁ־ל֖וֹ נָתַ֥ן בְּיָדִֽי׃

'But he [Joseph] refused and said to his master's wife, "Look, my master has no concern, because of me, for household affairs, for he has entrusted everything he owns to me."' (Gen. 39.8)

The earliest *derash* I have found on this *ṭaʿam* is in the late-eleventh-century *Leqaḥ Ṭov* of Tobias ben Eliezer, the Greek-speaking exegete associated with the Byzantine city of Kastoria (Ta-Shma 2005, 259–94; Mondschein 2009, 270–72; Cohen 2020, 166–67, 176–90). According to this explanation, the *ṭaʿam* reveals the manner in which Joseph refused the advances of Potiphar's wife: '"But he refused." Refusal upon refusal *ad infinitum,*

---

[6] On the interpretation of further features of the Masora, see Penkower (1982, xi, 31–40); Mondschein (2009, 270–72). On the interpretation of *tagin* and irregular letters in the *Sefer Torah*, see Razhabi (1978, 90–94, 120–23); Caspi (2015, 403–46). My thanks to Jen Taylor Friedman for drawing my attention to Caspi's study.

[7] In addition to those discussed below, see also Gellis (1982–2014, IV:94), and BnF MS Hébreu 5, fol. 1r. On the latter, see Wickes (1887, 85) and del Barco (2010, 42). On the interpretation of the Joseph narrative in rabbinic texts, see Kugel (1990).

as it is written with *pesiq* and *shalshelet*…' (Ben Eliezer 1884, I:198)[8]

As Aron Dotan (1967, 164–65, 343–44) and Nurit Reich (2006) have shown, *shalshelet* is also called *marʿim, marʿid,* and *mesulsal* in the Masora, names which characterise it as a distinctive raising of the voice or as a trill or tremolo.[9] Its association with a loud or repetitive melodic motif would explain the comment in the *Leqaḥ Ṭov*. The *shalshelet* on וַיְמָאֵ֓ן 'and he refused' therefore indicates not only how the cantor should recite the word, but also how direct speech was originally delivered and that Joseph himself spoke with prolonged and insistent determination.[10]

Several later exegetes used a similar method to explain the verse. The fourteenth-century Provençal commentator Joseph ibn Caspi (1280–ca. 1340), better known for his philosophical interpretations of the Bible, included *derash* on the *ṭeʿamim* in his *Maṣref la-Kesef* (Mesch 1975; Twersky 1979; Herring 1982, 125–

---

8 "וימאן. מיאון אחר מיאון הרבה פעמים, דכתיב בפסיק ובשלשלת. בדבר עבירה ממאנין, בדבר מצוה אין ממאנין". On the second part of the comment, 'Regarding a sin, one must refuse; regarding a commandment, one must not', see Genesis Rabbah 87.5 and Yalquṭ Shimʿoni 145 (ed. Hyman, 1973, 750). On the *paseq* that always accompanies the *shalshelet* in the twenty-one prose books, see Yeivin (1980, 188–89, no. 229).

9 The *shalshelet* is also discussed in Goren (1989; 1995, 66–77, 151–56); Morgenstern (1994).

10 The comment is closely echoed in the Midrash Śekhel Ṭov (Ben Solomon 1900–1901, I:239). On this work, see Cohen (2020, 193–205), the afterword in Ta-Shma (2005, 253–94), and Mondschein (2009, 272–77).

26; Ben-Zazon 2017, 87–95; Sackson 2017, 161–69).[11] He wrote that the *shalshelet* in Gen. 39.8 represents not determination, but rather Joseph's hesitation and wavering resolve in the face of great temptation:

> וימאן גם טעם השלשלת הוא מפרושי אנשי כנסת הגדולה שלמדו ממשה וכבר כתבתי זה על ויתמהמה ואין כן על וימאן אשר ביעקב שני פעמים. ואין תמה אם יוסף החכם פוסח בזה הענין המסוכן אם לפנים אם לאחור כי כן ראוי לכל חכם ואולי זולתו ששמו כשמו לקח דרך אחרת ומה היה נעלם מרבותי[נו] ז"ל שאמרו על יהודה שמלאך י"י דוחה אותו וביוסף אמרו ביקש עצמו ולא מצא. אשרי מי שידע להכיר מעלת דבריהם.
>
> "And he refused." The accent *shalshelet* is also among the explanations that the Men of the Great Synagogue learnt from Moses, about which I have already written regarding the word וַיִּתְמַהְמָ֓הּ 'and he hesitated' (Gen. 19.16). [The accent] is not above the word וַיְמָאֵן on the two occasions it refers to Jacob (Gen. 37.35; 48.19). There is no cause for surprise if the wise man Joseph hesitated (פוסח) with regard to this perilous matter, whether one way or the other, for this befits every sage (and maybe his namesake took another approach!).[12] For how could anything be concealed from our rabbis, of blessed memory, who said regarding Judah that an angel of the Lord was compelling him, but regarding Joseph that he checked himself and found that he could not [have intercourse]. Happy is the one who can fully comprehend their sublime words!

---

[11] On Ibn Caspi's treatment of the *ṭeʿamim*, see Rock (2007, §2.4). I am grateful to Dr Rock for kindly providing a copy of her dissertation.

[12] As suggested in the editions of Last (1905) and Rock (2007), this may be a self-deprecating reference on the part of the commentator.

(Staats- und Universitätsbibliothek Hamburg MS Levy 8, fol. 32b)[13]

By crediting the transmission of the cantillation marks to the Men of the Great Synagogue[14] while also endowing them with Mosaic authority, Ibn Caspi presents them as an authoritative source of information regarding the biblical narrative. To understand the significance of the *shalshelet* in question, Ibn Caspi refers the reader back to his interpretation of Lot's hesitant flight from Sodom and Gomorrah (Gen. 19.16), where the word וַיִּתְמַהְמָהּ 'and he delayed', is pointed with the same accent. There he explains that the *shalshelet*'s meaning lies in its shape (ענינה בצורתה) and that Lot's indecisiveness was manifested physically as he "was contorting his body (עושה תנועה מעוותת) forwards and backwards."[15] The presence of the accent in Gen. 39.8 underlies Ibn Caspi's attribution of the same vacillation and tortuous hesitation to Joseph, who, according to the interpretation in Midrash Tanḥuma and Genesis Rabbah, was saved from transgression only

[13] This manuscript underlies the editions of Last (1905) and Rock (2007), though the former prints a slightly different reading (ed. Last 1905, II:87–88).

[14] Ibn Caspi frequently refers to the Men of the Great Synagogue when explaining the accents, including in his comment on Gen. 1.1. The attribution is in accordance with the rabbinic association of the events of Neh. 8–9, including the reading of the Torah in such a way that it was understood (Neh. 8.8), with the activities of the Men of the Great Synagogue. See b. Nedarim 37b, b. Megillah 3a, and the texts examined in Schiffer (1977). Cf. Baḥya ben Asher's assertion of the Mosaic origin of the cantillation marks cited below.

[15] MS Hamburg 8, fol. 23b; cf. *Mishneh Kesef* (ed. Last 1905), II:57.

through divine intervention, as the miraculous appearance of his father's image rendered him impotent.[16] Ibn Caspi excuses Joseph for his wavering resolve, recalling the principle that sages are particularly susceptible to the evil inclination.[17]

A third explanation is that of Ibn Caspi's contemporary, Baḥya ben Asher of Saragossa.[18] Baḥya not only expounded the *shalshelet* in Gen. 39.8, but also supplied an explanation for his methods:

> וימאן ויאמר אל אשת אדניו הן אדוני. תחלת דבורו אמר לה: הן אדני, כלומר והלא אדני מצוי לך ומה את עושה לי. והטעם שבמילת 'וימאן' מורה על אסור הדבר ועל היותו נמנע אצלו ממאן בו בתכלית המיאון, שהרי מתוך הטעמים שבתורה אנו מבינים מה שלא נכתב בה, כענין התנועות שבאדם שמתוכם נדע כוונת לבו
>
> "But he refused and said to his master's wife, 'My master is here [...].'" [Joseph] began by saying to her, 'My master

[16] This is related to the statement that "there was no man (אין איש)" present in the house with Joseph and Potiphar's wife (Gen. 39.11) in Tanḥuma (printed) *Va-yeshev* 9 and Genesis Rabbah 87.7; cf. b. Sotah 36b and Rashi on Gen. 39.11. Cf. Levinson (1997, 279–81). Ibn Caspi contrasts Joseph's lack of resolve with that of his brother Judah, who, according to Genesis Rabbah 85.8, approached Tamar only reluctantly and through the coercion of the angel appointed over desire. Cf. the interpretation in Solomon ibn Parḥon's *Maḥberet he-ʿArukh* (1160–1161) of the *shalshelet* on Gen. 19.16 as an indication of confusion (בלבול). Ibn Parḥon (fol. 5a); Berlin (1991, 85).

[17] See b. Sukka 52a and also the *ʾaggadot* of Rabbi Meir and Rabbi Akiva, who were almost overcome by lust for the woman who turned out to be Satan in disguise (b. Kiddushin 81a). Cf. Boyarin (2009, 258–66; Clenman (2014); and Rosen-Zvi (2011, 112–19).

[18] On Baḥya, see Walfish (1993, 216–17).

> is here,' which is to say, 'Is my master not available to you? What need do you have of me?' And the cantillation mark on the word וַיְמָאֵ֓ן shows that the matter was forbidden and that he held himself back, refusing point blank. This is because we gain an understanding of what is not written in the Torah from the cantillation marks, just as one may perceive a person's inner intention from his movements (תנועות). (Ben Asher, ed. Chavel 1966, I:321)[19]

According to Baḥya, Joseph rejected Mrs Potiphar's advances by pointing to the immediacy of Potiphar's presence with the words *hen ʾadoni*, "My master is here." Potiphar's availability to his wife obviated any need of Joseph.[20] His determination in refusing her advances is indicated by the *shalshelet*. Baḥya then details his method of expounding the *ṭeʿamim* as sources of supplementary narrative information. His explanation hinges on a word play on תנועה, which refers both to 'movement' and 'direction' as well as to the 'vowels' and 'accents' (Wolfson 1989–90, 1, 3; cf. Martini 2010, 61–65). Just as actions may speak louder than words, so the accents that transform the biblical text into a dynamic melodic motif disclose meanings that would not otherwise be apparent.[21]

---

[19] Part of this comment was incorporated into the Minḥat Shay, possibly as an addition; see Norzi (2005–2006, 135).

[20] Cf. Genesis Rabbah 87.5 and Tanḥuma (printed) *Va-yeshev* 8.

[21] Baḥya also justified his interpretation of the two *ṭeʿamim* on זֶ֓֔ה 'this one' in Gen. 5.29 as follows:

> Do not think this matter is insignificant, since the whole Torah is replete with allusions and matters of a philosophical nature (ענינים שכליים). These were set forth providentially in anticipation of the one who investigates the divine

Besides interpreting unusual *ṭeʿamim* by means of *derash*, our three commentators all refer to the accents' conjunctive and disjunctive functions and use them to determine stressed syllables.[22] This is their principal significance in Rashi's commentary,[23] where they are frequently used to identify stressed syllables, as well as the grammatical and syntactic functions of particular words.[24] Abraham ibn Ezra likewise used the accents to

---

> Torah. In this regard the sages explained that the cantillation marks in the Torah were also handed down from Sinai, and they demonstrated this from what is written, "Giving the sense so that they understood the reading" [Neh. 8.8]. They expounded this as follows: '"Giving the sense" refers to the verses. "They understood the reading" refers to the cantillation marks.' (b. Nedarim 37b) (ed. Chavel 1966, I:98).

On Baḥya's exegetical use of the method of *śekhel*, see Walfish (1993, 201–2); Talmage (1999, 319); Van der Heide (1983, 153).

[22] See *Leqaḥ Ṭov* on Exod. 13.11 (cf. Cohen 2020, 194–95); Ibn Caspi on Gen. 1.1, 27; 3.23; 9.6; 18.21; and Baḥya on Gen. 1.1; Exod. 25.38; Lev. 10.9 (on 1 Sam. 3.3); Lev. 23.16; Deut. 25.19; 32.5. As has been shown by T. Cohen (1997–1998, 26, 43), even the accent *shalshelet* is accorded no special significance in Ibn Caspi's comment on Isa. 13.8, where he follows David Kimḥi in noting its disjunctive function (see the texts in M. Cohen 1996, 98–99). I am grateful to Tamir Cohen for providing a copy of his dissertation.

[23] Existing studies include Englander (1939, 402–3; 1942–1943); Shereshevsky (1972; 1982, 86–92); Kogut (1994, 42–54, 78–88, 148–90); Himmelfarb (2004; 2005); Banon (2006).

[24] It cannot be established with absolute certainty that Rashi did not treat the *ṭeʿamim* as sources of *derash* due to the lack of clarity regarding the correct text of his commentary (Grossman 2012, 75–78; Lawee

parse words and explain syntax in accordance with his commitment to grammatical exegesis,[25] and there are numerous such interpretations in the commentaries of David Kimḥi.[26] In contrast to this common exegetical approach to the accents, *derash* on the *ṭeʿamim* is a relatively unfamiliar medieval method of exegesis, being employed only in expositions that favour the *derash* and

2019, 15–20). However, the 45 comments on accentuation that I have examined in *Mikra'ot Gedolot 'Haketer'*, Bayerishe StaatsBibliothek Munich MS Cod. hebr. 5, and Fredman's edition of the commentary on Proverbs confirm that Rashi resorted to the accents to resolve questions of grammar and syntax. Examples include Gen. 18.20; 29.6; 41.35; 42.21; 46.26; Num. 11.8; Deut. 11.30; Ezek. 40.18; Hos. 11.6; Ps. 10.3; 150.5; Job 18.20; Eccl. 3.16. The apparent lack of *derash* on the accentuation could be explained by the absence of such interpretations in Rashi's sources of rabbinic exegesis. Cf. Kamin's (1980, 24) argument that, in Rashi's biblical commentaries, "the root [דר"ש] in its various forms indicates the source of the interpretation as taken from the Sages"; see also Kamin (1986, 136–57); cf. Grossman (2017; 2021, 112–14, 125–32, 256–81). Among the many studies of the relationship between midrashic interpretations and the plain meaning of Scripture (פשוטו של מקרא) in Rashi's commentary, see Gelles (1981, 9–27, 42–65, 114–16); Ahrend (1997); Touitou (2000); Grossman (2017, 84–96); Cohen (2020, 95–126; 2021).

[25] For instance, see his comments on Exod. 5.7; 18.3, 26; 29.35 (all in the Long Commentary); Mic. 4.8; Nah. 1.1; Ps. 20.10; 45.6; 64.7. The preface to Ibn Ezra's commentary on the Torah includes criticism of the methods of the *Leqaḥ Ṭov* (1977a, I:7, 10); cf. Mondschein (2009, 271–72). See also Wolfson (1988–1989, 3), and §6 of Ibn Ezra (1977b, 111). Cf. Kogut (1994, 90–94, 196–230).

[26] For instance, see his comments on Jdg. 6.16; 11.25; Isa. 28.17; 44.15; Jer. 8.5; 9.18; 22.14; 22.20; 31.7, 36.20; Ezek. 15.4; 33.6; Ps. 35.19; 116.6. Cf. Kogut (1994, 56–57, 95–102, 231–38).

with reference to exceptional accents, such as the rare *shalshelet*.[27]

Baḥya's statement that one may "gain an understanding of what is not written in the Torah from the cantillation marks" was most likely known to Moses Alsheikh of Safed, who read and cited Baḥya's commentary on Genesis,[28] and who made full use of this exegetical principle. Born around 1520, Alsheikh was of the second generation of the Sephardi community that settled in the Ottoman Empire (Alsheikh 1563, author's introduction) following the expulsions from the Iberian Peninsula in the 1490s. As shown in his many responsa, he was a student of Joseph Karo, a communal rabbi, and a preacher. But Alsheikh is celebrated for his biblical commentaries, an extensive corpus of exegesis that covers almost the entire Hebrew Bible. His discursive, homiletic style, and abundant use of midrash, have endeared him to generations of readers, and his commentaries remain popular to this day (see Shalem 1965–1966).

---

[27] Another example is the account of Lamech naming Noah, where two accents appear on the word זֶה 'this one' in Gen. 5.29 (Ben Eliezer 1884, I:32, and Baḥya's commentary, as noted above, n. 25). The two accents on קִרְבוּ 'come near' in Lev. 10.4 are expounded in interpretations attributed to Judah the Pious and Eleazar of Worms; see the editions of Konyevsky (1978–1981, II:225) and Lange (1980, 42). On mystical interpretations of the *ṭeʿamim*, see Wolfson (1988–1989; 1989–1990); Dan (1968, 70). On the interpretation of the accent *shalshelet* in the thirteenth- or early-fourteenth-century *Sod ha-Shalshelet*, see Idel (1988, 56–61); Fishbane (1994, 31).

[28] See Alsheikh's comments on Gen. 45.22; Prov. 30.29; Job 28.19; and Song 5.8.

Like Tobias ben Eliezer, Joseph ibn Caspi, and Baḥya ben Asher, Alsheikh considered the meaning of the *shalshelet* in the Joseph narrative. Ever the dutiful preacher, he formulated a moralising interpretation that exhorts the reader to determined refusal when faced with temptation, lest excuses or explanations be undermined by the wiles of the tempter:

> על כן ותמאן (וימאן) וילפת בשומעו כשלשלת שעל התיבה. והנה יוסף התנהג בחכמה והוא כי דרך אנשים בבא רשע או אשת כסילות לפתותו לדבר עברה והוא לא כן ידמה כי יתן טענות נגד המפתה להשתיקו אך לא זו הדרך להציל את נפשו מעשות רע כי יקרה יהיה המפתה איש לשון שבשפת חלקות ישחית דברי הנפתה הנעימים וילכד ברשתו אך אשר מוח לו בקדקדו לא יעשה כן כי אם מיד יחליט אומר למאן ולומ[ר] שלא יעשה בשום פנים גם כי ינוצח ואחרי כן אם ירצה יסדר ג[ם] כ[ן] טענות נגד המפתה וזה היה ענין יוסף כי ראשונה החליט וימאן כמי שקושר עצמו בשלשלת ואח[ר] כ[ך] אמ[ר] טענות... וזהו הן אדוני כו' ולא חשך כו' ואיך אעשה הרעה הגדולה הזאת להיות כפוי טובה לבשר ודם שאם כה אעשה אהיה גם כפוי טובה לה' וזהו וחטאתי לאל[ה]ים כאשר נרמז באומ[רו] וימאן בטעם שלשלת כאומר ברמז שהוא נותן שלשלת עון בצוארו
>
> "But he refused." This means that he shook[29] when he heard it, like the *shalshelet* upon the word. Indeed, Joseph behaved wisely. This is because it is human nature, when an evil man or a foolish woman (cf. Prov. 9.13) comes to entice [someone] to a sinful action that he does not intend to do (cf. Isa. 10.7), that he will counter the tempter with

[29] On the meaning of וַיִּלָּפֵת (Ruth 3.8), see Alsheikh's comments on Deut. 3.29–4.1; Prov. 10.8; 12.17; Ruth 3.8; Job 6.18; and the introduction to the commentary on Ecclesiastes. Given the definition in b. Sanhedrin 19b (cf. Targum Ruth 3.8) and the context of Joseph's seduction, there is also the possibility of double entendre. On humour in Alsheikh's commentaries, see his interpretations of Deut. 22.4–5 and Ps. 49.2.

> objections in order to silence him. But this is hardly the way to save oneself from doing evil. For it might so happen that the tempter is a smooth talker (cf. Ps. 140.12) who, with flattering lips (cf. Ps. 12.3–4), will sway the fine words of the one who is tempted, and he will be caught in his net. But the one who has a brain in his head will not act in this way, but rather will immediately resolve to refuse and say that he will not do so under any circumstances, even if overpowered. Thereafter, if he so desires, he can also list the objections to counter the tempter. This is what happened in Joseph's case. First, he made the resolve and "he refused," like one who binds himself with a chain (*shalshelet*). [Only] afterwards did he give the objections... This is the meaning of, "Look, my master [has no concern, because of me, for household affairs, for he has entrusted everything he owns to me. He is not greater in this house than I am,] nor has he withheld [anything from me except you, because you are his wife.] How could I do this great evil [and sin against God (*l-elohim*)?]" (Gen. 39.8–9) being ungrateful to a human being, and thereby also being ungrateful to the Lord. This is what is meant by "and sin against God." The same is indicated when it says "and he refused" with *shalshelet*, to indicate that he puts the chain of iniquity (*shalshelet ʿavon*) around his neck. (Alsheikh 1593, fol. 65b)[30]

Alsheikh begins by suggesting that the shape or melody of the *shalshelet* indicates Joseph's reaction to Mrs Potiphar's advances—he trembled at the very thought. The ensuing explanations hinge on the meaning of the word שלשלת 'chain'. Alsheikh associates Joseph's exemplary decision to refuse temptation out-

[30] The corrected reading וימאן is from the 1710 edition, fol. 58a.

right with the accent, suggesting that he resolved to reject Potiphar's wife as if bound by this 'chain' to his chosen course of action. Alsheikh finally turns to Joseph's commitment to proper behaviour not only towards his master, but also towards God, likening him to one who puts the שלשלת עוון 'chain of iniquity' around his neck. This is the phrase that Rashi used to explain the word קולר in the Babylonian Talmud (b. Shevuʿot 31a), which refers to the burden of personal responsibility that would be assumed by a witness who testifies in a fraudulent case (see Berkowitz 2006: 149, 278, n. 128; Sinai 2007). In suggesting that Joseph's words amount to a testimony, Alsheikh echoes midrashic expositions of Gen. 39.9, "How could I do this great evil and sin against God (*l-elohim*)?" as an oath by which Joseph committed himself to shun the opportunity for sin.[31] The *shalshelet* or 'chain' in the biblical text is the testimony to his vow before the divine judge.

For all the creativity and ingenuity of his interpretations, Alsheikh's focus on the rare accent *shalshelet* as the key to understanding the narrative resembles the exegetical approach of the medieval interpreters of Gen. 39.8 examined above. But Alsheikh and other sixteenth-century Sephardi commentators of the Ottoman Empire, including Abraham ben Asher and Solomon Alkabets, did not limit their expositions to a few exceptional

[31] See the interpretation of Gen. 39.9 as an oath in Tanḥuma (printed) *Va-yeshev* 8; Genesis Rabbah 87.5; Leviticus Rabbah 23.11; Ruth Rabbah 6.4.

ṭeʿamim.[32] Rather, they saw the accentuation more broadly as a source of information about biblical narratives. In order to examine this exegetical approach to the Masora, we will turn to three comments in Alsheikh's commentary on the book of Ruth, entitled *ʿEne Moshe* and first printed posthumously in Venice in 1601. The commentary is structured as a series of discourses on extended pericopes. Each begins with a list of שאלות 'questions' or קושיות 'difficulties' which Alsheikh subsequently resolves. This technique, for which Isaac Abravanel (1437–1508) is well known, is ubiquitous in late-medieval and early-modern Sephardi commentaries and homilies.[33] A barrage of questions arouses the reader's curiosity about whether the text really makes sense and whether the exegete can solve all the problems he has made for himself. Alsheikh does so by examining the minutiae of the biblical text, points he calls דקדוקים. His aim is to show that seemingly trivial details, when properly understood, contribute to overarching harmonious interpretations.

Alsheikh resorts to the *ṭeʿamim* to solve exegetical problems in the very first verses of Ruth:

(6) וַיְהִ֗י בִּימֵי֙ שְׁפֹ֣ט הַשֹּׁפְטִ֔ים וַיְהִ֥י רָעָ֖ב בָּאָ֑רֶץ וַיֵּ֨לֶךְ אִ֜ישׁ מִבֵּ֧ית לֶ֣חֶם יְהוּדָ֗ה לָגוּר֙
בִּשְׂדֵ֣י מוֹאָ֔ב ה֥וּא וְאִשְׁתּ֖וֹ וּשְׁנֵ֥י בָנָֽיו׃ וְשֵׁ֣ם הָאִ֣ישׁ אֱ֠לִימֶלֶךְ וְשֵׁ֨ם אִשְׁתּ֜וֹ נָעֳמִ֗י

---

[32] On Abraham ben Asher's interpretation of the *zaqef qaṭan* in Gen. 12.1, presented in the course of his exposition of Midrash Genesis Rabbah 39.1, see Williams (2016, 75). On Solomon Alkabets, see his comments on Ruth 1.11; 3.13, 17 (Alkabets 1992, 22, 188, 206).

[33] See Bland (1990); Saperstein (2014a); Williams (2015); Lawee (2008).

וְשֵׁ֣ם שְׁנֵֽי־בָנָ֣יו ׀ מַחְל֧וֹן וְכִלְי֛וֹן אֶפְרָתִ֕ים מִבֵּ֥ית לֶ֖חֶם יְהוּדָ֑ה וַיָּבֹ֥אוּ שְׂדֵֽי־מוֹאָ֖ב
וַיִּֽהְיוּ־שָֽׁם׃

‘And it came about (וַיְהִי) in the days when the judges judged that there was (וַיְהִי) a famine in the land. So a man of Bethlehem of Judah (מִבֵּית לֶחֶם יְהוּדָה) went to reside in the fields of Moab, he and his wife and his two sons. The man’s name was Elimelech, his wife was Naomi, and his two sons were Mahlon and Chilion. They were Ephrathites from Bethlehem of Judah (מִבֵּ֥ית לֶ֖חֶם יְהוּדָ֑ה). They came to the fields of Moab and were there.’ (Ruth 1.1–2)

Alsheikh begins by enumerating no fewer than ten קושיות ‘difficulties’ regarding these verses, asking why וַיְהִי ‘and it came about, there was’ and בֵּית לֶחֶם יְהוּדָה ‘Bethlehem, Judah’ are repeated, and why the family members are introduced once anonymously and then again by name. The eighth difficulty focuses on how Elimelech is introduced in verse two:

> הנה מהראוי להבין במקרא... ח' אומרו ושם האיש והיה די יאמ[ר] ושמו אלימלך...
>
> The following must be understood in this passage of Scripture... 8. The statement ‘the man’s name [was Elimelech],’ as it would have sufficed to say ‘his name was Elimelech.’ (Alsheikh 1601, fol. 3a)

Alsheikh here calls attention to an apparent tautology. Revealing his conception of Scripture as marked by perfect felicity of expression, in which no detail is superfluous, he asks why Ruth 1.2 states וְשֵׁ֨ם הָאִ֜ישׁ אֱֽלִימֶ֗לֶךְ when שְׁמוֹ אֱלִימֶלֶךְ would have been more concise.

Alsheikh's explanation revolves around two concerns: Elimelech's social status and the halakhic question of the circumstances in which one is permitted to leave the land of Israel. This latter is discussed with reference to the book of Ruth in b. Bava Batra 91a. On the one hand, Elimelech's departure at a time of famine suggests that scarcity of food is a permitted reason to leave the land of Israel. On the other hand, he and his sons die in the next three verses, suggesting that departure even in the direst of circumstances is forbidden.[34] Alsheikh seeks an explanation partly in the talmudic principle that "the Holy One, blessed be He, is exacting with his righteous ones to the extent of a hair's breadth" (Cf. b. Yevamot 121b; y. Sheqalim 48d (5.1), y. Betsa 62b (3.8); b. Bava Qamma 50a). Thus, even if departure from the land of Israel is tolerated in particular circumstances, Elimelech's social status meant that he was held to particularly high standards. But to demonstrate this, Alsheikh must show that Elimelech was indeed important or righteous, a detail not explicit in Scripture. He alludes to the rabbinic interpretations that Elimelech and his sons were "great men of their generation" and "leaders of their generation" (b. Bava Batra 91a; Ruth Rabbah 1.4) and adds insights of his own:

> אל תתמה על החפץ כי הלא אדם גדול היה כי ושם האיש כלומר האיש הרשום שהוא תואר איש שהוא גדול ככל אנשי[ם] שבמקרא וגם בה"א הידיעה וגם אלימלך כמ[ו] ש[אמרו] ז"ל שהיה אומר אלי תבא מלכות שעל רוב שלמותו היה אומר שאין ראוי למלכות ישראל כמוהו ולרמוז

---

[34] See also Sifra *be-Har* parasha 5.4 and Moses Maimonides, *Mishneh Torah, Hilkhot Melakhim u-Milḥamotehem* 5.9–12. Cf. *Encyclopedia Talmudica*, s.v. 'Ereẓ Israel', III:47; Safrai (2018, 78–79); Kanarfogel (1986); Saperstein (2014b, 281).

> רוממותו הוא טעם פז"ר גדו"ל... שעל ידי כן הקב"ה מדקדק עמהם עד גדר ש... נשפטו משפט מות וזהו וימת אלימלך וכו'...
>
> Do not be surprised at the matter, for was [Elimelech] not a great man? This is because 'the name of the man [was Elimelech]' (וְשֵׁם הָאִישׁ אֱלִימֶלֶךְ) means 'the designated man [was Elimelech]'. This is a way of describing a man as 'great', like all [who are styled] אנשים in Scripture. The use of the definite article also [indicates this], as does [the name] Elimelech. [This is] as the sages said, '[Elimelech] would say, "Kingship will come to me (אלי... מלכות)."' Because of his pre-eminence he would say that no one was better suited for the monarchy of Israel than he was. And to indicate his exalted position is the cantillation mark *pazer gadol*... On account of this, the Holy One, blessed be He, was strict with them to the extent that... they were sentenced to death. (Alsheikh 1601, fol. 4a)

Alsheikh demonstrates that each word of the phrase וְשֵׁם הָאִישׁ אֱלִימֶלֶךְ indicates Elimelech's high standing. שֵׁם shows that he is singled out as an important individual. Midrashic interpretations of the word אִישׁ treat individuals so designated as particularly righteous, such as the exposition in Genesis Rabbah 30.7 of Noah, the "man righteous and wholehearted" (Gen. 6.9).[35] Elimelech's name itself indicates his aspirations. Alsheikh relates the interpretation in Ruth Rabbah 2.4 that revocalises his name to show

[35] "Wherever the word *ʾish* occurs, it refers to a righteous man who forewarned [his generation]" (Theodor and Albeck eds. 1903–1936, 272). Cf. Numbers Rabbah 16.5. For Alsheikh, the same applies to אִשָּׁה, and he interprets the designation of Rebekah as הָאִשָּׁה with the definite article in Gen. 24.39 (*ad. loc.*) as an indication of her importance.

that he positioned himself to become Israel's first king by claiming that "kingship is mine", אֱלַי מַלְכוּת.

Alsheikh supports these interpretations by referring to a feature of the biblical text itself: the *ṭaʿam* on Elimelech's name. Though the disjunctive accent *pazer* is not unusual (it occurs 858 times in the prose books of the Hebrew Bible), it appears only here in Ruth (Price 1996, I:5, IV:831). In the public recitation of the book, the melodic motif unique to this verse and the pause indicated by the accent draw attention to Elimelech's name at the moment he arrives on scene. Alsheikh refers to this accent as *pazer gadol*, a name which holds the key to the interpretation that it "indicates [Elimelech's] exalted position": a 'great *pazer*' heralds the entrance of the great Elimelech.[36] It thus helps to explain the significance of the expression וְשֵׁ֣ם הָאִ֣ישׁ אֱֽלִימֶ֡לֶךְ and supports the overarching interpretation that, due to his importance, he was held to high standards and punished for leaving the land of Israel even at a time of famine.

Alsheikh resorts to the *ṭeʿamim* again in his comment on the narrative of Ruth gleaning in the field in chapter 2:

(7) וַיֹּ֤אמֶר בֹּ֙עַז֙ לְנַֽעֲר֔וֹ הַנִּצָּ֖ב עַל־הַקּֽוֹצְרִ֑ים לְמִ֖י הַנַּעֲרָ֥ה הַזֹּֽאת׃ וַ֗יַּעַן הַנַּ֛עַר הַנִּצָּ֥ב
עַל־הַקּוֹצְרִ֖ים וַיֹּאמַ֑ר נַעֲרָ֤ה מֽוֹאֲבִיָּה֙ הִ֔יא הַשָּׁ֥בָה עִֽם־נָעֳמִ֖י מִשְּׂדֵ֥ה מוֹאָֽב׃

[36] In his commentary on Lev. 23.27, Alsheikh similarly designates the *pazer* on the word אַ֡ךְ as *pazer gadol*; he does not use the term to refer to *qarne farah* (see Yeivin, 1980, 212–13, nos. 274–76). The interpretation of Ruth 1.2 is analogous to that of Est. 6.7, where the *zaqef gadol* on the word אִ֕ישׁ indicates the great importance of the individual concerned.

> 'Boaz said to his servant who was stationed over the reapers, "To whom does this young woman belong?" The servant stationed over the reapers answered and said (וַיַּ֫עַן... וַיֹּאמַ֑ר), "She is a young Moabite woman, the one who returned with Naomi from the fields of Moab."' (Ruth 2.5–6)

Alsheikh begins with the characteristic litany of questions. Among them, he asks why two verbs introduce the servant's reply, וַיַּ֫עַן and then וַיֹּאמַ֑ר, when one would suffice:

> ...ואף גם מלת ויען תראה מיותרת והיה די לומר ויאמר נערה מואביה כו'
>
> ...In addition, the word 'and he answered' (וַיַּ֫עַן) appears to be superfluous as it would have sufficed to say, 'And he said (וַיֹּאמַ֑ר), "She is a young Moabite woman."' (Alsheikh 1601, fol. 17a)

This question prompts an elaboration of the narrative. Alsheikh explains the role of the servant, his relationship to Boaz, and the particulars of their exchange. Because the servant was appointed or stationed "over" the reapers, Alsheikh describes him as standing on a platform to survey the harvest. He also develops interpretations from the Babylonian Talmud (b. Shabbat 113b) and Rashi's commentary (on Ruth 2.5), that Boaz asked about Ruth not because he habitually enquired whether young women were single, but because he noted how carefully she observed the halakhic regulations about gleaning. In the hands of Moses Alsheikh, this rabbinic interpretation germinates into an extended narrative in which the servant misinterpreted Boaz's intentions and so embarked upon a character assassination of Ruth to prevent his master from becoming entangled with a Moabite woman:[37]

> ויען הנער וכו' הנה דרך בעלי שדות להעמיד איש נצב על הקוצרים בל יתרפו במלאכתם ולהעמידו במקום גבוה יראה את כלם לבל ישמט איש מהם אשר לא יראנו ולבחור אותו מכל נעריו איש אשר כח בו להרים קול לקרובים ולרחוקים ומה גם בשדות גבר כבועז גדול ועצום בעושר ונכסים כי רבים אשר אתו קוצרי קצירו ואמר כי להשיב לו הרים קול לספר בגנות רות וזהו ויען הנער מלשון הרמת קול כמו וענית ואמרת ויען איוב ויאמר יאבד יום וכו' וקצת סעד לזה הוא הטעם אשר עליו מלמעלה הוא הרבי"ע וזהו ויען
>
> "And the servant answered and said..." The practice of field owners is to station a man appointed over the reapers so that they do not get lazy in their work. [They] station him in an elevated place [from which] he can see them all, so that no one will let [any grain] drop without him seeing it. [Owners] choose this individual from among all their servants, someone who has the strength to raise their voice to those near and far. This is particularly [important] in the fields of a great man like Boaz who had immense wealth and property, for many [people] were reaping his harvest with him. And it says that, in order to reply to [Boaz], he raised his voice to denigrate Ruth. This is the meaning of 'and the servant answered [and said]' (וַיַּעַן... וַיֹּאמַר). The expression indicates that he raised his voice, just as in the case of, "And you will answer and say (וְעָנִיתָ וְאָמַרְתָּ) [before the Lord your God, 'An Aramaean was seeking to destroy my father...']" (Deut. 26.5) and, "And Job answered and said (וַיַּעַן אִיּוֹב וַיֹּאמַר), ['Let the day on which I was born perish...']" (Job 3.2). And a little support for

[37] Contrast with the overseer's words in Ruth Zuta 2.7 and Targum Ruth 2.6, where he points out that Ruth is a convert.

> this may be [drawn from] the cantillation mark on the penultimate syllable, which is *revia*ʿ. This is the meaning of וַיַּ֫עַן. (Alsheikh 1601, fols 17b–18a)

According to Alsheikh, the two verbs וַיַּ֫עַן and וַיֹּ֫אמַר indicate that the overseer spoke loudly. Deut. 26.5 and Job 3.2 both introduce direct speech in this way, and Rashi's commentary explains on each occasion that the phrase indicates a raising of the voice.[38] Alsheikh appeals to the *ṭa*ʿ*am* on וַיַּ֫עַן to show that this interpretation holds true in the verse in question. This is one of several occasions in his commentary where he focuses on the melodic function of the disjunctive accent *revia*ʿ. Elsewhere he describes it as כמגביה קול ואומר 'like one who raises the voice' to communicate a particular interpretation.[39] Here it appears on the first word of the verse and introduces direct speech. Alsheikh therefore suggests that the accent indicates how the ensuing statement was delivered and that the servant shouted out an urgent warning to Boaz. This interpretation is in accordance with the exegetical technique observed above in the *Leqaḥ Ṭov*, which treats the cantillation marks both as musical signs for the cantor and as indications of how direct speech was originally delivered by biblical characters. By supporting the interpretation that the overseer was shouting, the *revia*ʿ helps Alsheikh to formulate a narrative that answers his initial question about an apparent tautology. He

[38] See the 1546–1548 Rabbinic Bible (Venice: Bomberg), fols 216b, 785a, and the texts discussed in Smelik (2013, 58–67).

[39] See, for instance, Alsheikh's comment on Gen. 24.7. Cf. Rashi's commentary on Gen. 1.1 and 37.20, where significant phrases 'speak' to the expositor, saying דרשני 'expound me' (Ben Isaac, 1982, 2, 134); regarding the latter, cf. Tanḥuma (Buber) *Va-yeshev* 13.

shows that there is no redundancy in the use of both וַיַּ֣עַן and וַיֹּ֔אמֶר, as the accent on the former reveals its distinctive shade of meaning.[40]

A final comment on the *ṭeʿamim* concerns the exchange between Ruth and Naomi after the harvest. The third chapter of Ruth begins:

(8) וַתֹּ֣אמֶר לָ֔הּ נָעֳמִ֖י חֲמוֹתָ֑הּ בִּתִּ֗י הֲלֹ֧א אֲבַקֶּשׁ־לָ֛ךְ מָנ֖וֹחַ אֲשֶׁ֥ר יִֽיטַב־לָֽךְ׃ וְעַתָּ֗ה
הֲלֹ֥א בֹ֙עַז֙ מֹֽדַעְתָּ֔נוּ אֲשֶׁ֥ר הָיִ֖ית אֶת־נַעֲרוֹתָ֑יו הִנֵּה־ה֗וּא זֹרֶ֛ה אֶת־גֹּ֥רֶן הַשְּׂעֹרִ֖ים
הַלָּֽיְלָה׃ וְרָחַ֣צְתְּ ׀ וָסַ֗כְתְּ ושמתי (K) וְשַׂ֥מְתְּ (Q) [שמל]תך (K) שִׂמְלֹתַ֛יִךְ
(Q) עָלַ֖יִךְ [וי]רדתי (K) וְיָרַ֣דְתְּ (Q) הַגֹּ֑רֶן אַל־תִּוָּדְעִ֣י לָאִ֔ישׁ עַ֥ד כַּלֹּת֖וֹ לֶאֱכֹ֥ל
וְלִשְׁתּֽוֹת׃[41]

'Naomi her mother-in-law said to her, 'My daughter (בִּתִּ֗י), should I not seek security for you, that you may be well? Now is not Boaz, with whose young women you were, our kinsman? He is about to winnow the barley at the threshing-floor tonight. Now wash, anoint yourself, put on your cloak and go down to the threshing-floor. Do not make yourself known to the man until he has finished eating and drinking.' (Ruth 3.1–3)

Among the קושיות, Alsheikh lists the following:

---

[40] A variant pointing of the word with the accent *darga* is attested in a number of manuscripts; see Wright (1864, 9 [second pagination]). However, the explicit reason for Alsheikh's reference to the accent of וַיַּ֣עַן is to support his account of the overseer's actions, rather than to assert the correct reading of the text.

[41] As printed in the 1546–1548 Rabbinic Bible (Venice: Bomberg), fol. 831a. See the footnote below regarding the pointing of בִּתִּ֗י.

...וגם מה בצע להגיד לנו שקראה בתי כי אין ספק לא שת לבו שמואל הנביא ברוח קדשו לכתוב לנו רובי דברים אשר אין לסיפור בהם חפץ

...Furthermore, what is the use of telling us that [Naomi] called [Ruth] "my daughter" (בִּתִּ֥י)? For without a doubt the prophet Samuel did not intend, by means of the holy spirit, to write lots of words for us which serve no purpose for the narrative. (Alsheikh 1601, fols 28a–28b)

Alsheikh here makes explicit a key assumption underlying his interpretations. Referring to the talmudic attribution of the book of Ruth to Samuel (b. Bava Batra 14b), he accords it the status of an inspired prophetic writing. This means that nothing is redundant and, as he asserts, every textual detail contributes to the book's narrative. In the comment that follows, this principle is applied both to the word בִּתִּ֥י and to its accent.

Alsheikh refers to a kabbalistic interpretation related by Naḥmanides and the *Midrash ha-Neʿelam* on Ruth. When Naḥmanides expounded Onan's failure to raise up offspring for his late brother, he referred to levirate marriage as "one of the great secrets of the Torah." Concealing the nature of this "secret" from the casual reader, Naḥmanides referred allusively to Ruth 4.17 and stated והמשכיל יבין 'and the wise will understand' (commentary on Gen. 38.8 in Ben Naḥman 1959, I:214–15; see Idel 1983; Wolfson 1989; 1993; Yisraeli 2006). This is a reference to the women of Bethlehem, who celebrated the birth of Obed by saying not "a son is born to Ruth" but rather "a son is born to Naomi." As explained in the *Midrash ha-Neʿelam*, this indicates that Ruth's son was in fact the reincarnation of her late husband Mahlon (*Midrash ha-Neʿelam* on Ruth, ed. Margaliot, 2007–2008,

89d–90a).[42] The "great secret" of levirate marriage, it would seem, is that the soul of the deceased is reborn in the child begotten of the union.

Because Ruth's marriage to Boaz would secure Mahlon's reincarnation, Naomi had a vested interest. This calls into question her motivation in arranging the rendezvous at the threshing floor. Alsheikh defends Naomi's altruism by explaining the word בִּתִּ֗י and its accent:

> על כן באה רוח הקדש להעמידנו על האמת ויאמ[ר] ותאמר נעמי כלומר אשר היא נעימה במעשיה עשתה כשמה עם היותה חמותה שאין דרכה לחזור אחר תועלת כלתה וזהו ותאמר לה נעמי חמותה והן זה הורת לה בנועם מיליה באמור אליה בתי וכו' וגם ידוקדק היות טעם זקף גדול במלת בתי כרומז לה עליה בתואר זה והוא לומר אל אהיה בעיניך באשר אני מצוה אותך כחמות עם כלתה כי לא כלתי את בעצם כי אם בתי כלומר כי רוח בני בקרבך וכבת לי תחשב ולמה לא אבקש הנאתך
>
> Therefore, the holy spirit came to show us the truth of the matter and said, "Naomi said". This indicates that she was as pleasant (נעימה) in her actions as her name suggests even though, being [Ruth's] mother-in-law, it was not in her nature to pursue the benefit of her daughter-in-law. That is the meaning of, "Naomi her mother-in law said to her." [Naomi] demonstrated this to [Ruth] with her pleasant words (בנועם במיליה) when she said to her, "My daughter (בתי)..." The cantillation mark *zaqef gadol* on the word בתי must also be examined precisely (ידוקדק) because it [likewise] indicates that Naomi had such [an attitude] towards Ruth. It is as if to say, "When I instruct you, do not think

[42] Cf. Zohar *Mishpatim* 2.99b and Zohar *Va-yeshev* 1.188a–b (ed. Matt, Wolski, and Hecker 2004–2017, III:148–50; V:38; *XI*:263–65). See Mopsik (1987, 16–21); Hallamish (1999); Fine (2003, 304–14); Werblowsky (1997, 112–15, 234–56).

> of me as a mother-in-law [talking] to her daughter-in-law, for you are not in fact my daughter-in-law, but my daughter. This is to say that the spirit of my son is inside you, and you should be considered as a daughter to me. Why would I not seek your benefit?" (Alsheikh 1601, fol. 28b)

This comment is an atomistic reading of the words נָעֳמִ֖י חֲמוֹתָ֑הּ בִּתִּ֞י. Naomi's name is mentioned explicitly in order to evoke the etymology in Ruth Rabbah that she was "pleasant (נעימה) in her actions" (Ruth Rabbah 2.5; 3.6). Her kind-heartedness prevailed over what Alsheikh considers to be the nature of the mother-in-law, who does not pursue her daughter-in-law's best interests.[43] This insight is supported by the word בִּתִּ֞י and its accent. In interpretations similar to that of the aforementioned *revia*ʿ, Alsheikh likens the *zaqef gadol* in his commentaries on Eccl. 9.10 and Est. 6.7 to "one who raises the voice" to declare a particular interpretation. In this case, the disjunctive accent on the initial word of Naomi's speech focuses attention on the expression that captures the true relationship between the women. Alsheikh rewrites Naomi's words to show that she considers Ruth her daughter and treats her accordingly. The word בִּתִּ֞י and its accent thus support the interpretation that Naomi arranged Ruth's liaison with Boaz purely out of concern for Ruth's wellbeing rather than as a selfish means to secure Mahlon's rebirth.[44]

---

[43] On the portrayal of the mother-in-law in rabbinic texts, see Ilan (2017, 120–22).

[44] A variant pointing of בִּתִּ֗י with the accent *revia*ʿ is attested in a number of manuscripts and printed editions, though, as noted in the case of וַיַּ֫עַן above, Alsheikh draws no attention to the different reading. See Gins-

By means of these three comments on the accentuation of Ruth, Alsheikh has opened up remarkable new vistas on a well-known narrative. Elimelech's *pazer* reveals his high social status. A *revia*ʿ shows that Boaz's servant was stationed on a platform, shouting to the harvesters and, in an unfortunate misunderstanding, even to his master. And a *zaqef gadol* shows that Naomi shunned selfishness and spoke to Ruth out of maternal compassion. These *ṭeʿamim* disclose information about the narrative that is not otherwise indicated in the text. In this respect, Alsheikh's comments resemble the aforementioned interpretations of Gen. 39.8, in which the *Leqaḥ Ṭov*, Ibn Caspi, and Baḥya ben Asher derived the details of Joseph's refusal of Potiphar's wife from the accent *shalshelet*.

An important difference between Alsheikh and his predecessors is that, rather than explaining peculiarities as he encounters them, he goes in search of *ṭeʿamim* that might serve as useful sources of narrative information. The accents he selects in Ruth are not unusual in themselves, though in a particular verse, *pazer*, *revia*ʿ, and *zaqef gadol* stand out from the most familiar sequences of *ṭeʿamim*.[45] Alsheikh ascertains their meanings from their names

---

burg (1926, 579); Wright (1864, 16 [second pagination]). In the Leningrad Codex (fol. 422a), the word is pointed with *gershayim*. This is also the reading of the 1601 edition of Alsheikh (1601, fol. 27b), in which the biblical text printed alongside the commentary obscures the meaning of Alsheikh's interpretation. On the significance of the accents and Zoharic references to the masoretic pointing among early modern Kabbalists, see Penkower (2010); Dweck (2011, 151–69); Rubin (2011).

[45] *Revia*ʿ occurs 8910 times in the prose books; *zaqef gadol* 1655 times (Price 1996, I:5).

and their melodic functions. But his discussions also draw on insights from *midrashim*, Rashi's and Naḥmanides's commentaries, and the *Midrash ha-Neʿelam*. Alsheikh uses the accents to support these explanations by showing that they may be derived directly from features of the biblical text. One reason for this is evident in the comment on the word בְּתִּ֞י, where Alsheikh states that the *zaqef gadol* should be "examined precisely (ידוקדק היות טעם זקף גדול)". As mentioned earlier, forms of לדקדק are used by Alsheikh and other contemporary Sephardi commentators to refer to the scrutiny of the biblical text to find answers to the קושיות, the questions raised in the pericope. That Alsheikh used the *ṭeʿamim* to this end was already apparent in his comments on the *pazer* on Elimelech's name and the *reviaʿ* on וַיַּ֗עַן. Both respond to questions about seemingly superfluous words. But the interpretation of בְּתִּ֞י makes explicit that Alsheikh counts the accents among the minutiae of the biblical text which, properly understood, demonstrate its overall coherence.

By appealing so readily to the *ṭeʿamim*, Alsheikh treats the accents as an essential and fundamental means by which biblical narrative is expressed. No longer are they a paratextual guide to the grammar and syntax of the words; nor are they occasional indicators of unexpected interpretations. Now they are treated as an integral part of the text itself, conveying information that is necessary to understand the narrative with clarity. The reader of the biblical text must therefore be constantly alert to the bearing that every accent, however commonplace, might have on the course of events in any given passage. This manner of reading the Hebrew Bible was enabled in many editions of Alsheikh's works that were issued in Venice by Giovanni di Gara, including the 1601 *editio princeps* of the commentary on Ruth, by the provision of a vocalised and accented text alongside the commentary.[46] This *mise en page* allows the reader to move from an encounter with the accented words of the biblical text to Alsheikh's questions regarding their significance and coherence, and finally to a problem-solving exegetical discourse that shows how studying the details of the accented text allows one to grasp its full meaning.

The idea that the *ṭeʿamim* indicate not only grammar and syntax, but also narrative information has resurfaced in several recent expositions of the Hebrew Bible. In their homilies on the Joseph narrative, Louis Jacobs, Jonathan Sacks, and Jonathan Magonet find common cause in interpreting the shape and quivering tone of the *shalshelet* in Gen. 39.8 as an indication of the protagonist's inner conflict, struggle, torment, and *crise de conscience*. For Jacobs (2004, 59–60), the *ṭaʿam* "expresses vacillation where we would expect firm resolve" and, for Magonet (2004, 27–28), Joseph was "fighting against the temptation to accept." Sacks (2009, 109–15) ascribes his interpretation to an

---

[46] Partly through the efforts of Alsheikh's son Ḥayyim, Di Gara issued Alsheikh's commentaries on Daniel (1591), Song of Songs (1591; 1606), Proverbs (1601), Ruth (1601), Lamentations (1601), Qohelet (1601), Job (1603), and Psalms (1605) with the biblical text printed alongside. This typographical complication was omitted from the earlier editions of the commentaries on Song of Songs (1563) and Daniel (1563) that were printed in the Ottoman Empire. The list of printed editions of Alsheikh's commentaries compiled by Naphtali Ben-Menaḥem is in Shalem (1965–1966, 237–74). See Benayahu (2001); Dweck (2010).

earlier exegete, Joseph ibn Caspi, developing his predecessor's interpretation that the *ṭaʿam* indicates a physical manifestation of wavering resolve by suggesting that it reveals "a psychological state of uncertainty and indecision." As the cantillation marks once again "raise their voices" to relay interpretations old and new, it is hoped that an understanding of the development of this expository technique and its relationship to earlier exegetical methods will enable a deeper appreciation of a chapter of the reception history of the Hebrew Bible, in which the Masora is treated as a means to "gain an understanding of what is not written in the Torah" (Ben Asher, 1966, I:321).

References

Ahrend, Moshe. 1997. 'L'adaptation des commentaires du Midrash par Rashi et ses disciples à leur exégèse biblique'. *Revue des Études Juives* 156: 275–88.

Alkabets, Solomon. 1992. *Sefer Shoresh Yishai: Perush ʿal Megilat Rut*. Jerusalem: Hivzon.

Alsheikh, Moses. 1563. *Ḥavaṣelet ha-Sharon*. Constantinople: Jabez.

———. 1593. *Sefer Torat Moshe*. Belvedere: Ashkeloni.

———. 1601. *ʿEne Moshe*. Venice: Di Gara.

———. 1710. *Sefer Torat Moshe*. Amsterdam: Proops.

Banon, David. 2006. 'L'exégèse de Rachi sur les *té'amim*'. In *Héritages de Rachi*, edited by René-Samuel Sirat, 127–36. Paris: Eclat.

del Barco, Javier. 2010. *Bibliothèque nationale de France: Hébreu 1 à 32: Manuscrits de la bible hébraïque*. Turnhout: Brepols.

Ben Asher, Baḥya. 1966. *Beʾur ʿal ha-Torah*. Edited by Charles Chavel. 3 vols. Jerusalem: Mossad Harav Kook.

Benayahu, Meir. 2001. 'Rabbi Isaac Gershon'. *Asufot* 13: 9–89. [Hebrew]

Ben Eliezer, Tobias. 1884. *Lekach-Tob*. Edited by Solomon Buber. 2 vols. Vilna: Romm.

Ben Isaac, Solomon. 1982. *Perushe Rash"i ʿal ha-Torah*. Edited by Charles Chavel. Jerusalem: Mossad Harav Kook.

Ben Naḥman, Moshe. 1959. *Perushe ha-Torah*. Edited by Charles Chavel. 2 vols. Jerusalem: Mossad Harav Kook.

Ben Solomon, Menaḥem. 1900–1901. *Midrash Śekhel Ṭov*. Edited by Salomon Buber. 2 vols. Berlin: Ittskovski.

Ben-Zazon, David. 2017. '"Parashat ha-Kesef" le-R. Yosef ibn Kaspi'. In *Five Early Commentators on R. Abraham Ibn Ezra*, edited by Howard Kreisel, 87–95. Beer-Sheva: Ben-Gurion University of the Negev Press.

Berkowitz, Beth. 2006. *Execution and Invention: Death Penalty Discourse in Early Rabbinic and Christian Cultures*. New York: Oxford University Press.

Berlin, Adele. 1991. *Biblical Poetry through Medieval Jewish Eyes*. Bloomington: Indiana University Press.

Bland, Kalman. 1990. 'Issues in Sixteenth-Century Jewish Exegesis'. In *The Bible in the Sixteenth Century*, edited by David Steinmetz, 50–67. Durham, NC: Duke University Press.

Boyarin, Daniel. 2009. *Socrates and the Fat Rabbis*. Chicago: University of Chicago Press.

Bregman, Marc. 2003. *The Tanhuma-Yelammedenu Literature*. Piscataway, NJ: Gorgias Press. [Hebrew]

Caspi, Ephraim. 2015. 'Meqorot Darshaniyim la-ʾOtiyot ha-Metuyagot ve-ha-Meshunot ba-Tora'. *Hitzei Giborim* 8: 403–46.

Clenman, Laliv. 2014. 'The Fire and the Flesh: Self-Destruction and the Male Rabbinic Body'. In *The Body in Biblical, Christian and Jewish Texts*, edited by Joan Taylor, 210–25. London: Bloomsbury.

Cohen, Menaḥem (ed.). 1996. *Mikra'ot Gedolot 'Haketer': Isaiah*. Ramat Gan: Bar-Ilan University Press. [Hebrew]

Cohen, Mordechai. 2020. *The Rule of Peshat: Jewish Constructions of the Plain Sense of Scripture and Their Christian and Muslim Contexts, 900–1270*. Philadelphia: University of Pennsylvania Press.

———. 2021. *Rashi, Biblical Interpretation, and Latin Learning in Medieval Europe: A New Perspective on an Exegetical Revolution*. Cambridge: Cambridge University Press.

Cohen, Tamir. 1997–1998. 'ʿAl Ṭaʿam ve-ʿal Ri"k'. MA thesis, Yaakov Herzog Teachers' Institute.

Dan, Joseph. 1968. *The Esoteric Theology of Ashkenazi Hasidism*. Jerusalem: Bialik Institute. [Hebrew]

Dotan, Aron. (ed.). 1967. *The Diqduqe ha-Ṭeʿamim of Aharon ben Moshe ben Asher*. Jerusalem: The Academy of the Hebrew Language. [Hebrew]

———. 2005. '*Paseq* in Antiquity'. In *Samaritan, Hebrew and Aramaic Studies: Presented to Professor Abraham Tal*, edited by Moshe Bar-Asher and Moshe Florentin, 121–33. Jerusalem: Bialik Institute. [Hebrew]

———. 2009. 'Masora's Contribution to Biblical Studies—Revival of an Ancient Tool'. In *Congress Volume Ljubljana 2007*, edited by André Lemaire, 57–69. Leiden: Brill.

Dweck, Yaacob. 2010. 'Editing Safed: The Career of Isaac Gershon'. *Jewish Studies Quarterly* 17: 44–55.

———. 2011. *The Scandal of Kabbalah.* Princeton, NJ: Princeton University Press.

Encyclopedia Talmudica: A Digest of Halachic Literature and Jewish Law from the Tannaitic Period to the Present time, Alphabetically Arranged. Edited by Meir Bar-Ilan and Shlomo Josef Zevin, translated by Isidore Elstein and Harry Freedman. 6 vols. Jerusalem: Talmudic Encyclopedia Institute, 1969–.

Englander, Henry. 1939. 'Grammatical Elements and Terminology in Rashi'. *Hebrew Union College Annual* 14: 387–429.

———. 1942–1943. 'A Commentary on Rashi's Grammatical Comments'. *Hebrew Union College Annual* 17: 427–98.

Fine, Lawrence. 2003. *Physician of the Soul, Healer of the Cosmos: Isaac Luria and His Kabbalistic Fellowship.* Stanford, CA: Stanford University Press.

Fishbane, Michael. 1994. *The Kiss of God: Spiritual and Mystical Death in Judaism.* Seattle: University of Washington Press.

———. 2013. 'Midrash and the Meaning of Scripture'. In *Midrash Unbound: Transformations and Innovations*, edited by Michael Fishbane and Joanna Weinberg, 13–24. Oxford: Littman.

Fredman, Lisa (ed.). 2019. *Rashi's Commentary on the Book of Proverbs: Edited with Introduction and Notes.* Jerusalem: World Union of Jewish Studies. [Hebrew]

Freedman, David Noel (ed.). 1998. *The Leningrad Codex: A Facsimile Edition*. Grand Rapids, MI: Wm. B. Eerdmans.

Friedeman, Caleb et al. (eds). 2021. *A Scripture Index to Rabbinic Literature*. Peabody, MA: Hendrickson.

Gelles, Benjamin. 1981. *Peshat and Derash in the Exegesis of Rashi*. Leiden: Brill.

Gellis, Jacob. 1982–2014. *Sefer Tosafot ha-Shalem*. 17 vols.; Jerusalem: Mifal Tosafot Hashalem.

Ginsburg, Christian (ed.). 1926. *The Writings: Diligently Revised According to the Massorah and the Early Editions*. London: British and Foreign Bible Society.

Goren, Zekhariah. 1989. "ʿAl ha-Mashmaʿut ha-Parshanit shel Ṭaʿam "ha-shalshelet"'. *Tura*: 83–92.

———. 1995. *Ṭaʿame ha-Miqra ke-Farshanut*. Tel-Aviv: Hakibbutz Hameuchad.

Grossman, Avraham. 2012. *Rashi*. Translated by Joel Linsider. Oxford: Littman.

———. 2017. 'Rash"i ke-Darshan Meqori'. In *Transformations in Medieval Jewish Society*, 386–407. Jerusalem: Bialik Publishing.

———. 2021. *Rashi and the Jewish-Christian Polemic*. Ramat Gan: Bar Ilan University. [Hebrew]

Hallamish, Moshe. 1999. *An Introduction to the Kabbalah*. Translated by Ruth Bar-Ilan and Ora Wiskind-Elper, 281–309. Albany: State University of New York Press.

Heinemann, Isaac. 1970. *Darkhe ha-ʾAggada*. Jerusalem: Magnes Press.

Herring, Basil. 1982. *Joseph Ibn Kaspi's Gevia' Kesef: A Study in Medieval Jewish Philosophic Bible Commentary*. New York: KTAV.

Himmelfarb, Lea. 2004. 'On One Masorah in Rashi's Biblical Commentary'. *Sefarad* 64: 75–94. [Hebrew]

———. 2005. 'On Rashi's Use of the Masorah Notes in his Commentary to the Bible'. *Shnaton: An Annual for Biblical and Ancient Near Eastern Studies* 15: 174–78. [Hebrew]

Hyman, Arthur (ed.). 1973. *Yalqut Shimʿoni ʿal ha-Torah le-Rabbenu Shimʿon ha-Darshan: Sefer Bereshit*. Jerusalem: Mossad Harav Kook.

Ibn Ezra, Abraham. 1977a. *Perushe ha-Torah*. Edited by Asher Weiser. 3 vols. Jerusalem: Mossad Harav Kook.

———. 1977b. *Sefer Ṣaḥot*. Edited by Carlos del Valle Rodriguez. Salamanca: Universidad Pontifica.

Ibn Parḥon, Solomon. 1844. *Lexicon Hebraicum*. Edited by Salomon Stern. Pressburg: Shmid. [Hebrew]

Idel, Moshe. 1983. '"We Have No Kabbalistic Tradition on This"'. In *Rabbi Moses Naḥmanides: Explorations in His Religious and Literary Virtuosity*, edited by Isadore Twersky, 51–73. Cambridge, MA: Harvard University Press.

———. 1988. *The Mystical Experience in Abraham Abulafia*. Albany: State University of New York Press.

Ilan, Tal. 2017. *Massekhet Hullin: Text, Translation, and Commentary*. Tübingen: Mohr Siebeck.

Jacobs, Louis. 2004. *Jewish Preaching: Homilies and Sermons*. London: Vallentine Mitchell.

Kahana, Menahem (ed.). 2011–2015. *Sifre on Numbers: An Annotated Edition*. 4 vols. Jerusalem: Magnes Press. [Hebrew]

Kamin, Sarah. 1980. 'Rashi's Exegetical Categorization with Respect to the Distinction between Peshat and Derash'. *Immanuel* 11: 16–32.

———. 1986. *Rashi's Exegetical Categorization in Respect to the Distinction between Peshat and Derash*. Jerusalem: Magnes Press. [Hebrew]

Kanarfogel, Ephraim. 1986. 'The ʿAliyah of "Three Hundred Rabbis" in 1211: Tosafist Attitudes toward Settling in the Land of Israel'. *Jewish Quarterly Review* 76: 191–215.

Khan, Geoffrey. 2013. *A Short Introduction to the Tiberian Masoretic Bible and Its Reading Tradition*. 2nd edition. Piscataway, NJ: Gorgias Press.

Kogut, Simcha. 1994. *Correlations between Biblical Accentuation and Traditional Jewish Exegesis: Linguistic and Contextual Studies*. Jerusalem: Magnes Press. [Hebrew]

Konyevsky, Ḥayim (ed.). 1978–1980. *Rokeach: A Commentary on the Bible by Rabbi Elazar of Worms*. 3 vols. New York: Bnei Brak. [Hebrew]

Kugel, James. 1990. *In Potiphar's House: The Interpretive Life of Biblical Texts*. Cambridge, MA: Harvard University Press.

Lange, Itzhak (ed.). 1980. *Ṭaʿame Masoret ha-Miqra: Le-Rabi Yehuda he-Ḥasid*. Jerusalem: Ben-Arzah.

Last, Isaac (ed.). 1905. *Joseph ibn Caspi's Mishneh Kesef*. 2 vols. Cracow: Fischer. [Hebrew]

Lawee, Eric. 2008. 'Isaac Abarbanel: From Medieval to Renaissance Jewish Biblical Scholarship'. In *Hebrew Bible/Old Testament: The History of Its Interpretation. Volume II: From the Renaissance to the Enlightenment*, edited by Magne Sæbø, 195–99. Göttingen: Vandenhoeck & Ruprecht.

———. 2019. *Rashi's Commentary on the Torah: Canonization and Resistance in the Reception of a Jewish Classic*. Oxford: Oxford University Press.

Levinson, Joshua. 1997. 'An-Other Woman: Joseph and Potiphar's Wife—Staging the Body Politic'. *Jewish Quarterly Review* 87: 269–310.

Liebermann, Saul. 1962. *Hellenism in Jewish Palestine*. 2nd edition. New York: Jewish Theological Seminary of America.

Loewinger, David. 1960. 'The Aleppo Codex and the Ben Asher Tradition'. *Textus* 1: 59–111.

———. 1972. Review of G. Weil, *Massorah Gedolah: iuxta codicem Leningradensem B19a*. *Kiryat Sefer* 47: 601–5. [Hebrew]

Magonet, Jonathan. 2004. *A Rabbi Reads the Bible*. 2nd edition. London: SCM.

Margaliot, Reuben (ed.). 2007–2008. *Sefer Zohar Ḥadash*. Jerusalem: Mossad Harav Kook.

Martín-Contreras, Elvira. 2003. 'Comments on Textual Details: Relationships between Masorah and Midrash'. *Journal of Jewish Studies* 54: 62–70.

Martini, Annett (ed.). 2010. 'Introduction'. In *Yosef Giqaṭilla: The Book of Punctuation*, 19–162. Kabbalistic Library of Giovanni Pico della Mirandola 4. Turin: Nino Aragno Editore.

Matt, Daniel C., Nathan Wolski, and Joel Hecker. 2004–2017. *The Zohar: Pritzker Edition*. 12 vols. Stanford, CA: Stanford University Press.

Mesch, Barry. 1975. *Studies in Joseph ibn Caspi: Fourteenth-century Philosopher and Exegete*. Leiden: Brill.

Mondschein, Aharon. 2009. '"The Masoretes Fabricated Explanations for Full and Deficient Spellings": On Abraham Ibn Ezra's Struggle Against the (Ab)use of Biblical Spelling as an Exegetical Tool'. *Shnaton: An Annual for Biblical and Ancient Near Eastern Studies* 19: 245–321. [Hebrew]

Mopsik, Charles. 1987. *Le Zohar: Livre de Ruth*. Lagrasse: Verdier.

Morgenstern, Yossi. 1994. 'Ha-Shalshelet ke-Ṭaʿam Mefaresh'. *Tura* 3: 251–54.

Norzi, Jedidiah. 2005–2006. *Minḥat Shay on the Torah*. Edited by Zvi Betser. Jerusalem: World Union of Jewish Studies. [Hebrew]

Ofer, Yosef. 2019. *The Masora on Scripture and its Methods*. Berlin: De Gruyter.

Penkower, Jordan. 1982. 'Jacob ben Ḥayyim and the Rise of the Biblia Rabbinica'. PhD dissertation, The Hebrew University of Jerusalem. [Hebrew]

———. 2010. *The Dates of Composition of the Zohar and the Book Bahir*. Los Angeles: Cherub Press. [Hebrew]

Price, James. 1996. *Concordance of the Hebrew Accents in the Hebrew Bible*. 5 vols. Lewiston, NY: Edwin Mellen.

Razhabi, Yitzhak. 1978. 'Irregular Letters in the Torah'. In *The Script of the Torah and Its Characters*, edited by Menahem

Kasher, 1–234. Torah Shelemah 29. Jerusalem: Beth Torah Shelemah. [Hebrew]

Reich, Nurit. 2006. 'The Names of the Accent *Shalshelet*'. *Massorot* 13–14: 203–24. [Hebrew]

Revell, E. J. 2000. 'The Interpretative Value of the Massoretic Punctuation'. In *Hebrew Bible/Old Testament: The History of Its Interpretation. Volume I/2: The Middle Ages*, edited by Magne Sæbø, 64–73. Göttingen: Vandenhoeck & Ruprecht.

Rock, Avigail. 2007. 'R. Yosef Ibn Kaspi's Biblical Exegesis: Exegetical Methodology and a Critical Annotated Edition of *Mazref la-Kesef* on Genesis. PhD dissertation, Bar-Ilan University. [Hebrew]

Rosen-Zvi, Ishay. 2011. *Demonic Desires:* Yetzer Hara *and the Problem of Evil in Late Antiquity*. Philadelphia: University of Pennsylvania Press.

Rubin, Aaron. 2011. 'Samuel Archivolti and the Antiquity of the Hebrew Pointing'. *Jewish Quarterly Review* 101: 233–43.

Sacks, Jonathan. 2009. *Covenant & Conversation: A Weekly Reading of the Jewish Bible. Genesis: The Book of Beginnings*. New Milford, CT: Maggid Books.

Sackson, Adrian. 2017. *Joseph ibn Kaspi: Portrait of a Hebrew Philosopher in Medieval Provence*. Leiden: Brill.

Safrai, Zeʾev. 2018. *Seeking out the Land: Land of Israel Traditions in Ancient Jewish, Christian and Samaritan Literature (200 BCE – 400 CE)*. Leiden: Brill.

Saperstein, Marc. 2014a. 'Cultural Juxtapositions: Problematizing Scripture in Late Medieval Jewish and Christian Exegesis'. In *Leadership and Conflict: Tensions in Medieval and*

Early Modern Jewish History and Culture, 113–39. Oxford: Littman.

———. 2014b. 'The Land of Israel in Pre-Modern Jewish Thought: A History of Two Rabbinic Statements'. In *Leadership and Conflict: Tensions in Medieval and Early Modern Jewish History and Culture*, 271–90. Oxford: Littman.

Schiffer, Ira Jeffrey. 1977. 'The Men of the Great Assembly'. In *Persons and Institutions in Early Rabbinic Judaism*, edited by William S. Green, 237–76. Missoula, MT: Scholars Press.

Shalem, Shimʿon. 1965–1966. *Rabbi Moshe Alshekh.* Jerusalem: Ben Zvi-Institute.

Shereshevsky, Esra. 1972. 'The Accents in Rashi's Commentary'. *Jewish Quarterly Review* 42: 277–87.

———. 1982. *Rashi: The Man and his World.* New York: Sepher-Hermon Press.

Shinan, Avigdor (ed.). 1984. *Midrash Shemot Rabba: Chapters I–XIV*. Jerusalem: Dvir. [Hebrew]

———. 1994. 'The Midrashic Interpretations of the Ten Dotted Passages of the Torah'. In *The Bible in the Light of its Interpreters*, edited by Sara Japhet, 198–214. Jerusalem: Magnes Press. [Hebrew]

Sinai, Yuval. 2007. 'Judicial Authority in Fraudulent-Claim Cases (*din merume*)'. *Jewish Law Annual* 17: 209–66.

Smelik, Willem. 2013. *Rabbis, Language and Translation in Late Antiquity*. Cambridge: Cambridge University Press.

Talmage, Frank. 1999 (1986). 'Apples of Gold: The Inner Meaning of Sacred Texts in Judaism'. In *Apples of Gold in Settings of Silver: Studies in Medieval Jewish Exegesis and Polemics*, edited by Barry Walfish, 108–50. Papers in Medieval Studies 14. Toronto: Pontifical Institute of Mediaeval Studies. Originally published in *Jewish Spirituality I: From the Bible through the Middle Ages*, edited by Arthur Green, 313–55. New York: Crossroad.

Ta-Shma, Israel. 2005. 'Midrash Lekah-Tov: Its Background and Character'. In *Studies in Medieval Rabbinic Literature: 3. Italy & Byzantium*, 96–114. Jerusalem: Bialik Institute. [Hebrew]

Theodor, Julius, and Chanoch Albeck (eds.). 1903–1936. *Midrash Bereshit Rabba*. 3 vols. Berlin: Ittskovski.

Touitou, Elazar. 2000. 'Darko shel Rashi be-Shimusho be-Midreshe Ḥaz"al: ʿIyun be-Ferush Rashi li-Shemot 1:8–22'. *Talele ʾOrot* 9: 51–78.

Twersky, Isadore. 1979. 'Joseph ibn Kaspi: Portrait of a Medieval Jewish Intellectual'. In *Studies in Medieval Jewish History and Literature*, 3 vols., edited by Isadore Twersky, I:231–57. Cambridge, MA: Harvard University Press.

Van der Heide, Albert. 1983. 'PARDES: Methodological Reflections on the Theory of the Four Senses'. *Journal of Jewish Studies* 34: 147–59.

Walfish, Barry. 1993. *Esther in Medieval Garb*. Albany: State University of New York Press.

Werblowsky, R. J. Zwi. 1997. *Joseph Karo: Lawyer and Mystic*. Philadelphia: Jewish Publication Society of America.

Wickes, William. 1887. *A Treatise on the Accentuation of the Twenty-One So-Called Prose Books of the Old Testament*. Oxford: Clarendon.

Williams, Benjamin. 2015. 'Doubting Abraham Doubting God: The Call of Abraham in the Or ha-Sekhel'. *Melilah* 12: 31–42.

———. 2016. *Commentary on Midrash Rabba in the Sixteenth Century: The* Or ha-Sekhel *of Abraham ben Asher*. Oxford: Oxford University Press.

Wolfson, Elliot. 1988–1989. 'Biblical Accentuation in a Mystical Key: Kabbalistic Interpretation of the *Te'amim*: Part 1'. *Journal of Jewish Music and Liturgy* 11: 1–16.

———. 1989. 'By Way of Truth: Aspects of Naḥmanides' Kabbalistic Hermeneutic'. *AJS Review* 14: 103–78.

———. 1989–1990. 'Biblical Accentuation in a Mystical Key: Kabbalistic Interpretation of the *Te'amim*: Part 2'. *Journal of Jewish Music and Liturgy* 12: 1–13.

———. 1993. 'Beautiful Maiden Without Eyes: *Peshat* and *Sod* in Zohardic Hermeneutics'. In *The Midrashic Imagination: Jewish Exegesis, Thought, and History*, edited by Michael Fishbane, 155–203. Albany: State University of New York Press.

Wright, Charles. 1864. *The Book of Ruth in Hebrew*. London: Williams & Norgate.

Yeivin, Israel. 1980. *Introduction to the Tiberian Masorah*. Translated and edited by E. J. Revell. Missoula, MT: Scholars Press.

Yisraeli, Oded. 2006. 'The Kabbalistic *remez* and Its Status in Naḥmanides' Commentary on the Torah'. *The Journal of Jewish Thought and Philosophy* 24: 1–30.

DOES SAADYA REFER TO THE ACCENTS IN HIS INTRODUCTION TO THE PENTATEUCH?[236]

Joseph Habib

In his article 'The Tension between Literal Interpretation and Exegetical Freedom', Haggai Ben-Shammai (2003, 38, n. 42) raised the possibility that the famous medieval rabbinic scholar Saadya Gaon (882–942) directly refers to the biblical accents and their function of joining and separating words. The relevant passage comes from Saadya's introduction to his long commentary on the Pentateuch (henceforth SIP). A thorough analysis of the passage was beyond the scope of Ben-Shammai's article. Saadya does not explicitly mention the accents in SIP, but what is clear is that Saadya attaches exegetical importance to the grouping of words in a passage. The purpose of this article is to determine whether or not Saadya has specifically the accents in mind.

[236] The content of this article formed part of my PhD research, which was funded in part by the Faculty of Asian and Middle Eastern Studies, University of Cambridge, and in part by the University of Haifa's Valler Doctoral Fellowship. I warmly thank them for their generosity and support.

 https://doi.org/10.11647/OBP.0330.10

1.0. Saadya Gaon and the Importance of His Testimony

If the phenomenon that Saadya describes in SIP does indeed relate to the accents, this is significant because (1) Saadya had direct contact with the Tiberian Masoretes and (2) the question of the original function of the biblical accents remains unanswered (see, recently, De Hoop 2008; Shoshany 2009; Park 2014; Pitcher 2020). Saadya's account would therefore furnish testimony relevant to the function of the accents contemporary with the Tiberian Masoretes.

Saadya, known in Arabic as Saʿīd ben Yūsuf al-Fayyūmī, was born in Egypt around 882 CE (the most authoritative biography remains Malter 1921). Throughout his life, Saadya's creative mind and wide range of knowledge allowed him to make foundational contributions to a number of intellectual fields, including biblical exegesis, grammar, poetry, and *halakha* (Brody 2006 [Hebrew]; 2013 [English]). Saadya's capacity as a scholar led to his appointment as head—Gaon—of the struggling Babylonian academy (ישיבה *yeshiva*) in Sura in 928 (Brody 1998, 237–238).[237] His most significant contribution to biblical exegesis was

[237] It was once thought that it was Saadya's involvement in the calendar controversy that erupted in 921/2 CE between the Babylonian and Palestinian *yeshivot* that led to his appointment as Gaon. On the basis of a fresh examination of the sources, Stern (2019) has demonstrated that Saadya's role in the exchange between the two academies was marginal.

his translation of, and commentary on, most of the Bible, conventionally known as the *tafsīr*.[238]

Before his appointment as Gaon, Saadya spent about ten years in the city of Tiberias. For some of that time, he was the student of one Abū Kathīr Yaḥyā ben Zakariyyā, whom the Muslim historian al-Masʿūdī (893–956) describes as a “Tiberian scribe (*al-kātib al-ṭabarānī*)” and as an expert in Bible translation.[239] In that time, Saadya would have been exposed to a variety of reading traditions within different masoretic circles (Dotan 1996).

---

[238] The appellation *tafsīr* was not used by Saadya himself, but has become accepted among scholars; I thank Ronny Vollandt for pointing this out to me. There is not yet general consensus as to when Saadya began this project or how it developed. See Zewi (2015, 28–29) for a recent discussion of the different arguments.

[239] See de Goeje (1894, 112–13) for the original source; see also Gil (1992, 176–78), Polliack (1997, 11–12). The second source from which Saadya’s time in Palestine is known is a letter he wrote to his three students. The scenario was as follows: Saadya and one R. David were both in Babylon. R. David received a letter from Saadya’s students, who requested letters from the Babylonian academy regarding the calendar controversy of 921/2 CE, in which Saadya played a small part (Stern 2019, 288; many thanks to Prof Ronny Vollandt for this reference). Puzzled as to why his students had not written to him instead, Saadya wrote back to them: כסבור אני כי לא כתבתם אליו מבַלעדַי בלתי כי דימיתם כי עד עתה עודני בארץ ישראל ‘I believe that you only wrote to him, rather than to me, because you assumed that until now I was still in the land of Israel’ (text and translation from Stern 2019, 308–9; this fragment was published earlier by Schechter 1901, 60, fol. 1v, lns 6–8 for the original letter fragment; see also Brody 2013, 26 for comment on the letter).

Saadya's intellectual connection with the Masoretes is evident in a number of places throughout his works. Traces of the *masora* are seen in Saadya's grammar book *The Book of Elegance of the Language of the Hebrews* (Dotan 1997, 34–35). In his chapter on vowels, Saadya clearly derives material from the masoretic treatise now known as *ʾOḵla we-ʾOḵla* and refers to it as 'the *masora*' (אלמאסרה; Dotan 1997, 433). There he tells his reader to consult 'the *masora*' and then lists words in which the final *he* is not pronounced with *mappiq*, nearly all of which are found in a list in *ʾOḵla we-ʾOḵla*.[240] Dotan (1997, 35–36) notes that Saadya drew heavily from the קונטרסי המסורה *qunṭrese ha-masora*, i.e., masoretic treatises, when formulating his rules for *shewa*.[241] Another point of contact between Saadya and the Masoretes is reflected in a disagreement among them. At one point in the grammar (Dotan 1997, 410), Saadya objects to a masoretic formulation of the rule for fricativisation of the בגדכפ"ת letters. Saadya states that the rule should be that this realisation depends on whether the previous word ends in a vowel, not, as some Masoretes formulated the rule, on whether the previous word ends in the letters א, ו, י, or ה (see Ofer 2019, 234).

---

[240] See Díaz Esteban (1975, 85–86) or the list in the treatise. The second part of the treatise was published by Ognibeni (1995).

[241] The term *qunṭrese ha-masora* was coined by Dotan (1967, 13) to refer to instances which represent the first attempts at formulating systematic rules based on the *masora*. They were variously copied individually, as a group, or found in the pages of other books, but never formed a standalone work, such as that of *Diqduqe ha-Ṭeʿamim* (Dotan 2005, 20).

Regarding the accents specifically, Saadya composed some of his works in the style of Biblical Hebrew, complete with Tiberian vowel and accent signs. One such work is the Hebrew introduction to his dictionary of Biblical Hebrew, entitled *Ha-ʾEgrōn* 'The Thesaurus' (ed. Allony 1969). Saadya's use of the accents generally conforms to the rules with which modern scholarship is familiar (Revell 1974, 125, and, more recently, Hitin-Mashiah 2011, though Revell also notes many peculiarities in Saadya's use of accents). It differs only in small details, which is to be expected, given the fact that Saadya lived and worked nearly three centuries before Maimonides proclaimed the Ben Asher tradition as authoritative (Penkower 1981; Ofer 2019, 144–46). This would have therefore been a time when various sub-traditions of the Tiberian Masoretic reading tradition would have existed side-by-side. The reason given by Saadya himself for his use of accents in his works is "so that its (i.e., the text's) reading may be easier and its memorisation more possible (ליכון אסהל לקראתה ואמכן להפטֹה)" (Yeivin 1959, 48). Saadya is probably pointing here to some kind of aural (and oral) phenomenon that he would have expected the reader to hear in their mind's ear (Habib 2021, 35). It is still not clear exactly what he is referring to, but Revell (1974, 125ff.) has argued that Saadya must have thought of the accents as an organic part of Biblical Hebrew.

Given Saadya's geographical, chronological, and intellectual proximity to circles of the Masoretes, any comment he offers on the accents would afford scholars valuable insight into "one of the most neglected fields in the study of Hebrew graphemes" (Dotan 1970, vii). If Saadya does indeed have the accents in mind in SIP, then the passage should receive serious consideration in future scholarship on the accents.

2.0. Analysis of SIP

The passage in question comes from what is conventionally known as Saadya's 'long commentary' on the Pentateuch—an exegetical work that consists of translation of biblical verses embedded within a 'long commentary'.[242] The passage, along with my translation, follows.[243]

Zucker (1984, 19)	Lines	
ואלקסם אלראבע מן אלמוצ̇חאת אלגואמע̇ הי אלצ̇מאת פאן משהורהא אלאכ̇ד̇	17	The fourth part of those things that clarify obscurities is the joining/ grouping of words. So, the commonly accepted sense of it (a verse) is taking [it]

[242] A name for the 'long commentary' is not extant (Ronny Vollandt, personal correspondence). Saadya called his translation of the Pentateuch devoid of commentary *ikhrāj maʿānī naṣṣ al-tawrāt* 'extraction (i.e., edition) of the meanings of the text of the Torah' (see Vollandt 2015, 82–83); this is known in scholarly parlance as Saadya's 'short *tafsīr*'. The remainder of the biblical books that Saadya translated and commented upon each bear their own unique title consistent with the content of the book (Vollandt 2015, 82). Saadya titles his commentary on Isaiah, for example, *kitāb ʾal ʾistilāḥ l-ʾal-ṭāʿa*, which, according to Ben-Shammai (1991), should be understood as 'The Book of the Endeavour towards Improvement of Worship'.

[243] In all translations of Judaeo-Arabic texts that follow, square brackets '[]' indicate an editorial addition to make the text more readable; round brackets '()' indicate an editorial comment for clarification and biblical references.

כמה צׄמתה וד̇אך באן יכון כל כלמאת צׄמת פי אלקראה̈ תג̇על מעני ואחד פי	18	according to the way it is arranged to-gether. This because all the words that are joined together in the reading should considered to have one meaning in
אלתפסיר ולא יפרק בינהא וכד̇לך לא יולף פי אלתפסיר בין אלכלמאת אלמפרקה̈	19	the interpretation, and they should not be divided. Similarly, words that are separated should not be joined together in interpretation,
כמא אקול פי תפסיר שרפים עומדים ממעל לו אן אלפרק כביר בין אן תצׄם	20	just as I will say in the interpretation of שְׂרָפִ֨ים עֹמְדִ֤ים ׀ מִמַּ֣עַל ל֔וֹ (Isa. 6.2) that there is a big difference between whether two words
כלמתין עלי חדה̈ וכ[למה̈] עלי חדה̈. ואן אחתאג̇ פי אלתכ̇ריג̇ לתצׄר אלמעאני	21	are joined together or one word stands apart from the others. If there is need to deviate [from the accepted meaning] so that the sense [units] are broken apart (lit., harmed)—
אן יפרק מא הו מצׄמום או יולף מא הו מפרוק פי אלקראה̈ ג̇אז ד̇לך כמא	22	[i.e.,] if that which is joined is sepa-rated, or that which is separated is joined in the reading—that is possible, just as
יפרק ויצׄם קולה הן האדם היה כאחד ממנו לדעת טוב ורע חתי יסתקים אלמעני וכד̇לך פי תאליף ובמנורה ארבעה גביעים משקדים כפתריה ופרחיה יריד משקדים	23 24	the phrase וַיֹּ֣אמֶר ׀ יְהוָ֣ה אֱלֹהִ֗ים הֵ֤ן הָֽאָדָם֙ הָיָה֙ כְּאַחַ֣ד מִמֶּ֔נּוּ לָדַ֖עַת ט֣וֹב וָרָ֑ע (Gen. 3.22) is sep-arated and joined in order that the in-terpretation be correct. This is also the case in the joining of וּבַמְּנֹרָ֖ה אַרְבָּעָ֣ה גְבִעִ֑ים מְשֻׁקָּדִ֕ים כַּפְתֹּרֶ֖יהָ וּפְרָחֶֽיהָ: (Exod. 25.34; 37.20). [The word] מְשֻׁקָּדִ֕ים is intended to be

עלי אלאול לא עלי אלת̇אני ומא הו נט̇יר ד̇לך ואלקסם.	in the first [part], not within the second, as well as that which is similar to that division (i.e., the other verses like this one. [Exod. 25.33; 37.19, 20]).

The text that precedes this passage is missing from the manuscript and, therefore, the broader context of the passage is unavailable. The opening lines make it clear enough, though, that it may be interpreted as a self-contained paragraph. Evidently this passage constitutes but one item in a list which deals with how to “clarify obscurities (אלמוצ̇חאת אלגואמץ̇)” (ln. 17) one encounters in the Biblical text. In this analysis, I will focus on three key terms which must be properly understood in order to determine whether or not Saadya is referring in this passage to the accents.

2.1. *Ḍammāt*

The fourth item in this list of the principles that “clarify obscurities” Saadya designates with the term אלצ̇מאת *al-ḍammāt* (ln. 17). I have translated this term ‘joining/grouping of words’. One method employed by Saadya to clarify obscurities is appeal to *al-ḍammāt*—the joining and grouping of words. The grouping of words in the context of disambiguating the sense of a passage would correspond to the accents’ function of joining and separating words. This may indeed be what Saadya intended. Though Ben-Shammai (2003, n. 41) states that he has not come across the word *ḍammāt* elsewhere in Saadya’s corpus, I have found one further instance of Saadya’s use of this word with what seems like a similar meaning, on the basis of which the sense of the term may be clarified.

Zucker (1984, 103)	Lines	
ויקאל אן פי ג̇מעה אלרג̇ל בעץ̇ אלי בעץ̇ בקו אתה ובניך וג̇מע אלנסא	27	It is said that in its (i.e., Scripture's) grouping the men together in the phrase אַתָּ֨ה וּבָנֶ֛יךָ אִתָּֽךְ 'You and your sons with you'[244] (Gen. 6.18) and the grouping of the women
בעצ̇א אלי בעץ̇ בקו ואשתך ונשי בניך חט̇ר עליהם אלג̇שיאן טול מא אקאמו	28	together in the phrase וְאִשְׁתְּךָ֥ וּנְשֵֽׁי־בָנֶ֖יךָ 'And your wife and your son's wife' (Gen. 6.18) forbids sexual relations for the duration of which they are
p. 104		
פי אלתאבות [והו] קול קריב. ויקויה מא עכס הדה **אלצ̇מאת** ענד אלתכ̇ריג̇ פצ̇ם	1	in the ark. This statement is likely to be correct (lit. close [to the correct interpretation]). That which is opposite this **grouping of words** in [the account of] their exiting [the ark] strengthens this [interpretation]. So, [there], it joins
[אל]זוג̇ אלי זוג̇תה בקו אתה ואשתך ובניך ונשי בניך	2	the husband to his wife in the phrase אַתָּ֕ה וְאִשְׁתְּךָ֛ וּבָנֶ֥יךָ וּנְשֵֽׁי־בָנֶ֖יךָ 'You and your wife and your sons and your sons' wives' (Gen. 8.16).

Saadya argues here that one may interpret the actual grouping of words used in Gen. 6.18 as a prohibition which God gave to Noah to abstain from sexual relations while on the ark. To support this claim Saadya points to the account of their exiting

244 In Gen. 6.18 the word אִתָּֽךְ is at the end of the verse, not after אַתָּ֨ה וּבָנֶ֛יךָ.

the ark (Gen. 8.16) and says that the *ḍammāt* there is the opposite (עכס; p. 104, ln. 1)—Noah is grouped with his wife (אַתָּ֕ה וְאִשְׁתְּךָ֛) and his sons are grouped with their wives (וּבָנֶ֥יךָ וּנְשֵֽׁי־בָנֶ֖יךָ). Since they are leaving the ark, there is no longer concern for their sexual relations while inside. In this context, the word *ḍammāt* obviously refers to the grouping of the items within both lists. We therefore see similarity in this use of the term *ḍammāt* with what is found in SIP, in that both indicate the grouping of words.

The use of *ḍammāt* in the commentary on the Genesis passages does not reflect the grouping of words according to the accents. I will argue below that this is actually a crucial clue for the question addressed in this essay. First, however, it should be noticed that in both places Saadya's interpretation is based on a 2 + 2 division of the list, whereas the accents divide both lists into 1 + 3.

	Gen. 6.18: Entering	Gen. 8.16: Exiting
Saadya	אַתָּ֕ה וּבָנֶ֛יךָ וְאִשְׁתְּךָ֥ וּנְשֵֽׁי־בָנֶ֖יךָ	אַתָּ֕ה וְאִשְׁתְּךָ֛ וּבָנֶ֥יךָ וּנְשֵֽׁי־בָנֶ֖יךָ
Accents	אַתָּ֕ה וּבָנֶ֛יךָ וְאִשְׁתְּךָ֥ וּנְשֵֽׁי־בָנֶ֖יךָ	אַתָּ֕ה וְאִשְׁתְּךָ֛ וּבָנֶ֥יךָ וּנְשֵֽׁי־בָנֶ֖יךָ

In both verses, the list falls within the domain of the accent *silluq*. The accents which divide *silluq*'s clause are *zaqef* (main division) and *ṭifḥa* (minor division). In both lists the sequence of accents is the same—the *zaqef* (*gadol*) accentuates the first item of the list (אַתָּ֕ה in both cases), leaving the next three items to be grouped together and terminating in *ṭifḥa*. If, for Saadya, the *ḍammāt* were based on the accents, it would create a difficulty for his commentary on Gen. 6.18. There, the accents group Noah's sons (וּבָנֶ֛יךָ) with the women (וְאִשְׁתְּךָ֥ וּנְשֵֽׁי־בָנֶ֖יךָ).[245]

It appears that the *ḍammāt* Saadya refers to reflects rabbinic tradition, rather than the accents (the reason for which will be made clear below). The Babylonian Talmud states:

> ומנין דנאסרו דכתיב ובאת אל התיבה אתה ובניך ואשתך ונשי בניך אתך וכתיב צא מן התיבה אתה ואשתך ובניך נשי בניך אתך וא״ר יוחנן מיכן אמרו שנאסרו בתשמיש המטה
>
> From where do we know that they were prohibited [from sexual relations on the ark]? From that which is written, "And you will come to the ark—you, and your sons, and your wife, and your sons' wives with you" (Gen. 6.18). And it is [also] written: "Go out from the ark—you, and your wife, and your sons and your sons' wives with you" (Gen. 8.16). R. Johanan said, "From here they said that they were prohibited from sexual relations on the ark" (b. Sanhedrin 108b.14).

This interpretation is paralleled in the Jerusalem Talmud:

> ר׳ יודה בר פזי ר׳ חנין בשם ר׳ שמואל בר רב יצחק נח בכניסתו לתיבה נאסרה לו תשמיש המיטה מ״ט ובאת אל התיבה אתה ובניך ואשתך ונשי בניך אתך וביציאתו הותרה לו תשמיש המיטה מ״ט צא מן התיבה אתה ואשתך ובניך ונשי בניך אתך
>
> R. Judah b. Pazi, R. Hanin on behalf of R. Samuel b. Rav Issac [say], "When Noah entered the ark sexual relations were forbidden to him. [For,] what is the meaning of, "And you will enter the ark—you, and your sons, and your wife

---

[245] The word וּבָנֶ֛יךָ is out of necessity accented with the minor disjunctive *teḇir*, because *ṭifḥa*'s clause can only contain three words (see Wickes 1887, 89; cf. Breuer 1989, 45).

> and your sons' wives with you" (Gen. 6.18)? When he (Noah) came out, he was permitted to have sexual relations. [For,] what is the meaning of, "Go out from the ark—you, and your wife, and your sons and your sons' wives" (Gen. 8.16)? (y. Taʿanit 7a.1)

This parallel suggests that, even if Saadya's use of *ḍammāt* in SIP above refers to the grouping of words by the accents, here the term was used to mean the grouping of words according to the interpretation of the Oral Law. This apparent contradiction in usage by Saadya is elucidated by a passage in his *Kitāb al-ʾamānāt wal-ʾiʿtqādāt* 'The Book of Beliefs and Opinions'. At the beginning of his chapter on resurrection, Saadya explains that any given scripture may be interpreted in a way other than its apparent (*ẓāhir*) sense for one of four reasons. As his fourth reason, he states: "Anything to which tradition applies a condition, we will interpret it in agreement with the reliable tradition (ומא גאת בה אלאת֗אר בשריטה עליה פנפסרה תפסירא יואפק אלאת֗אר אלצאדקה)" (Qafiḥ 1969, 220, lns 6–8). The case of Gen. 6.18 is one where this exception clearly applies. This raises an important point—*the exception highlights the rule.* If tradition allows for an interpretation of Gen. 6.18 which departs from the 'apparent' (*ẓāhir*) grouping of words (*ḍammāt*), one must ask what the 'plain' or 'apparent' (*ẓāhir*) grouping of words is from which the tradition's interpretation departs? What is it that governs this grouping of words? The accents are one obvious possibility. But, again, Saadya never explicitly says this.

In sum, in his commentary on Gen. 6.18 Saadya used the term *ḍammāt* to refer to groupings of words that were not reflected by the accents. This grouping was based rather on rabbinic tradition. The question arises whether this was the principle of grouping that Saadya referred to also in SIP cited above. This may have been the case. Another possibility, however, is that Saadya used the term by default to refer to groupings reflected by the accents where no other factors were at play, but used it to refer to other types groupings when these were sanctioned by rabbinic tradition.

2.2. *Mašhūr*

Returning to the passage in SIP, the next idea which may point to Saadya's use of the term *ḍammāt* as referring to the accents is the word משהור *mašhūr* 'commonly accepted' (ln. 17). Elsewhere in his introduction to Genesis, Saadya uses the term *mašhūr* to clarify the meaning of the word *ẓāhir* 'apparent'. He says, אעני אלמשהור פי מא בין אהל לגתה ואלכת̇יר אלאסתעמאל '[By *ẓāhir*] I mean that which is commonly known (*mašhūr*) among native speakers of the language, as well as that which is used frequently' (Zucker 1984, 18, lns 1–2). Ben-Shammai (2003, 37) highlights the twofold nature of Saadya's description of *mašhūr* in another passage.[246] On the one hand, the frequency with which words occur in a written text is measured by their distribution throughout that text. On the other, Saadya's equation of *mašhūr* with *ẓāhir* points to the fact that features which later readers of a text can declare *mašhūr*, based on a measurement of their distribution, must reflect what the *ẓāhir* 'plain sense' of that feature was to the lan-

[246] See also Ben-Shammai (1991, 380) for a brief discussion of *mašhūr*.

guage's original users. It seems to me that Ben-Shammai is drawing attention to the fact that for Saadya, *mašhūr* included the idea of what something would have meant to the native speakers of Biblical Hebrew. This meaning becomes 'commonly known' among the readers of Biblical Hebrew only on the basis of its distribution (and, necessarily in this case, its frequency) throughout the Biblical text.

In SIP, Saadya says that the *mašhūr* of a given verse includes its interpretation according to the 'grouping' of its words (*ḍammatihi*; lns 17–18). If we apply the aforementioned definition of *mašhūr* here, the implication is that adhering to the *ḍammāt* of a passage of Scripture yields its original understanding/interpretation (*mašhūr*). This raises an important question—how would Saadya have known the divisions of a passage that reflect a so-called 'native speaker's' original understanding of Biblical Hebrew? One clear possibility is the prosodic divisions reflected by the accents, if these were considered by Saadya to be an integral component of the spoken language. If, against Ben-Shammai's suggestion, we were to understand *mašhūr* with the meaning of 'commonly accepted', this could be equated with the default interpretation of groupings of words on the basis of the accents.

2.3. *Al-qirāʾa*

The final important term for understanding SIP is אלקראה̄ *al-qirāʾa* 'the reading' (ln. 18). After the statement about *mašhūr*, Saadya elaborates and explains that the purpose of the *ḍammāt* 'grouping of words' is so that "words which are joined together in the reading (אלקראה̄; ln. 18) would have one meaning in the interpretation (אלתפסיר; ln. 19).[247] The challenge here lies in determining whether the term *al-qirāʾa* 'reading' is being used in a specific or general sense. The former would most likely denote the oral/musical recitation of the accents, while the latter would not. The determination must be made on the basis of Saadya's use of this word in other places.

Saadya's use of *al-qirāʾa* in his introduction to the Psalms strongly suggests that the intention is indeed oral recitation.[248] There Saadya explains that "the people would sing praises to God with it (the Psalms) according to five stipulations (אלקום כאנוא יסבחון בה פי אלקדס עלי כ̇מסה שרוט)" (Qafiḥ 1966, 30, lns 9–10). Although the text of the third stipulation is fragmentary, enough has been preserved to understand that Saadya is arguing that the instruments to be used in the accompaniment to any particular psalm must be chosen on the basis of the psalm's superscription. For example, any superscription which contains לְאָסָ֑ף 'for/by Asaph' (e.g., Ps. 53.1; 74.1; 75.1; etc.) must be accompanied by a cymbal, due to the Bible's association of the two in the verse וְאָסָ֖ף בַּֽמְצִלְתַּ֥יִם מַשְׁמִֽיעַ 'And Asaph sounds the cymbals' (1 Chron. 16.5). In the final part of this stipulation Saadya states:

---

[247] "The accents are probably indicated here by the Arabic term *al-qirāʿa,* i.e., recital" (Ben-Shammai 2003, n. 42).

[248] On Saadya's introduction to the Psalms and for a translation of it see Soklow (1984).

ובאלהדי לא יג̇וז אן יקאל עלי שי אלבתה אלא אן יכון עלי סביל אלקראה ואלתלאוה

When it (the superscription) is silent (i.e., when no instrument can be ascertained from it), it is not possible for it (the Psalm) to be said with anything at all, except that it be (said) in the manner of reading (*al-qirāʿa*) or recitation (*al-tilāwa*). (Qafiḥ 1966, 32, lns 12–14)[249]

In other words, if no instrument is mentioned or hinted at in the superscription, the psalm should not be accompanied by an instrument, but instead either be 'read' or 'recited'. The significance of this passage for the meaning of the word *al-qirāʾa* lies in its relationship to the other manner of reading the text, indicated by אלתלאוה *al-tilāwa*. That is, it appears that these two words reflect alternative manners of reading the biblical text—in this case the Psalms. Earlier in the same introduction, in the section which introduces the first stipulation, this distinction is clarified:

פאלאול מנהא אן כל מזמור מענון לקום מן אללוים ילזמהם הם אן יקולוה ולא יג̇וז לגירהם אן יקולה אלא תלאותה פקט

The first among them (the stipulations) is that every *psalm* which is ascribed to the Levites requires them to say it (the psalm). Anyone besides them is not allowed to say it *unless (they say) its recitation only*. (Qafiḥ 1966, 30, lns 10–13; emphasis mine: JH).[250]

[249] Cf. Soklow's (1984, 163) idiomatic translation: '…a mute Psalm cannot be put to any tune at all, it can only be read or recited.'

[250] Cf. Soklow's (1984, 158–59) translation: 'The first of these is that every psalm is addressed to a group of Levites who were required to chant it. No one other than they could chant it, only recite it.'

As Qafiḥ explains in his apparatus to this text, Saadya is stipulating that a psalm which is associated with the Levites can be musically chanted only by a Levite. If anyone else recites the psalm, they must simply read it without chanting. The term *al-tilāwa* 'recitation' here must therefore refer to reading without chanting. Returning to the text of the third stipulation, it stands to reason that this same term *al-tilāwa* 'recitation' must be juxtaposed with a term meaning to read with musical chanting—*al-qirāʾa* 'reading'. For Saadya, then, at least some instances of *al-qirāʾa* 'reading' refer specifically to the act of chanting the text with melodies.

These considerations suggest that it is reasonable to understand Saadya's use of *al-qirāʾa* in SIP (Zucker 1984, 19, ln. 18) in specific reference to the musical cantillation of a text. The context can certainly accommodate this interpretation. The joining and separation of words is indeed one function of the accents. As we have seen, the meaning of *al-qirāʾa* includes a musical element—a feature that also clearly applies to the cantillation of the accents.

2.2. Analysis of Biblical Passages from SIP

We have seen that the terms *ḍammāt* 'grouping of words', *mašhūr* 'commonly known', and *al-qirāʾa* 'reading' can all have nuanced meanings in the writings of Saadya. If these meanings are applied to the passage under consideration, it seems that Saadya is saying something to the effect of the following: one way of resolving an obscurity in the text is by considering the grouping of its words (*ḍammāt*). This arrangement reflects the way in which the original users of Biblical Hebrew (or those in the Rabbanite community) would have uttered (or understood) the obscure passages (=*mašhūr*). Specifically, this arrangement refers to the way in which words are joined and separated in the oral performance (*al-qirāʿa*) of the text. The accents may be the common denominator of all these ideas, and so it is highly likely that this passage refers to them despite the fact that Saadya does not mention them explicitly.

Saadya tells his readers that he will illustrate this principle in his commentary on Isa. 6.2. Unfortunately, that specific portion of his commentary on Isaiah has not survived. But other statements by Saadya on this verse do survive. In the very same passage, Saadya specifies that "there is a great difference between whether two words are joined together or one word stands apart from the others" (SIP lns 20–21). A discussion of Isa. 6.2 also appears in Saadya's commentary on Prov. 25.11. Below is Saadya's translation of Isa. 6.2 followed by the discussion of this verse in his commentary on Proverbs.[251]

(1) שְׂרָפִ֨ים עֹמְדִ֤ים ׀ מִמַּ֙עַל֙ ל֔וֹ שֵׁ֧שׁ כְּנָפַ֛יִם שֵׁ֥שׁ כְּנָפַ֖יִם לְאֶחָ֑ד בִּשְׁתַּ֣יִם ׀ יְכַסֶּ֣ה פָנָ֗יו וּבִשְׁתַּ֛יִם יְכַסֶּ֥ה רַגְלָ֖יו וּבִשְׁתַּ֥יִם יְעוֹפֵֽף׃

'The Seraphim standing above were His. Each had six wings. With two it (i.e., one of the Seraphim) would cover up its face, and with two it would cover up its feet, and with two it would fly.' (Isa. 6.2)

---

[251] All of my translations of biblical passages reflect the division of the accents unless otherwise stated or shown.

Ratzaby (1993, 14)	Lines	
ולה מלאיכה וקוף פי	3	And [belonging] to Him were angels standing in
אלעלו סתה אגׄנחה לכל ואחד באתׄנין יסתר	4	the heights. Each one had six wings. With two he would hide
וגׄהה ובאתׄנין יסתר רגׄליה ובאתׄנין יסעי	5	his face and with two he would hide his feet and with two he would fly to and fro.
Qafiḥ (1976, 199)		
ואן תצׄם כל גׄמאעה מן אלכלאם אלדׄי	23	[The second consideration of arranging words according to the way they should be arranged with regard to phrasing is that] those groups of words which are required to be joined together
צׄמה עלי מא תוגׄבה אלמעאני פאן צׄמת עלי	24	by the meaning are joined together. If they are joined differently, it (the different
כׄלאף דׄלך אפסדהא	25	joining) distorts it (the meaning).
וכדׄלך	31	Similar is the
קול שרפים עומדים ממעל לו אדׄא צׄם תׄלאתׄ	32	phrase שְׂרָפִ֨ים עֹמְדִ֤ים ׀ מִמַּ֙עַל֙ ל֔וֹ. If he/it combines three
כלמאת עלי חדה ואלראבעה עלי חדא כאן	33	words together and the fourth by itself, then the
אלקול אן אללה לה מלאיכה פי אלסמא, ואן	34	phrase becomes, ‘Behold, God has angels in the heavens.’ And if

p. 200		
הו צ̇ם את̇נתין עלי חדה ואת̇נתין עלי חדה	1	he/it joins two words together and two words together,
פקאל שרפים עומדים ת̇ם קאל ממעל לו צאר	2	so that it says שְׂרָפִ֨ים עֹמְדִ֤ים ׀ and then it says מִמַּ֙עַל֙ ל֔וֹ, then this
ד̇לך כפרא אד̇ ג̇על אלמלאיכה פוק כ̇אלקהם	3	[interpretation] becomes blasphemous, because the angels are set above their Creator.

The context of this discussion is Saadya's commentary on תַּפּוּחֵ֣י זָ֭הָב בְּמַשְׂכִּיּ֣וֹת כָּ֑סֶף דָּ֝בָ֗ר דָּבֻ֥ר עַל־אָפְנָֽיו׃ 'Like apples of gold in a silver fixture is a word spoken in the proper way' (Prov. 25.11). Here, Saadya discusses at length what it means for something to be spoken properly. One of the requirements for proper speech, Saadya says, is that "words which are required to be joined together by the meaning (מא תוג̇בה אלמעאני) are joined together" (Qafiḥ 1976, 199, lns 23–24). Failure to do so results in a distortion of meaning (lns 24–25).

In order to illustrate the aforementioned point Saadya discusses the first clause of Isa. 6.2 שְׂרָפִ֨ים עֹמְדִ֤ים ׀ מִמַּ֙עַל֙ ל֔וֹ. He explains that if the words are joined 3+1, then the interpretation is that "God has angels in heaven (אללה לה מלאיכה פי אלסמא)" (Qafiḥ 1976, 199, ln. 34). That is, ל֔וֹ 'to him' is the predicate of the phrase. The subject is שְׂרָפִ֨ים 'Seraphim' followed by an asyndetic relative clause that modifies it—עֹמְדִ֤ים ׀ מִמַּ֙עַל֙ '(Seraphim which are) standing above'. This is the interpretation reflected in Saadya's translation (Ratzaby 1993, 14, ln. 3). Saadya then states that arranging the clause 2+2, represented by the translation 'Seraphim were standing above him', is blasphemous, because it implies that the "angels are set above their creator" (Qafiḥ 1976, 200, lns 2–3). While שְׂרָפִ֨ים 'Seraphim' serves as the grammatical subject in either case, the predicate in the 2 + 2 division is עֹמְדִ֤ים '(were) standing' modified by the prepositional phrase מִמַּ֙עַל֙ ל֔וֹ 'above Him'.

According to Wickes's principle of continuous dichotomy, the accents, like Saadya's translation, also reflect a 3 + 1 grouping of this phrase. The entire phrase is governed by the accent *zaqef* on the word ל֔וֹ. The primary division within *zaqef*'s domain is indicated by the accent *pašṭa* on the word מִמַּ֙עַל֙, since there is no *revia*ʿ present.[252] The result of this division is that ל֔וֹ is set apart from the words שְׂרָפִ֨ים עֹמְדִ֤ים ׀ מִמַּ֙עַל֙.[253]

---

[252] 1 Kgs 7.3a offers an example of מִמַּ֙עַל֙ with *pašṭa* preceded by *revia*ʿ (i.e., one of the ways in which a 2 + 2 grouping could have been accented in Isa. 6.2). As a result, מִמַּ֙עַל֙ forms a compound modifier with what follows: וְסָפֻ֣ן בָּאֶ֗רֶז מִמַּ֙עַל֙ עַל־הַצְּלָעֹת֙ אֲשֶׁ֣ר עַל־הָֽעַמּוּדִ֔ים 'And it was covered with cedar above the sides which were on pillars.'

[253] My analysis here is contra Ben-Shammai's (2003, 38). Later in the passage, Saadya mentions that if the sense requires it, תכריג *takrīj* 'deviation' is permissible (Zucker 1984, 19, ln. 21), and Ben-Shammai counts this verse as one of those instances. That is, he observes Saadya grouping the phrase 3 + 1 and says this is an example of *takrīj* since מִמַּ֙עַל֙ ל֔וֹ are "joined by the accents." There are two problems with this analysis. First, for these two words to be joined together by the accents a *revia*ʿ must be present before the *pašṭa*. Second, Saadya discusses *takrīj* only after he cites Isa. 6.2. This suggests that he chooses Isa. 6.2 to illustrate the salient point of the passage—that the *mašhūr* 'commonly accepted sense' of a passage is to take it according to the proper arrangement of its words; that is, he did not choose Isa. 6.2 to illustrate the exception.

Saadya's explicit reason for this grouping is theological: the 2+2 division of the verse would be blasphemous because "the angels are set above their Creator" (Qafiḥ 1976, 200, ln. 3). Additionally, Saadya prefaced this section by saying that word groupings are determined by the 'meaning' (אלמעאני; Qafiḥ 1976, 199, ln. 24). Thus, while Saadya's translation and interpretation reflect the division of the accents, they are the product, according to his own words, of theological and semantic considerations. These considerations also provide a degree of cohesion for the ideas of *ḍammāt* and *mašhūr*, as, instead of accents, words in the Bible are grouped according to notions of theologically or semantically correct reading (*ḍammāt*). These are the ways in which the native speakers of Biblical Hebrew/speakers within Saadya's community would have understood the obscure passages (*mašhūr*). In order to resolve this ambiguity we should ask whether the same theological reservations would necessarily require that the words be grouped in a particular way. I suggest that this is not the case. Saadya could easily have chosen another grouping of words to safeguard against a blasphemous interpretation.

The treatment of this same passage by the Karaite exegete Yefet ben Eli, which is given below, makes it clear that he has the same theological reservations as Saadya. But his interpretation of Isa. 6.2 does not reflect the division of the accents. This indicates that, even given the same reservations, one's decision concerning the semantic grouping of words need not match the grouping reflected by the accents.

fol. 72r

וקו יֹשֵׁב עַל כִּסֵּא רָם וְנִשָּׂא ערף אנה ראי אלכָבוֹד עלי	2	As for the phrase יֹשֵׁב עַל־כִּסֵּא רָם וְנִשָּׂא ‘Sitting on the throne high and lifted up’ (Isa. 6.1), it makes known that he (Isaiah) saw the *glory* upon
כרסי מרתפע גִדא וקד בייַן יַחֶזְקֵאל אן אלכרסי שביה	3	a chair highly lifted up. *Ezekiel* already clarified that the chair resembles
באלגֿוהר אלמהא כקו וּמִמַּעַל לָרָקִיעַ אֲשֶׁר עַל רֹאשָׁם	4	the sapphire jewel, as it says וּמִמַּעַל לָרָקִיעַ אֲשֶׁר עַל־רֹאשָׁם
כְּמַרְאֵה אֶבֶן סַפִּיר דְּמוּת כִּסֵּא וקו וְשׁוּלָיו מְלֵאִים	5	כְּמַרְאֵה אֶבֶן־סַפִּיר דְּמוּת כִּסֵּא ‘Above the firmament which was over their heads, having an appearance like sapphire, was the likeness of a throne’ (Ezek. 1.26). Now, the phrase וְשׁוּלָיו מְלֵאִים
אֶת הַהֵיכָל ידל עלי אנה ראי אלכָבוֹד פוק סטח אל	6	אֶת־הַהֵיכָל: ‘and his hems filled the temple’ (Isa. 6.1), refers to the fact that he saw the glory above the top of the roof of the
כרסי[254] מן פוק אלהֵיכָל פכאנה שוּלֵי הַכָּבוֹד עלי אלהֵיכָל	7	temple [even though it surrounds the *temple* because this is the way of everything which is filled from something—it is set above it],[255] over the *temple*. So, it is as if the *hems of the glory* are over the *temple*

254 כרסי] IOM Ms. A 143 fol. 78r, ln. 3 אלהֵיכָל.

255 Added from IOM Ms. A 143 fol. 78r, lns 3–5 ואנהא מחיטה באלהֵיכָל לאן כדי סביל כל שי ממלו מן אלשי יפצֿל עליה.

וחואליה פראי כְבוֹד יְיָ האיל עטים פאמא יְחֶזְקֵאל	8	and around it. So, he (Isaiah) saw the *glory of the Lord* [as something] very enormous, whereas *Ezekiel*
ראי אלכָבוֹד עלי אלכְרוּבִים וקו שְׂרָפִים עֹמְדִים ממַעַל	9	saw the *glory* on the *cherubim*. The phrase שְׂרָפִים עֹמְדִים ׀ מִמַּעַל לוֹ
לוֹ יריד בה מלאיכה וקוף קדאם אלכָבוֹד פוק אלהֵיכָל	10	(Isa. 6.2) intends, 'angels [which] stood before the *glory* above the temple.'
IOM Ms. A 143 fol. 78r		
וקוֹ מִמַעַל לוֹ הו אשאראה	13	The phrase מִמַּעַל לוֹ (Isa. 6.2) is a reference
אלי שי תקדם דכרה פי אלפסוֹ אלמתקדם והי[256] תלת	14	to something whose mention came before in the previous *verse*, and it is three
אשיא כסֵא וְכָבוֹד וְהֵיכאל פלא יגוז יקול מִמַעַל	15	things—*throne,* and *glory* and *temple.* Now, it is not possible to say '*above*
ללכָבוֹד אד הם כדמה לה ולא יגוז <אן יכונו> פוק אלכרסי	16	*the glory'* because they (the angels) are His servants. Nor is it possible that they are over the chair
fol. 78v		
מעה בקי אן יכון[257] פוק אלהֵיכָל פכאן אלכרסי מעלק	1	with Him. It remains that they are over the *temple*. So, the chair was suspended

[256] אלי שי תקדם דכרה פי אלפסוֹ אלמתקדם והי] RNL Evr. Arab. I 568 fol. 72r, lns 15–16 אלי מא תקדם.

[257] מעה בקי אן יכון] RNL Evr. Arab. I 568 fol. 72r, ln. 18 אנמא.

פוק אלהֵיכָל פי אלהוא ואלשְׂרָפים קדאם רגִל אלכרסי	2	over the *temple* in the air and the *Sera-phim* were before the feet of the chair,
וקוף קדאם אלכָבוֹד[258]	3	standing before the *glory*.

Yefet's interpretation of the phrase in question reflects a 2+2 division. He says that the intended sense behind שְׂרָפִ֨ים עֹמְדִ֤ים ׀ מִמַּ֙עַל֙ ל֔וֹ is 'angels standing before the Lord *above the temple*' (RNL Evr. Arab. I 568 fol. 72r, lns 9–10; emphasis mine: JH). His insertion of the prepositional phrase קדאם אלכָבוֹד 'before the *Glory*' makes it clear that the following phrase פוק אלהֵיכָל 'above the *temple*' reflects his understanding of the Hebrew words מִמַּ֙עַל֙ ל֔וֹ as in the same prepositional phrase, viz., closely bound. He interprets the referent of ל֔וֹ as the temple.

Yefet has the same theological reservations as Saadya in this verse, but resolves them by exegesis in light of the context and in light of other Scripture. He explains that מִמַּ֙עַל֙ ל֔וֹ 'above it' refers to something in the previous verse—either the throne (כִּסֵּ֖א), the Lord Himself (אֲדֹנָ֛י), or the temple (הַהֵיכָֽל). The first two options are ruled out on theological grounds. The angels can neither be over the Lord nor His throne, because they would then be positioned higher than the Lord Himself. This leaves only the option that the angels are standing over the temple in front of the Lord (IOM Ms. A 143 fol. 78r, ln. 13–fol. 78v, ln. 3). Yefet's exegesis illustrates his understanding of the phrase in light of its context.

258 ואלשְׂרָפים קדאם רגִל אלכרסי / וקוף קדאם אלכָבוֹד] RNL Evr. Arab. I 568 fol. 72v, lns 1–2 ואלשְׂרָפִים קדאמה וקדאסה וקדאם אלכבוד וקוף.

The reason Yefet understands the Lord and His angels to be above the temple in the first place is because of his exegesis in light of other Scripture. Earlier in the commentary (not shown), Yefet connects Isaiah's vision of the Lord with that of Ezekiel's (Ezek. 1.16–21). The difference, Yefet says, is that in Ezekiel's vision, the Lord is departing from the temple, whereas in Isaiah's vision the Lord is dwelling in the temple.[259] In both visions God's throne is on high. This is indicated in Isaiah's vision by the phrase רָ֥ם וְנִשָּׂ֑א 'high and lifted up' (Isa. 6.1) and in Ezekiel's by וּמִמַּ֗עַל לָרָקִ֙יעַ֙ אֲשֶׁ֣ר עַל־רֹאשָׁ֔ם כְּמַרְאֵ֥ה אֶֽבֶן־סַפִּ֖יר דְּמ֣וּת כִּסֵּ֑א 'Above the firmament which was over their heads, having an appearance like sapphire, was the likeness of a throne' (Ezek. 1.26), from the latter of which Yefet also deduces that the throne in Isaiah's vision must be made of sapphire (RNL Evr. Arab. I 568 fol. 72r lns 3–5). Yefet then accommodates the phrase וְשׁוּלָ֖יו מְלֵאִ֥ים אֶת־הַהֵיכָֽל 'and His hems filled the temple' to this scenario: if one thing fills something else, by definition it is then above it.

Yefet's exegesis of this passage illustrates that theological considerations do not force one to read the words as grouped in a particular way. Both Saadya and Yefet express the same theological reservations regarding this verse. Yefet resolves this tension by considering the context and other Scripture. Saadya resolves it by recourse to the *ḍammāt* of the verse. This gives further support to the idea that Saadya's conception of *ḍammāt* 'grouping

[259] The grounds for Yefet's claim that the Lord is departing the temple in Ezekiel's vision are the presence of the אוֹפַנִּים 'wheels' (see Ezek. 1.15–21), which Yefet interprets as depicting God on a מֶרְכָּבָה 'chariot' (RNL Evr. Arab. I fol. 71v, lns 3–8).

of words' may very well be determined by the grouping of the accents.

2.2.1. *Takrīj*

The next section of SIP concerns the term *taḵrīj* 'deviation'. After Saadya illustrates how the *mašhūr* 'commonly accepted' sense of a passage may be understood according to its *ḍammāt* 'grouping of words', he says that if there is need for 'deviation' from this principle in order to make the meaning clearer, then this is permissible (lns 21–22). Saadya defines *taḵrīj* as separating that which is joined and joining that which is separated (ln. 22). He then offers two examples that respectively illustrate these two processes—Gen. 3.22 and Exod. 35.34. The crucial task for the present discussion is discerning the basis for the exegetical tradition from which Saadya deviates. If Saadya's exegesis of these verses reflects a deviation from the clear division of the accents, then this makes it even more probable that the idea of *ḍammāt* indeed refers specifically to the accents.

(2) וַיֹּ֣אמֶר ׀ יְהוָ֣ה אֱלֹהִ֗ים הֵ֤ן הָֽאָדָם֙ הָיָה֙ כְּאַחַ֣ד מִמֶּ֔נּוּ לָדַ֖עַת ט֣וֹב וָרָ֑ע וְעַתָּ֣ה ׀ פֶּן־
יִשְׁלַ֣ח יָד֗וֹ וְלָקַח֙ גַּ֚ם מֵעֵ֣ץ הַֽחַיִּ֔ים וְאָכַ֖ל וָחַ֥י לְעֹלָֽם׃

'Then the LORD God said, "Behold, the man has become like one of us in knowing good and evil. Now, lest he reach out his hand and take also of the tree of life and eat, and live forever."' (ESV, Gen. 3.22)

RNL Evr. Arab. II C 1 fol. 6r	Line	
תם קאל אללה הודא אדם קד צאר	13	Then God said, 'Behold! *Adam* has become
כואחד מנה מערפה אלכיר ואלשר	14	as one from whom (is) the knowledge of good and evil.
ואלאן כילאי מד ידה פיאכד מן	15	And now, lest he stretch forth his hand and take from
שגרה אלחיוה איצֿא ויאכל ויחיא	16	the tree of life as well, and eat, and live
אלי אלדהר	17	for eternity.'
Zucker (1984, 79)		
וקולה תבארך הן האדם היה כאחד ממנו לדעת טוב ורע כשף לנא בה מוצֿע	19	Now the Blessed One's phrase הֵ֣ן הָֽאָדָם֙ הָיָה֙ כְּאַחַ֣ד מִמֶּ֔נּוּ לָדַ֖עַת ט֣וֹב וָרָ֑ע (Gen. 3.22) reveals to us the reason (lit., 'place') for the rebuke of *Adam*. It is because [it is as if the Lord said] 'He (Adam) himself has
אלזגֿר עלי אדם והו אנה קד צאר כאסתאדֿ נפסה וכאן מסתגניא ען אלאזדיאד מן	20	become like a master of himself. And he (Adam) was no longer in need of additions from among
תעלימי פקד וגֿב טרדה. ומחץֿ כאחד ממנו לדעת טוב ורע כאחד מן הו מן נפסה	21	My teachings.' So, it required his banishment. כְּאַחַ֣ד מִמֶּ֔נּוּ לָדַ֖עַת ט֣וֹב וָרָ֑ע (Gen. 3.22) is literally translated as, 'Like one who by himself
יערף אלכֿיר ואלשר	22	knows good and evil.'

The question here is how to understand the words כְּאַחַ֣ד מִמֶּ֔נּוּ. The accents join these two words together. This is indicated by the conjunctive accent *munaḥ* on the word כְּאַחַ֣ד. The word-unit מִמֶּ֔נּוּ is divided from what comes after by the disjunctive accent *zaqef*. According to the division of the accents, the following form, לָדַ֖עַת 'knowing' must be analysed as an infinitive which elaborates on the immediately preceding clause.[260] The accents, therefore, reflect an interpretation such as the following: 'Behold! The man has become like one of us (in what way?), knowing good and evil.'[261] Any *taḵrīj* 'deviation' from the division of the accents must divide between the two words כְּאַחַ֣ד מִמֶּ֔נּוּ in some way.

Indeed, Saadya's translation and commentary reflect an interpretation based on a division between כְּאַחַ֣ד and מִמֶּ֔נּוּ. The Hebrew form מִמֶּ֔נּוּ may be analysed as the (doubled) preposition מִן 'from' plus either the 3MS suffix (= 'from him') or the 1CPL suffix (= 'from us'). The interpretation which results from the joining of the two words by the accents requires this to be understood as 'from us' (e.g., ESV and LXX). Saadya, however, translates according to the former—מנה *minhu* 'from him'. He then translates the Hebrew form לָדַ֖עַת as a noun—מערפה *maʿrifa* 'knowledge'—that is in construct with what follows (אלכיר ואלשר; ln. 14). This suggests that Saadya analysed the Hebrew מִמֶּ֔נּוּ לָדַ֖עַת ט֥וֹב וָרָֽע as an

[260] See Joüon and Muraoka (2006, 407) for this function of the preposition -לְ.

[261] This corresponds to the LXX translation of this verse: καὶ εἶπεν ὁ θεός Ἰδοὺ Αδαμ γέγονεν ὡς εἷς ἐξ ἡμῶν τοῦ γινώσκειν καλὸν καὶ πονηρόν 'And God said, "Behold! Adam has become like one of us, knowing good and evil"'. The genitive article followed by an infinitive modifies the meaning of a previous verb. See Smyth (1920, §2032).

asyndetic relative clause modifying the head אַחַ֣ד 'one' (in the phrase כְּאַחַ֣ד). In the relative clause מערפה אלכיר ואלשר 'knowledge of good and evil' is the compound subject and מנה 'from him' is the predicate (as I have translated above in ln. 14); the knowledge of good and evil comes from man himself, with no outside intervention. His translation is therefore a deviation (*takrīj*) from the division of the accents.

Furthermore, Saadya's commentary suggests that his *takrīj* in Gen. 3.22 is a deviation from the accents. He says that God rebukes Adam, because Adam has become like one who already knows everything (כאסתאדׂ lit. 'a teacher/master'; ln. 20). Adam no longer needs God to teach him good and evil (lns 20–21). This interpretation reflects an understanding of כְּאַחַ֣ד as not bound to what follows. Saadya offers his own literal translation (מחץׄ) in what follows (lns 21–22), which confirms the above analysis of his understanding of the Hebrew syntax—כְּאַחַ֣ד is followed by an asyndetic relative clause. This is indicated by the fact that Saadya inserts the Arabic relative pronoun מן *man* in his literal translation—Adam is like one who (מן *man*) knows good and evil by himself. In both syndetic and asyndetic relative clauses in Biblical Hebrew, the word being modified is usually set off from its modifier by a disjunctive accent.[262] This strongly suggests that Saadya interpreted a break between כְּאַחַ֣ד and מִמֶּ֔נּוּ, contra the division of the accents.

---

[262] E.g., asyndetic: וְ֝אַשְׁרֵ֗י דְּרָכַ֥י יִשְׁמֹֽרוּ׃ 'Happy are those who keep My ways' (Prov. 8.32); syndetic: ...וַיֹּ֖אמֶר הָֽאָדָ֑ם הָֽאִשָּׁה֙ אֲשֶׁ֣ר נָתַ֣תָּה עִמָּדִ֔י 'And the man said, "The woman which you gave to be with me..."' (Gen. 3.12).

It seems, therefore, that in Gen. 3.22 the *takrīj* ‘deviation’ to which Saadya refers is a deviation away from the division of the accents. The process in this *takrīj* was, as he says in SIP, to separate that which is joined together. The words that are joined together are כְּאַחַד מִמֶּנּוּ. In this particular phrase both the vocalisation and the accents join these words together—אַחַד is the form normally used in construct relationships whereas אֶחָד is typically the absolute form.[263] Using the example of Gen. 3.22 alone, it is not certain whether the division from which Saadya deviates is that based on the accents or the vocalisation. The next example of *takrīj* that Saadya gives strongly supports the interpretation of the term as referring to deviation from the accents.

(3) וּבַמְּנֹרָה אַרְבָּעָה גְבִעִים מְשֻׁקָּדִים כַּפְתֹּרֶיהָ וּפְרָחֶיהָ׃
‘On the Menorah shall be four cups. Its knobs and its flowers shall be almond-shaped’ (Exod. 25.34/37.20)

This verse is one of חמש מקראות בתורה אין להן הכרע ‘five verses in the Torah for which no decision has been reached’ (b. Yoma 52a.10–52b.1). The question here is whether the word מְשֻׁקָּדִים should be grouped with what comes before or after. The former yields the translation ‘Four almond-shaped cups [shall be] on the Menorah.’ The latter produces the translation I have offered above (Breuer 1989, 369; Kogut 1994, 35). All the major Tiberian codices group מְשֻׁקָּדִים with what comes after by placing an *ʾatnaḥ* on the previous word גְּבִעִים, thereby grouping מְשֻׁקָּדִים with what

[263] Ibn Ezra draws attention to the significance of the vocalisation of this phrase (Kogut 1994, 41–42). Al-Fāsī’s also considers the difference between these forms to be one of contextual status (Skoss 1936, I:61–62).

comes after. Morphosyntactically, both options are possible. Grouped with what comes before, מְשֻׁקָּדִים is an MPL attributive adjective modifying MPL גְּבִעִים. Grouped with what comes after, מְשֻׁקָּדִים may be analysed as the predicate of כַּפְתֹּרֶיהָ וּפְרָחֶיהָ, both MPL. Therefore, if Saadya's translation reflects a division whereby מְשֻׁקָּדִים is grouped with what is before (גְּבִעִים), then that which Saadya is deviating from—the commonly accepted sense (*mašhūr*)—must be the division of the accents.

RNL Evr. Arab. II C 1 fol. 175v (25.34)	Lines	
ופי דאת אלמנארה ארבע גאמאת	17	And as for the Menorah, four almond-shaped cups—
וקיל בואטי מלוזאת ותפאפיחהא	18	it is also said 'vessels'—and its apples
וסואסנהא	19	and its lilies.

RNL Evr. Arab. II C 1 fol. 214v (37.20)	Lines	
ופי דאת אלמנארה ארבע	17	And as for the Menorah, four
גאמאת מלוזאת ותפאפיחהא	18	almond-shaped cups and its apples
וסואסנהא	19	and lilies.

I have found no extended commentary on these verses, but Saadya's translations reflect a division whereby מְשֻׁקָּדִים is grouped with what comes before it, suggesting that the *takrīj* 'deviation' contrasts with the division of the accents. This corresponds to the second kind of *takrīj* mentioned in SIP above—joining together that which is separated.

Saadya's translation differs from the division of the accents in terms of (1) the grammatical agreement of גְּבִעִ֣ים מְשֻׁקָּדִ֔ים in the Arabic translation and (2) the addition of an extra -ו 'and' conjunction to the Arabic translation of כַּפְתֹּרֶ֖יהָ. Saadya's translation is virtually identical in both instances. The lone exception is the addition of another gloss for the word גְּבִעִים 'cups'—בואטי 'vessels' in his translation of 25.34.[264] Saadya translates the Biblical Hebrew masculine noun phrase גְּבִעִ֣ים מְשֻׁקָּדִ֔ים into the Arabic feminine plural phrase גאמאת מלוזאת. Before the word תפאפיחהא 'its apples' (= כַּפְתֹּרֶ֖יהָ) Saadya adds the conjunction *waw*, setting it apart from what precedes. I agree with Kogut (1994, 143) here, who says that the sense of Saadya's translation seems to be that the Menorah contains three things: (1) four almond-shaped cups, (2) its apples, and (3) its lilies.[265] In any case, this is clearly an example of *takrīj* as תאליף *taʾlīf* 'joining' (SIP ln. 24).

Since Saadya listed Gen. 3.22 and these verses in Exodus as examples of *takrīj*, both examples must be deviating from the same thing—the accents. Gen. 3.22 is an example of separating that which is joined together (SIP, ln. 22) and the Exodus passages are examples of joining together that which is separated (SIP, lns 22, 24).

---

[264] See Ratzaby (1998, 340 lns 14–15) for Saadya's explanation for this alternate gloss.

[265] Kogut's description of Saadya's approach must be slightly refined for the sake of accuracy. He claims that Saadya here chooses the tradition of division of this verse which was 'rejected' (נדחתה). It is clear from the present discussion, though, that Saadya is not 'choosing' a tradition, but rather deviating (*takrīj*) from one.

3.0. Conclusion

The above analysis suggests that the accents are indeed what Saadya is referring to in SIP as a means of clarifying obscurities. While Saadya does not explicitly mention them, the accents strongly correlate with every key part of the description. Saadya's use of the term *ḍammāt* in Gen. 6.18 points to a particular grouping of words in that verse according to the Oral Law. Saadya's exegetical principle of recourse to the Oral Law where the *ẓāhir* 'apparent meaning' is unsatisfactory raises the question of what the *ẓāhir* (i.e. default) grouping of words was for Gen. 6.18. The simplest answer is the accents, since they divide the verse in the way which Saadya was trying to avoid. The way in which the original users of Biblical Hebrew/those in Saadya's community would have understood a verse (*mašhūr*) facilitates the arrangement of words into groups (*ḍammāt*). But what feature of the text purports to reflect the word groupings of biblical verses as they were originally understood? The accents are the best candidate. This original manner in which words were arranged must be maintained so that what is joined together in 'the reading' (*al-qirāʾa*) will be joined in meaning. We saw that the term *al-qirāʾa* has a special meaning of reading with chant or oral performance, since Saadya used the word *al-tilāwa* to refer to reading without chant or, perhaps, plain reading. How does a reader know what to chant/perform? The best candidate is the accents. When Saadya illustrated the correct use of this interpretive device in Isa. 6.2, the proper arrangement of words reflected the division of the accents. When giving an example of *taḵrīj* whereby one must break apart that which the *mašhūr* joins together, Saadya gave Gen. 3.22. Here Saadya interpreted as separate what *the accents* join together. For the example of *taḵrīj* whereby one must join what the *mašhūr* separates, Saadya gave Exod. 25.34. There, he joined together *what the accents* separated.

References

Allony, Nehemya, ed. 1969. *Ha-ʾEgron: Kitāb Uṣūl al-Šiʿr al-ʿIbrānī by Rav Seʿadya Gaʾon*. Jerusalem: The Academy of the Hebrew Language. [Hebrew]

Ben-Shammai, Haggai. 1991. 'Saadya's Introduction to Isaiah as an Introduction to the Books of the Prophets'. *Tarbiz* 60/3: 371–404. [Hebrew]

———. 2003. 'The Tension between Literal Interpretation and Exegetical Freedom: Comparative Observations on Saadia's Method'. In *With Reverence for the Word: Medieval Scriptural Exegesis in Judaism, Christianity, and Islam*, edited by Jane Dammen McAuliffe, Barry D. Walfish, and Joseph W. Goering, 33–50. Oxford: University Press.

Breuer, Mordechai. 1989. *The Accents of the Bible in the Twenty-One Books and in the books of Job, Proverbs, Psalms*. Jerusalem: Ḥorev. [Hebrew]

Brody, Robert. 1998. *The Geonim of Babylonia and the Shaping of Medieval Jewish Culture*. New Haven, CT: Yale University Press.

———. 2006. *Rav Saadya Gaon*. Jerusalem: The Zalman Shazar Center. [Hebrew]

———. 2013. *Sa'adyah Gaon*. Translated by Betsy Rosenberg. Portland, OR: The Littman Library of Jewish Civilization.

Díaz Esteban, Fernando. 1975. *Sefer ʾOklah Wĕ-ʾOklah: Colección de Listas de Palabras Destinadas a Conservar La Integridad Del Texto Hebreo de La Biblia Entre Los Judios de La Dad Media.* Textos y Estudios 'Cardenal Cisneros' 4. Madrid: Consejo Superior de Investigaciones Científicas.

Dotan, Aaron. 1967. *The Diqduqe ha-Ṭeʿamim of Aharon ben Moshe ben Asher: With a Critical Edition of the Original Text from New Manuscripts.* 3 vols. The Academy of the Hebrew Language Texts and Studies 7. Jerusalem: The Academy of the Hebrew Language. [Hebrew]

———. 1970. 'Prolegomenon'. In *Two Treatises on the Accentuation of the Old Testament: Taʿame Emet on Psalms, Proverbs, and Job; Taʿame Kaf-Alef Sefarim on the Twenty-Only Prose Books, by William Wickes.* New York: KTAV Publishing House, Inc.

———. 1996. 'Masoretic Schools in the Light of Saadya's Teaching.' In *Proceedings of the Twelfth International Congress of the International Organization for Masoretic Studies*, edited by E. J. Revell, 1–9. Scholars Press.

———. 1997. *The Dawn of Hebrew Linguistics: The Book of Elegance of the Language of the Hebrews by Saadia Gaon.* 2 vols. Jerusalem: World Union of Jewish Studies. [Hebrew]

———. 2005. *The Awakening of Word Lore: From the Masora to the Beginnings of Hebrew Lexicography.* Jerusalem: The Academy of the Hebrew Language. [Hebrew]

Gil, Moshe. 1992. *A History of Palestine, 634–1099.* Translated by Ethel Broido. Cambridge: Cambridge University Press.

de Goeje, Michal Jan (ed.). 1894. *Kitāb al-Tanbīh wal-ʾIshrāf by Abū al-Ḥasan ʾAlī ben al-Ḥusāyn ben ʿAlī al-Masʿūdī*. Bibliotheca Geographorum Arabicorum 8. Leiden: Brill.

Habib, Joseph. 2021. 'Accents, Pausal Forms and Qere/Ketiv in the Bible Translations and Commentaries of Saadya Gaon and the Karaites of Jerusalem'. PhD dissertation, University of Cambridge.

Hitin-Mashiah, Rachel. 2011. 'Biblical Accents in the Preface of the *ʾEgron* (Thesaurus) by Rav Seʿadya Gaʾon'. In *Israel: Linguistic Studies in the Memory of Israel Yeivin*, edited by Rafael I. Zer and Yosef Ofer, 113–128. Jerusalem: The Hebrew University Bible Project. [Hebrew]

de Hoop, Raymond. 2008. 'Stress and Syntax, Music and Meaning: The Purpose and Function of the Masoretic Accentuation System'. *Journal of Northwest Semitic Languages* 34/2: 99–121.

Joüon, Paul, and Takamitsu Muraoka. 2006. *A Grammar of Biblical Hebrew*. Subsidia Biblica 27. Rome: Pontifical Biblical Institute Press.

Kogut, Simcha. 1994. *Correlations between Biblical Accentuation and Traditional Jewish Exegesis*. Jerusalem: Magnas Press. [Hebrew]

Malter, Henry. 1921. *Saadia Gaon: His Life and Works*. Philadelphia: Jewish Publication Society of America.

Ofer, Yosef. 2019. *The Masora on Scripture and Its Methods*. Fontes et Subsidia ad Bibliam pertinentes 7. Berlin: De Gruyter.

Ognibeni, Bruno. 1995. *La Seconda Parte del Sefer ʾOklah WeʾOklah: Edizione del Ms. Halle, Universitätsbibliothek Y B*

40 10, Ff. 68–124. Textos y Estudios 'Cardenal Cisneros' 57. Madrid: Instituto de Filología del CSIC, Departamento de Filología Bíblica y de Oriente Antiguo.

Park, Sung Jin. 2014. '"Pointing to the Accents in the Scroll": Functional Development of the Masoretic Accents in the Hebrew Bible'. *Hebrew Studies* 55: 73–88.

Penkower, Jordan S. 1981. 'Maimonides and the Aleppo Codex'. *Textus* 9/1: 39–128.

Pitcher, Sophia Lynn. 2020. 'A Prosodic Model for Tiberian Hebrew: A Complexity Approach to the Features, Structures, and Functions of the Masoretic Cantillation Accents.' PhD dissertation, University of the Free State.

Polliack, Meira. 1997. *The Karaite Tradition of Arabic Bible Translation: A Linguistic and Exegetical Study of Karaite Translations of the Pentateuch from the Tenth and Eleventh Centuries C.E.* Leiden: Brill.

Qafiḥ, Yosef (ed. and trans.) 1966. *Tehilim ʿim Tirgum u-Ferush ha-Gaʾon Rabbenu Seʿadya ben Yosef Fayumi*. Jerusalem: American Academy of Jewish Research.

——— (ed.). 1969. *Kitāb al-Mukhtār fī al-Amānāt wal-Iʿtiqādāt (Sefer ha-Nivḥar ba-ʾEmunot u-va-Deʿot)*. Jerusalem: Sura.

——— (ed. and trans.). 1976. *Mishle ʿim Tirgum u-Ferush ha-Gaʾon Rabbenu Seʿadya ben Yosef Fayumi*. Jerusalem: Ha-Vaʿad le-Hotsaʾat Sifre Rasag.

Ratzaby, Yehuda. 1993. *Tafsir Yeshaʿya le-Rav Seʿadya*. Kiryat Ono: Mekhon Moshe.

———. 1998. *Sefer Perushe Rav Seʿadya Gaʾon le-Sefer Shemot: Maqor ve-Tirgum*. Jerusalem: Mosad ha-Rav Kook.

Revell, E. J. 1974. Review of *Seadya Gaon, "Ha-Egron: Kitab Usul as-Shi'r al-'Ibrani"*. *Journal of Semitic Studies* 19: 123–29.

Schechter, Solomon. 1901. 'Geniza Specimens.' *The Jewish Quarterly Review* 14/1: 37–63.

Shoshany, Ronit. 2009. 'The Biblical Accents' Original Purpose'. In *Masʾat Aharon: Linguistic Studies Presented to Aaron Dotan*, edited by Moshe Bar-Asher and Chaim E. Cohen, 469–86. Jerusalem: The Bialik Institute. [Hebrew]

Skoss, Solomon L. 1936. *The Hebrew-Arabic Dictionary of the Bible Known as Kitāb Jāmiʿ al-Alfāẓ (Agrōn) of David Ben Abraham al-Fāsī the Karaite (Tenth Cent.)*. 2 vols. Yale Oriental Series Researches 20. New Haven, CT: Yale University Press.

Smyth, Herbert Weir. 1920. *A Greek Grammar for Colleges*. New York: American Book Company.

Sokolow, Moshe. 1984. 'Saadiah Gaon's Prolegomenon to Psalms'. *Proceedings of the American Academy for Jewish Research* 51: 131–74.

Stern, Sacha. 2019. *The Jewish Calendar Controversy of 921/2 CE.* Leiden: Brill

Vollandt, Ronny. 2015. *Arabic Versions of the Pentateuch: A Comparative Study of Jewish, Christian, and Muslim Sources*. Biblia Arabica 1. Leiden: Brill.

Wickes, William. 1887. *A Treatise on the Accentuation of the Twenty-One So-Called Prose Books of the Old Testament.* Oxford: Clarendon Press.

Yeivin, Israel. 1959. 'The Accentuation of Rabbinic Texts with *Ṭeʿamīm*'. *Lĕšonénu* 24/1–2: 47–69.

Zewi, Tamar. 2015. *The Samaritan Version of Saadya Gaon's Translation of the Pentateuch: Critical Edition and Study of MS London BL OR7562 and Related MSS*. Biblica Arabica 3. Leiden: Brill.

Zucker, Moshe, ed. 1984. *Perushe Rav Seʿadya Gaʾon li-Vreshit*. New York: Bet ha-Midrash le-Rabanim ba-Ameriqa.

INDEX

accents, x, xxi, 11–12, 14, 52, 66, 182, 243, 245, 263, 279, 289, 295, 297, 306, 318, 330, 336, 340, 342–45, 361–62, 377–78, 381, 384, 386–91, 393–94, 397–98, 403, 405–10

accentuation, xix, xxi, 1–2, 5, 7, 9, 11–12, 14, 126, 174, 176, 182–83, 197, 289, 307, 326, 329–30, 337, 344, 349, 361

ʾalef, 163, 167, 169–70, 183–84, 197

Alsheikh, Moses, xxi, 330, 345–54, 356–64

Arabic, v, ix–x, xviii, 24, 117–20, 125, 146, 156, 158, 189, 203–4, 214–17, 237, 239, 240–42, 290–91, 293, 378, 382, 391, 406, 409, 414–15

ʾatnaḥ, 267, 275, 280–81, 303–17, 322–23

ʾatnaḥta, 294

ʿayin, 164, 170–71, 173

ʾazla, 294

Babylon, 23, 145, 254, 335–36, 379

Babylonian Masora, xvi, 2, 19, 24–25, 40, 46, 65, 72–73

Babylonian *ṭeʿamim*, 289

begadkefat, 243

Byzantine, v, xvii, 112, 163, 165–67, 170–71, 173, 181, 183–85, 187, 190–96, 198, 337

cantillation, xi–xii, xix, xxi, 31, 243–48, 251–55, 257–62, 264–66, 269–73, 275–81, 283–85, 289, 295–96, 329–30, 334, 340, 342–43, 345, 352, 356, 359, 364, 393

codex, xi–xii, xv–xvi, 1, 5, 7, 9–10, 12–14, 24, 26–29, 53, 56, 66, 71, 75–80, 83, 86, 90, 92, 95, 96, 98–99, 103–4, 106–9, 163–67, 183, 185, 189, 191, 194, 197, 205, 213, 236, 238–39, 291, 294–96, 334, 407

codicology, viii, xviii, 84, 164–65, 184, 187, 189–90, 192, 197–99

conjunctive accent, 58, 176–77, 181–82, 243, 245, 294–95, 315, 317, 343, 405
construct, 245–50, 252–58, 260, 274–75, 279, 282–83, 405, 407
dagesh, xvii, 126, 163–64, 169, 170, 172–81, 183–84, 197, 214, 242
ḍammāt, 384, 386–90, 393, 398, 402–3, 410
darga, 294, 357
defective, 35, 39, 4–44, 62, 67, 69, 99, 125, 147
deḥi, 314–17
derash, xxi, 330, 337–38, 343
disjunctive accent, 176–78, 182, 243, 245, 264, 275, 278–81, 294–95, 303–7, 309, 312–15, 319, 343, 353, 356, 360, 387, 405–6
Extended Tiberian, xvii, 197–98, 201
Firkovitch collections, 79, 204
galgal, 294
geresh, 257, 292, 294
guttural, 55, 125, 171, 173, 179, 183, 196–97, 214, 221, 224–25, 227, 232, 234, 236
ḥaṭef, xviii, 30, 173, 188–90, 205, 207–9, 211, 219, 234–36, 238–39
ḥet, 54, 164, 170–73
ḥireq, 54–55, 62, 167, 185, 186, 188–89, 235
ḥolem, 52
iconicity, 128
imperfect performance, xviii, 204
interchange, 135, 137, 146, 165, 172, 184–90, 199, 206, 215, 217, 237
interpretation, x–xi, xv, xix, 2, 4–5, 47–48, 116, 148, 155, 174, 244, 247, 250, 254, 256–62, 266–68, 281, 283, 285, 329, 331–34, 336–37, 340–42, 344–46, 348–49, 353–54, 356, 358, 360–63, 383, 385–88, 390–91, 393, 396, 398, 401, 405–7
Karaite, v, x, xviii, 18, 203–5, 213, 236, 239, 240–42, 291, 325, 398, 413–15
ketiv, v, xvi, xvii, xix, 75–76, 78, 80, 83, 98, 102–4, 106–7, 110, 115–33, 135–36, 138–39, 141–42, 144–54, 204, 207, 210, 234, 243–44, 284

lamed, 51, 172, 175, 178–80, 182–83
legarmeh, 294
mappiq, 170, 277–78, 380
maqqef, 14, 306, 316, 335
mašhūr, 389–90, 393, 397–98, 403, 408, 410
masora magna, 3, 24, 41, 76, 81, 192, 334, 336
masora parva, xvi, 3, 40–41, 76, 78, 80–81, 84, 95–101, 106–7, 109–10, 145, 192
Masoretes, vii, xi, xix, 14, 18, 204, 236, 244, 273, 275, 278, 281, 284, 299, 311, 318, 329, 372, 378, 380–81
Masoretic Text, 1, 19–20, 118, 218, 243, 284, 300, 329, 333
mayela, 294, 303
merkha, 14, 294, 317
midrash, vi, x, xx, 329–32, 334, 336, 338, 340, 345, 349, 358, 362, 364–65, 367, 371, 374–76, 416
*mille*ʿ*el*, 294
*millera*ʿ, 294
Nehardea, 28, 73
nequddot, 292–93, 320
niqqud, 243, 292
nun, v, xvi, 75–77, 80, 84, 86, 92–96, 100, 105, 110, 134, 175–76, 178–80, 182–83
palaeography, vii, viii, 82, 185, 187, 191–92, 194, 196–99
Palestinian *ṭe*ʿ*amim*, 300, 320
Palestinian *Yeshiva*, xi, 204
Palestino-Tiberian, xvii, 164–65, 197
parallelism, 254, 295, 305, 307–8, 310, 320, 321
parasha, 57–59, 61, 333, 351
parashiyyot, 57
paratextual, 84–85, 92, 108–9, 362
pashṭa, 8, 306
pataḥ, 30–31, 52, 172–73, 185–86, 188–90, 206–12, 214–19, 221, 225, 227, 229–30, 232, 234, 237, 260
pausal, x, 15, 243, 245, 263–65, 267–69, 271, 285–86, 304, 330, 413
pazer, 294, 352–53, 361
Pentateuch, vi, xvii, xxi, 19, 24–25, 71–72, 83–84, 95, 100–1, 112, 118, 144, 156–57, 377, 382, 414–16
peshaṭ, 330
pesiq, 338

pisqa, 47, 57–60
piyyuṭ, 292
plene, 6, 33–40, 42–45, 47–49, 55, 63, 65, 67– 68, 146, 151
poetry, xx, 295–96, 303, 307, 309, 313–14, 321, 326, 378
puncta extraordinaria, 331
qameṣ, 185–86, 188–89, 206, 208, 211–12, 214–18, 224–25, 229, 233–34
qere, v, xvi–xvii, xix, 11, 75–76, 78, 80, 83, 96–99, 101–4, 106, 107, 110, 115–20, 122–32, 135–36, 139, 141–42, 144–45, 147–54, 204, 244, 284, 331
qirāʾa, 390–93, 410
rafe, 30, 126, 163, 169–70, 199
resh, 6, 175, 179–80
reviaʿ, 294, 314–16, 356, 360–61, 397
reviaʿ mugrash, 314–16
Ruth, 19, 298, 346, 348–55, 357–61, 363, 368, 372, 376
Saadya Gaon, vi, x, xxi, 377–82, 384–91, 393–94, 396–98, 401–3, 405–13, 416
Samaritan, v, viii, xvi, 115–18, 121, 123, 125, 127, 133–34, 136–38, 140–41, 143–44, 147, 149, 151–54, 156–58, 160, 366, 373, 416
samekh, 63, 175–76, 178
segol, 6–7, 55, 185–86, 188–89, 206–9, 211, 213–14, 216–18, 223–24, 228, 232, 254, 271, 335
ṣere, 185–86, 188–89, 213
sevirin, 51
shalshelet, xxi, 329–30, 337–43, 345–48, 361, 363, 368
shewa, xvii–xviii, 163–64, 170–73, 175, 180–81, 183–86, 188–90, 197, 205, 219, 227, 229, 234–36, 238–39, 260–61, 271, 380
shureq, 189
silluq, 275, 294, 303–5, 307, 312, 314–16, 386
siman, 6–7, 60, 242
sof-pasuq, 30
stress, xv, 7–11, 15, 275, 289, 294, 306, 315–17
suppletion, 128, 134
Sura, 28, 73, 276, 378, 414
syllable, xviii, 10–11, 14, 119, 121, 124, 166, 169, 171–74, 176–77, 179, 181, 183–84, 186, 196–97, 205, 213, 225, 234–36, 238–39, 243, 304–5, 315–17, 330, 343, 356

takrīj, 397, 403, 405–10
ṭarḥa, 14
taw, 8, 179
ṭeʿamim, 243, 289–90, 292–93, 294–97, 299, 301–9, 311–15, 317–21, 329–30, 336, 338–39, 342–43, 345, 349, 353, 357, 361–63
telisha, 9–10, 294, 335–36
ṭeres, 294
tevir, 257, 279–80, 294, 322
Tiberian pronunciation tradition, 55, 179, 204, 213–14, 234
Tiberias, xi–xii, 23, 108, 204, 379
ṭifḥa, 294, 303, 305, 307, 312–14, 322
tosafot, 297
transcriptions, xviii, 203–5, 239
verse length, 297–99, 301–2
vocalisation, xiii, xv, xvii–xix, 1–2, 5, 7, 9, 31, 49, 53–55, 62–63, 80, 104, 108, 115, 126, 150, 164, 169, 171, 185, 190, 192, 196–99, 205–6, 213–14, 218, 236, 239, 243–48, 251–54, 257, 259–63, 265, 269, 271, 274, 276–78, 281, 283–85, 407
waw consecutive, 9
yetiv, 294, 306
yod, 234–35
zaqef gadol, 353, 359–61
zaqef qaṭan, 264, 267, 279–80, 294, 304–7, 309, 311, 313, 318, 322–23, 349, 353, 359–61, 386, 397, 405
zarqa, 247, 294
zayin, v, xvi, 75–76, 78, 80, 84, 86, 92–96, 100, 105, 110, 175–76, 184

Cambridge Semitic Languages and Cultures

General Editor Geoffrey Khan

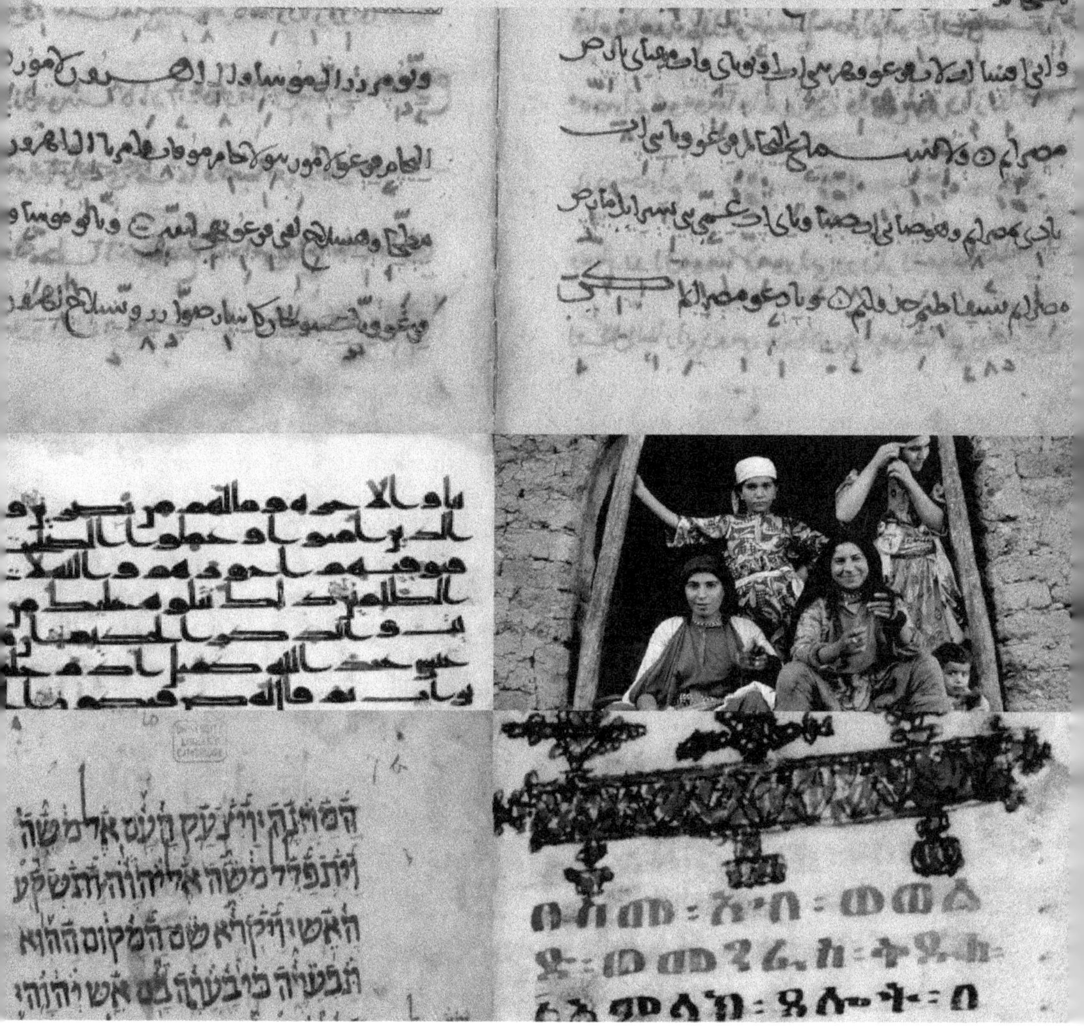

About the series

This series is published by Open Book Publishers in collaboration with the Faculty of Asian and Middle Eastern Studies of the University of Cambridge. The aim of the series is to publish in open-access form monographs in the field of Semitic languages and the cultures associated with speakers of Semitic languages. It is hoped that this will help disseminate research in this field to academic researchers around the world and also open up this research to the communities whose languages and cultures the volumes concern. This series includes philological and linguistic studies of Semitic languages, editions of Semitic texts, and studies of Semitic cultures. Titles in the series will cover all periods, traditions and methodological approaches to the field.

This is the first Open Access book series in the field; it combines the high peer-review and editorial standards with the fair Open Access model offered by OBP. Open Access (that is, making texts free to read and reuse) helps spread research results and other educational materials to everyone everywhere, not just to those who can afford it or have access to well-endowed university libraries.

Copyrights stay where they belong, with the authors. Authors are encouraged to secure funding to offset the publication costs and thereby sustain the publishing model, but if no institutional funding is available, authors are not charged for publication. Any grant secured covers the actual costs of publishing and is not taken as profit. In short: we support publishing that respects the authors and serves the public interest.

UNIVERSITY OF CAMBRIDGE
Faculty of Asian and Middle Eastern Studies

You can find more information about this serie at:
http://www.openbookpublishers.com/section/107/1

Other titles in the series

Diachronic Variation in the Omani Arabic Vernacular of the Al-ʿAwābī District
From Carl Reinhardt (1894) to the Present Day

Roberta Morano

https://doi.org/10.11647/OBP.0298

Sefer ha-Pardes by Jedaiah ha-Penini
A Critical Edition with English Translation

David Torollo

https://doi.org/10.11647/OBP.0299

Neo-Aramaic and Kurdish Folklore from Northern Iraq
A Comparative Anthology with a Sample of Glossed Texts, Volume 1

Geoffrey Khan, Masoud Mohammadirad, Dorota Molin & Paul M. Noorlander

https://doi.org/10.11647/OBP.0306

Neo-Aramaic and Kurdish Folklore from Northern Iraq
A Comparative Anthology with a Sample of Glossed Texts, Volume 2

Geoffrey Khan, Masoud Mohammadirad, Dorota Molin & Paul M. Noorlander

https://doi.org/10.11647/OBP.0307

The Neo-Aramaic Oral Heritage of the Jews of Zakho

Oz Aloni

https://doi.org/10.11647/OBP.0272

Points of Contact
The Shared Intellectual History of Vocalisation in Syriac, Arabic, and Hebrew

Nick Posegay

Winner of the British and Irish Association of Jewish Studies (BIAJS) Annual Book Prize

https://https://doi.org/10.11647/OBP.0271

A Handbook and Reader of Ottoman Arabic

Esther-Miriam Wagner (ed.)

https://doi.org/10.11647/OBP.0208

Diversity and Rabbinization

Jewish Texts and Societies between 400 and 1000 CE

Gavin McDowell, Ron Naiweld, Daniel Stökl Ben Ezra (eds)

https://doi.org/10.11647/OBP.0219

New Perspectives in Biblical and Rabbinic Hebrew

Aaron D. Hornkohl and Geoffrey Khan (eds)

https://doi.org/10.11647/OBP.0250

The Marvels Found in the Great Cities and in the Seas and on the Islands

A Representative of ʻAǧā'ib Literature in Syriac

Sergey Minov

https://doi.org/10.11647/OBP.0237

Studies in the Grammar and Lexicon of Neo-Aramaic

Geoffrey Khan and Paul M. Noorlander (eds)

https://doi.org/10.11647/OBP.0209

Jewish-Muslim Intellectual History Entangled

Textual Materials from the Firkovitch Collection, Saint Petersburg

Camilla Adang, Bruno Chiesa, Omar Hamdan, Wilferd Madelung, Sabine Schmidtke and Jan Thiele (eds)

https://doi.org/10.11647/OBP.0214

Studies in Semitic Vocalisation and Reading Traditions

Aaron Hornkohl and Geoffrey Khan (eds)

https://doi.org/10.11647/OBP.0207

Studies in Rabbinic Hebrew

Shai Heijmans (ed.)

https://doi.org/10.11647/OBP.0164

The Tiberian Pronunciation Tradition of Biblical Hebrew

Volume 1

Geoffrey Khan

Winner of the 2021 Frank Moore Cross Book Award for best book related to the history and/or religion of the ancient Near East and Eastern Mediterranean

https://doi.org/10.11647/OBP.0163

The Tiberian Pronunciation Tradition of Biblical Hebrew

Volume 2

Geoffrey Khan

Winner of the 2021 Frank Moore Cross Book Award for best book related to the history and/or religion of the ancient Near East and Eastern Mediterranean

https://doi.org/10.11647/OBP.0194

www.ingramcontent.com/pod-product-compliance
Lightning Source LLC
Chambersburg PA
CBHW051107230426
43667CB00014B/2474
9781800649194